RITUAL AND THE IDEA OF
EUROPE IN INTERWAR WRITING

For My Parents

Ritual and the Idea of Europe in Interwar Writing

PATRICK R. QUERY
United States Military Academy, USA

Routledge
Taylor & Francis Group

LONDON AND NEW YORK

First published 2012 by Ashgate Publishing

Published 2016 by Routledge
2 Park Square, Milton Park, Abingdon, Oxon OX14 4RN
711 Third Avenue, New York, NY 10017, USA

First issued in paperback 2017

Routledge is an imprint of the Taylor & Francis Group, an informa business

British Library Cataloguing in Publication Data
Query, Patrick R.
 Ritual and the idea of Europe in interwar writing.
 1. Ritual in literature. 2. National characteristics in literature. 3. Group identity in literature.
 4. National characteristics, European. 5. Politics and literature – History – 20th century.
 6. Literature and society – History – 20th century. 7. Catholic Church – In literature.
 8. Bullfights in literature. 9. Verse drama, English – 20th century – History and criticism.
 I. Title
 820.9'353'09042-dc23

Library of Congress Cataloging-in-Publication Data
Query, Patrick R.
 Ritual and the idea of Europe in interwar writing / by Patrick R. Query.
  p. cm.
 Includes bibliographical references and index.
 ISBN 978-1-4094-4608-8 (hardcover: alk. paper)
 1. Politics and literature—Europe—History—20th century. 2. Ritual in literature.
 3. Group identity—Europe—History—20th century. 4. Europe—In literature.
 I. Title.
 PN51.Q34 2012
 809'.93358—dc23

                                                                         2012014718

ISBN 13: 978-1-138-10798-4 (pbk)
ISBN 13: 978-1-4094-4608-8 (hbk)

Contents

Acknowledgments

The painter Stanley Spencer, a contemporary of the poet David Jones, was the source of what Jones considered the most "apt expression of the artist's business" he ever heard. The expression was simply: "All must be safely gathered in" (EA 243). I think a similar ideal characterizes the less exalted business of writing a big book of literary criticism. What more apt way to express, too, the goal of acknowledging the host of people who over a period of years have played a part in the book's creation? Here I will gather in many, but not all, and suggest in a small way how much they have meant to me.

I am grateful first to David Chinitz, under whose unerring direction at Loyola University Chicago I began the research that led me to this project, and whose example and support remain near the heart of my professional life. I thank Joyce Wexler, too, for guidance in those early stages, and Allen Frantzen for his counsel and his friendship. Loyola's Crown Fellowship was an invaluable aid in my early research and writing process. I am indebted to Neil Davison for providing me with an enduring model of scholarly excellence, and to early mentors Linc Kesler, Michael Oriard, Audrey Eyler, David Seal, Charles Bergman, and James Albrecht.

Ann Donahue has been a marvelous editor to work with throughout the process: disarming, generous, and patient—ideal qualities for shepherding a first-time author. I thank her and her Ashgate colleagues Seth F. Hibbert, Whitney Feininger, and Juleen Eichinger. This book has also benefitted in significant ways from the feedback provided by two anonymous readers at Ashgate and an anonymous expert on David Jones. For their perceptive and thorough criticism I offer my sincere thanks.

A number of friends at West Point have been keenly supportive during the process of bringing this book to publication, and I especially want to thank Tony McGowan and Peter Molin for many helpful conversations that helped hone the ideas contained in it, and them and their families for making the Hudson Valley feel like home. I am grateful, too, to Rick Kerin, Scott Krawczyk, and Brian Imiola for leading a thoroughly hospitable Department of English and Philosophy, and to Karin Roffman, Rebecca Wisor, John Nelson, Mike Edwards, Bob Tully, Linda Kerin, Justin Gage, Jesse Zuck, and many other colleagues and their families for kindnesses of all kinds. Additional thanks for generosity and camaraderie are due to my fellow members of the Evelyn Waugh Society, particularly John H. Wilson, and of the T.S. Eliot Society, particularly Anthony Cuda. My friend Charles Andrews has been an incomparable ally for many years, and I owe him a great debt as well, as I do Katie and Cullen Sheppard, Rana and Hugh Liebert, and Jodi and John Cabrera, the kinds of friends one has to be lucky to find at just the right time.

One of the most enjoyable aspects of this project has been developing as an aficionado of the bullfight. Much remains for me to learn about this mysterious art, but I am immensely grateful to my friend Ismael Ibáñez Rosales for my early and ongoing education in *toreo* and, with Ana Altemir Giral, for locating the wonderful cover image in the Zaragoza archives. Special thanks are due as well to the author and former *torero* Barnaby Conrad, to Gil Arruda of the Taurine Bibliophiles of America, and to the family of Ignacio Sánchez Mejías

This book is dedicated to my parents, Richard and Pamela Query, to whom I will always be grateful for their willingness to encourage my interest in any and all subjects, including the study of literature. My in-laws, George and Kathleen Sayler, deserve special mention, too, for their support and love as well as an abiding interest in and encouragement of my work, which has buoyed me for years. My children, Fiala Kathleen and Joaquin Richard St. Patrick, are the greatest joys in my life, next to one person: my wife, Michelle. No one knows more about this project than she does, and there is no way I can imagine of repaying, or even of articulating, the debt I owe her for what she has given me and what she has been to me, but I am happy to spend a lifetime trying.

A portion of Chapter 1 appeared in *T.S. Eliot, Dante, and the Idea of Europe*, edited by Paul Douglass (copyright 2011), and is reproduced here by permission of Paul Douglass. An early and modified version of Chapter 3 appeared in *Modern Drama* 51 (2008) and is reprinted with permission from University of Toronto Press Incorporated (www.utpjournals.com).

List of Abbreviations

Works of T.S. Eliot

4Q   *Four Quartets*
ASG *After Strange Gods*
CC   *Christianity and Culture*
CPP   *The Complete Poems and Plays, 1909-1950*
FR   *The Family Reunion*
OPP   *On Poetry and Poets*
SE   *Selected Essays*
SP   *Selected Prose*
SPO   *Selected Poems*
SW   *The Sacred Wood*
TCC   *To Criticize the Critic and Other Writings*

Works of W.B. Yeats

AV   *A Vision*
CP   *Collected Plays*
CPO   *Collected Poems*
E   *Explorations*
EI   *Essays and Introductions*

Works of W.H. Auden

P   *Plays, and Other Dramatic Writings, 1928–1938* (ed. Mendelson)

Works of D.H. Lawrence:

MM   *Mornings in Mexico*
PS   *The Plumed Serpent*

Works of Graham Greene:

LR   *The Lawless Roads*
PG   *The Power and the Glory*

Works of Evelyn Waugh

EAR *Essays, Articles, and Reviews* (ed. Gallagher)
RUL *Robbery Under Law*

Works of David Jones

DG   *The Dying Gaul and Other Writings*
DGC *Dai Greatcoat*
EA   *Epoch and Artist*
IP   *In Parenthesis*

Introduction
Making, Watching, and Using Ritual

The second epigraph to Rebecca West's 1941 book *Black Lamb and Grey Falcon* is a passage from Shakespeare's *Henry V* in which Fluellen says: "I tell you captain, if you look in the maps of the 'orld, I warrant you sall find, in the comparisons between Macedon and Monmouth, that the situations, look you, is both alike."[1] A few pages into the book's Prologue, in which West surveys the history of the Balkans, she describes "a news film which had shown with extraordinary detail the actual death of the King of Yugoslavia" (14). One of the final scenes, in particular, resonates for West:

> Now there is no jolly priest confident that he has the sacred mysteries well in hand ... All these men look as the King looked at his coming, as if there lay behind the surface of things a reality which at any moment might manifest itself as a eucharist to be partaken of not by individuals, but by nations ... They are intensely surprised that the eucharist was of this nature, but the King of Yugoslavia had always thought it might be so. (17)

Finally, she reflects a bit later on the difference between Croat doctors and English ones:

> [T]here was in their minds no vista of shiny hospital corridors, leading to Harley Street and the peerage, with blameless tailoring and courtesy to patients and the handling of committees as subsidiary obligations, such as appears before most English doctors. There was no sense that medical genius must frustrate its own essential quality, which is a fierce concentration on the truth about physical problems, by cultivating self-restraint and a conventional blankness which are incompatible with any ardent pursuit. These people had an air of pure positiveness which amounted to contentiousness. They might have been bull-fighters. They were bull-fighters, of course. The bull was tuberculosis. (76)

The first thing that unites this otherwise heterogeneous and apparently idiosyncratic group of references—to drama, Catholicism, and bullfighting—is that all three represent the invocation of a cultural form not part of the immediate situation in an attempt to render that situation intelligible, an allusion to something tangible and (more or less) familiar to make sense of the intangible and unfamiliar. This is a common enough operation, to be sure, the fashioning of metaphors as footholds in alien territory. It has affinities, moreover, with the "mythical method" that, according to T.S. Eliot, James Joyce's *Ulysses* established for all subsequent narrative writing

---

[1]   The first epigraph in *Black Lamb and Grey Falcon* is a passage from Jean Cocteau's play *Les Chevaliers de la Table Ronde*.

(SP 178). But West is also performing a more specialized operation. Just as the tenor of the metaphors above is always the likeness of Balkan culture to other parts of Europe, she has also chosen for her metaphors a common vehicle, the apparent heterogeneity of which diminishes with the realization that verse drama, the Eucharist, and the bullfight are all instances, at their core, of ritual practice.

The appearance of idiosyncrasy in West's choices diminishes, too, in light of the surprising frequency with which these three forms appear, often in combination, in the writing of West's contemporaries. The idea of invoking ritual—and particularly these three forms—as a means of framing explorations into unfamiliar cultural territory occurred to a number of other British and Irish writers of the 1920s and 1930s. Indeed, it occurred to a number of those, besides West, whose writing has helped to form our understanding of the age. In West's case, the unfamiliar territory she was attempting to access was Yugoslavia, with a particular eye toward the implications of the Balkan story for Great Britain and the rest of Europe. Although the first term in that formula, Yugoslavia, was different for most of West's contemporaries, the concern for Europe was broadly consistent, taking precedence over even the psychological, the sexual, the religious, or the aesthetic. Shared, too, was the habit of attaching questions of European identity to ritual forms.

It must be noted that West's three references above do not amount to a sustained or even deliberate mediation on ritual. The allusion to Shakespeare is a quotation only; it does not dwell upon *Henry V* as verse drama, less still as ritual. Her invocation of the matador does not necessarily imply more than a superficial sense of the ritual of the bullfight, and the lower-case "eucharist" evinces the readiness with which that form, too, is employed as metaphor while being evacuated of much of its orthodox ritual signification. West gets the first word in this study because her use of ritual in the space of the first few pages of *Black Lamb and Grey Falcon*—one of the great twentieth-century works on the idea of Europe— exemplifies the sometimes glancing but nonetheless productive familiarity with ritual characteristic of any number of West's British and Irish contemporaries which, when sustained, narrowed, and deepened by a group of them, became the framework for a nuanced and moving exploration of what Eliot called "the mind of Europe." Eliot, W.B. Yeats, and others whose writing pursued an engagement with ritual as a clue to the mind of Europe, nonetheless betray some of the imprecision, limitations, and dangers of that engagement. The cultural depth and texture that ritual affords as material for writing, but also the fitful success with which that material is managed and deployed, are two hallmarks of a literary phenomenon spanning the interwar years, a phenomenon in which West is implicated and Eliot is at the center.

One is struck in each of West's allusions above by the level of specificity of her references, by her choice of such concrete and local particulars to try to clarify the reader's view of a vast and nebulous object. Part of the impetus behind the present study is the recognition that, for an important group of British and Irish writers between the world wars, no representations of European identity would be meaningful so long as they remained safely superficial, that abstractions would never serve to pinpoint or nurture the idea of Europe so effectively as the particulars of Europe's local cultures. What Timothy Reiss calls the "hope of cultural community" (24) that has always existed in the back of the mind of Europe was, for these writers, brought closer to reality not by the erasure or denial of cultural difference but by the identification of what is shared in the culturally particular. It is an audacious thing to invoke Shakespeare and bullfighters as cultural signifiers in, of all places, Croatia. Considering how many of her contemporaries made similar moves, though, with reference to other European places, and the insights they gained as a result, such audacity begins to look more like real utility.

The three ritual forms West invokes and upon which this study is based—verse drama, the bullfight, and the Mass—have deep, though not unambiguous, roots in European history and possess a complex appeal for writers from across the English Channel. Although Europe possesses, of course, a great many other notable and revealing rituals, these three forms are of particular interest for at least three reasons. First, they conform to the anthropological definition I have chosen, and which I will elucidate fully below, of ritual as a communal, repeated but non-habitual action attached to a sacred space and to long tradition. Second, as publicly produced actions necessarily involving the participation of a number of persons, in which the individual and the group must interact, they partake of much of the same logic as politics proper. They represent a kind of political testing ground, situated in what Eliot called "the pre-political area" (TCC 144), that cultural sphere on which politics must draw but that also functions at a certain remove from the stiff polarities and demands for immediate results native to the political sphere. Third, verse drama, bullfighting, and Catholicism drew more attention than other ritual forms from some of the most important British and Irish writers of the interwar era, including all of those named above in addition to Louis MacNeice, Stephen Spender, Cecil Day Lewis, George Orwell, and Aldous Huxley. The writing these and other authors produced between the world wars constitutes a special body of work linking some of the rituals of Europe to a wide range of political meaning. Where they have been left out, other rituals or pseudo-rituals that might have provided excellent material for this study have most often failed to meet one or more of these three principles of selection. The pilgrimage, the pageant play, and the political rally, in particular, fall only slightly outside my chosen scope, as do some rituals of Judaism and Islam. Likewise, other authors who would have made interesting additions to the current list of subjects have usually had to be excluded because their engagement with one or more of the rituals falls chronologically outside the scope of the interwar years.[2]

---

[2]   That is, the historical period and the rituals of verse drama, bullfight, and Mass came first in the development of this book's topic, and individual authors either adhered to or fell away from that focus. Although several women writers are treated in Chapter 5, their absence from the list of primary subjects above was an unexpected consequence—one in need of further investigation itself—of the paired historical and formal emphases.

Ritual keeps, clarifies, illuminates, and disseminates the key characteristics of a society. But, in the hands of modern writers, it also scrutinizes, repositions, and at times subverts those characteristics. One of my working hypotheses has been that the inherent dialecticism of ritual creates a framework in which some of the most pressing oppositions of the European idea interact and overlap in ways that challenge the usual sense of the rigid political dichotomy of the interwar period. Although ritual in general, and each of these three forms in particular, has been popularly associated with at least a political conservatism and even the extreme Right wing, the literature in question suggests an idea of Europe that is surprisingly inclusive politically. That interwar Europe was fiercely divided politically between communism and fascism, leaving little room in between for liberalism and little interest in democracy, has become a commonplace. In 1928, Eliot, neither a communist nor a fascist himself, wrote: "it is manifest that any disparagement of 'democracy' is nowadays well received by nearly every class of men, and any alternative to 'democracy' is watched with great interest" ("Literature" 287). Just as both sides of the divide, Eliot's "reactionaries and communists" (287), tended toward the ritual performance of their political ideals, writers of radically different political stripes were attracted to the old rituals of Europe for their modern political potential.

The Idea of Europe

In a 1990 lecture, part of a Turin conference on European cultural identity, Jacques Derrida wrote: "I am European, I am no doubt a European intellectual, and I like to recall this, I like to recall this to myself, and why should I deny it? In the name of what?" (*Other Heading* 82). He did not answer his own question, but he did acknowledge one potential deterrent to the continued investigation of European identity: the savor of conservatism that seems to accompany the project.[3] "[T]he very old subject of European identity has the venerable air of an old, exhausted theme. But perhaps," he continued, beginning to suggest not only a way but also a reason to ask the European question anew,

> this 'subject' retains a virgin body. Would not its name mask something that does not yet have a face? We ask ourselves in hope, in fear and trembling, what this face is going to resemble. Will it still resemble? Will it resemble the face of some

---

[3]   Although conservative commentaries are outnumbered in contemporary critical (especially literary) debates by the kinds of deconstructive approaches taken up in this Introduction, the seemingly intuitive association of "Europe" with ideals of order, tradition, and hierarchy remains, likely a function of residual cultural memories or a perceived rhetorical necessity. For an articulation of the conservative position on European cultural identity, see *The Future of the European Past* (ed. Hilton Kramer and Roger Kimball), a product of *The New Criterion*. The essays in this collection focus on the diagnosis of a "crisis" in European culture brought on, for instance, by the influence of popular culture, and on the defense of European "tradition" in a fairly narrow sense.

persona whom we believe we know: Europe? And if its non-resemblance bears the traits of the future, will it escape monstrosity? (5)

This study proposes that the accepted answers—both conservative and progressive—to the question "What is Europe?" mask one of the faces of Europe. During the 1920s and 1930s, that face, I hope to show, resembled nothing so much as the reconciliatory action of three of Europe's own ritual forms.

Before returning to the interwar period, some discussion of the European idea in broader (though necessarily abbreviated) terms may be useful. Although the question of European identity has been asked for as long as, or longer than, the word "Europe" has existed, the proffered answers have not changed a great deal.[4] Bernard Crick, in his Foreword to the collection *The Idea of Europe in Literature*, surveys several, though not all, of the usual suspects. From the Zeus-abducting-Europa myth he derives the answer, Europe is not Asia.[5] A second historically popular though relentlessly debated possibility is: Europe is Christendom.[6] And, if one entertains this possibility, one must also consider whether Europe is actually the Roman Empire. Europe might also be the spiritual offspring of the Enlightenment, "felt," according to Andreas Michel, "in such philosophical ideas as reason, liberty, and equality, in political ideals such as democracy and human rights, as well as in the enterprises of science and technology" (232).[7] This view is related to that of Edmund Husserl (and many others) that the essence of Europe is traceable to the philosophical spirit of sixth- and seventh-century B.C. Greece,[8] and to that of Benedetto Croce (whom Denis de Rougemont calls a "good European" (390)) that liberty and humanism are the core ideas of European identity (358). The famous political divide of the years between the world wars

---

[4]   In his seminal book, *The Idea of Europe*, Denis de Rougemont identifies the first mention of "Europe" as Hesiod's c. 900 B.C. and "the first mention of Europe as not just a geographical but a human entity" as that found in the sequel to Isidore de Seville's *Chronicle* c. 754. He devotes some six pages as well to sketching the main lines of etymological hypothesis concerning the term *Europe* itself (3, 25–30).

[5]   De Rougemont names Hippocrates as the "first to describe Europe and to compare it with Asia" (3).

[6]   Today, for instance, the idea of the European Union as a Christian club continues to present an unofficial obstacle to Turkey's inclusion. See the work of Omer Taspinar. Jacques Derrida critiques Jan Patočka's interpretation of the philosophical birth and development of Europe, which "traces ... a genius of Christianity that is the history of Europe" (*Gift* 3), but Europe-as-Christianity is also the third "mystery," after "orgiastic" and "Platonic," in Derrida's own theory of European "responsibility" (2–34).

[7]   Michel understands all of these enlightenment associations to be subsumed within "the idea of Europe ... as a marker for the European project of universal emancipation ... The idea of universal emancipation shapes the claims of the enlightenment" (232).

[8]   Husserl famously explicated this view in his "Vienna Lecture" of 1935, "Philosophy and the Crisis of European Man." In Husserl 269–300.

was matched, de Rougemont argues, by one focused on a particular aspect of European cultural history:

> Two great schools of cultural historians differed violently with each other on this score during the so-called interwar period (1919–1939). One, programmatically optimistic, continued the tradition of the Enlightenment, of Promethean science and technology, and regarded Europe as a creation of the Renaissance. The other, pessimistic more by allegiance than by nature, regarded the great centuries of the Catholic Middle Ages (from the eleventh to the thirteenth) as the only Europe worthy of the name. The Europe of Man and the future *vs.* the Europe of Christendom and the past? What we have here is rather a polemic between two parties both genuinely concerned with saving the present-day Europe—a Europe threatened from without by the rise of 'quantitative empires,' and from within by age-old divisions. But to which of the saints should we appeal? Or to which of the scientists? (380–81)

More starkly still, Michel compels his audience to consider the possibility that the spirit of "universal emancipation," coupled with a history of slavery, colonialism, and holocaust, indicates that the meaning of Europe amounts to "a geopolitics of exploitation" (233). Each of these possibilities, of course, like each of the potential answers enumerated by Crick, whatever its particular advantages, is riddled with too many blind spots, exclusions, and false assumptions to satisfy on its own.[9] Crick, though, offers a further response that suggests the special contribution literary scholarship can make to the European question: Europe is ambiguous. It is a "core of meaning," he writes, "around which clusters of ... associations revolve ... a magnetic field around which particulars revolve" (x). Underscoring the importance of the literary to a full understanding of European politics, he argues "how much more our perceptions of national identity and of political and social justice are shaped by literature than by formal history ... [I]maginative literature," he continues, "is both the main source of most people's understandings of 'Europe' and a potent factor from way, way back in the construction of the concept" (xii). Thus, not only does the capacity for ambiguity allow literature to comprehend more of an ambiguous Europe than, say, "formal history"; literature may be largely responsible for the European concept itself, including its ambiguity.

The literature under investigation here shows British writers drawing upon that ambiguity and pressing it to new lengths. These writers' interest in ritual tends to draw their focus not to the traditional centers of liberal European *esprit*—Paris, Vienna, Switzerland, the Low Countries, for instance—but to some of Europe's

---

[9]   For just one example, to cite Anthony Pagden: "[N]either the Roman Empire, nor Christendom was, of course, identical with 'Europe.' Much of the Roman Empire lay in Asia and in North Africa. Christianity had begun as an Asian religion, and the first Christian churches had been established on the North African littoral" ("Conceptualizing" 45). Neither does de Rougemont ignore the "symmetrically similar errors committed by both schools" in the interwar Catholic-versus-Enlightenment debate. Instead, he defers to Christopher Dawson to complicate and correct the narrower positions.

physical and traditional peripheries, such as Ireland, Wales, and Spain, and in several cases as far afield as Mexico and Japan, all of which become enfolded in a fluid, complex, and portable picture of European cultural identity. At least since Edward Said's *Orientalism*, it has been necessary to account for the non-Western *other* in any and all accounts of European self-imagining. As Robert M. Dainotto demonstrates in *Europe (In Theory)*, Eurocentrism (a thorny term I will explore more fully below) is rendered problematic not only "from the outside but from the marginal inside of Europe itself" (4).[10] "A modern European identity," he writes, "begins when the non-Europe is internalized—when the south, indeed, becomes the sufficient and indispensable *internal* Other: Europe, but also the negative part of it." Dainotto's focus is southern Europe in the eighteenth and nineteenth centuries; that of the present study is somewhat broader geographically, somewhat later historically. It does not attend to all or even most of the "marginal inside" of Europe, leaving Eastern Europe, the Balkans, and the extreme North, for instance, all but untouched. However, by foregrounding the Celtic, Hispanic, and other margins of Western Europe, it does attempt to complicate, as do the works of both Said and Dainotto, at least one "lofty" but also "parochial" version of the idea of Europe (Dainotto 4–5).

An idea of Europe constructed at Europe's margins—geographical, cultural, historical—necessarily invites a great deal of ambiguity as to the limits of European coherence. The ritual emphasis, however, has the effect of tethering such ambiguity to concrete reality, to the visible evidence of discrete places, objects, and bodies in action, rather than encouraging a meditation on the idea of Europe that is entirely free-floating, nebulous, hypothetical. As Reiss argues:

> Writing does not dwell in a disembodied arena where there is no place for light and shadow, croissants and gouda, political dirt and concrete cultural dissension, gray ghosts of low clouds over polders, the gloom of broken San Sebastian bullfights, and the horror of half-wit soccer battles. It feeds on and lives in what Yourcenar calls 'the frightful smell of humanity,' caught up in 'life itself, with its chaos of formless and violent occurrence.' (16)

As with writing, so with ritual and, as Reiss implies, with the idea of Europe. However, in verse drama, the bullfight, and the Mass, much of that "chaos" and "formlessness" is given shape, and writers interested in these rituals often turn to them as a means of ordering violence without banishing ambiguity.

The tolerance of ambiguity is crucial to the argument of this study, not only because the cultural complexity of Europe seems to demand it but also because ritual meaning itself, as will be discussed below, is inherently ambiguous. Rather than insist on an answer to the question, What is Europe?—which in its implication

---

[10]   Dainotto's focus is on the traditionally assumed backwardness of southern Europe in the eyes of the north: indeed, "PIGS": Portugal, Italy, Greece, and Spain (2). The debt crises of 2010 and 2012, with their epicenter in Greece but implicating Italy, Spain, and Portugal as well, are a timely reminder of another kind of southern European marginality.

of essentials does imply an unproductive cultural conservatism—I will instead ask, What does an idea of Europe expressed in the literature of ritual contain? What cultural material adheres to it, and what falls away? How well does this idea of Europe experienced in ritual respond to the cultural and political demands of the interwar period? I will treat the concept of European identity rather as Derrida recommends: "Like the fission reaction it propagates in our discourse, the paradox of the paradox should lead us to take the old name of Europe at once very seriously and cautiously, that is, to take it lightly, only in quotation marks, as the best paleonym, in a certain situation, for what we recall (to ourselves) or what we promise (ourselves)" (82).

In his introduction to the *PMLA* special issue, "Literature and the Idea of Europe," Reiss chooses *memory* and *imagination* as his operative terms, echoing Derrida's "what we recall" and "what we promise."[11] The articulation of any notion of European identity, Reiss argues, involves acts of selective remembering. What Europe means depends on what parts of the history of Europe one chooses to remember. And any remotely comprehensive idea of Europe must include the parts of European history and culture that argue against any positive identification. European culture, after all, is full of much that is, supposedly, *not* Europe, just as European history is fraught with violence of all kinds perpetrated against (and by) its global neighbors and between its own constituent parts.[12] "Both associations," Reiss writes, "—with imperialism and with internal violence—show how the very idea of Europe falls ambiguously between the exclusive and the inclusive, how 'Europe' has always foundered over its identity and its relations with others" (19). Derrida argues that the fissures and wounds of Europe are inseparable from its cohesion:

> Hope, fear, and trembling are commensurate with the signs that are coming to us from everywhere in Europe, where, precisely in the name of identity, be it cultural or not, the worst violences, those that we recognize all too well without yet having thought them through, the crimes of xenophobia, racism, anti-Semitism, religious or nationalist fanaticism, are being unleashed, mixed up, mixed up with each other, but also, and there is nothing fortuitous in this, mixed in with the breath, with the respiration, with the very 'spirit' of the promise. (6)

---

[11]   Similar pairs abound in modern philosophical formulations of the idea of Europe. Bruno Snell writes that the question "'What do I want to do?' is in [the Western] mind always linked with the further question 'Who am I, and what have I been?'" (qtd. in de Rougemont 370).

[12]   "Claimed historical unities," argues Craig Calhoun, "tend to be constructed on the basis of highly selective readings of history" (52). As an "alternative to selfsameness as a way of approaching large-scale collective identities," Calhoun follows Ludwig Wittgenstein in suggesting that one should "think of Europe as a field of multiple, overlapping, and sometimes even conflicting identities." From such a field, European "similarity" does emerge, "not from a lowest common denominator nor from rigidly enforced boundaries but from characteristics that many Europeans hold in common without any being definitive of the whole" (52).

Skeptics take these troubling associations as evidence of the impossibility of formulating any meaningful idea of Europe in a world from which official imperialism has been banished and in which the ties of international commerce supersede those of historical or cultural identification. The history of Europe is, in Reiss's words, "fraught with conflict over national and international identity, individualism and community, sovereignty and collectivity" (19), a fact that might be taken to invalidate any notion of a European "identity." Yet what Luigi Barzini calls "the European Dream" has obstinately survived.[13]

Its most vocal adherents, moreover, have often been non-Europeans. Susan Sontag, an American "of European-Jewish descent," writes, "One might think that the notion of Europe would have been thoroughly discredited, first by imperialism and racism, and then by the imperatives of multi-national capitalism. In fact, it has not" (285–87).[14] On the contrary, such tensions are what make the articulation of such a notion possible in a critical landscape in which all identity is multiple and riven with conflict, in which what contributes to identity and what is excluded from it are interdependent.[15] The ambiguities of Europe—"of struggling sovereignties, of constituting identity, of the relation between European cultures and war and between them and what and whom they exclude" (Reiss 21), and of Europeans themselves as "foreigners in their own land, caught between an identity they are losing and the identity of an other that invites at the same time as it frightens them" (Gambaudo 225)—constitute the new basis for critical inquiry into the idea of Europe.[16] Thus the present study prefers to conceive of "Europe" as a *way* instead

---

[13]   Barzini's "European Dream" describes the desire, "many centuries old," of seeing Europe politically unified on the basis of its "irrational, emotional" sense of identification (11). Among those who have championed it, Barzini cites Kant, Voltaire, Rousseau, Bentham, Garribaldi, "obdurate conservatives such as Klemens Metternich and revolutionary apostles such as Pierre Proudhon." Ètienne Balibar ends his influential essay "World Borders, Political Borders" with the challenge: "Europe impossible: Europe possible" (77).

[14]   In her essay "The Idea of Europe," Sontag touches upon some historical and political implications of the European idea, but her appeal is primarily lyric: "If I must describe what Europe means to me as an American, I would start with liberation. Liberation from what passes in America for a culture. The diversity, seriousness, fastidiousness, density of European culture constitute an Archimedean point from which I can, mentally, move the world. I cannot do that from America, from what American culture gives me, as a collection of standards, as a legacy. Hence Europe is essential to me" (286).

[15]   Jacques Derrida argues that the spiritual development of Europe, from orgiastic to Platonic to Christian mystery, is itself a study of changing models of "incorporation and repression, what occurs between one conversion and another" (*Gift* 10).

[16]   In interpreting Derrida, Andreas Michel offers his own litany of "sinister historical events and conceptions involving Europe," including "slavery, colonialism, the holocaust, classism, sexism, and homophobia" (232). All of these, writes Michel, "occurred, for the most part, concurrently with the project of universal emancipation" and thus "seem to have been compatible with, perhaps even sanctioned by the idea of Europe." Like Derrida, Timothy Reiss, and Sylvie Gambaudo, however, Michel sees such troubling associations not merely as validating the anti-Eurocentric viewpoint but, rather, as suggesting the complexity, even the paradox, with which modernity itself is faced as it comes to terms with its Eurocentric elements.

of an object, and to approach the analysis of a body of literature as an attempt to create what Reiss calls "a field of relations that incorporates [European] identity, while denying such identity any singular accumulation of properties" (27). No monolithic "Europe" will emerge, but rather a pattern of literary representation suggestive of a complex and surprisingly fluid relation between the constituent parts of Europe and, at times, with its geographical and spiritual others.[17]

This formulation borrows the language of modern globalization studies, and the present discussion of the idea of Europe relocates some of the critical inquiries globalization has occasioned. The "relatively new culturalist orientation" to globalization theory has in recent years prompted scholars to find new ways of addressing what Paul Jay calls a "growing deterritorialization of culture" (37–38). Jay observes that globalization theory has mobilized and capitalized on the "relatively recent interest in culture as a fluid, mobile, transnational phenomenon that predates and often ignores nation-state boundaries" (37). One scholar pressing for the idea of the mobility of culture is James Clifford, who argues, "We need to conjure with new localizations like 'the border,' specific places of 'hybridity and struggle, policing and transgression'" (109). Places, that is, like modern Europe.[18]

If there has been a critical reluctance to allow "Europe" an important place in literary globalization studies, it may be because what Derrida calls "the exhausted programs of *Eurocentrism* and *anti-Eurocentrism*, these exhausting yet unforgettable programs" (12) have continued to exert influence past their former usefulness. The current moment demands a more nuanced, more flexible model, and that model has begun to take shape in the writing of a few important theorists. Carlos Fuentes does much in a very few words to reconfigure the landscape. The "'other face,'" of Europe, he argues, "is 'Ibero-America … whose colours are also Amerindian and African' and which is as close in spirit as 'Europe beyond the Danube is [as] a physical fact'" (qtd. in Reiss 19). Fuentes's boldness is compelling, but to some critics it overlooks the problem of power relations.[19] These critics, says Jay, argue that "globalization theory too easily colonizes discrete local cultures, subordinating them to sweeping formulations that are often Eurocentric" (41–42). What happens, as Dainotto has asked, when the cultures in question are all European, either "in spirit" or in "physical fact"? Globalization theory, with its emphasis on the dynamic interaction of local and global cultures, puts pressure on

---

[17]   Craig Calhoun similarly concludes, "Europe is constructed out of both categorical similarities and relational ties, but no one set of these reaches all Europeans without joining a range of non-Europeans as well" (52).

[18]   The language of globalization made its way into European studies long ago, even if the reverse is only slowly taking place. As Ètienne Balibar argued in a 1999 lecture in Greece: "We must privilege the issue of the border when discussing the questions of the European people and of the state in Europe because it crystallizes the stakes of politico-economic power and the symbolic stakes at work in the collective imagination: relations of force and material interest on one side, representation of identity on the other" ("Borders" 73).

[19]   See, for example, Enrique Dussel, "Eurocentrism and Modernity" 75 n.15.

the idea of Europe, challenges it, forces its continuous reevaluation (and Europe returns the favor), but it does not erase it. The term "Europe" names a unique phenomenon that globalization theory must account for if it is to fully realize its potential: a model of cultural identification that transcends economics and politics, extending beyond the nation-state but not to the entire globe, one that bespeaks internationalism even as it resists sweeping internationalization. Anthony Pagden writes: "Europeans are, I suspect, unusual in sharing in this way a sense that it might be possible to belong to something larger than the family, the tribe, the community, or the nation yet smaller and more culturally specific than 'humanity'" ("Conceptualizing" 53). Europe is a unique and essential third term in the local-global dyad, one that any reasonably thorough discussion of globalization cannot afford to ignore.[20]

Work on the relationship among individual, national, and transnational identity in modern Europe has been steadily increasing in the past two decades, and the coming together of this discourse and that of globalization studies seems inevitable. "Despite its ostensibly self-evident quality," writes Lars-Erik Cederman, "Europe belongs to the most elusive and contested entities in today's international system" (1). As Étienne Balibar has declared: "[W]e are dealing with "triple points" or mobile "overlapping zones" of contradictory civilizations rather than with juxtapositions of monolithic entities. In all its points, Europe is multiple" ("Borders" 74). Recent symposia have considered the idea of Europe in terms of Gilles Deleuze and Félix Guattari's theory of the nomadic self spread across multiple national territories. And there has been growing discussion (pushed to a new level of interest in Dainotto's work) of the ways the traditional peripheries of Europe—especially Ireland and, more recently still, Turkey and even Iceland—figure in the European whole.

One of the most wide-ranging book-length studies of the European idea published in the last decade is the collection edited by Pagden, *The Idea of Europe: From Antiquity to the European Union* (2002). Pagden's own chapter "Europe: Conceptualizing a Continent" very neatly illustrates key terms that have long governed debates on the meaning of Europe: language, religion, the rule of law, the city, the idea of exceptionality, and others. His is a historical-political survey, not a literary study, but its concern with identity does recommend it as a contextual aid to my own investigations. The same can be said of *The Meaning of Europe: Variety and Contention with and among Nations* (ed. Mikael af Malmborg and Bo Ström), a fascinating collection in which each essay considers the influence of the

---

[20] Jürgen Habermas sees a special significance for the European idea "in a complex global society," namely, the lesson that "it is not just the divisions that count, but also the soft power of negotiating agendas, relations, and economic advantages ... The EU already offers itself as a form of 'governance beyond the nation-state,' which could set a precedent in the postnational constellation" ("February 15" 293–94). In another place, he cites Mario Telò and Paul Magnette, who write: "The Union may be seen as a laboratory in which Europeans are striving to implement the values of justice and solidarity in the context of an increasing global economy" (qtd. in Habermas, "Why" 12).

European idea on the process of self-identification of a different nation.[21] Another important and even more recent collection, *Myths of Europe* (2007), edited by Richard Littlejohns and Sara Soncini, is especially relevant to the present study because it focuses substantially on literature and because its essays collectively cast a wide geographical net, from India to Ireland. The books' readings of literature are unlike my own in that they both cover the whole of Western history and are explicitly concerned with answering questions of twenty-first-century European identity. Its use of myth, while narrowing the discussion somewhat, describes a far wider field of investigation than does my own use of ritual. Still, in the questions it asks regarding the relationship between traditional inheritance and modern-day efforts at identity formation, *Myths of Europe* helpfully prepares some of the ground for my own, more acutely focused exploration.

Seamus Deane, like the contributors to *The Meaning of Europe*, looks at Europe through the lens of one locality—in this case, Ireland. Although some of Deane's ideas helped to inspire the present study, they also represent one of the key viewpoints from which opposition to my own premises may come. Deane's Field Day Theatre Company represents one of the most tangible and pertinent manifestations of the patterns of thought being explored here. Deane and the other Field Day founders have made it their business "to engage in the action of establishing a system that has an enabling, a mobilizing energy, the energy of assertion and difference" (15). Deane has made a career out of defending cultural particularity against the seemingly overwhelming discursive barrage of "diversity." His own work has focused on Ireland, but it is representative of a whole movement having as its aim the "repossession" of colonial and post-colonial writers "for an interpretation ... governed by a reading of the conditions in which their work was produced and in the [culturally specific] conditions in which it was read" (11). He has labored to restore their Irish particularity to, for instance, Yeats and James Joyce, who "had been (mis)read in the light of what was understood to be English or British literature, international modernism, the plight of humankind in the twentieth century ... to repossess their revolutionary and authoritative force for the here and now of the present in Ireland" (11). By extension, Deane has deplored what he sees as the recent rush in Ireland toward integration and internationalism, a movement that he sees, with the wisdom of considerable firsthand experience, as symptomatic of the clandestinely oppressive claims of global diversity. In 1990 his anxiety centered on the eagerness of the Irish Republic to embrace "all of those corporate, 'international' opportunities offered by the European Economic Community and the tax-free visitations of international cartels" (14).[22] To resituate

---

[21] *Engaging Europe: Rethinking a Changing Continent* (2005), edited by Evlyn Gould and George J. Sheridan, Jr., is concerned primarily with pedagogical questions, but its essays do provide very useful inroads to the idea of contemporary Europe. The book also features a most helpful bibliographic essay.

[22] In the intervening two decades, Ireland of course shot to the forefront of both European *and* global economic cooperation, and then its star predictably fell somewhat. Whether the cultural results of the process for Ireland will be what Deane feared remains

Ireland in a global, or at least European, context in which all the meaningful Irish "lesions and occlusions are forgotten, in which the postmodernist simulacrum of pluralism supplants the search for a legitimating mode of nomination and origin, is surely to pass from one colonizing experience into another," he argued (19). With this and with all of Deane's views thus far enumerated the current project is entirely in sympathy. It is, predictably, on the question of Europe that differences begin to emerge.

Deane's anxiety over the loss of cultural particularity in the face of European integrative measures is characteristic of the conservative position on the idea of Europe (and, for that matter, on the institution of the European Union). It is not my intent, in selecting a wider lens through which to view not only Ireland but also Great Britain, Spain, and other countries in the context of Europe, to elide or minimize difference, nomination, or origin, blending all into a bland (and false) picture of European "unity in diversity." On the contrary, this study centers on origins, in the form of some ancient rituals that interwar literature invokes, and on the shock of difference that invariably accompanies a writer's ingress to another country. Every effort to show the political multiplicity of which these forms are capable in the context of interwar Europe, and the ways in which they create connections between nations, will have to address the very real ways in which the same forms isolate and divide nations. Likewise, the emphasis on border-crossings, travel, and cultural exchange is chosen especially for what it *can* reveal about origin, nationality, and difference. As Susanne Fendler and Ruth Wittlinger rightly acknowledge, "the nation-state is still the most important political (f)actor in the context of European integration" ("Contribution" xix). It has long been (and probably still is) the most important "(f)actor" in European literary production as well.[23] Deane, speaking of Irish particularity, insists, "Nature may be a cultural invention, but it is nonetheless powerful for that" (17). At the other extreme is the view of Friedrich Nietzsche, who a century earlier decried "the morbid estrangement which the lunacy of nationality has produced ... between the people of Europe ... Europe wants to become one" (*Beyond Good and Evil* 120). Somewhere between them lies the idea of a European internationalism that

to be seen, but the presence of the usual multinational corporations in Ireland has already begun to suggest a certain amount of at least superficial homogenization. It is estimated today that of Ireland's population of 4.2 million, some 500,000 are immigrants, the majority from Eastern Europe, Asia, and Africa.

[23] Jürgen Habermas, who advocates a positive political unity for Europe, does so fully aware of the role of nationalism in Europe's identity. "[W]hat," he asks, "could hold together a region characterized more than any other by the ongoing rivalries between self-conscious nations? ... Europe is composed of nation-states that delimit one another polemically. National consciousness, formed by national languages, national literatures, and national histories, has long operated as an explosive force" ("February 15" 294). Yet he sees this history, and Europe's responses to it, as the basis for the idea of Europe in the 21st century: "The acknowledgement of differences—the reciprocal acknowledgement of the Other in his otherness—can also become a feature of common identity" (ibid. 294).

contains nationalism without erasing it, a whole that maintains the integrity of each part. While the powerful political movements of the interwar period espoused a view similar to Nietzsche's, those who asserted it, especially the Nazis, did so in the teeth of an equally powerful inclination *against* pan-Europeanism. The perfect balance between the parts of Europe and an idea of its wholeness has throughout history been impossible to strike on the ground. Yet the provisional modeling of such a balance remains an attractive, and important, project for literary and cultural studies. Reiss concludes: "Neither community, as some kind of party-led mechanism, nor individualism, as some foundational absolute, can stand alone. Their interplay may be sensed first in aesthetic culture" (27). The special utility of European ritual is that, although it does exist in "aesthetic culture," it is also rooted in the public, material culture of Europe, so its modeling of "interplay" brings the observer a step closer to the elusive political reality.

Ritual and Literature

When one moves from anthropological, sociological, and religious analyses into studies of literary texts, there is at once a noticeable slippage in the precision with which ritual functions as a critical category, and an exponential expansion of the territory covered by the term. René Girard's enormously influential work— particularly in *The Scapegoat* (1986) but also *Violence and the Sacred* (1977) and *Things Hidden Since the Beginning of the World* (1987)—identifying the sacrificial scapegoat mechanism as a foundation of Western literary texts is partly responsible, for, very much in the manner of the Freudian Oedipal propositions it was designed to challenge, it established the precedent of totalizing the local object of inquiry—the scapegoat ritual—as a template for virtually all forms of human cultural practice. In the process, Girard shifted the focus from the individual psyche to the human community, and his formulations have proven very attractive indeed to scholars interested in transcending the critical hegemony of Freudian Oedipal codes.

Two recent books, William A. Johnsen's *Violence and Modernism* and Thomas Cousineau's *Ritual Unbound*, provide representative examples of the kind of investigations of modern literature, especially fiction, to which the Girardian hypothesis has led scholars. They are useful here both for their articulation of some of the principles that guide this study and for delineating the ways in which my own method differs from Girardian readings. First, Johnsen usefully points up the distinction between an interest in ritual and an interest in the primitive. Following Girard and Northrop Frye, he refuses the common view of "a 'return' of myth in modern times ... the usual literary journalism which talks of a psychological or cultural neoprimitivism" (ix). Like Girard and Frye, Johnsen is "careful to keep the relation of the primitive to the modern schematic, saying that myth ... [is] the logical (not necessarily chronological) origin of literature" (ix). Cousineau agrees that "the modernist use of ritual elements cannot be interpreted as simply an act of recovery. Rather, it amounts to a profoundly critical act" (16). The verse drama, the bullfight, and the Mass wear a badge of the past fairly prominently. They all have long histories and, in the context of modern Europe, stand out for that reason. Twentieth-century writers' interest in these particular rituals naturally implies a certain amount of chronological looking-back, at least a superficial sense of the tradition behind the forms. Yet Yeats, Eliot, W.H. Auden, and others held virtually no interest in what Johnsen calls "some atavistic return to origins" (2).

Both Johnsen and Cousineau use the expansive analytical mode, characteristic of contemporary Girardian applications, which is quite different from mine. Based on a correct identification of the modern "secularization of violent myth and ritual" (Johnsen 18), this expansive mode tends to metaphorize ritual, making it possible to see ritual in all manner of human activity, diminishing, I would argue, the revelations that ritual in a stricter sense still holds. The underlying premise of the former view is that the ritual mechanism which once ordered sacrifice has been sublimated (to borrow from Sigmund Freud) as modern human patterns of organization and exclusion, and that the scapegoat ritual, as the basis for every cultural form, is visible in all of them. For Johnsen it includes, for instance, both "private, domestic, or social interactions ... and global relations" (x). For example, among the "forms of ritual exclusion" in Conrad's *Heart of Darkness*, Cousineau includes the way that "the members of the company affirm their solidarity through the judgment whereby they designate Kurtz as a pariah, and Marlow constructs a community of civilized white males by excluding black Africans and European women" (20). Similarly, the fact that "Lily, as a woman, should not intrude upon a male preserve" in *To The Lighthouse* is, according to Cousineau, part of Virginia Woolf's "portrayal of a community that resorts to exclusionary, sacrificial practices" (Cousineau 21). Even the social divisions depicted in Dickens's *Our Mutual Friend* are "ritualized exclusions" (Cousineau 24). Once ritual becomes metaphor, its potential applications, it would seem, are endless. Cousineau does acknowledge that "[t]he sacrificial rituals that we find in these novels are not so much observable communal practices as they are hypothetical constructions that have been projected upon the stories by their narrators" (17). His interest, like Johnsen's, is in unpacking the ritual significance not only in the stories themselves but also in the self-conscious narrative techniques of modernism, including the effects that point of view and authorial framing have on the way readers interpret those "rituals." Thus, "when Nick Carraway refers to Gatsby's death as a 'holocaust,' we recognize in his choice of this term his desire to construct a sacrificial scene that does not apply in an obvious and unarguable way to the actual circumstances of Gatsby's death" (Cousineau 17). Cousineau and Johnsen are both far more interested in the Girardian social themes of violence, victimization, and exclusion than in any quality or feature described by ritual alone. The objects of my attention, however, are precisely those "observable communal practices," cases in which the presence of ritual is "obvious and unarguable," or nearly so. If Cousineau, Johnsen, and others are interested in the ritualization of everyday life, to borrow another phrase from Freud, I am interested in those rituals that persist deliberately apart from the everyday. The whisky-priest hero of Graham Greene's novel *The Power and the Glory* reflects upon the action of the Mass saying "everything in time became a routine but this" (PG 71), suggesting that, rather as Europe is resistant to the full diffusion and flattening of qualities globalization seems to herald, real ritual is distinguished by its resistance to the unreflective everyday.

When dealing with ritual in literature, one must come to terms with Girard's thesis. However, owing to the wide applicability of that thesis, a great deal more in literature has come to be called ritual than either Girard's original subject or what the present study intends. Certain literary scholars weary of being told that everything is sex have in turn begun to suggest that virtually every social act in literature is ritual—or sacrifice, or exclusion, or some other hastily applied synonym. For instance, in a Modernist Studies Association panel a few years ago, one participant proposed that bombing London during World War II was a ritual. Whether such scholars are right or wrong is not truly the concern of this study. I would suggest, however, that neither Girard's scapegoating thesis nor its many permutations in literary analyses of all kinds do an adequate job of explaining the attraction of modern writers to rituals in the stricter, anthropological sense. Even if ordinary modern social behaviors fulfill and replace the imperatives of the ancient sacrificial ritual (the way that sublimation or neurosis fulfills and replaces Oedipal desires), actual, formal enactments of that ritual still persist. And why, to press further, were they so attractive to British and Irish writers of the interwar period? Verse plays, bullfights, and Masses are not like the living creatures, assumed to exist only in fossil form, that occasionally emerge from the sea or the woods, confounding accepted explanations of present reality; they have never ceased to exist in plain sight, right alongside the processes of cultural substitution that are supposed to have displaced them.

Anthropologists do not always agree on the definition of ritual, but even in their disagreements there is a firmer and more satisfying basis for understanding than is offered by the bulk of current literary scholarship putatively concerned with ritual. I have chosen to rely primarily on the definitions of ritual offered by scholars of anthropology and religion because these more systematically formulate the kinds of deliberate formal structures that characterize the rituals here under investigation. Besides bespeaking an idea of Europe in a less diluted form, the verse drama, the bullfight, and the Mass partake so much more fully of the logic of true ritual than do the sundry social interactions for which ritual is often invoked as a metaphor that they stand apart and require separate attention. They retain something akin to what Walter Benjamin called the "aura" that adheres to original works of art but not to their innumerable mechanical reproductions (221).[24] In the

---

[24]   "[T]hat which withers in the age of mechanical reproduction is the aura of the work of art. This is a symptomatic process whose significance points beyond the realm of art. One might generalize by saying: the technique of reproduction detaches the reproduced object from the domain of tradition" (221).

modern European world, these rituals do something that most other "observable communal practices," much less "hypothetical constructions" thereof, do not: create a space apart from the flow of ordinary experience wherein the temporal and relational dynamics of ordinary experience are transcended and thus seen anew: "everything in time became a routine but this."

The prevailing definitions of ritual—and there are many—from anthropological-religious quarters tend to agree upon a few key points, beyond which exist broad differences of opinion and emphasis. Perhaps the most basic point of agreement among these definitions is that ritual is action.[25] This distinguishes ritual from myth, from which it derives, and from symbol, with which it is frequently carried out. Still, the relationship among myth, ritual, and symbol is so intimate that there is considerable latitude for movement among the three terms, though not so much as seems to be allowed between ritual and its associated terms in the literary-Girardian schema. In common usage, ritual is often used to name what is more accurately called *habit* as well as the behaviors associated with obsession, what Freud called "neurotic ceremonials" (430). True ritual is like both of these forms in that it is a formal, repetitive action, but in most anthropological and religious scholarship is distinguished from them by virtue of its being essentially collective and maintaining a special location.[26] As Jan Koster argues, "Like the words and idioms of language, ritual acts belong to the socio-cultural repertoire of a community" (212). Koster's theory of ritual centers on the simultaneous processes of "ego-reduction" and "collective identity-building (*communitas*)" inherent in ritual (223).[27] A ritual *location* or what George Mosse calls a "sacred space" (208) has been one of the defining elements of ritual since the earliest times and can be nearly as constitutive of the effects of ritual as is the action itself. Indeed, in his excellent essay "Ritual Performance and the Politics of Identity" (2003), Koster deliberately pays "just as much attention to the ubiquitous presence of ritual space as to the rituals themselves" (214). Verse drama, bullfighting, and Roman Catholic rite encourage the observer to do likewise, as the spaces of their enactment are

---

[25]   Catherine Bell's interrogation of the ostensible divide between action and thought in ritual is considerably more nuanced than this, but she nonetheless takes action as a starting point for the discussion of ritual (19–23).

[26]   Sigmund Freud underscores the first difference. The "compulsions and prohibitions" of neurotics, he writes, "apply ... to the subject's solitary activities and for a long time leave his social behaviour unaffected. Sufferers ... are consequently able to treat their affliction as a private matter and keep it concealed for many years" (430). Moreover, such actions are marked by a "greater individual variability ... in contrast to the stereotyped character of rituals" (431).

[27]   The terms here may call to mind Benedict Anderson's *Imagined Communities* as well as the more recent and also influential *A Shrinking Island* (2003) by Jed Esty. While both of these books relate in interesting ways to my own argument, the primacy in Anderson and Esty of the concept of *nationalism* is ultimately the key difference that kept them from figuring more prominently in my investigation.

integral to their meaning and to their engagement with European culture, and distinguish them from everyday activities.

Finally, true ritual is differentiated from habit or obsessive practices, as well as from play, in that ritual requires at least an implied connection to tradition, to the maintenance and adaptation of a collective action over time. From even this limited sense of tradition it is but a small step to perhaps the most disputed element of ritual: belief. Most contemporary formulations of ritual choose to downplay the extent to which belief in the supernatural is essential to it. According to Koster, "the presence or absence of religion is irrelevant in the most basic theoretical characterization of ritual" (214). In doing so, they are opposing such theorists as Victor Turner, who holds that ritual cannot exist apart from its "religious component" (79). Thus, Turner defines ritual as "prescribed formal behavior not given over to technological routine, having reference to beliefs in invisible beings or powers regarded as the first and final causes of all effects" (79).[28] He credits Auguste Comte, Godfrey and Monica Wilson, and Ruth Benedict for this definition, as against Sir Edmund Leach and others who "would eliminate the religious component."[29] He might also have credited Eliot, who wrote in 1925: "For you cannot *revive* a ritual without reviving a faith. You can *continue* a ritual after the faith is dead—that is not a conscious, 'pretty' piece of archaeology—but you cannot *revive* it" ("Ballet" 443). The question then arises whether two of the rituals at the heart of this study—the bullfight and the drama in verse—ought to be considered rituals at all. In the 1920s and 1930s these forms were enacted quite apart from any explicit spiritual, much less religious, meaning, no matter the spiritual framework a Yeats, for instance, might believe his plays to imply. The modern verse drama and the bullfight may well both have descended from the ancient sacrificial religious rites of the ancient Greeks,[30] but their official spiritual associations had long since fallen away, nor were most writers much concerned with restoring them. The modern bullfight is most certainly not the cult of Mithras, and *Murder in the Cathedral* is not a sacrificial rite. Yet this realization did not keep Yeats, Eliot, and many others from trying to reconstitute ritual forms as meaningful tools in the formation and articulation of modern European cultural identity, or from referring to the objects of their attention in terms of their ritual qualities.

This may be because verse drama and the bullfight, no matter how little they retained of their original spiritual signification, retained their attractiveness as

----

[28]   Similarly, and much earlier, Henri Hubert and Marcel Mauss define ritual as "establishing a means of communication between the sacred and the profane worlds" (97).

[29]   Sigmund Freud, too, implicitly upheld the connection between true ritual and belief, using "rituals," "religious observances," and "religious ceremonial" as synonyms, all distinguished from neurotic compulsions and prohibitions precisely because the "minutiae" of the former "are full of significance and have a symbolic meaning," while the latter "seem foolish and senseless" (431). Although "the true meaning" of neurotic ceremonial may be accessed through psychoanalysis, it is nonexistent as concerns the world beyond the individual, and is most often not available to the neurotic subject's own conscious mind.

[30]   The directness with which any or all of them derives from some originary sacrificial ritual is relentlessly debated. For the key terms of the debate, see Dahl 4.

symbolic frameworks onto which new meanings might be overlain. The more they were emptied of their official religious associations, the more capable they were of being filled with new associations, and it is this potential upon which writers frequently seized. Cousineau speaks of an "unpurged mythic residue" that clings to modernist narrators' treatments of ritual, a residue that explains their partial endorsement of scapegoating mechanisms (18). This residue, I hope to show, also clings to verse drama, bullfight, and Mass, which is why they are always saying more on a greater number of levels to interwar writers than can more mundane or practical, more efficient, cultural forms. That these forms retain at least a savor of the mythic or sacred distinguishes them within what Mary Karen Dahl calls "the desacralized context of the modern world" (9), where "political modes of thought have usurped the relationship to power that religious or mythological modes traditionally hold" (131). The "mythic residue" that surrounds these rituals augments the symbolic power that they retain by virtue of their ritual structure, even absent a specific context of belief. What has fallen away of spiritual dogma is replaced by the political, the social, the cultural, even the spiritual reconceived—whatever the preoccupations of the modern moment may be. Even the Mass, which, far more than the others, retains and implies an established element of belief, is capable of picking up, for instance, a secular idea of Europe. Faith may endure, but it does not preclude rationality from gaining a foothold in the symbolic territory of ritual. Belief, in other words, cannot be said to exist as an absolute quality of these rituals as they are conceived in literature, yet the space that belief once occupied (and may, to a greater or lesser extent, still occupy) is essential to their persistent efficacy as symbolic actions.[31]

Some of the most helpful attempts to define ritual have made a point of avoiding the kinds of pseudo-scientific conclusions that would presume to fix ritual as an absolute concept. Instead, as David Kertzer does in *Ritual, Politics, and Power* (1988), many contemporary theorists have emphasized ambiguity and multiplicity as the only truly fundamental characteristics of ritual.[32] Out of this acceptance of

---

[31]   Claude Lévi-Strauss articulates a similar idea in *The Savage Mind*: "In totemism, therefore, function inevitably triumphs over structure. The problem it has never ceased presenting to theorists is that of the relation between structure and event. And the great lesson of totemism is that the form of the structure can sometimes survive when the structure itself succumbs to events" (97). Ritual, of course, is an appendage of totemism. Europe's rituals present an interesting challenge for Lévi-Strauss's thesis because Europe "has chosen to explain [itself] by history" instead of totemism, resulting in a "'totemic void,' for in the bounds of Europe and Asia there is a remarkable absence of anything which might have reference to totemism, even in the form of remains" (97). I think that verse drama, bullfight, and Mass may be among the few exceptions that prove Lévi-Strauss's rule.

[32]   This is opposed to the view, for instance, of Johnsen, whose Girardian commitment leads him to be critical of "discussions of symbolic action that prematurely terminate themselves in the circular answers of ambivalence, human duplexity, and undecidability" (6).

ambiguity emerges a preference for viewing ritual as a mode, a way, instead of as an object to be classified. Ritual, writes Kertzer,

> is not an entity to be discovered. Rather, ritual is an analytical category that helps us deal with the chaos of human experience and put it into a coherent framework. Thus, there is no right or wrong definition of ritual, but only one that is more or less useful in helping us understand the world in which we live. My own use of the term reflects my goal of shedding light on how symbolic processes enter into politics and why these are important. (8)

Kertzer shares this tolerance of the multivalence of ritual with Kenneth Burke, who posited not only ritual but also each human creative product as "a strategy for encompassing a situation" (Burke 109). Catherine Bell has also made the case for ritual as a *way*, as opposed to a thing. Her emphasis, shared by Kertzer and others, is on ritual as a way of orchestrating the interaction of oppositions. "[R]itual," she writes, "is a type of critical juncture wherein some pair of opposing social or cultural forces comes together," for example, "belief and behavior, tradition and change, order and chaos, the individual and the group, subjectivity and objectivity, nature and culture, the real and the imaginative ideal" (16). She defines ritual as "a dialectical [as opposed to dichotomous] means for the provisional convergence of those opposed forces whose interaction is seen to constitute culture in some form ... a medium of integration or synthesis for opposing sociocultural forces" (23). This notion of dialecticism has been present in critical formulations of ritual since the modern, systematic study of culture emerged in nineteenth-century anthropology, and it helps in understanding the complex functions of ritual in an apparently polarized European political climate.

Like the idea of "Europe," the idea of "ritual" tends to be associated automatically with a conservative, even reactionary politics. Seen from a rarely critical but nonetheless influential point of view, ritual conjures outmoded social hierarchies, irrationality, fear, exclusion, and violence, and thus has little to contribute to the modern progressive ideals based on inclusivity, reason, and nonviolence. To many contemporary observers, such cultural forms as bullfight and Mass savor of an unproductive and embarrassing past-ness and are best left behind by enlightened and forward-looking Europe. Yet such a view seems incomplete in light not only of the wide range of political uses to which modern writers put the ritual forms of Europe but also of the broad and flexible political meanings of ritual itself. Scholars of ritual continue to argue that the political signification and utility of ritual extend far beyond the right wing and can be (and have been) powerful tools of innovation and opposition.

Few such scholars deny that for all the "creative potential" it may possess, ritual also has a "conservative bias" (Kertzer 12), owing to the slowness with which ritual forms tend to change, as well as their dependence on a sense of continuity over time. These characteristics form the basis of what Eliot—and many others, including contemporary theorists of ritual—calls tradition. But Eliot's sense of tradition also famously made room for innovation, for the contribution of what he called "the individual talent." A similar dialectic of continuity and change makes ritual both the bastion of the past and the gateway to the new.[33] Indeed, Kertzer insists that its conservatism is precisely what gives ritual its potency as an agent of change (12). Like the communal requirement described above, conformity to tradition and, indeed, to formal rules of enactment are essential to the effects of ritual, yet the human element of that enactment necessarily creates a space where dissent and change become possible, even inevitable. "The impact of a particular enactment of a ritual," writes Kertzer, "is a product of its past performances" (12). The past, that is, makes possible, rather than overrides, the possibilities inherent in the present. Turner argues:

> The rules 'frame' the ritual process, but the ritual process transcends its frame … [I]n the 'carrying out,' I hold, something new may be generated. The performance transforms itself. True, as I said, the rules may 'frame' the performance, but the 'flow' of action and interaction within that frame may conduce to hitherto unprecedented insights and even generate new symbols and meanings, which may be incorporated into subsequent performances. Traditional framings may have to be reframed—new bottles made for new wine. (79)

What is true on the formal level turns out to be equally true on the political level. Koster emphasizes the tribal thrust of ritual, its function in defining and enforcing the sense of *communitas* upon which society depends (223), but his argument underestimates the innovatory power that individual participation in ritual necessarily carries with it. "Ritual space," Koster argues, "excludes both individual differentiation and the symbolic presence of other tribes. Instead, it stands for the visceral emotions of ego-loss and *communitas*, which are alien to critical thinking and democracy" (239). The felt sense of *communitas* can be very real, but it is not always overwhelming, and while true ritual may have very little in common with democracy, the human element of ritual guarantees some level of critical thinking. As Kertzer notes, consensus may be a goal of ritual, "[b]ut rites are not simply stylized statements of belief. Participation in ritual is politically important even where participants interpret the rites differently" (67). While "solidarity" may be possible, it is practically impossible for politics, since it speaks a different language from ritual action, to overcome entirely "the very ambiguity of the symbols employed in ritual action" and achieve "consensus" (69). The political multivalence of ritual, then, is very likely a product of the form of ritual itself. As a performance based upon the symbolic interaction of opposites,

---

[33]   Adrian Shubert argues in his important study *Death and Money in the Afternoon* that, as a landmark instance of "commercialized mass leisure … the bullfight that had emerged in the eighteenth century was not archaic and atavistic but fully modern" (14–15). The terms of his further claim that "[t]he modern bullfight emerged from the confluence of elite and popular cultures" will be discussed in Chapter 5.

even within the limited territory it sets itself, it is better suited to creating a sense of dialectic interaction than of univocal control.[34]

The association of ritual with conformity and with political control is not baseless, but it is far from absolute. Historically, ritual has been enlisted, successfully, by both those in power and those in search of it. "True, kings use ritual to shore up their authority," writes Kertzer, "but revolutionaries use ritual to overthrow monarchs. The political elite employ ritual to legitimate their authority, but rebels battle back with rites of delegitimation. Ritual may be vital to reaction, but it is also the life blood of revolution" (Kertzer 2). This much was demonstrated with surprising clarity in the interwar period in the fashioning of fascism on the pseudo-ritual model of socialism. Kertzer notes: "Indeed, it was from observing the socialist enemy that Hitler recognized the value of symbols and rituals to the revolutionary cause" (164). In the early stages of Nazism, ritual served as a tool for insurrection; after Hitler's triumph, it became a means of consolidating power, illustrating once more how the multiple political implications of ritual derive from its necessary ambiguity.

Ritual, it begins to appear, is built to do in miniature what an idea of Europe requires on a grand scale.[35] The terms of ritual and the idea of Europe are so alike as to suggest a potent and abiding relationship between the two, and so alive as to call into question the notion of relegating either or both to the museum of the past. Both are dynamic *ways* of thinking through the inevitable tensions and contradictions of social experience. Both include and exclude powerfully yet ambivalently while resisting the tendency toward bland homogenization and minimization of difference. The connection between them, however, is more than a theoretical one. The specific rituals of verse drama, bullfight, and Mass have historically—and thus dialectically and imperfectly—participated in the subtle work of mediating between (though not always reconciling) European parts and wholes, individuals and communities, inside and outside, maintaining tradition through present innovation. These rituals, both for their form and their historical content, are a uniquely situated lens for viewing the crises of European identity.

---

[34]   Jacob Korg's argument in *Ritual and Experiment in Modern Poetry* depends on seeing ritual as inherently conservative, static, "embody[ing] tradition and communal agreement" (2–3). He associates ritual with "what is conventionally expected of poetry" and experiment with the deviation from that expectation (3). The dialectical anthropological view, in which ritual *is* partly experiment, makes such a distinction more difficult.

[35]   One metaphorical use of the term *ritual* is too provocative to neglect here. In "Eurocentrism and Modernity," Enrique Dussel "summarize[s] the elements of the myth of modernity" beginning with Europe's assumption of its own superiority, moving to the inevitable violence upon other civilizations that proceeds from this assumption, and noting that "This violence, which produces, in many different ways, victims, takes on an almost ritualistic character: the civilizing hero invests his victims ... with the character of being participants in a process of redemptive sacrifice" (75). That is, an (if not the) apotheosis of the idea of modernity itself and thus of Europe, is ritual action. Such an idea must for now be held in abeyance, as the possible macro- beyond the present microanalysis.

As both reactionary and revolutionary, they speak for both sides of the interwar European political divide as well as to both sides of Derrida's European equation: "what we recall" and "what we promise." In interwar writing, these rituals perform aspects of cultural memory—feared, longed for, or both—and frame some imaginations of what the future might hold. The verse drama, the bullfight, and the Mass remind interwar writers of some of the dynamics of the creation of the European idea and help them to imagine its future, allowing them to anchor their memories of and desires for European identity to present action.

Making, Watching, and Using Ritual

> "The *whole* of anything is never told; you can only take what groups together."
> —Henry James

This study examines the perpetually contested idea of Europe, as it takes shape in the imaginations of interwar British and Irish writers. During the politically unstable interwar years, these writers feared European cultural disintegration and sought to synthesize or reconcile various antinomies which they saw as essential parts of the mind of Europe: the general and the culturally particular, the center and the periphery, Europe and non-Europe, past and future, tradition and innovation, individual and community, nation and continent, sacred and profane, political Right and Left. As vehicles for syntheses, they turned to rituals, whether for the content of their writing (as, for example, did D.H. Lawrence, Greene, and many poets of the Spanish Civil War), its form or style (as did David Jones), its mode (Eliot, Yeats, and Auden), or its conceptual and logical ground (Jones, Greene, and Evelyn Waugh). Especially in the cases of the various dramatists, with their high hopes for ritual as a form of cultural renewal, their successes were perhaps outweighed by failures. Nonetheless, all the texts examined herein reveal the complex and often positive functions that rituals can play, contrary to their reputation, with some, as serving only reactionary, even fascistic, ends.

Neither verse drama, nor bullfighting, nor Catholicism speaks for all of Europe. Nor does ritual as a whole. Nor, indeed, does any single cultural form, but in order to open up something as large as the idea of Europe, one needs to choose a key. Europe has been conceived throughout recorded history, in different combinations, and with varying viability, as a political, a cultural, a geographical, a spiritual, and an economic entity. I have chosen ritual as my key because it seems to touch a number of these categories without affording any one of them disproportionate significance, and because the ineluctable locality of ritual simultaneously highlights commonality, precisely the kind of operation Europe is forever trying to perform. Verse drama, the bullfight, and Catholic ritual provide controlled spaces in which the dynamic interplay of oppositions that constitute European identity are visible in miniature.

Several of the writers under consideration in this study, particularly Eliot, Waugh, and Jones, speak often and explicitly about the idea of Europe. Others, for example Greene, do not. However, just as ritual provides a more dynamic sense of a given culture than do abstract ideas, and just as the localities of Europe provide a more concrete sense of the European whole than do vague generalizations about European *esprit*, so does the work of one European author often serve to illumine the idea of Europe, even when that is not his or her primary subject. Indeed, talking about Europe as such often leads to abstraction rather than to the particular details that animate, and constitute, European culture. Such is not generally the case for the writers in this study, who are most often focused on the hard material they find close to home and who—as creative artists with a measure, great or small, of Modernist sensibility—prefer specificity to abstraction. The mind of Europe exists nowhere if not in the minds and, as Crick suggests, the writing of individuals.

The opening section treats three prominent poets-turned-dramatists whose interest in the idea of Europe as a cultural whole coalesces with the sense that ritual drama is the best vehicle for establishing a connection between art and society. When they are creating plays, these three writers—Yeats, Eliot, and Auden—see themselves as makers of ritual. Their interest in the European idea links them to most of the other writers covered in this study; their engagement with ritual, however, is unique in its attempt to make ritual—or at least aspects of it—manifest in time and space. Although his career as a playwright began later than Yeats's, Eliot comes first in this section because his writing on the mind of Europe cuts so close to the heart of the concerns of this study. Chapter 1 looks at the ways in which Eliot's verse drama of the interwar period reflects his commitment to European unity in diversity. Eliot believed that poetic language functions as the steward of a people's "sensibility" and that the English language, because it contains more of the "mind of Europe" than any other, is the privileged language to safeguard European culture. His own plays, especially *Murder in the Cathedral* and *The Family Reunion*, reveal him trying to get the English language to do justice to this responsibility, to nurture a common sensibility of Europe through the careful manipulation of local particulars of language and theme. I argue that while Eliot's fundamentally Christian notion of European identity excludes a great deal that has contributed historically to the idea of Europe, those very exclusions clarify the terms on which the idea of Europe has been and must be debated. Eliot's religious commitment does not prevent him from advocating true cultural diversity in Britain and in Europe; rather, religion provides him with a basis, however limited, on which to objectify the very concepts of unity and diversity.

In the second chapter, I argue that Yeats's verse drama after the Easter Rising begins with a tentative exploration of ritual as a means of revivifying modern life and evolves according to ritual imperatives toward tragedy and the ideal of sacrificial death. Through the particularity of Irish themes and settings, Yeats gains access to what he believes is the mystical core of Europe, largely obscured in the modern period. In looking to the Noh drama of Japan and to Indian mysticism for models, Yeats also hints that any comprehensive spiritual idea of Europe requires the East for its completion. In the 1930s, his aesthetic and political views bring him into the orbit of European fascism, but his final two plays, *Purgatory* and *The*

Death of Cuchulain, ironically undercut the conclusions toward which fascism, and Yeats's drama, seems to point.

The third chapter, on Auden, rounds out the section on verse drama. Here I argue that Auden's experimental verse plays, born out of a commitment to ritual apparently similar to Yeats's and Eliot's, offer a useful measure of the difficulty of imagining European cultural cohesion in the interwar period. Auden's plays employ a host of formal strategies to recreate the conditions of ritual, with some success. More explicitly than either Eliot's or Yeats's, Auden's plays, especially those written in collaboration with Christopher Isherwood, also wrestle with the problem of European atomization and the meaninglessness of modern life. The solutions the plays offer, while often dramatically compelling, ultimately do not extend beyond the cultural limitations and disorders they describe, a shortcoming Auden later came to see in terms of the absence of tradition.

The second section deals with the uses of the Spanish bullfight in English writing of the 1920s and 1930s. The writers covered here, unlike Eliot, Yeats, and Auden, are not practitioners of ritual; they do not make bullfights but rather observe them. They are the audience of the bullfight, a position that, as will be discussed, is likewise essential to the production of meaning in this ritual. Bullfighting, perhaps the most idiosyncratic of the major ritual forms of Europe, is ideally situated to reveal the utility of the local in defining the characteristics of the collective through a combination of affirmation and opposition. Chapter 4 focuses on Lawrence's two primary bullfighting works, the first chapter of his novel *The Plumed Serpent*, and his short story "None of That!". From a vantage point in Mexico, part of what Enrique Dussel calls the "first periphery" of Europe (67), Lawrence is forced to consider European identity in light of what it has engendered in the New World. The ritual of the bullfight, imported from Europe but integral to Lawrence's perception of Mexico, provides a site where Lawrence's main convictions and anxieties about culture are given concrete form. His initial inability, like that of the heroine of *The Plumed Serpent*, to understand the ambiguities of the bullfight is one indication of his inability to conceive of ritual as a meaningful part of European culture. "None of That!", however, provides a more sophisticated interpretation of the rhythm of the bullfight, corresponding to a subtler and richer evocation of the basic ambiguity of European identity.

Chapter 5 argues that the symbolic uses of the bullfight by British writers in 1930s Spain are so varied and complex as to transcend any simple and purely contemporary political associations. Most observers saw the Spanish war as a microcosm of the cultural conflicts defining interwar Europe, and many poets, including Spender, Jack Lindsay, George Barker, Roy Campbell, and Day Lewis, saw the bullfight as a microcosm of the war. To writers from all over Europe, the bullfight stood as a kind of shorthand for Spain itself, and the way they viewed the bullfight was tied to their sense of the relation of Spain to the rest of Europe. The ritual, even imperfectly understood by English-speaking writers, encompassed and figured not only the Spanish Civil War but also what Eliot called the "international civil war of opposed ideas" concurrently consuming Europe.

The inherent ambiguities of form and of meaning in the bullfight map usefully onto the political, cultural, and even spiritual anxieties of the era.

Like the verse dramatists but unlike the writers of the bullfight, Greene, Waugh, and Jones have the practitioner's insight into their subject, Catholic ritual. Like the latter group only, their art does not involve them in the production of a ritual, only in its observation and its representation. So Greene, Waugh, and Jones sit in interesting ways between the extreme positions available to writers working with ritual, and it may be useful to consider them the custodians of ritual, those whose knowledge enables them to critique actual and potential appearances of Catholic ritual, as well as to propose them, directly or indirectly. Chapter 6, on Greene and Waugh, opens this final section. Although its unifying cultural reach is not co-extensive with the whole of European diversity, compared to English-language verse drama and the Spanish bullfight, Catholic ritual has had a far more pervasive and cross-cultural impact on the formation of European identity. For British Catholic writers, Catholicism affords a unique means of objective contact with a perceived European cultural collectivity that extends well beyond the geographical boundaries of Europe, indeed to the New World. In the late 1930s, Greene and Waugh each traveled to Mexico to report on, among other things, the persecution of the Catholic Church. I argue that, like Lawrence, both writers, in looking at Mexico, found Europe. That they did so invites accusations of Eurocentrism, but this chapter asserts that in the late 1930s, Europe was as involved in a process of self-imagining as any of the societies of the "new" world and, moreover, that the increased objectivity afforded by viewing Europe from abroad is a necessary prerequisite to the success of that process. Greene's and Waugh's observations are as different as their politics and their Mexican narratives, yet both authors end up articulating a notion of European identity anchored to the same Roman Catholic ritual tradition. Following up on what was begun in Chapter 4 by taking the question of Europe to a culture both a descendant of and a foil to the European imagination, this chapter shows the idea of Europe to be wider, more complex, and more engaged with world culture than its (somewhat arbitrary) geographical boundaries might suggest. At the same time, it shows that Catholic ritual itself can encompass a range of political commitment nearly matching that of the ultra-political 1930s.

Chapter 7 argues that the part-Welsh David Jones writes from a position straddling the kinds of oppositions that have emerged in the previous chapters: periphery and center, part and whole, local and international. In *In Parenthesis*, Jones takes up heterogeneous pieces of European cultural history and weaves them into something like a figure of European unity in diversity. *In Parenthesis*, set amid the scenery of the first great dissolution for twentieth-century Europe, the Great War, employs ritual models ranging from Welsh mythology to Catholic liturgy to suggest a pattern underlying the chaos of the war. This pattern does not rationalize the war itself, much less the experience of the trenches, but it does describe the scaffolding on which an individual observer might hang an idea of European identity. Jones uses Catholicism, or, more specifically, sacramentalism, as the key with which to open up part of the hidden core of Europe. What he calls "the Catholic thing" and "the Welsh thing" lead Jones in *In Parenthesis* to an approximation of a European thing.

The Conclusion addresses an issue that may have begun to nag at some point in the foregoing chapters, which is the sense of the failure, or at least the decline, of ritual as a productive means of considering European identity around the end of the 1930s. Do the turns in Eliot's and Auden's dramatic careers, the end of Yeats's, the closing up of literary frontiers at the end of the Spanish Civil War, the apotheosis and then near obliteration of European fascism in World War II, the increasing marginality of Waugh's social views, and Greene's ostensible turn away from an emphasis on Church ritual in his fiction indicate a project that had failed? The Conclusion also does what the rest of the chapters have deliberately avoided doing, which is suggest some ways in which the ideas raised by this literary phenomenon of the 1920s and 1930s might fruitfully be considered in light of the face contemporary Europe wears. In the interest of focus and depth, the body of the analysis has been constrained to approximately the years 1919–1939, and if the reader's mind has not leapt often or at all in the course of that analysis to the cultural contours of twenty-first-century Europe, here it is invited to do so.

Interchapter:
Ghosts

Those familiar with the whole of Eliot's dramatic writing consistently remark upon the chasm that seems to exist between his theoretical formulations and the plays, whether read or performed. Eliot was well aware of the failure of his plays to meet the high standards for a modern poetic drama set out in his critical writings, yet he never considered success an impossibility. As he wrote in a 1932 *Criterion* "Commentary": "I have myself no great taste for lost causes. I mean that if I believe in a cause I find it impossible to believe that the cause is lost. If it really appears to me to be lost, then I must stop and examine, whether I have really cared purely for its essence, or whether I have attached myself ... to an impermanent form" ("[July 1932]" 677). Nor was he ashamed to acknowledge the specific shortcomings of his verse plays. His 1951 essay "Poetry and Drama" includes a litany of the failure of each of his plays to solve the problem of finding a viable verse form for the modern theatre. Virtually all of his critical writing about verse drama is couched in the language of potentiality, not actuality; his seminal essays bear titles such as "The Possibility of a Poetic Drama," "The Need for Poetic Drama," "The Aims of Poetic Drama."

In the same way, Yeats's verse plays, which, like Eliot's, did achieve a measure of real-world success, cannot but appear today as the remains of a civilization that never quite came into existence. The story of the Abbey Theatre in the first four decades of the twentieth century is also the story of the persistent, promising, but ultimately frustrated attempt to secure a place for poetic drama in modern Europe. Even the verse plays of Auden, which Eliot called "the forerunner of contemporary poetic drama," almost immediately became a "distant episode" in Auden's career once he stopped writing them in 1939 (qtd. in Mendelson, *Plays* xvi; Hogg ii). For two decades, the ideal of a modern drama in verse, drawing on the ritual origins of European drama, drove some of the most important writers in English to write verse plays. In 1939, however, more quickly than it had arrived, the ritual ideal seemed to all but vanish, like a ghost.

"Yet," as Eliot wrote, "nothing is more dramatic than a ghost" (SE 39). Ghosts are everywhere not only in these plays but also in the critical discourse that surrounds them. The ghostly figures that link the past to the present in Eliot's *The Family Reunion*, Auden's *The Ascent of F6*, and virtually all of Yeats's interwar plays are the dramatic expression of the playwrights' desire to revive not only a literary but also a cultural form. The possibility of a poetic drama haunts the first half of the twentieth century like a ghost, an image of a richer, stranger European past constantly tantalizing poets with the promise of a more meaningful sense of artistic purpose, a more satisfying relationship of art and life. To many contemporaries of Yeats, Eliot, and Auden, this ghost bespoke only the past, but for these authors it also offered a bracing vision of the future of Europe. In her essay "The Waking of Medieval Theatricality," Helen Solterer describes the mystical importance Roland Barthes and other actors in 1930s France attributed to the theatre. She speaks of Barthes's "profound desire to establish a connection with the dead" through performance, a desire consistent with the fundamental "wish to experience once more what is no longer" that the theatre satisfies (356).

Yeats's theory of dreaming back, explicated in *A Vision*, expresses the formula that framed not only his own verse drama project but also those of Eliot and Auden. The dead, in Yeats's system, are able to dream themselves back into the present as ghosts and to collaborate with the living to restore spiritual order on both planes (224–31, passim). This principle echoes G.K. Chesterton's pronouncement, later to become a favorite of Auden's, that tradition amounts to a "democracy of the dead," that present wholeness requires the participation of those who are of the past (48). Virtually the same idea is expressed in purely literary-historical terms by Eliot in "Tradition and the Individual Talent." Living writers, he argues, collaborate with past ones to make European literature signify and cohere.

The notion of dreaming back provides the explicit thematic basis of many of Yeats's interwar plays, but it also explains his, Eliot's, and Auden's effort to rejuvenate verse drama as a form. All of their plays are in a sense the ghosts of the European past dreaming themselves back into the present, desperate for contact but almost always denied it. Yeats's dramatic ghosts come close to communion with the living, who see in ghosts—equally present and past, earthly and spiritual—the figure of reconciliation that living tradition affords, but communion is invariably frustrated. The verse plays of Yeats, Eliot, and Auden likewise beckoned to the public of the 1920s and 1930s as they do to contemporary readers, hinting at a reconciliation of past and present but always holding that object, for reasons this section will try to identify, just beyond reach.

Each of these three playwrights pursued ideals of ritual verse drama and of European identity throughout the interwar period, but in the year 1939, each fundamentally altered or relinquished those ideals, for very different reasons. In each case, the reason has as much to do with an idea of Europe—which, in 1939, could not have been other than under strain—as with the evolution of a dramatic vision. Yeats had been trying to mobilize the mystical riches of Ireland in order to restore Europe's spiritual self. Eliot was expressly interested in how to honor European variety while maintaining a common European cultural order. Auden could see Europe in the process of fragmenting itself, and he wrote with an eye toward saving it from disintegration. The three dramatists are united by a commitment to ritual, but the plays they produced out of that commitment are remarkably heterogeneous. Yeats's plays build toward the full confrontation of blood sacrifice that is the apotheosis of ritual. Eliot's explore the ritual function of poetic language, manipulating dramatic speech to maximize the ability of language to revivify culture. Auden's plays experiment with the ritual integration of audience and performance, with ways of getting drama to reinforce, even create, community. The ways these writers weave together ideas of Europe and ideas of drama reveal, in their variety as well as their unity, that verse drama may not have been able to save interwar Europe, but it did exercise—and at times exorcise—parts of the mind of Europe much larger than the contemporaneous political ideologies vying for control of Europe's future.

Chapter 1
That the Pattern May Subsist:
Eliot, English, and the Mind of Europe

In a famous 1929 essay, Eliot wrote of Dante's poetry, "What we should consider is not so much the meaning of the images, but the reverse process, that which led a man having an idea to express it in images" (SE 204). A similar notion motivates this chapter, namely: What we should consider is not the meaning of all of these modern verse plays, but what led a man having an idea of Europe to try to express it in dramatic verse. It is difficult to disagree with David E. Chinitz's overall assessment of Eliot's lifelong experiment with dramatic verse, "the revival" of which, he writes, "was an almost total loss" (151). This judgment, unflinching as it is, is supportable on any number of levels and rings with special justice because in the same chapter Chinitz not only has positively valued Eliot's motive for fighting the quixotic fight for a modern drama in verse but also has perceived the cultural machinery that rendered Eliot's failure all but inevitable. Chinitz's praise for Eliot is based primarily on the righteousness of the attempt to make the stage accessible for modern poetry, and on Eliot's refusal to withdraw into artistic isolation and elitism in the face of the generally unsatisfying response to his dramatic efforts. However much he identified with the misunderstood, ridiculed, at times overly valued hero, Eliot was no Coriolanus (one of his Shakespearean heroes) who turned bitterly toward exile—"Despising, / For you, the city, thus I turn my back: / There is a world elsewhere" (*The Tragedy of Coriolanus* 3.3.134-36). Eliot chose to stick, to maintain his engagement with a temperamental culture and fickle audiences. For him, "the ideal towards which poetic drama should strive ... [was] an unattainable ideal" (OPP 93). As Chinitz notes, "Eliot did not *expect* to succeed—not, at least, according to the usual aesthetic definitions of success" (150). He did succeed, however, in articulating critically, and at times demonstrating dramatically, how such a form as verse drama might serve to catch up some threads of language, ritual, tradition, and innovation behind not only British but also European culture.

Although he continued to write poems between 1922, the year of *The Waste Land*'s publication, and 1939, the year of the Second World War's beginning and *The Criterion*'s end, Eliot's primary creative project in this period was not poetry per se, but drama. Along with cultural theorization, dramatic writing, both creative and critical, received the bulk of his attention. As he was always adamant about the relationship that necessarily exists between one's creative, critical, and social endeavors, it is reasonable to expect to find an important reciprocity between Eliot's own dramatic writing and his extensive work on European cultural identity. Although this relationship emerges more subtly than that between his criticism and his great European poems, *The Waste Land* and *Four Quartets*, once discerned it becomes clear that Eliot's dramatic ideas and his idea of Europe were nearly inseparable.

More consistently and explicitly than any other writer in this study, Eliot devoted his energy and attention in the interwar period to the exploration and elucidation of an idea of Europe, and specifically to the question of European unity in diversity. In his role as editor of *The Criterion*, he oversaw one of the most important discourses on the condition of European culture, the possibilities for its enrichment, and the forces vying for its destruction. "One of the ideas which characterizes our age," he wrote in a 1927 "Commentary,"

> may be called The European Idea ... It is a hopeful sign that a small number of intelligent people are aware of the necessity to harmonize the interests, and therefore to harmonize the ideas, of the civilized countries of Western Europe. We are beginning to hear mention of the reaffirmation of the European tradition. It will be helpful, certainly, if people will begin by believing that there is a European tradition; for they may then proceed to analyse its constituents in the various nations of Europe; and proceed finally to the further formation of a tradition. (97–98).[1]

It is likely that, in his keenness, Eliot overestimated the degree to which a European tradition seemed relevant or desirable to Europeans outside of his own intellectual circle. This circle, though, was still broad enough to include some of the preeminent European thinkers of the day—Henri Massis, Jose Ortega y Gasset, Jorge Guillen, Christopher Dawson, Karl Mannheim—as well as continental periodicals similar to *The Criterion*, all of which amounted to "visible evidence of a community of interest, and a desire for co-operation ... which has been growing steadily since 1918" ("Commentary [Jan. 1930]" 182). Besides, Eliot's own analytical powers were such that they tended to invest the *Criterion* view with an aura of almost objective reality. Both in his own Commentaries and in the solicitation and publication of the writings of important continental authors, Eliot attempted, according to Peter Ackroyd, "to express, if not create, a genuinely European consciousness" (248). It is undeniable that this "notion of a European intellectual and cultural order ... was being asserted at a time when political events began to destroy the illusion of a common European identity." However, rather than underscoring Eliot's ostensible penchant for embracing lost causes, this circumstance is one reason why his cultural criticism—and the life of *The Criterion*, which "covered nearly the same period that we call the years of peace"—serves as such a useful index of European thought between the wars (Eliot, CC 192).[2]

---

[1]   In this passage as well as others, "Europe" and "the civilized countries of Western Europe" seem virtually synonymous in Eliot's mind (which Western European countries, one wonders, were uncivilized? Spain? Ireland?). This easy elision of Eastern and Central Europe from the "Idea of Europe," though not absolute, is a notable and problematic feature of Eliot's formulations on the subject, early and late.

[2]   For a useful discussion of what Eliot generally excluded from his vision of Europe, see Moody, "The Mind of Europe" 22.

The *Criterion* project sets effective terms for engaging the question of interwar European cultural identity not because of its typicality or even its breadth, but because of its clearly maintained sense of purpose, its well-defined preferences and exclusions. Eliot himself acknowledged that the journal's intended diversity of perspectives—within approximately "classical" parameters—had deteriorated by 1939 to near one-dimensionality, owing to "the gradual closing of the mental frontiers of Europe." In the end, *The Criterion* "tended to reflect a particular point of view, rather than to illustrate a variety of views on that plane" ("Unity" 194, 196). What J.S. Cunningham observes about *The Waste Land* applies equally well to Eliot's interwar cultural critique: "[T]he redeeming creative art occurs, or seeks to occur, within the zone of what variously excites it, resists it, or is fundamentally hostile to it" (84).

As Eliot wrote in "East Coker" (1940), "There is only the fight to recover what has been lost / And found and lost again and again: and now, under conditions / That seem unpropitious" (4Q 31). Not even the extreme in unpropitious conditions, the Second World War, fundamentally altered his commitment to an ideal of European cultural cohesion; on the contrary, it clarified his sense of his own role in the pursuit of it. "The man of letters," he wrote in 1944, "is not concerned with the political or economic map of Europe; but he should be very much concerned with its cultural map"; this after five years of watching Europe tear both maps apart ("Man of Letters" 383).[3] Indeed, in a post-war radio addresses in, of all places, Berlin (1946), he was still able to assert that "the health of the culture of Europe ... is possible because there is a common element in European culture, an interrelated history of thought and feeling and behaviour, an interchange of arts and ideas" (CC197). This chapter traces the parallel development of Eliot's dramatic ideal and his idea of Europe in "the years of peace." Using the evidence of his own prose writings and his plays from *Sweeney Agonistes* to *The Family Reunion*, it follows Eliot's search for a ritual form of drama that might contribute to the cultural health of Europe, a search that led Eliot to some of his most important conclusions about the relationship of art to European identity.

---

[3]   In a 1926 *Criterion* essay, "Defence of the West," Henri Massis wrote of "the danger of Asiaticism" threatening Europe by means of German mysticism and "[t]his new assault by the East on the Latin inheritance" (4.2.231). Eliot's own thought admitted a limited permeability between East and West: "The frontiers of culture are not, and should not be, closed. But history makes a difference" ("Unity" 191). In *Notes Toward the Definition of Culture*: "European culture has an area, but no definite frontiers: and you cannot build Chinese walls. The notion of a purely self-contained European culture would be as fatal as the notion of a self-contained national culture" (CC 136). One cannot help but be struck by the similarity of the terms of debate in Eliot's time and our own. In light of attacks in European capitals by Islamic extremists, the European Union's deliberations regarding the admission of Turkey, and the growing tension regarding the integration of Muslim communities into European culture, the contemporary import of what a classical idea of Europe excludes should be obvious.

United in Diversity

In two poems bracketing the First World War, Eliot made his first literary overtures toward an idea of Europe. The tentative references to Elizabethan drama, to Donne and Marvell, the exploratory inclusion of lines from Laforgue, and the famous women, so discomfiting to Prufrock, who "come and go / Talking of Michelangelo," anticipate the cacophony of languages, literatures, and cultural fragments that comprise *The Waste Land* ("Stetson! / You who were with me in the ships at Mylae!"). Together, "Prufrock" and *The Waste Land* are the clearest early articulation of a theme that runs throughout Eliot's poetry, prose, and drama: the attempt to make sense of modern experience in the context of the cultural inheritance of Europe. Although it has come to stand for not only Eliot's but at least one whole generation's frustration at the futility of the effort, the abortive European union that is *The Waste Land* is far from Eliot's last word on the issue. Twenty years later, after his notion of European unity was objectified as a Christian unity, the voices that jar and clash in that poem coexist with far greater stability and harmony in *Four Quartets*. Even an essay prior to *The Waste Land*, "Tradition and the Individual Talent" (1919), already points toward a more comprehensive, more inclusive structure for the reconciliation of Europe's competing voices—historical, social, regional, and literary.

That the birth of the *The Criterion* is precisely coincident with the first appearance of *The Waste Land* helps in understanding the direction which Eliot's literary exploration of the idea of Europe was to take in the interwar years. In the first pages of the very forum he would use over the next sixteen years to try to build up a coherent European consciousness, Eliot published the century's first great poetic illustration of European *in*coherence. For *The Waste Land* is, among many other things, a demonstration of European linguistic disunity, Europe's voices—including those not of European origin—clanging against one another in a frustrated attempt to be heard and to find a place in the whole. A.D. Moody argues that the poem depicts the chaotic state not only of "the mind of Europe" but also of Eliot's own mind as it struggled to represent so vast a tradition. It reveals

> the mind of the poet unable to digest what it knows of Europe, and breaking up under the shock of the scope and complexity of its culture. In this variation upon Eliot's theory, *The Waste Land* becomes an expression of the mind of Europe as it exceeded the mind of the individual poet; or to be more precise, as his power to register it exceeded his power to interpret it. (25)

The complexity of European culture was no doubt brought home to Eliot by the specific circumstances troubling Europe in the wake of the First World War, the time of *The Waste Land*'s composition—circumstances to which the poem repeatedly alludes. Much of the poem is, as Stan Smith emphasizes, a poetic response to the breakup of Central Europe following the Treaty of Versailles, a fragmentation fueled by "destitution" and emergent nationalisms and that Eliot referred to—with a characteristic lack of charity toward nationalist movements—as "the 'Balkanisation' of Europe" (Letters 351). Eliot wrote that "[t]he problem of nationalism and the problem of dissociated personalities may turn out to be the same" qtd. in Smith 168), and Smith is following this suggestion in associating the fragmentation of Central Europe with a "Balkanisation of the spirit" in Eliot and others, and painfully apparent in *The Waste Land* (180).[4] The seeming disorder of the poem, though, as has been remarked (perhaps too often and with overmuch certainty), simultaneously suggests the possibility of order. Its structures of harmony, though obscure, beckon from behind its surface chaos, hinting at the unifying orthodoxy that would come increasingly to define Eliot's views in ensuing years, when European unity became concretized in his mind as a Christian unity. In this poem, writes Cunningham, as in much of Eliot's writing between the wars, "a difficult but true coherence is won from, but still within, distracted and demoralized states of awareness" (85). In a sense, the poem itself demonstrates the need for projects like *The Criterion*, for environments in which multiple European voices might productively coexist. At the same time, it treats the question of European literary order with far more wariness than the confident assertions in "Tradition and the Individual Talent." Demonstrating poetically the idea that "the whole of the literature of Europe from Homer … has a simultaneous existence and composes a simultaneous order" proved far more difficult than formulating the abstract concept (SW 49). It is from this difficulty that the bulk of Eliot's interwar writing proceeds, in methodical pursuit of the "mind of Europe" so confidently posited in the early essay (51).[5]

Still, the belief that a common tradition, however difficult to express creatively, united Europe remained at the heart of Eliot's thought in the interwar period and, indeed, long after. One other belief complicated and completed the first and begins to explain how Eliot's dramatic efforts in these years correspond to his idea of Europe. In his 1946 Berlin address, entitled "The Unity of European Culture," he asserted:

> For the health of the culture of Europe two conditions are required: that the culture of each country should be unique, and that the different cultures should recognise their relationship to each other, so that each should be susceptible of influence from the others. And this is possible because there is a common element in European culture, an interrelated history of thought and feeling and behaviour, an interchange of arts and of ideas. (197)[6]

---

[4] How interesting, and useful, that Étienne Balibar, decades after Eliot, argues: "Either Europe will recognize in the Balkan situation not a monstrosity grafted to its breast, a pathological 'aftereffect' of under-development or of communism, but rather an image and effect of its own history and will undertake to confront it and resolve it and thus to put itself into question and transform itself" ("Borders" 74).

[5] Eliot was quite explicit about this difference, writing in *After Strange Gods* (1934) that "in one's prose reflexions one may be legitimately occupied with ideals, whereas in the writing of verse one can only deal with actuality" (30).

[6] For a thorough and recent discussion of this address, see John Xiros Cooper's chapter "T.S. Eliot's *Die Einheit der Europäischen Kultur* (1946) and the Idea of European Union" in *T.S. Eliot, Dante, and the Idea of Europe,* edited by Paul Douglass (2011).

As central to Eliot's notion of European unity as the belief in a "common element" was the conviction that only through commitment to constituent cultural particularities, and not through any "emotional summons to international brotherhood" could true unity be realized ("Commentary [Jan. 1930]" 182; "[Apr. 1938]" 478). In *Notes Toward the Definition of Culture* (1948), he argued that a Europe without obvious cultural differences would be "no culture at all," just as, in the British Isles, "[i]t would be no gain whatever for English culture, for the Welsh, Scots and Irish to become indistinguishable from Englishmen" (CC 136; 129). He was steadfast in maintaining the necessity of unique cultural points of view, as opposed to a bland European homogeneity, and he invariably preferred to learn those points of view from their respective sources. "[T]he European idea," he wrote in 1926, "the idea of a common culture of Western Europe ... may appear under a different light" in France, Italy, Spain, Great Britain, or Germany ("Commentary [Apr. 1926]" 222). Not even the events leading up to the Second World War could shake his commitment to locality. In one of the final Commentaries, he wrote that "[w]hat we need in the Press is not merely more foreign news, but presentation of foreign opinion, and unbiassed explanation of how the foreigner comes to hold this opinion" ("Commentary [July 1938]" 689). Holding to this difficult position of diversity in unity allowed him to strive "to keep the intellectual blood of Europe circulating throughout the whole of Europe," to restore "that higher community which existed ... throughout the middle ages," while also asking, "Would it not be better at present for each people to concentrate attention on what it can do at home?" ("Commentary [Jan. 1932]" 271). With impressive resolve, Eliot maintained his *both-and* view, and only when European atomization was actualized by the early salvos in the Second World War was the *Criterion* forced to back off its assumption "that there existed an international fraternity of men of letters, within Europe: a bond which did not replace, but was perfectly compatible with, national loyalties, religious loyalties, and differences of political philosophy" (CC 195–96). Even after the war, Eliot made the theme of variety-within-unity a foundation of *Notes Toward the Definition of Culture*, his most sustained work on the subject of cultural dynamics, British, European, and global.

While what Eliot called "the gradual closing of the mental frontiers of Europe" (CC 194) may have killed the *Criterion* project, it did not drastically alter his own approach (mirrored in that of his literary review) to "The European Idea" or "the problems of contemporary civilization" ("Commentary [June 1928]" 291). Afterwards, as before, the same principle of fidelity to the local with an eye toward the European governed his ideas of politics, economics, and art, indeed of "everything that can be examined in a critical spirit" (291). In an October 1937 "Commentary," he wrote that "I cannot think of art as either national or international ... but as racial and local; and an art which is not representative of a particular people, but 'international,' or an art which does not represent a particular civilization, but only an abstract civilization-in-general, may lose its sources of vitality" (82). His own art being literature, he added that "it is obvious that the limitation of a particular language is the condition of a writer doing anything at all" (83). Even local language, though, depends for its life on the interaction of its constituent parts. He argued that "the future vitality" of English literature "will depend very much upon the vitality of its parts," including English, Irish, Scottish, Welsh, American, and Jewish ("A Commentary [Oct. 1935]" 611). So even as the aforementioned closing of the frontiers of Europe began to substitute a purely local consciousness for any idea of common European identity or tradition, Eliot remained committed to the integrity of European cultural particulars—its individual talents, as it were—including its local languages and literary forms.

The question that opens the essay "The Aims of Poetic Drama" (1949)—"Why should anyone want to write a play in verse, instead of in prose?"—is one Eliot had been addressing for years and would continue to address. In this case, late in his career, he still maintains that "poetry is the normal form for serious drama" and that "everything that prose can do in the theatre, verse can do; but … there is a dramatic range possible to verse, greater than that open to prose" ("Aims" 10, 15). Much earlier, he had answered the question from a different angle. In 1920, with the brashness typical of his criticism at that time, he wrote in "The Possibility of a Poetic Drama" that "the majority, perhaps, certainly a large number, of poets hanker for the stage; and second, that a not negligible public appears to want verse plays. Surely there is some legitimate craving, not restricted to a few persons, which only the verse play can satisfy" (SW 60). After experiencing firsthand the difficulties of modern playwriting, he would write with greater circumspection about that public in subsequent years. In "A Dialogue on Dramatic Poetry" (1928), though, he could still suggest that "the craving for poetic drama is permanent in human nature" (SE 43).[7] Another contention in this essay, gradually refined, would continue to shape his verse drama project and to join it to his vision of European civilization. All great European poetic forms, he wrote, "found their perfection by serving particular societies … Nevertheless, the drama is perhaps the most permanent, is capable of greater variation and of expressing more varied types of society, than any other" (61). As he developed as a dramatist, he appears to have continued to believe the second half of that claim, but it is the first part, about the societal particularity of poetic forms, indeed of all great art, to which he would most often return. For instance: "[W]e tend to think of each of the greater peoples as excelling in one art rather than another: Italy and then France in painting, Germany in music, and England in poetry" (CC 191).[8] Still, for any art to

---

[7]   Of course, this sentiment is voiced by only one of the several imaginary participants in "A Dialogue on Dramatic Poetry," so it need not be taken at face value as Eliot's own. Still, as David E. Chinitz has written, "*each* interlocutor" in the essay "displays aspects of Eliot and voices positions he adopts or considers in various essays" (218 n.12).

[8]   Eliot's choice of Italy, France, Germany, and England as the "greater peoples" of Europe is not surprising, but a statement like this ought to remind us of Eliot's essentially hierarchical idea of Europe, one that frequently coalesced around those nations with the most wealth and might in the early twentieth century.

flourish, "the local tradition, the common European tradition, and the influence of one European country upon another" must all operate simultaneously. This view helped Eliot conceive of his own dramatic efforts—English in form, language, and scene—in the context of his broader concern with Western civilization. The dual assertion is an indication of the nuanced way he would come to think of the place of drama in society and of the relationship between local literary production and the wider "mind of Europe."

The Use of Poetry

In the 1932–1933 series of Harvard lectures published as *The Use of Poetry and the Use of Criticism*, Eliot famously posited that "[E]very poet would like ... to be able to think that he had some direct social utility ... He would like to convey the pleasures of poetry, not only to a larger audience, but to larger groups of people collectively; and the theatre is the best place in which to do it" (154). Whether or not every poet shares Eliot's hankering for the stage is less important than the idea, expressed in no uncertain terms in "The Social Function of Poetry" (1943), that poetry "makes a difference to the society as a whole ... it makes a difference to the speech, to the sensibility, to the lives of all the members of a society, to all the members of the community, to the whole people, whether they read and enjoy poetry or not" and that the deterioration of language resulting from the absence of great poets invariably leads to the deterioration of culture (OPP 8–12). The more contact ordinary people have with the great poetry in their language, the more direct will be the positive difference poetry can make in society. The theatre, by virtue not only of its larger audiences but also by its relationship, even more intimate than that of poetry, with ordinary speech, has the greatest potential to affect the living language and thus the sensibility of a public. Ideally, poetic drama will "bring poetry into the world in which the audience lives and to which it returns when it leaves the theatre" (OPP 87). Rather than "transport the audience into some imaginary world totally unlike its own, an unreal world in which poetry is tolerated," poetic drama should do the opposite: transport poetry into the daily life of the audience, that their speech, their sensibility, and their local culture might be revitalized.

    Eliot's answer to the question of why one should want to write a verse play, then, is at times given in terms of simple supply and demand, at others by invoking the call to social usefulness.[9] The "sensibility" of a people, the characteristic ways in which it thinks and feels, is the province of poetry in the life of a civilization. By demanding a certain rhythm, a new verse form privileges a particular vocabulary,

---

    [9]   He also offers purely aesthetic justifications for the use of verse in drama. In another of his most conclusive statements, he argued that "poetry both imposes a form to which the author must submit himself, and releases more unconscious force, than prose can; and this in the end is, I think, the reason why only dramatic poetry can give us the full satisfaction that we ask of the theatre" ("Aims" 16).

which is why it has the power to alter the language of a nation and, thus, its sensibility. The social utility of poetry is dependent not on its direct engagement with social or political concerns but, rather, on its ability to "preserve ... extend and improve" the local language that is the conduit and repository of the sensibility of a people (OPP 9). The quality and range of a people's thought and feeling, in other words, have a living relationship with those of its language, the custodian of which is poetry. Poetry "does, in proportion to its excellence and vigour, affect the speech and sensibility of the whole nation" (OPP 12). Although "[t]he influence of poetry, at the furthest periphery [of a society], is of course very diffused, very indirect, and very difficult to prove," it will nonetheless be understood to exist in any "healthy society" in which "there is a continuous reciprocal influence and interaction of each part upon the others," in other words, in a classically ordered society (OPP 12).

Eliot uses this classical conception as a kind of physiology to explain the linkages between poetry and local language, including his own practice of poetic drama and its place in British society. He applies precisely the same terms to the question of European cultural and linguistic relations. In an ingenious turn, he suggests that "[t]he whole question of the relation of countries of different language but related culture, within the ambit of Europe, is ... one into which we are led, perhaps unexpectedly, by inquiring into the social function of poetry" (OPP 12). The conceptual terrain that opens out from this question is difficult, but Eliot was tireless in trying to find the order in it. So, for instance, he writes that although poetry, bound as it is to local speech, "differs from every art in having a value for the people of the poet's race and language, which it can have for no other," it is also true that "a reciprocal influence and stimulus ... a constant give and take" between the several cultures of Europe is essential to the health of each local language. Poetry may be "a constant reminder of all the things that can only be said in one language, and are untranslatable," but it also occasionally affords special access into foreign cultures by virtue of the emotional signature of its rhythms (OPP 13–14). Owing both to this untranslatable aural quality and to the tradition of European multilingualism, the poetry of each nation affects all the others and the European whole. Indeed, "no one nation, no one language, would have achieved what it has, if the same art had not been cultivated in neighboring countries and in different languages" (CC190). An additional level of sensitivity will result from the poet's having learned "at least one foreign language as well as one can learn any language but one's own," but ultimately one's duty is to one's own. If the local language the poet speaks is sufficiently healthy, it will already contain a good deal of what unites the culture of Europe. "The variety is as essential as the unity," and, as it happens, the English variety may be the best at expressing the European unity (OPP 13).

His abiding commitment to multilingualism did not preclude Eliot from recognizing and extolling the unique poetic merits of his own language among the several languages of Europe. In his postwar Berlin address, he gave his full, but diplomatic, support to the claim "that English, of all the languages of modern

Europe, is the richest for the purposes of writing poetry" (CC 187). The primary reason for this richness, in Eliot's view, is not any feature that isolates English from other European languages but, rather, "that it is a composite from so many different European sources," from Greek and Latin to Germanic, Anglo-Saxon, and Celtic (CC 189). It is precisely the status of English as the repository of so much European linguistic history that privileges it as the vehicle for poetry; in its breadth and variety, English contains more of the mind of Europe than the more narrowly derived languages of the continent. Thus Eliot uses English, as in a line from *Murder in the Cathedral*, "That the pattern" of Europe "may subsist" (22). As Moody observes, for Eliot "there is more to the English language than just English or British culture … [i]t affords its users access to the mind, that is, to the cultural traditions, of Europe … Eliot's achievement," he argues, "was to discover his mind of Europe already at home in the English language" (29–30). Likewise, Eliot (once a banker) saw England itself as uniquely situated to act as a kind of European cultural clearinghouse. In a wartime address to the Anglo-Swedish Society on "The Nature of Cultural Relations," he suggested that "London, as the capital of a country which has the Celtic world on its border from the south-west to the north, the Scandinavian to the east, the plattdeutsch to the south-east, and the Latin to the south, is suited to be one of the great *entrepôts* of culture for Europe" (15).[10] He was convinced equally that "Europe is, culturally, a whole, of which no part can flourish in isolation," and that only by the work of poetry in nourishing local language could local culture be preserved. Therefore, Eliot could set about writing poetic plays in his native language, confident that that language contained more than any other of the mind of Europe, and that in his service to his language, he was doing all that one might for European culture.

Toward Ritual Drama

There is even more, however, to Eliot's choice of verse drama as his preferred medium for safeguarding European culture than the service of poetry to local language and the increased access to a public afforded by the stage. For Eliot, the theatre is not just a good way to get a lot of people to hear poetry; it also provides the setting for ritual, in which art, language and bodies interact to fulfill a necessary societal function that poetry alone cannot. In 1923, Eliot wrote, "The drama was originally ritual," and the ritual impulse, although it became less conspicuous

---

[10] Elsewhere, Eliot also wrote of England's unique position between Europe and America. "Britain is related on the one hand to the rest of Europe and on the other hand to an Empire which from a cultural point of view, includes the United States of America ... she is the only member of the European community that has established a genuine empire ..." ("A Commentary [Mar. 1928]" 194). Here he is obviously guilty of the Iberian-Latin American omission criticized by Enrique Dussel and Carlos Fuentes, but his inclusion of the United States does suggest that he was not thinking in the most narrowly Eurocentric mode.

over time, was at the heart of his dramatic vision, particularly in the interwar years ("Beating" 12). It may fairly be said that one arc traced by Eliot's career is toward a more realistic, less ritualistic form of drama—*The Elder Statesman* is a long way from *Sweeney Agonistes*—but it is equally true that each step he took away from overt ritualism was also an attempt to achieve more effectively some of the true aims of ritual—the preservation of the past, the renewal of the present, the ordering of relations between the spiritual and material worlds—in a society hostile to both ritual and its necessary counterpart, tradition.

For ritual, as will be discussed in the following chapter, bridges the gap between the material and the immaterial worlds. In Eliot's verse drama, the immaterial corresponds to an emotional "fringe of indefinite extent ... beyond the nameable, classifiable emotions and motives of our conscious life;" and to the "planes of reality" that exist not "*out* of character, but in some way *beyond* character" (OPP 93). It also implies the spiritual: "What poetry should do in the theatre is a kind of humble shadow or analogy of the Incarnation, whereby the human is taken up into the divine" ("Aims" 12). Access to this other plane is provided by the "unconscious" effect of poetic rhythm and style (OPP 77). Yeats, as will be seen, brings the spiritual world into everyday life by foregrounding strange images and staging his hieratic plays in such intimate everyday spaces as drawing rooms. Eliot opts to keep his plays in the theatre but to so manipulate the relationship between his dramatic verse, conveyor of unconscious emotional effects, and the language of everyday speech that the two should become all but indistinguishable.

Eliot's first dramatic effort, *Sweeney Agonistes*, sought to bridge this gap by plunging poetic drama into a mélange of popular forms, "vaudeville, music hall, melodrama, burlesque, jazz, and minstrelsy" (Chinitz 107). It was written in the years (1924–25) immediately after his *Criterion* essays "Marie Lloyd" (1922) and "Dramatis Personae" (1923), in which Eliot made the case for a ritualistic yet popular form of modern drama, one that might integrate art and ordinary lived experience. However, *Sweeney*'s integrative strategy quickly became unsatisfactory for Eliot. As much as the "vernacular sources" of the play might provide that contact with everyday life that is essential to the poet's refinement of language and sensibility, the language they provided was hardly that great reservoir of European cultural tradition Eliot believed English to be:

> There's no telephones
> There's no gramophones
> There's no motor cars
> No two-seaters, no six-seaters,
> ....
> I seen it in the papers
> You seen it in the papers
> They *dont* [*sic*] all get pinched in the end. (CPP 80–83)

A statement he made later in life helps explain why his subsequent plays employed quite a different strategy. In "American Literature and the American Language" (1953), he wrote:

It is, of course, a necessary condition for the continuance of a literature, that the language should be in constant change. If it is changing it is alive; ... But when a change occurs such as that which led to the supersession of Latin by French, Italian, Spanish and Portuguese, the new languages have to grow up from the roots of the old, that is, from the common speech of uneducated people, and for a long time will be crude and capable of expressing only a narrow range of simple thoughts and feelings. (49)

The language of *Sweeney Agonistes*, despite the implication of its subtitle's reference to Aristophanes, is very much "the common speech of uneducated people."[11] It is, moreover, largely derived from American English, a language still in the process of growing to maturity, and from slang, which never does so. What Eliot's next plays make clear is that he was not ready to accept that English had reached the point at which it must succumb to the limitations of a modern popular vernacular insufficient to contain a wide range of "thoughts and feelings." Although the inroads made by *Sweeney* are considerable, both in suggesting how ritual might be actualized in a modern form and in realizing the fertilizing potential of American speech on the English language, Eliot was too steeped in the best literature in his language to concede its "supersession" by the exciting but, for the time being, cruder and narrower American-English derived language of the music hall.[12] For all its novelty and avant-garde interest, the language of *Sweeney* was not very promising for Eliot because it prematurely cast off tradition in favor of the purely new and its comparatively shallow cultural capacity.[13]

That he had not yet given up on the more traditional resources of the English language is made plain in the verse of his next play, *Murder in the Cathedral* (1935).[14] It has often been remarked that the theme and tone of this play signal Eliot's outlook following his conversion to Anglo-Catholicism. Less often noted is how thoroughly it reflects Eliot's clarified sense of the importance of tradition, particularly linguistic tradition, in the social utility of verse drama. The "literary" weight of much of the play's idiom is not merely the result of a temperamental high seriousness attendant upon the author's newfound orthodoxy. It is the music produced by the strategic use of the capacity of his native language to suggest order. As we have seen, the richness of the English language subsists, according

---

[11]   It is instructive that the original title, "Wanna Go Home, Baby?" was only changed to "Sweeney Agonistes" and the epigraphic material citing Aeschylus, Aristophanes, and St. John of the Cross only added in 1933, apparently in an effort to refigure the play in terms of Eliot's classical conception of European literary history.

[12]   On the American derivations of the play's slang, see Chinitz 112.

[13]   My focus here is primarily on language, but for a very insightful treatment of *Sweeney* as performance, see Julia Daniel's essay "'Or It Might Be You': Audiences in and of T.S. Eliot's *Sweeney Agonistes*" in *Modern Drama* 54 (2011).

[14]   I am not dealing here with *The Rock* (1934) because, while its versification is an interesting study in Eliot's development in writing for the stage, it is hardly, as Eliot acknowledged, a dramatic work at all. See OPP 98–99.

to Eliot, in its ability not only to assimilate new material but also to maintain the linguistic tradition behind "the mind of Europe." In "The Music of Poetry" (1942), he argues that the "music of a word … arises from its relation first to the words immediately preceding and following it, and indefinitely to the rest of its context; and from another relation, that of its immediate meaning in that context to all the other meanings which it has had in other contexts, to its greater or less wealth of association" (OPP 25). In this sense the lines of *Sweeney Agonistes* appear definitely impoverished, while it is clear from a glance at any page of *Murder in the Cathedral* that the playwright has selected a vocabulary with a far greater "wealth of association":

> Now is my way clear, now is the meaning plain:
> Temptation shall not come in this kind again.
> The last temptation is the greatest treason:
> To do the right deed for the wrong reason.
> The natural vigour in the venial sin
> Is the way in which our lives begin.
> Thirty years ago, I searched all the ways
> That lead to pleasure, advancement and praise.
> Delight in sense, in learning and in thought,
> Music and philosophy, curiosity,
> The purple bullfinch in the lilac tree,
> The tilt-yard skill, the strategy of chess,
> Love in the garden, singing to the instrument,
> Were all things equally desirable. (44)

Even this short passage is shot through with the accumulated signification of centuries. The word-group *temptation, sin, tree, garden* evokes the core myth of Western civilization. The litany of pursuits—*learning, music, philosophy*, nature, sport, *love*, even *chess*—speaks to the West's more earthly imagination of itself. Even the music of the line "The purple bullfinch in the lilac tree," balanced between soft Latinate adjectives (*purple, lilac*) and sturdy Anglo-Saxon nouns (*bullfinch, tree*), captures the rich order in diversity behind Europe and inside English.[15] The language suggests how much respect Eliot accords the cultural inheritance of the English language, on the level of rhythm, tone, and the individual word.

Eliot's own account of how he arrived at the style of *Murder in the Cathedral* reveals another level of meaning in the language of the play, although it understates the strategic significance of his eventual choice. In order to both "take my audience

---

[15]   A. David Moody provides an interesting analysis of how Eliot, particularly in *Four Quartets*, used the associative resources of English words derived respectively from Latin, Greek, and Anglo-Saxon to express an order in the mind of Europe. For example, "the facts of experience tend to be given in a basic or elementary Anglo-Saxon; while the search for their meaning, the metaphysical investigation of them, is carried forward in a discourse largely derived from the classical component of the language" (28). The first Quartet, "Burnt Norton," was built around passages excised from *Murder in the Cathedral*.

back to an historical event" and "bring home ... the contemporary relevance of the situation," he arrived at a linguistic *via media* between the archaic and the purely contemporary. "The style," he writes in "Poetry and Drama," "... had to be *neutral*, committed neither to the present nor to the past" (OPP 85). He might better have said, "committed *both* to the present *and* the past," in light of his solution: a "vocabulary and style" dynamically poised between "unintelligible ... Norman French and Anglo-Saxon" and "modern conversation" (84). He decided to write while keeping in mind "the versification of *Everyman*, hoping that anything unusual in the sound of it would be, on the whole, advantageous."[16] His ostensible ambition in making this specific choice was to avoid any form reminiscent of the derivative English nineteenth century, but in banking on the "unusual" aural effect of *Everyman*'s influence, he was also implicitly tapping into the ability of his audience to recall, even unconsciously, the depth behind their own language. "Tradition," Eliot wrote two years before the first performance of *Murder in the Cathedral*, "is of the blood, so to speak, rather than of the brain: it is the means by which the vitality of the past enriches the life of the present" (ASG 32). The versification of the play is essentially an appeal to tradition, which opens into the general through its purchase in the local. To whom besides an English audience would the rhythms of *Everyman*, a fifteenth-century morality, sound sufficiently strange yet familiar to situate the experience of Eliot's play both in the present and the past? Grover Smith observes that, moreover, the long, alliterative lines of the choral passages are "obviously allied to Old and Middle English" verse forms (194). The term "allied" is well chosen, because one must assume that, for Eliot, to associate his language with another, older form goes beyond mere mimicry of superficials and implies, rather, a deliberate effort to capitalize on the resources of meaning of the older form, conveyed down through centuries by way of the unconscious signification of poetic rhythms. The "importance of the unconscious effect of the verse upon us" is not merely that it increases the enjoyment of a poetic play, but that it subtly invokes the levels of tradition behind the verse (OPP 81). While Eliot eventually felt "the versification of the dialogue in *Murder in the Cathedral*" to have "only a *negative* merit," it had the positive, if unnamed, merit of adding a layer of unconscious association to a modern idiom through recourse to the rhythms of ancestral ones (OPP 85). The play's versification *allies* the past and the present, bringing the linguistic order of a past in which England and Europe were closer to their common sources of unity to bear on a present in which such unity seems a mirage. It is the stylistic equivalent of foregrounding the contemporary relevance in the story of St. Thomas á Becket, a story that works close to the core of some British ideas of social and religious order. The Second Priest is soon disabused of his temporary belief that "Our Lord is at one with the Pope, and also the King of France. / We can lean on a rock, we can feel

---

[16]   Grover Smith notes that Eliot's "principal debt" to *Everyman* "appears in the rhyming passages of the Tempters' dialogues with Becket, where the sharp, irregularly assorted stresses, four to the line, mimic skillfully the meter of the old play" (194).

a firm foothold …" (*Murder in the Cathedral* 17). His words, though, bespeak the ideal condition long but, Eliot hoped, perhaps not completely forgotten by a contemporary English audience, and of which they might be reminded by the old rhythms buried in their own language.

While audiences have always found the verse of *Murder in the Cathedral* a bit too conspicuous, there can be no doubt that the play goes to great lengths to bring poetry into their world. In addition to the careful selection of a verse form, the other primary means of doing so is in the employment of a Greek-style chorus. Although Eliot was not entirely satisfied with the chorus, it is worth examining because it reveals much about his vision not only of verse drama but also of the kind of society in which verse drama could thrive. Besides all the practical reasons he gives in "Poetry and Drama," the use of a chorus is a natural one for "a poet," such as Eliot, "writing for the first time for the stage" because it is an effective means of stimulating the audience members' belief that "*I* could talk in poetry too!" (OPP 86–87). Eliot sees his chorus, in the Greek manner, as a mediator between the action and the audience. By providing an example of the effect of dramatic action on ostensibly ordinary people—here the "excited and sometimes hysterical women" of Canterbury—the chorus demonstrates the possibility of such people expressing intense emotion in verse (OPP 86). The Canterbury women's uncertainty (like that of the speakers who introduce Yeats's final plays) mirrors that of the audience. Their early questions, in addition to establishing the foreboding atmosphere of the play, approximate those in the audience's mind at the production of such an unusual play:

> … Here let us wait.
> Are we drawn by danger? …
> … What danger can be
> For us, the poor, the poor women of Canterbury? What tribulation
> With which we are not already familiar …
> … Some presage of an act
> Which our eyes are compelled to witness, has forced our feet
> Towards the cathedral. We are forced to bear witness. (*Murder in the Cathedral* 11)[17]

The ability of such language to influence that of a contemporary audience might seem slim, given the choruses' generally distant relation to everyday speech. However, the verbal style is not so remote from the familiar as it might at first appear. Indeed, its style would seem quite recognizable to an audience familiar with Anglo-Catholic liturgy. For instance, as Grover Smith points out, the "terminal

---

[17] As the play was originally produced in Canterbury Cathedral and is still frequently played in churches, the doubling effect of the chorus's speech can be even more pronounced. So it is in *The Family Reunion*, in which the Chorus speak of themselves as actors: "Why do we feel embarrassed, impatient, fretful, ill at ease, / Assembled like amateur actors who have not been assigned their parts?" (CPP 231).

chorus is conspicuously indebted to Anglican ritual, including perhaps the English 'Gloria in excelsis' and the 'Benedicite, omnia opera'" (193). The play as a whole continues the experiments with ritual that characterize *Sweeney Agonistes* while raising ritualism to a new level by anchoring it to a recognized ritual form, the Anglo-Catholic Mass.[18] *Murder* is Eliot's best attempt to get poetic language and local life to interact in such a way that, unlike in *Sweeney*, the cultural depth contained in the language is not sacrificed. Such a maneuver at once helps Eliot situate his drama within an established, "credible order" and keep his dramatic verse within the scope of what is accessible to a wide public (OPP 94). The move toward liturgy, as Chinitz argues, evinces not archaism or snobbery, but Eliot's "recogni[tion of] religious ritual as community property," and thus a desire to keep his poetry meaningfully involved in social life (135–36). The Mass is, after all, "a cultural form no less familiar to contemporary audiences than, say, music hall" (136). Rather than distancing the play from a contemporary audience, then, the association actually renders the experience of the play less strange.[19] In allying the play with Anglican liturgy, Eliot borrowed the authority of a publicly accepted (if threatened) ritual form, sowing his effort at linguistic reconciliation in perhaps the only remaining ground in which people would tolerate not only poetry but also the suggestion of permanent order.

Some recent critics have focused on the related theme of the impulse toward community in Eliot's verse drama. Randy Malamud's book on Eliot's "Communities of Drama" sees in a whole host of Eliot's dramatic maneuvers a striving toward "the succor of community beneficence" (3). Thus the Chorus in *Murder in the Cathedral*, Becket's sermon, and the Knights' direct address to the audience serve to create a tentative sense of community both onstage (as with the Chorus and Knights) and between the audience and actors, as well as between the depicted past and the contemporary world. Malamud identifies in these devices Eliot's full exploitation of "a Brechtian sensibility," foregrounding the role of the audience as spectators and the actors' as performers (74). Like Brecht, Eliot believed "that the essential consequence of a play is its impact on the audience and that dramatic historical analysis must serve to bring the past into the present with an eye toward using its lessons to affect and improve the future" (Malamud 74). True enough, and certainly Eliot's work, early and late, is concerned, up to a point, with the establishment of sympathetic communities and the potential of art to effect real-world change. Such a use of the past is a foundation of Eliot's interest in ritual. However, in its enthusiasm to endow Eliot with a great deal more fellow-feeling than he has historically been accorded, Malamud's analysis, with its happy

---

[18]   See Matthiessen 162.

[19]   The opposite possibility also exists, however. As will be seen in the chapter on David Jones, a paradox of modern poetry is that by appealing to an objective tradition a poem can often appear more strange, more subjective. However, the degree to which those objective traditions, such as Christianity, had deteriorated as a source of social coherence by the 1930s is, I would argue, most often overstated by literary critics.

conception of "community," understates how far away from ordinary liberalism, not to mention from Brechtian socialism, Eliot's classicism and idea of European order took his drama.

Malamud observes that the effect of an Eliot Chorus is effectively to "deconstruct" the drama (98). Specifically, it deconstructs the expectations of traditional realistic performance and the willing identification by the audience with the performers on stage. Such is precisely the aim, formally, of the Brechtian "epic theatre." Malamud, however, also makes this crucial observation: that once the drama has been sufficiently deconstructed, Eliot has the audience "firmly in his power" (98). Clearly, matters of control were central to Eliot's dramatic program. Even in that populist appreciation, "Marie Lloyd," he singled out their ability to "control an audience" as the best music-hall performers' primary talent (SE 369). Brecht, of course, had in mind to unlock the *audience's* power of social criticism and free-thinking by severing the traditional ties of illusion and identification. He hoped his audiences would leave the theatre more keenly and critically aware of the material conditions of their lives. Eliot, however, hoped his audiences would leave the play aspiring to speak in poetry—aspiring, in other words, to speak as people conscious of the wide intellectual and emotional range of their language. Brecht's intention is truly popular, revolutionary in the Marxist sense. Eliot's, too, is revolutionary, but its populist overtones are balanced by its classicist tendencies toward authority, tradition, and, above all, order, the same characteristics that describe the idea of Europe in which his dramatic project is situated. Just as, in the Church, order is protected by an elite, the clergy, the literature of a people, according to Eliot, is best presided over by those, such as himself presumably, trained in its language. In a 1929 "Commentary," he wrote that "[i]n our ideal Platonic Republic, of course, the country would be governed by those who can best write and speak its language—those, in other words, who can best think in that language" (378). Further, "the development of culture," he argues in "The Social Function of Poetry," "does not mean bringing everybody up to the front … : it means the maintenance of such an *élite*, with the main, and more passive body of readers not lagging more than a generation or so behind" (OPP 11). The notion that order in art, and by extension in society, depends on the authority of a few is precisely the feature of Eliot's thought that shifts it away from the truly "popular" or "communal."

Eliot's hope in *Murder in the Cathedral* is not to meet the audience on equal terms or, like Brecht, to set loose the audience member's own capacity to critique the world but, rather, to inspire his or her participation, through language, in an ordered vision of cultural identity. The play, like the famous "DA" concluding *The Waste Land*, and like Marie Lloyd, gives to, sympathizes with, but finally controls its audience. The successful verse dramatist, in Eliot's view, orchestrates the sensibility of the public through the vehicle of the theatre, involving drama and reality in a symbiotic relationship intent on the maintenance and revivification of Western culture. This "spiritual" component of the drama is akin to that of a Church ritual like the Mass, and both derive at least as much from authority as from community. Chinitz argues that the Mass, in its familiarity and communal nature, constitutes "a form of popular culture" (136). However, the Mass is also the embodiment of order, both social and artistic. In addition to being "community property," Catholic liturgy manifests the sense of tradition and hierarchy that are as essential to Eliot's view of art and society (and art in society) as the need to keep poetry close to everyday life (136). Eliot's enlistment of liturgy, while making his vision of a poetic drama more comprehensible to a public, also inscribes in the drama a code, a practice of understanding, based on order, tradition, and authority. The communal impulse he imports from Church ritual is not gained at the expense, in other words, of the basic imperative of order implicit in that form. As Grover Smith notes, one key effect of the verse of *Murder in the Cathedral* is the overall "feeling of structural orderliness" in the play (193). And Eliot makes clear that in these matters of order, the line between art and society is utterly permeable: "It is a function of all art to give us some perception of an order in life, by imposing an order upon it" (OPP 93).

Eliot's plays, particularly *Murder in the Cathedral*, intensify the relationship between order-in-art and order-in-life by gathering the audience into the ritual unfolding onstage. W.B. Worthen argues, "Eliot's dramaturgy strategically designs the spectator's performance as essential to the meaning of the theatrical event" (271). The moments in *Murder in the Cathedral* when the normally accepted boundaries between stage and audience are punctured are attempts "to inscribe the spectator's performance in the play's design" (Worthen 271). In Eliot's project of cultural rejuvenation, the play's the thing, whether in the collaboration of audience and actors during the time span of the performance, or in the refined sense of tradition and language the play imparts to the playgoers to take home with them. "The poetic theater," says Worthen, "... works to figure and thematize the audience's performance, to enable both actor and audience to become 'part of the act,' to discover a 'vital flame' enabled precisely by the artifice of performance itself, their mutual 'work of acting'" (262). By doing so, it seeks to do the reverse: to enable the play—order, language, and unconscious stimulation to forgotten regions of sensibility—to become a part of reality, that "our own sordid, dreary world would be suddenly illuminated and transfigured" (OPP 87). Its transfiguration, Eliot hoped, would be a function of the recollection by the public that it is heir, through its language and the poetry that nurtures it, to a wide range of sensibility, as well as to a cultural tradition that promises "serenity, stillness, and reconciliation" by uniting them to their own past and thus that of the European whole (OPP 94).

Eliot understood fairly early that, given *Murder in the Cathedral*'s formal novelty, specialized audience, and historically remote subject matter, continued writing in this mode would be untenable for the achievement of his related dramatic and cultural aims:

> [P]eople are prepared to put up with verse from the lips of personages dressed in the fashion of some distant age: therefore they should be made to hear it from people dressed like ourselves, living in houses and apartments like ours, and using telephones and motor cars and radio sets ... And audiences ... expect poetry to be in rhythms which have lost touch with colloquial speech. (OPP 87)

The better to "bring poetry into the world in which the audience lives," he knew that his next play must have "a theme of contemporary life, with characters of our own time living in our own world" (OPP 87). In his later plays, Eliot would move so far in this direction as almost to efface their poetry, not to mention their ritual resemblance, altogether. While *The Family Reunion* (1939) clearly indicates the shift, like *Murder in the Cathedral* it does not surrender to purely vernacular speech, nor does it entirely abandon ritual. It does, however, reveal the scales of Eliot's ritual vision beginning to tip in the direction of everyday life, and away from such mysteries as suggested by liturgical forms. The goal, to restore to a contemporary audience a sense of cultural order and wholeness, has not changed; rather, the dramatic means of delivering that sense has become a bit more like community property.

In *The Family Reunion*, Eliot attempts to get poetic language to act on ordinary experience by narrowing the divide between them, bringing the verse closer to "the speech which [the poet] finds around him, that with which he is most familiar" (OPP 24). The verse of *The Family Reunion* is certainly not "transparent," however (OPP 79). Even the non-choral passages, whose rhythm is generally unobtrusive, frequently ascend to an intense poetic pitch and employ a syntax laden with ritual resonance. The play as a whole retains some of the incantatory gravity as well as spiritual signification of *Murder in the Cathedral*. In the passage below, the syntax is drawn from part of the ritual core of the West. Spring is "an issue of blood / A season of sacrifice" because of the Christian ritual celebration of Christ's death and resurrection at Easter. Blood sacrifice and the return of the dead, besides being the foundational themes of Christianity, are precisely those celebrated in its oldest and most important ritual, the Mass:

> Spring is an issue of blood
> A season of sacrifice
> And the wail of the new full tide
> Returning the ghosts of the dead
> Those whom the winter drowned
> Do not the ghosts of the drowned
> Return to land in the spring?
> Do the dead return? (FR 58)

Eliot tries to camouflage such flights between passages of more mundane language, the better to keep the attention of the audience away from the fact of the verse:

> Well, as for me,
> I would never go south, no, definitely never,
> Even could I do it as well as Amy:
> England's bad enough, I would never go south,
> Simply to see the vulgarest people—
> You can keep out of their way at home;
> People with money from heaven knows where—
> … Dividends from aeroplane shares. (FR 13)

The combination of styles is Eliot's attempt to do the ritualistic work of affecting present reality by melding it with poetic or spiritual reality. Its awkwardness, later apparent to Eliot, is rather like that expressed in one chorus: "why should we be implicated, brought in and brought together?" (FR 42). Why, in other words, should ordinary people be implicated in "some revelation" apparently beyond their capacity or concern? Although the ordinary is required for ritual revelation, every step away from the traditional ritual framework of Christianity once more begs the question of why one should then be implicated in such an undertaking. The effect of mixed styles, as might be expected, struck Eliot much later as "defective," as did the ghosts the play uses toward a similar end (OPP 89).

What is interesting about *The Family Reunion* is that it incorporates at least three other means of recuperating what ritual significance might be lost by vernacularizing theme and language and placing the action in the present. The most conspicuous is the presence of ghosts. As he had written in 1928, "nothing is more dramatic than a ghost," and in *The Family Reunion*, ghosts do much of the work of tethering the drama to the ritual origins so important to Eliot (SE 39). Their relationship to the present world of the play—"wherever I am not looking, / Always flickering at the corner of my eye, / Almost whispering just out of earshot— / And inside too ..." is precisely that of Eliot's ideal dramatic verse to contemporary speech, designed such that "more is heard than is spoken" (FR 55; 93). While he had to sacrifice some of the associative weight of the idiom of *Murder in the Cathedral*, he made up some of the ground by including the Eumenides, who, like the verse rhythms in the previous play, demonstrate that "all past is present" (FR 28). They do so in the immediate context of the action of the play by continually reminding Harry of his past deeds and the curse that burdens his family. Moreover, their appearance is linked to the construction of Wishwood as the kind of sacred space on which ritual depends and which Eliot, having taken his plays out of the church, no longer enjoys by default. Harry asks: "They were always there. But I did not *see* them. / Why should they wait until I came back to Wishwood? There were a thousand places where I might have met them! / Why here? why here?" (FR 24).The answer, as Yeats knew, is that ghosts, like rituals, have a symbiotic relationship with sacred spaces. Borrowed from Aeschylean tragedy, these Eumenides are also a survival of the past of Europe, an iconic link to the classical ritual theatre underlying all this modern experimentation. Eliot eventually found his Eumenides, as onstage characters, to be too much of a distraction, and decided that they would function better on the margins of consciousness. "When the loop in time comes—and it does not come for everybody— / The hidden is revealed, and the spectres show themselves" (FR 18). His decision that "[t]hey must, in future, be omitted from the cast, and be understood to be visible only to certain of my characters, and not to the audience" is more technical than conceptual (OPP 90). In this, his final play in the ritualistic mode, the ghosts, even as merely verbal indices, have important work to do.

The second technique is the constant discursive return to the idea of ritual unification of past, present, and future, the condition of "living on several planes at once," that ghosts, like the echo of an ancestral verse form, represent (CPP 266).

The dead, in a truly unified experiential order, do return in order to suggest the reconciliation of present and past. The theme of the presence of the past is written everywhere into the characters' dialogue, both in the abstract and in the specifics of Harry's relationship to Wishwood and to the memory of his misdeed ("I am the old house / ... / In which all past is present" (FR 28)). It might even be said that Agatha's admission, "I can guess about the past and what you mean about the future; / But a present is missing, needed to connect them," is the ultimate justification for ritual and, indeed, for Eliot's ideal verse drama (FR 95-96).

The third technique is what Eliot, in "Poetry and Drama," called the "trance-like state" into which characters occasionally enter and in which they speak their most poetic lines (OPP 88). In two cases this state is the occasion of a "lyrical duet" of the kind Auden employed in *On the Frontier*, "isolated" from the main current of the dialogue. The last of these duets, between Agatha and Mary, takes place as part of a modern approximation of ritual, the blowing out of birthday candles, heightened by liturgical vocabulary and by having the speakers process somberly around the cake:

> This way the pilgrimage
> Of expiation
> ....
> By intercession
> By pilgrimage
> By those who depart
> In several directions
> For their own redemption
> And that of the departed—
> 　　May they rest in peace. (FR 131)

Such interludes, even without the choreography, are a rather heavy-handed attempt to get ritual into the play, and Eliot later found this device, too, "defective." For the time being, though, it enabled him to suggest, albeit mechanically, the multiple planes of reality he wanted his drama to imply.

After *The Family Reunion*, Eliot did not publish another play for ten years, a gap that, in the context of his career, clearly suggests the end of a phase. His own sense of an ending is painfully obvious in his final *Criterion* "Commentary": "It will perhaps need more severe affliction than anything we have yet experienced, before life can be renewed. As the state of arts and letters is a symptom of decline, so it might be a symptom of a true revival. But in any case, the immediate future is not bright" ("[Jan. 1939]" 274). The next play he did write, while commercially successful, revealed that no such "revival" had been in the offing. The style of *The Cocktail Party* showed just how much of the ritual ideal Eliot had left on the threshold of World War II, the same point at which the "'European mind', which one had mistakenly thought might be renewed and fortified, disappeared from view" ("[Jan. 1939]" 271). As suggested in the next chapter, 1939 appears to have been the year in which the possibility of ritual drama died in Europe. Certainly, *The*

Family Reunion has much more in common, aesthetically, with its truly ritualistic predecessor, *Murder in the Cathedral*, than with the more naturalistic sitting-room dramas beginning with *The Cocktail Party*.

A *Via Media*

As Chinitz points out, many critics have bemoaned the fact that Eliot's later plays never delivered on *Sweeney Agonistes*'s promise of a "fascinating and original expressionist drama," but here they are substituting their own ambitions for Eliot's (149). Any even marginally thorough reading of Eliot's writing *about* verse drama will reveal that his own project had quite a different aim, although this one, too, turned out largely to be an unrealized potential. In the case of the plays, this is attributable to his capitulation to the institutional realities of the modern theatre, as well as to the drastically altered political climate in the wake of World War II. In "yielding ... to the demands of the existing theater," Eliot chose to forego further adventures in radical modernist-style experimentation. In the face of the justifiable wariness of his culture about the possibility of European cultural "order" and of the legitimacy of any classical notion of tradition and authority, Eliot chose to forego the fullest exploration of verse drama as a modern ritual form (Chinitz 148). While the weird pageantry and cultural ideas of European fascism had once been tolerated, if viewed with suspicion, the full revelation of Nazi atrocities had rendered the idea that Europe could be ordered by an imaginative recuperation of ancient spirituality and the ritualization of experience far too abhorrent to push very hard in that direction.

Like Yeats and fascist dramatic politics, Eliot was involved in the European pattern of trying to restore ritual to European life. Eliot's own skepticism about fascism, though, was so thorough and consistent as to render the question of his relationship to it almost moot. However, the specific ways his own thought diverges from that of abstract fascism are instructive in understanding how broad and complex the potential uses of ritual in an idea of Europe are, notwithstanding the general recoil from them in response to revelations about fascist practice. Eliot's fundamental objection to the fascist governments of both Italy and Germany was that both arose out of no credible European tradition, and to the exclusion of any notion of European cultural intercourse. In an April 1926 "Commentary," he addressed the problem of modern Italy's relation to the Roman Empire with its implication of European order:

> [T]he Roman Empire does concern us, but ... whatever use may be made of that idea in Italian politics as an incentive to local action is a local matter which does not concern—in either way—those persons who are interested primarily in European ideas. The old Roman Empire is an European idea; the new Roman Empire is an Italian idea ... The general idea is found in the continuity of the impulse of Rome to the present day. It suggests Authority and Tradition, certainly, but Authority and Tradition (especially the latter) do not necessarily suggest Signor Mussolini. (222)

As he later wrote in *The Family Reunion*, "the future can only be built / Upon the real past"; thus, Italian fascism promised no future (CPP 228). A movement that also cuts one nation off from "the European idea—the idea of a common culture of western Europe," is entirely contrary to Eliot's vision, both at this relatively early date and in 1939 at the onset of the dismemberment of Europe. Contributing to *The Criterion*'s demise, he wrote, was the fact that "the newer German writers had less and less to say to Europe; ... they were more and more saying what could be understood, if understood at all, only in Germany" (CC 194).[20] One recalls Eliot's belief that the special strength of the English language lay in its comprehension of European multiplicity and notes that not even the possession of this supposedly privileged poetic language could diminish his appreciation for European variety.

It might be argued that while Yeats's cultural outlook is characterized by the opposition and interplay of binaries, Eliot's is defined by the kind of multiplicity advocated in his dissertational theory of points of view (and illustrated, for example, in "A Dialogue on Dramatic Poetry"). Great Britain, he argues, "is ... not only a part [of Europe], she is a mediating part: for Britain is the bridge between Latin and Germanic culture in both of which she shares" ("Commentary [Mar. 1928]" 194).[21] His desire for European wholeness to be inclusive of all its parts extends even to the Western hemisphere, with Britain as a "*via media*" between Europe's ancient and modern selves (194). He sees Britain as uniquely positioned linguistically, culturally, and geographically to help restore Europe to the kind of "serenity, stillness, and reconciliation" it so desperately needs. And he sees verse drama, in utilizing the resources of both poetic language and ritual action, as the best means of restoring the mind of Europe to Britain.

---

[20]   Eliot's vision of Europe shares this disapproval of nationalism with that of his hero, Dante. See de Rougemont 55–58.

[21]   David Jones, as discussed in Chapter 7, similarly situates Britain as the pivot on which Europe turns, but he adds the Celtic world to the Latin and Germanic.

Chapter 2
For European Purposes:
Yeats and Fascism Revisited

The verse plays Yeats wrote in the last two decades of his life all explore the reconciliation through ritual action of the oppositions dividing human experience and confounding full unity of being. For Yeats, the use of ritual is a return to the past but also a plan for the future. Michael Valdez Moses astutely observes the dual character of Yeats's aims, arguing that Yeats's desired reclamation of ancient myths, legends, and ritual, his plan to revive the spirit of ancient tragedy, "promised to be at once a radically retrograde and a revolutionary nationalist cultural phenomenon" (565).[1] However, national identity is only one of Yeats's concerns in trying to create a ritual drama. Wherever he looks for ritual models in Ireland, Yeats finds Europe. This expanding frame of reference, particularly after the 1916 Easter Rising, helps to explain the trajectory of Yeats's verse-drama project, which brought him to a form of drama capable at once of gathering in key elements of European cultural memory and of questioning the future those elements seemed to promise.

The unique cultural permeability of Yeats's approach is especially apparent because the rituals he celebrates and uses as dramatic guides—Irish, Greek, Japanese—are almost invariably without a specific content. The form is what concerns him, the action undertaken as ritual, frequently implying a supernatural component but rarely naming a supernatural object. A remarkable passage in the 1919 essay "If I Were Four-and-Twenty" provides an example:

> But if I were four-and-twenty, and without rheumatism, ... I think I would go—though certainly I am no Catholic and never shall be one—upon both of our great pilgrimages, to Croagh Patrick and to Lough Derg ... ; no congregation has climbed to the Rock of Cashel since the stout Church of Ireland bishop took the lead roof from the Gothic church to save his legs: *but Europe has nothing older than our pilgrimages.* In many little lyrics I would claim that stony mountain for all Christian and pagan faith in Ireland ... Mountain and lough have not grown raw and common; pillage and ravage could not abate their beauty; and the impulse that gathers these great companies in every year has outlasted armorial stone. (E 266–67, my emphasis)

It makes little difference to Yeats what religion the Irish pilgrimages endorse; indeed, he loves the potential associations of pagan and Christian practices and

---

[1]   For more on how the content of Yeats's plays based on the Ulster cycle of myths fulfills this radical dualism, see Moses 567, 569–78.

places. The same attitude characterizes his use of Japanese Noh drama. While he is intrigued by the specific religious content of these plays, he never feels bound by it. Its brand of "intellectual subtlety is perhaps Buddhist," he writes, but he happily moves to the Irish associations it conjures in his mind (EI 232). What is important to Yeats about pilgrimage and about Noh (or any theatrical form) is the "impulse," not the dogma.[2] It is enough that the act of pilgrimage, a ritual action attached to a geographical sacred space, brings the past into contact with the present and the natural with the supernatural. The place is genuinely and specifically Irish; the ritual, though, is enacted in Ireland and Europe at once. "Europe has nothing older than our pilgrimages," which, for Yeats, remind Europe of its sacred self as though from a remote corner of its mind.

Pilgrimage, which unites particular (place) and universal (meaning), demonstrates the reconciliatory power of ritual that Yeats found so attractive for the metaphysical reasons most often cited by critics. However, he also found in ritual reconciliation a model for European coherence. His entire *oeuvre* represents a painstaking search for the point at which antitheses intersect: death and life, memory and desire, dream and reality, soul and body, natural and supernatural, individual and collective, time and eternity. In the latter part of his career, Yeats uses drama to articulate that search, then to suggest its resolution. He offers certain actions *in* the plays as well as the overall event *of* the plays as rituals with the potential to transform not only the experience of the theatre but also the cultural life of Europe by restoring to both the ritual element that once clarified their meaning and might do so again.

This chapter traces Yeats's construction of a ritualistic drama from the time of the Easter Rising to his death in 1939. It begins by looking at some of the spiritual, aesthetic, and cultural ideals that led Yeats to pursue a ritual type of drama, and the principles drawn from the Japanese Noh that shaped his early plays. It then situates Yeats's dramatic project in the context of his evolving idea of Europe in the interwar period, emphasizing the points at which his political ideas and those of European fascism overlap. It ends, however, with a sequential reading of Yeats's plays which shows that his work with ritual drama seems to have led him to a reconsideration of the real-world utility of ritual, a reconsideration marking a point at which Yeatsian verse drama and fascism finally diverge. Yeats's final plays, both in their form and in their subject matter, reveal his engagement with Greek dramatic models. They bring his vision of ritual drama to completion even as his own innovations subvert the imperative of sacrifice on which the Greek drama is based.

---

2   Even *A Vision*, which, as a metaphysical system, seems to establish a good deal of spiritual content, is ultimately a form and achieves its coherence as such: interlocking gyres and spirals mapped onto layered circles, for example, pure forms, are the frames on which all history and meaning hang.

"Precise Inexplicable"

As Theodor Adorno has written, Western civilization methodically divested itself of enchantment beginning with the Enlightenment, which established unequivocally that "there shall be neither mystery nor any desire to reveal mystery" (2). Henceforth, "anything which does not conform to the standard of calculability and utility must be viewed with suspicion" (Adorno 3). Yeats bemoaned this condition throughout his career. His preoccupation with mystery and the supernatural—second only to his preoccupation with Irish national identity, and intimately linked to it—dominates both his drama and his writing about the theatre. "As life becomes more orderly, more deliberate," he wrote in 1904, "the supernatural world sinks further away" (E 17). This view had not changed much by 1919: "Logic is loose again, ... and ... the wild beast cannot but destroy mysterious life" (E 277). However, ongoing experimentation with the supernatural through séances, his wife's automatic writing, and his work toward *A Vision* strengthened his belief that the "wild beast" of logic might be matched and overcome by the return of mystery, perhaps as part of the natural rhythm of human history. This optimism is evident in the Introduction to *The Cat and the Moon* (1926), where he writes, "Perhaps now that the abstract intellect has split the mind into categories, the body into cubes, we may be about to turn back toward the unconscious, the whole, the miraculous" (E 404). At the same time, his notion of what such a revivified sense of mystery might mean for human experience became clearer. In the Introduction to *The Words Upon the Window-Pane* (1934), he writes, "All about us there seems to start up a precise inexplicable teeming life, and the earth becomes once more, not in rhetorical metaphor, but in reality, sacred" (E 369). To make the earth really sacred is the end. The paradoxical unity expressed in the adjective phrase "precise inexplicable" is the one on which the means, ritual action, is based.

Although Yeats's drama had been evolving around a more-or-less consistent set of principles for years, it became truly ritualistic after his encounter with the Noh theatre of Japan, beginning in 1913. His friend Ezra Pound's work in editing Ernest Fenellosa's Noh translations provided the occasion for some examination and discussion of the hieratic Japanese form Pound and Yeats found both revelatory and relevant to modern European dramatic practice. Yeats's essay "Certain Noble Plays of Japan" was written in April 1916, so it coincided almost exactly with the Easter Rising and is dominated by many of the same reflections the Rising had stimulated. The essay implies the course Yeats's drama would follow toward the eventual representation of the sacrificial death that is the apogee of ritual. In his first four dance plays (published as *Four Plays for Dancers* (1920)), death is brought onstage either rhetorically or through the appearance of dead persons "dreaming back" into the settings of their lives, but no one dies. In his last plays, though, Yeats's vision of ritual drama reaches its logical end, and blood is shed.

Perhaps, considering how often his dance plays borrow the formal arrangement of the Noh, Yeats was insufficiently modest in announcing, "I have invented a form of drama, distinguished, indirect, and symbolic" (EI 221). In fairness, though, the plays he wrote after the Noh model are not, as Masaru Sekine notes, truly Noh plays, nor, as Sekine often fails to note, were they intended to be. In addition to shoring up a formal framework, the Noh legitimized some of Yeats's dearest thematic concerns: place, death, and bodily action—all of which have supernatural significance in the Noh and in Yeats's Noh-inspired plays. In combination, these themes formed the ritual core that positioned the Noh as at once in public life and a symbolic refinement of it. As Yeats wrote approvingly:

> These plays arose in an age of continual war and became a part of the education of soldiers. These soldiers, whose natures had as much of Walter Pater as of Achilles, combined with Buddhist priests and women to elaborate life in a ceremony, the playing of football, the drinking of tea, and all great events of State, becoming a ritual. (EI 235)

Gaelic people and the writers of Noh plays share the "idea of the 'sacred space,'" defined by George Mosse as "a place that could be filled only with symbolic activity" (208). The feeling for place in Noh drama revived and affirmed Yeats's longstanding "ambition of helping to bring again to certain places their old sanctity and romance" (EI 233). He enthused that "[t]hese Japanese poets feel for tomb and wood the emotion, the sense of awe that our Gaelic-speaking countrypeople will sometimes show when you speak to them of Castle Hackett or of some holy well" (232).

The Dreaming of the Bones (1919), the play that hews most closely to the Noh model, is also the most explicit in evoking Irish details of setting and story, but, like a key in a lock, its small particulars give access to a comparative vastness. Those particulars, which Natalie Crohn Schmitt thoroughly records, deliberately locate the play in a recognizable Irish landscape, but one already brimming with supernatural import. "In the western countryside," she writes, "dotted with ruins and the remembered sites of ancient rituals, including some that are still celebrated, the distinction between past and present, dream and reality, sacred and profane, is unclear" ("Haunted" 339). County Clare is the specific locale, in the vicinity of landmarks including Muckanish, Finvara, Aughanish, Bailevelehan, and "the ruined Abbey at Corcomroe" (CP 279). This index of place names lends the play a sense of familiarity, even for a non-Irish audience, based on a sense of present and concrete reality. However, the audience, like the hero of the play, is soon disabused of its realist expectations, including the sense of security implied by all the local geography. "Like wine that fills to the top / A grey-green cup of jade," the spirits of the dead often fill this landscape to the point of overflowing (CP 276).[3]

The Noh's use of stylized and largely inexpressive masks, by refuting the dramatic impulse toward realistic "vitality," seemed to Yeats indicative of the kind

---

[3]   Natalie Crohn Schmitt writes, based on personal experience, that "the strange and desolate Burren" in which the play is set is "so haunting that it is easy to think of it as haunted" ("Haunted" 350). She quotes F.A.C. Wilson, who "observes that the Burren is 'clearly an apt environment for a ghost play'" (353).

of knowledge that "makes us gaze with so much emotion upon the face of the Sphinx or the Buddha": the knowledge that full "being is only possessed completely by the dead" (EI 226). Yeats endorses the idea, articulated in 1907 by Gordon Craig, that the kind of mimetic facial expressiveness valued so highly by realism provides only a superficial depiction of life. Masks, in contrast, seem to invite the presence of both "exquisite life and acceptance of death" (236). Furthermore, the expressive potential denied by masking the human face is recuperated, even exceeded, in the Noh by concentrated bodily movement, an arrangement Yeats would find increasingly amenable over the next two decades. "Our bodies," he wrote near the end of his life, "are nearer to our coherence because nearer to the 'unconscious' than our thought" (E 446–47). In the Noh essay, he asserted that "[w]e only believe in those thoughts which have been conceived not in the brain but in the whole body" (EI 235). In Noh practice, little of importance is lost by covering the performers' faces, for "deep feeling is expressed by a movement of the whole body" (EI 226). At the end of his essay, Yeats powerfully intertwines art, body, death, and the divine: "It is still true that the Deity gives us, according to His promise, not His thoughts or His convictions but His flesh and blood, and I believe that the elaborate technique of the arts, seeming to create out of itself a superhuman life, has taught more men how to die than oratory or the Prayer Book" (EI 235). That Yeats should choose to enunciate his ultimate dramatic views in the language of Roman Catholicism is perhaps less strange than it might first appear, considering the ritual synthesis shared by the Noh drama, the Catholic Mass, and the plays Yeats began to write beginning in 1916.

All of Yeats's late verse plays explore ritual communion not only thematically but also in their own formal qualities. They attempt to construct the theatrical space and action themselves as elements of a ritual shared by the audience. This is the point at which the Yeatsian poetic drama begins to demonstrate its cultural purpose. Through the unique arrangement and integration of theatrical forms in his mature poetic plays, he hoped to reconnect art to normal lived experience. As he wrote in 1930, "I disliked the isolation of the work of art. I wished through the drama, through a commingling of verse and dance, through singing that was also speech, through what I called the applied arts of literature, to plunge it back into social life" (E 300). A primary difference between ordinary dramatic performance and ritual is that ritual breaks down the separation between performance and audience, between play and "social life." In the 1904 issue of *Samhain* Yeats was emphatic about this: "Ritual, the most powerful form of drama, differs from the ordinary form, because everyone who hears it is also a player" (E 129).[4]

Certain technical innovations in Yeats's new drama bring the performance and its audience into intimate proximity. The ideal stage for *At the Hawk's Well* (1917) and its successors is simply "any bare space before a wall" in an ordinary home. The best lighting "is the lighting we are most accustomed to in our rooms. These

---

[4]   Auden, as will be seen in the next chapter, began writing verse plays out of a similar idea, one that would undergo considerable revision over time.

masked players seem stranger when there is no mechanical means of separating them from us" (CP 136). When the Old Man enters, he enters "through the audience," as though either he were one of them or the audience were actually performers (CP 138). These paradoxes situate the performance in the territory of ritual, binding the familiar and the unfamiliar without diminishing either. As Schmitt puts it, "it is critical to Yeats's view of reality that both the real world and the unreal are present at once, not that one is transformed into the other" ("Haunted" 358). In each play, what masks, music, poetic speech, and stylized action make strange, the intimacy and familiarity of the setting anchor to the known.

Using limited theatrical space—first in the Abbey main stage and then in the Abbey's experimental Peacock theatre—as an advantage rather than a hindrance, Yeats experimented with formal and thematic means of connecting the audience and the performers. As in earlier plays, characters enter through the audience. Anticipating a technique Eliot would soon use in *Murder in the Cathedral*, Yeats includes deictic language that implicates the audience and even has a Musician address the audience directly. Yeats also makes ingenious use of Greek convention by using the nameless onstage characters, visible and invisible, to perform the role of chorus. *A Full Moon in March* (1935) takes up this work of bringing the audience and the performance into closer proximity. The Attendants open the play by speaking as though they were not characters at all:

> *First Attendant.*   What do we do?
> What part do we take?
> What did he say?
>
> *Second Attendant.*   Join when we like,
> Singing or speaking. (CP 390)

The Attendants fulfill the normal choral role of mediating between the audience and the stage action, but, as Richard Taylor notes, they are also "more overtly anti-illusionistic than usual" (143). They demolish almost entirely the expectation of realism. The illusion they do create, however, is that the audience is no different from themselves, that they are all equally involved in what is about to take place. All have gathered to fulfill some purpose unbeknownst to them. This illusion signals the play as less a conventional performance than a ritual in which audience and performers alike are collaborators.

"For European Purposes"

Before the decks were cleared and many creative attempts at reconciliation were shelved—by World War II and by the gradual consolidation of power by the Irish Free State along Celtic-Catholic lines—the attempt to reconcile European oppositions of self and nation, nation and continent, thought and action, past and present through dramatic ritual still seemed relevant, even if the time had not been exactly propitious for the hieratic form chosen by Yeats. His verse plays of the interwar period model problems typical not only of Ireland but also of other European countries, then as well as now: how to reconcile the national part to the European whole without compromising the integrity of either, what use to make of a past that seems to divide European nations as often as it unites them, what cultural material from among centuries of history to preserve and what to destroy. Deployed from the periphery of Europe, this drama speaks eloquently to the imagination of Europe itself. Donald Davie's declaration that "the wonder of Yeats's career is his having made poetry of world significance out of a landscape so much at the edge of things, so unrepresentative in the twentieth century, as the landscape of Ireland" hints at a recognition of this dynamic (qtd. in Schmitt, "The Landscape Play" 272). Striking, though, is Davie's omission of Europe from his formulation; he includes no middle term between Ireland and "world." Without Europe, one might ask, what is Ireland at the edge of, "things"? Furthermore, situating Ireland within Europe, even on the edge of it, suddenly makes much of what seems "unrepresentative of the twentieth century" in Yeats appear representative, perhaps even formative, of the century. It is far less a "wonder" that Yeats's work could achieve "world significance" in light of its purchase in European cultural practices and imaginative patterns.[5]

The limitations in the prevailing views of Yeats's politics are more the result of confining his political vision to the immediate Irish situation than to too easily casting aside its Irish particularity. This dialectic between universal and particular, a foundation of ritual that energized the whole of Yeats's career, has been reproduced in the critical literature on Yeats from his death even to the present. A 1939 essay in which Gordon Bottomley praises Yeats's cosmopolitan significance and range follows immediately upon one in which another contemporary, Richard Hayes, eulogizes Yeats as Ireland's native son:

> We in Ireland remember with no little pride that the many-sided activities of that long and full life were always centred in his native country ... In other days the flower of Ireland's sons forsook her, offering their swords to Europe. He saw now an equal tragedy when her intellect and imagination were given to another country ... [Our] nation—even if she eventually becomes Irish-speaking and self-centred—will remember Yeats ... as one of her great architects. (10–11)

It is doubtful Yeats would have enjoyed being lionized by an "Irish-speaking and self-centred" Ireland (in other words, a provincial one), but the sentiment of the passage has proven durable and influential. It anticipates, albeit with much less subtlety, the arguments of modern critics such as Seamus Deane, who fight against what they see as a veritable imperialism of literary appropriation.

Using a wider lens, one capable of seeing Ireland in the context of Europe, puts some of the apparent contradictions in Yeats's politics into clearer perspective.

---

[5]   This elision of Europe is replicated in more recent criticism, notably by Edward Said, as I will discuss in the following section.

The connection between his work and the early stages of Irish rebellion are comparatively well understood, with Yeats's own assessments having served as a guide: "The fall of Parnell ... freed imagination from practical politics, from agrarian grievance and political enmity, and turned it to imaginative nationalism, to Gaelic, to the ancient stories, and at last to lyrical poetry and to drama" (E 343). An issue which has been insufficiently remarked is how Yeats's own writing responded to the return of efficacious and official political structures to Ireland following the Anglo-Irish War and Irish Civil War. The last two decades of Yeats's life coincided with the first two decades of Irish independence and, as Moses has observed, with Yeats's "deepening discomfort with the direction of Irish political nationalism in particular, and (from 1922 onward) with the institutions of the Irish Free State in general" (563). It is partly this state of affairs that broadened the political scope of his work.

Yeats's later plays reveal a widening, not a narrowing gyre of political concern, and an idea not only of Ireland but also of Europe. His concern for the political life of his own country is inseparable from his concern for that of Europe, but, like his fellow Celticist David Jones, Yeats always looks to local particulars for evidence of the European whole. In support of this position, he invokes his eighteenth-century heroes: "Study the great problems of the world, as they have been lived in our scenery, the re-birth of European spirituality in the mind of Berkeley, the restoration of European order in the mind of Burke" (E 337). He conceives of the respective struggles of Ireland and Europe only in relation to those of the other, closing a circle where history (and most literary scholarship) has seen only a binary, when it has seen any relationship at all.[6]

As Mexico does for Lawrence, Greene, and Waugh, Ireland affords a kind of object lesson in the European struggle to recover meaningful identity. In Yeats's interpretation, the Irish lesson for Europe in the interwar period, as it has been argued to be in other historical periods from the early Middle Ages on, is twofold: first, that the preservation of the past—often with an attendant supernatural commitment—through ritual systems is the best guarantee of a spiritually rich present and future; and second, that fidelity to the unique character of the local affords the truest access to the universal. It has been acknowledged countless times in readings of modern Irish culture and literature that the self-conscious invocation of myths, holy sites, and rituals keeps the past productively alive in the Irish present. The crucial but almost always missed point is that this legacy is not only Irish but also European. Yeats's Ireland—mythic, sacred, ritualistic—completes modern Europe both as its antithesis and as its past, rather as East completes West in *A Vision.* Yeats had one eye on Ireland and the other always on Europe. His recovery and reanimation of Ireland's ancient myths was crucial to the formation of a national imagination and identity for Ireland, to be sure. However,

---

[6]   This part-whole dynamic is replicated in miniature in Yeats's predicament, which has received far more critical attention, as an Anglo-Irishman in Ireland. See Lyons 64; Foster 452–54; O'Faolain 106.

this project of recovery is European precisely to the extent that it is rooted in the specifically Irish.

At the outset of the Irish Literary Revival, Standish O'Grady identified Ireland as a kind of cultural custodian for Europe in his *History of Ireland (1878–80)*. As A. Thomas Cavano writes,

> O'Grady describes Ireland's unique place in Europe as having maintained a cultural continuum, through legend and myth, that corresponds to the ruins, castles, mounds, and standing stones still visible on the landscape. Ireland, he says, has preserved her past even better than Greece. While most of this history in Europe is lost, Ireland is still culturally integrated with its landscape. (417)

Through O'Grady, Cavano makes Ireland's landscape also Europe's landscape, Ireland's history Europe's history.

Although less concerned with physical landscape, Eliot had a similar idea in mind in his 1923 essay, "*Ulysses*, Order and Myth." Here he describes the process whereby the individual artist deeply rooted in the particulars of his own time and nation necessarily and simultaneously transcends those boundaries. Eliot flings the door wide open, and skips Europe in extrapolating from Ireland to universality, although it is doubtful his use of the term "universal" was meant to include more than the Western world. Thus, James Joyce's *Ulysses* and Yeats's later plays are the more "universal" for being resolutely Irish. Eliot singles out Yeats as "the first contemporary" to adumbrate the method, adopted by Joyce, of "manipulating a continuous parallel between contemporaneity and antiquity" which, Eliot predicted, would transform the whole of European literature (SP 177). Whether it did is debatable, but two things are clear. First, for interwar Europe (as, indeed, for Europe at many different times, including the present), Ireland came to stand for the impulse behind such a "mythical method" (SP 178). Second, the same impulse became increasingly visible in interwar Europe in the "whole complex of interests and modes of behaviour and society of which literature is a part" most glaringly in the mystical and pseudo-mythical politics of fascism (SP 177). Irrespective of origins, Ireland epitomized and shared with Europe a cultural proclivity that partially shaped two decades of European literature and politics.

The European link becomes especially important in talking about Yeats's later plays. There is, for instance, the simple fact that there was no native verse-drama tradition in Ireland, that Yeats's experiment in the form was based primarily on, in addition to Japanese, European, especially Greek, models. His friend Bottomley wrote that "the real significance" of Yeats's dramatic "masterpieces … seems to be that they had returned to the Greek principle of construction" (13). In importing the form, Yeats was simultaneously importing a European logic and a system of signification beyond the tradition of his own country. Without question, he then recast this material in the image of his native culture and experience, putting verse drama at the service of local, Irish aims, but his interest in the form links the Irish playwright to a European tradition. Acknowledging this fact need not dilute the Irish particularity of the plays; rather, it lets in sufficient air for the latter subject to breathe and restores to Yeats the paradoxes that make him unique even as they connect him to a larger whole. Eliot, for one, was more than willing to live with such paradoxes about Yeats. "[I]n beginning to speak as a particular man," wrote Eliot, "he is beginning to speak for man ... in becoming more Irish, not in subject-matter but in expression, he became at the same time universal" (OPP 301).

Yeats felt that the political situation which fostered the growth of a literature with specifically Irish political concerns had culminated in the Anglo-Irish war:

> The modern literature of Ireland, and indeed all that stir of thought which prepared for the Anglo-Irish war, began when Parnell fell from power in 1891. A disillusioned and embittered Ireland turned from parliamentary politics; an event was conceived; and the race began, as I think, to be troubled by that event's long gestation. (*Autobiographies* 559)

The relative stability (after the ensuing Irish Civil War), not to mention the Free State, that resulted from the war's conclusion presented a much different political landscape and, accordingly, an altered relationship between literature, politics, and the nation. Edward Said describes such a period in post-colonial terms as the one "after the last border has been crossed, the last sky flown in" (232). It was also a time in which Yeats's dramatic vision solidified and in which his creative and political thought increasingly connected Ireland to Europe and the world. After 1916, Yeats's political-dramatic development shows a remarkable consonance with that of Europe as a whole, both seeming to draw sustenance from common sources. "Perhaps some day," he wrote in 1916, "a play in the form I am adapting for European purposes may excite once more, whether in Gaelic or in English, under the slope of Slieve-na-mon or Croagh Patrick, ancient memories" (EI 236).

Fascism and Drama

In the Introduction to *Fighting the Waves* (1934), a prose reworking of *The Only Jealousy of Emer* (1919), Yeats reflects that it had been circumstances beyond Ireland which had facilitated the resurgence of Irish literature since the turn of the century:

> [W]e could not, considering that every man everywhere is more of his time than of his nation, have long kept the attention of our small public, no, not with the whole support, and that we never had, of the Garrets and Cellars. Only a change in European thought could have made that possible. (E 373)

That change had by 1934 helped Yeats reach the apex of his public fame, notwithstanding his own sense of being increasingly "out of fashion and out of date" (CP 438). Indeed, his thought was perhaps never more in consonance with a primary strain of "European thought" than in the 1930s, nor was his attention ever more focused on problems of European identity. As he wrote in "Tomorrow's Revolution," "[t]he danger is that there will be no war, that the skilled will attempt nothing, that the European civilisation, like those older civilisations that saw the triumph of their gangrel stocks, will accept decay" (E 425). When he wrote these words, much of English-speaking Europe had indeed gravitated away from the ideal of a ritualized reality, although the presence of General Eoin O'Duffy's Blueshirts in Ireland and Sir Oswald Mosley's British Union of Fascists indicate that the impulse had anything but died out in the islands. The places where this ideal was truly flourishing, moreover, were not so far away in Italy, Spain, and Germany.

The writers of the younger generation, who comprised the ascendant element of the times to which Yeats felt himself opposed, were also some of his greatest admirers. Nor did their leader, Auden, fail to recognize that the spirit of fascism was no aberration in modern Europe. Looking back on the 1930s, Auden recalled the "wild enthusiasm" that greeted the Nazi rise to power,

> not in some remote barbaric land outside the pale, but in one of the most highly educated countries in Europe, a country one knew well and where one had many friends. Confronted by such a phenomenon, it was impossible any longer to believe that the values of liberal humanism were self-evident. Unless one was prepared to take a relativist view that all values are a matter of personal taste, one could hardly avoid asking the question: 'If, as I am convinced, the Nazis are wrong and we are right, what is it that validates our values and invalidates theirs?' ("Missing" 305)[7]

Even before the rise of continental fascism, Yeats's spiritual education had helped fortify his belief that the change which appeared to be upon Western civilization was integral, rather than anomalous, to it. "My instructors," he wrote in *A Vision*, "certainly expect neither a 'primitive state' nor a return to barbarism as primitivism and barbarism are ordinarily understood; *antithetical* revelation is an intellectual influx neither from beyond mankind nor born of a virgin, but begotten from our spirit and history" (262). Whatever was slouching toward Bethlehem to be born in the interwar years, he was given to understand, had not very far to travel, being itself a product of "European thought."

Two primary questions, then, remain. On what basis is Yeats's late dramatic work in sync with "European thought" in the interwar period, and on what basis does it diverge? European fascism is the strain of "European thought" with which Yeats's later plays share the most. Yeats's dramatic vision and fascism have roots in similar spiritual, artistic, and imaginative soil; both bespeak and are visible manifestations of a desire to make meaning out of the contradictory experience of modern life through ritual. At the same time, however compelling Yeats may have found the imaginative forms on which fascism is based, his late plays and prose

---

[7]   In "The Idea of a Christian Society," Eliot remarked in similar terms the apparent hollowness of liberalism. "If then, Liberalism disappears from the philosophy of a people, what positive is left? ... We are in danger of finding ourselves with nothing to stand for except a *dislike* of everything maintained by Germany and/or Russia" (CC 15).

contain indications that, in the end, he found those forms untenable as political solutions. As Joseph Chadwick deftly asserts, fascism "comes very close to fitting ... the political and poetic strategies W.B. Yeats deploys in his later work," but this fit is "slightly flawed ... close but not perfect" (869). Although the fit is slightly better between fascism and Yeats's late plays (as opposed to his poetry), it remains imperfect. The points of incongruity between them, rather than negating or disproving a relationship, give it needed critical depth. Chadwick wisely asks "not whether Yeats was a fascist, but rather how and to what degree his work is involved with fascism" (871). However, rather than using fascism merely as a referent, and even more wary of what Paul Morrison calls the "specious totalization" (5) to which the term lends itself, I ask not whether Yeats was a fascist but, rather, how and to what degree Yeats's verse drama and fascism are involved in a European pattern of ritualizing life, one in which writers of much different political profiles were often engaged, as the surrounding chapters suggest. The point to be reached is one from which ambivalence provides the clearest view, where post-colonialism is not only liberatory, fascism is not alien, and nationalism does not preclude internationalism. At the same time, simple inconclusiveness will not satisfy. While Deborah Fleming is not altogether wrong in arguing that Yeats's "political vision defies explanation," his actions do not (xvi). Yeats acts politically, through drama, in ways that are complex but not inexplicable. The crossover in the 1920s and 1930s, in Ireland and Europe, between drama and politics is so pronounced that Yeats's work as a dramatist deserves a privileged place in the discussion of his politics, just as political questions figure prominently in the discussion of his plays.

What I have called the Irish lesson found fertile ground in continental European fascism. As for Yeats, his political outlook in the 1920s and 1930s is shot through with the energy and logic of the radical right wing, and much of his writing during this period lends the local habitation if not the name of fascism to that vision.[8] Considerable critical debate has focused on sorting out the relationship, often

---

[8]   Paul Morrison is correct that in many critical applications, "the word [fascism] itself is a specious totalization" (5). Without question, the term has come to encompass far more (and sometimes far less) than it should to be of real use in critical discussion; but there have been occasional exceptions. In a review of V.K. Narayana Menon's *The Development of William Butler Yeats*, George Orwell wrote: "Translated into political terms, Yeats's tendency is Fascist. Throughout most of his life, and long before Fascism was ever heard of, he had had the outlook of those who reach Fascism by the aristocratic route" (*Collected Essays* 273). Orwell's argument is perhaps the most unflinching on the subject of Yeats's relation to fascism, but it is also important for the connection it attempts to make between politics, social and religious views, and literary form: "The subject-matter and imagery of a book can be explained in sociological terms, but its texture seemingly cannot. Yet some such connection there must be" (271). In this instance he suggests that Yeats's "wayward, even tortured style of writing and his rather sinister vision of life" are intimately joined (271).

resulting only in confusion.[9] This confusion includes not only widespread misuse of the term "fascism" but also certain nervous attempts to reject the usefulness of conceptual fascism altogether. For example, Elizabeth Cullingford's claim that Yeats's work "escapes simple political labels because it is essentially dialectical" is entirely defensible. Her further claim that Yeats's literary, philosophical, and political thought culminated in "the acceptance of diversity," revealing "the inappropriateness of the label 'fascist'" is not (viii).

However, the fascist note is far from being the only political one that sounds in Yeats's late verse plays or in the critical literature about them. For each gesture these plays make toward the cruelest, most violent, most exclusive political ideals of the West, there is a corresponding one opening East, toward the spiritual and artistic currents of Asia, without the wisdom of which Yeats saw Europe doomed only to slouch ineffectually toward its desired rebirth as a meaningful whole. One of the resolutions towards which Yeats's late philosophy points—and on which the metaphysical system of *A Vision* is based—is "the marriage of symbolic Europe and symbolic Asia, the one begetting the other" (203). In a 1932 review, he describes his sense that, delve as he might into the "fibrous darkness" of Irish folklore and mysticism, "there was always something lacking" in his search for a complete philosophical synthesis (EI 429). It was only upon reading *An Indian Monk*, by Shri Purohit Swami, that "I found all I wanted" (EI 429). Taking a broad view of European art in the same essay, he finds that the apparently eternal opposition of East and West imperfectly hides an underlying

---

[9]   In 1965, Conor Cruise O'Brien, as part of a more sustained and intricate argument, wrote that "Yeats the man was as near to being a Fascist as the conditions of his own country permitted" (41). His essay "Passion and Cunning: An Essay on the Politics of W.B. Yeats" provoked far more controversy than Orwell's and continues to do so. (O'Brien also refused to let this essay gather dust. He not only chose to name his 1988 collection of essays "Passion and Cunning," after the Yeats piece but also included the original essay as the only one from a previous period. The rest "all ... appeared within the last four or five years" (1). The Yeats essay, he noted, "gave a certain amount of offence to Yeats scholars and others at the time and it has continued to be a subject of controversy."). As might be expected, in the process of objecting to O'Brien's main premise, critics have tended to overlook some of the essay's most important insights. Not least among these is the refusal to treat Yeats's political opinions as an aberration of any kind. (Orwell shared this conviction. He approvingly quoted Menon, "'If the greatest poet of our times is exultantly ringing in an era of Fascism, it seems a somewhat disturbing symptom'" and added, "It is a disturbing symptom, because it is not an isolated one" (276)). Of even greater importance, O'Brien has evidence to support the claim that "[pro-Fascist] opinions were quite usual in the Irish Protestant middle class to which Yeats belonged (as well as in other middle classes) in the 1920s and 30s" (41–42). David Carroll has been similarly judicious in talking about "literary fascism." He argues that, far from being aberrational, fascism is in fact a version of "Western cultural ideals in general," the culmination of a "European intellectual tradition" (4). Resituating Yeats in the historical moment of interwar Europe makes it increasingly difficult to see his politics as anomalous. It is surprising, then, that so few critics have capitalized on the further opportunity to link Yeats to Europe that the later verse plays provide.

unity: "We have borrowed directly from the East and selected for admiration or repetition everything in our own past that is least European, as though groping towards our common mother" (EI 433).[10]

This suspicion was affirmed in no uncertain terms by Yeats's encounter with the Noh theatre. In "Certain Noble Plays of Japan" (1916), he extols the model for his subsequent dramatic efforts. The hieratic Noh form not only fulfills Yeats's desire for a theatre of "nobility and strange beauty"; it also links him with "half-Asiatic Greece" as well as "our own Irish legends and beliefs, which once, it may be, differed little from those of the Shinto worshipper" (EI 229, 232, 236). This cultural receptivity is only one part of the complexity and depth of the Yeatsian idea of Europe. At the very least, it precludes the ready application of the "fascist" label to Yeats's outlook during the rise of European fascism proper, even if certain other characteristics seem to necessitate, or at least legitimize, doing just that.

Deane bridges the divide somewhat by equating "so-called fascism" with "the colonialist mentality" (*Celtic* 49). This is a highly insightful strategy, albeit one that, as alluded to in the Introduction, ultimately keeps Yeats and Ireland on too short a tether. In both respects, Deane's argument is like one of the most influential recent critical interventions in Irish studies, Edward Said's reinterpretation of Yeats as "a poet of decolonization" (230). In *Culture and Imperialism*, Said places Yeats's poetry in opposition to the "general European effort to rule distant lands and peoples" in discourse as in political economy (xi). His depiction of Yeats as postcolonial hero has in one sense widened the political implications of Yeats's work and seems largely to have succeeded in rescuing Yeats from the acquisitive and deadening hands of English literary canon formation. Said's argument works beautifully up to a point. This point is the early 1920s, the period approximately coincident with Ireland's political independence, a period during and after which Said can see only "Yeats's slide into incoherence and mysticism ... his rejection of politics, and his arrogant if charming espousal of fascism" (230). The question of fascism causes Said particular discomfort. He wants to reconcile Yeats's "unacceptable and indigestible reactionary politics" including "his outright fascism" to the poetry of liberation he admires (Said 228). He seeks "a *third* nature" to describe Yeats, "not pristine and pre-historical ... but deriving from the deprivations of the present" (Said 226). Where he finds the solution is in a fundamental feature of postcolonial experience itself: "That neither Yeats nor Fanon offers a prescription for making a transition *after* decolonization to a period when a new political order achieves moral hegemony is symptomatic of the

---

[10]   In a 1926 *Criterion* essay, Henri Massis saw this relationship in a much more sinister light, calling it the "crisis of Western civilization and the danger of Asiaticism ... the most complete rupture of equilibrium that the world has ever known ... this new assault by the East on the Latin inheritance" (4.2.224–31). This view was much more typical of the age. His sense of Germany "perpetually hesitating between Asiatic mysticism and the Latin spirit" provides a useful point from which to reassess the connection between Yeats and fascism (231).

difficulty that millions of people live with today" (Said 236). Yeats is incoherent on the subject, in other words, because he lives in the phase of post-colonialism after outright rebellion, when all is chaotic, when "conventional nationalism [has been] revealed to be both insufficient and crucial" (Said 224). The redeeming feature of Yeats's writing in this period, as Said sees it, is that it articulates the inherent contradictions of literary nationalism and roughly points the way to "new forms of verbal expression" it cannot achieve (236).

There is every reason to concur with Said's conviction that "we should think of Yeats ... as an Irish poet with more than strictly local Irish meaning and applications" (233). Such is, to the letter, an underlying contention of this chapter. However, his recourse to the descriptor "incoherence" admits an inherent limitation of Said's approach, one shared to a lesser degree by Deane. It is strange that Deane, who sees in the late plays the full flowering of Yeats's political and aesthetic views, should also describe the latter part of Yeats's career as "marked by incoherence and by an almost wilful [*sic*] mysticism" (*Celtic* 49). In intimately related endeavors—Said to liberate Yeats from Europe, Deane to particularize him as Irish—both critics artificially limit him to postcolonial confines, within which there is little to remark about Yeats's later work but that it is incoherent.

In addition to tracing their origins to approximately the same years, Yeats's ritualistic drama and European fascism were born out of similar events—the Easter Rising and the Great War, respectively. The Rising provided Yeats with the image of sacrificial death he was to explore in depth after 1916, even ending his final play with an evocation of Pearse and Connolly in the Post Office. If Parnell's fall in 1891 gave shape to the previous major phase of Yeats's literary career, Easter 1916 did the same for the next one. And if Parnell's fall turned Irish literature away from politics, the Easter Rising brought it back. As several critics have observed, the Rising was a kind of crucible for Yeats's late—and most important—playwriting. Moses writes,

> By the beginning of April 1916, when Yeats undertook his first crucial steps in his avant-garde theatrical revolution, his interest in *political* drama seemed on the wane. However, the events of Easter week changed utterly his artistic ambitions, and once more imparted to his subsequent dance plays the urgency and power of political tragedy. (574)

In doing so, the Rising was imparting a power widely felt to be contained in itself. In the events of Easter week, the overlap between the political and the artistic, particularly the dramatic, was almost immediately apparent. Doomed to failure from the beginning, the Rising, with "priority given to gestures above practicalities," may have been more a "blood-sacrifice ritual" than a military maneuver (Foster 482, 484). Neither those who participated in it nor those who observed it from a distance showed any hesitation in endowing Easter 1916 with spiritual, aesthetic, and dramatic significance far exceeding its military value. One participant, Ernie O'Malley, recalled, "I was in a whirl; my mind jumped from a snatch of song to a remembered page of economic history" (39). Michael Collins, the most prominent political figure to emerge in the wake of the Rising, noted, disapprovingly, that the event "had the air of a Greek tragedy about it," that the whole operation was "couched in poetic phrases" (qtd. in Coogan 54). Yeats shared Collins's suspicion of poeticized rebellion, but it did not keep him from drinking deeply of the spirit of the Rising and allowing it to infuse his dramatic writing.

At the end of his last play, Yeats poses the famous question: "What stood in the Post Office / With Pearse and Connolly?" One answer is: the daemon and image of Yeats's mature drama (CP 446). For Yeats, the Easter Rising seemed to reconcile, imperfectly but movingly, the whole range of oppositions concurrently dominating his thought. In the Rising, thought was manifested in action, hatred was wedded to love, life was promised out of sacrificial death, all at the historical intersection of remembered oppression and the desire for freedom. Years afterwards, he would write that "the sense of spiritual reality comes whether to the individual or to crowds from some violent shock" (E 399). Easter 1916 was the shock that, coupled with his study of Japanese theatre, delivered Yeats a new form of expression for that reality.

In an even more literal way, the experience of World War I provided models for European fascism. Both Mussolini and Hitler consistently cited the war in their construction of the ideal fascist community. Mussolini aspired to create "a *trincerocrazia*, a 'trenchocracy'," in 1920s Italy (Eksteins 309). In *Mein Kampf*, Hitler wrote that the war was "the greatest and most unforgettable time of my earthly experience" (qtd. in Eksteins 306); Modris Eksteins points out that "Hitler drew from this formative war experience the basic inspiration and organizational guidelines for his vision of a society of the future" (307). A disciple of Hitler's affirmed that "Only by understanding the *Fronterlebnis* (the front experience) can one understand National Socialism" (qtd. in Eksteins 307). Not excluding its horror and its danger, the Great War front-line experience fledged the experience and the aesthetic of fascism, based on such ideals as male camaraderie, rigid hierarchy, the imperative of violent action, and the constant and intimate presence of death.

Both fascism and Yeatsian ritual drama are based in part on a cult of the ecstatic moment contained within, or following immediately upon, action. Schmitt points out that "[m]any of Yeats's plays, the later ones in particular, are very brief because Yeats wished them to be in effect an extended moment, the moment of tragic ecstasy, the spiritual condition he wished to evoke" ("Haunted" 355). Yeats himself saw drama as "a moment of intense life. An action is taken out of all other actions; it is reduced to its simplest form" (E 153). As in the visual arts, the form of the late plays "is essentially spatial" and thus momentary (Schmitt, "Haunted" 355). In the manner of Greek theatre, the plays tend to explore one dramatic situation rather than emphasize the progressive development of a plot over time. They are, in other words, synchronic as opposed to diachronic, operating more on the level of image than narrative, and thus, as Yeats felt, they make their claims primarily on the basis of emotion, not rational formulation, of unconscious response, not conscious reflection, and of the spiritual as opposed to the intellectual (McCormack 378;

Richard Taylor 145).[11] "[A]ll emotional unities," he wrote in 1919, "find their definition through the image, unlike those of the intellect, which are defined by the logical process" (E 273). Nor was Yeats unaware of the political utility of emotion: "Intellectual agreements, propagandas, dogmas, we have always had, but emotional agreements, which are so much more lasting and put no constraint on the soul, we have long lacked" (E 266). Their indirection, rhythm, and basis in image are some of the means by which Yeats's verse plays invite the audience into such "emotional agreements." Without oversimplifying the comparison, it may be said that fascism is essentially a system of "emotional agreements." Roger Griffin, the preeminent theorist of the relationship between fascism and theatre, explains that fascism is essentially "anti-rational," meaning that it makes its greatest claims on the level of emotional response, not based on the conclusions of

> the rationalist and political tradition of the Enlightenment ... The central emphasis on the affective and subjective sense ... of belonging to a supra-individual reality, leads to an all-pervasive use of myths, symbols and rituals, designed to replace the primacy of individualism and reason by a transcendental community and faith. (15 17)

Its elaborate rituals and symbols, its saturation of public life with the aesthetic of the regime, are intended to do what its flimsy logical underpinnings cannot: inspire the people to emotional identification and willing participation.

The image and the moment are in a sense eternal because they do not change. For the same reason, though, like masks and like the isolated action that functions irrespective of time, they are also deathly. Although they had lost the Great War, both Mussolini and Hitler saw the value of the war experience in the act of war itself, not in its outcomes. Through imaginative remembering, the war could be fixed as an ideal and eternal "moment" outside of the temporal and the mundane. Thus they could make the war represent something other than defeat in their conceptual systems. "What was important," writes Eksteins, "was the act of assertion, of conquest, of victory, of struggle, and of dynamic life in war," not the material markers of victory or conquest after the fighting stops (307). In Nazi Germany, "[i]t was the act, the declaration, the theatrical pronouncement that was important, not the content" (Eksteins 313). Sean O'Faolain identifies the same

---

[11]   In this tendency they are consistent with Sean O'Faolain's assessment of Irish rebellion. "[I]t is ... true of our Irish rebels," he writes, "that it was upon the emotional content of the [French] Revolution that they seized and not on its intellectual content, with the result that the whole of Irish patriotic literature ever since has ... concerned itself with matters of sentiment rather than thought" (128). One wonders how Yeats fits into this tradition, given his abiding concern with balancing passion and thought. Still, his late verse plays, much colder, harder, and less "sentimental" than his pre-1916 work, appeal far more to the heart than to the head. If anything, his early conviction that the theatre should "substitute for the movements that the eye sees the nobler movements that the heart sees" grew in clarity after the Rising (E 109).

spirit in the Irish "Rebel" as a type: "There was only one thing at which the Rebel wished to be a success and that was at rebelling. Death did not mean failure so long as the Spirit of Revolt lived ... Always we seem to be excellent at the thing, but not good at the idea" (121–26). Though himself an intellectual, Yeats often expressed his admiration for men of action, Irish and European. "When I think of Swift, of Burke, of Coleridge, or Mallarmé," he writes in 1930, "I remember that they spoke as it were sword in hand, that they played it, as a politician cannot though he stand in the same ranks, with the whole soul" (E 301). During his own (and only) public affiliation with a fascist movement as such, the Irish Blueshirts, in the early 1930s, Yeats remarked his pleasure at living "in a country where men will always act. Where nobody is satisfied with thought" (*Letters of W.B. Yeats* 812). To many of his countrymen, notably those involved in the Rising, but not to himself, it mattered little that action, far more often than thought, led to violent death.

Yeats's plays and fascist spectacle alike aspire to the kind of energetic release and spontaneous community formation that the Rising and the Great War unmistakably foregrounded. Just as Yeats believed that in the key features of Easter 1916, including sacrificial death, a poetic sense of purpose, and the crystallization of a common identity, "A terrible beauty is born" (CPO 180), European fascism found its justification and ideal in the "total mobilization of society in the interests of a greater metaphysical good" occasioned by the Great War (Eksteins 307).

At the Hawk's Well (1917) establishes this theme of momentary action through indirection, through the suspense attached to an action that never happens. The central action in this play and the others in *Four Plays for Dancers* is really the deferral of a hoped-for action. Here it is the Old Man's and Cuchulain's thwarted desire to witness the filling of a magic well and to drink from it. In the next two plays, *The Only Jealousy of Emer* and *The Dreaming of the Bones*, the anticipated event is likewise a union of the material world with the eternal in the form of a kiss. All such actions, in that they unite the natural (a dirty well, a human body) with the supernatural (eternal life, ghosts), would represent a supreme ritual consummation of the earthly with the divine. In each case, though, the ritual action is frustrated, the opportunity missed. At the same time, each play makes clearer that the end of such ritual union is, in fact, death. In *Emer*, the Woman of the Sidhe, come to lure Cuchulain away ("for the Sidhe / Are dexterous fishers and they fish for men / With dreams upon the hook"), takes on a seductive shape ("I was that bird of prey, and yet / I am all woman now"), performs a ritual dance, and invites him to complete the reconciliation of physical and spiritual that opens up eternity:

> Time shall seem to stay his course;
> When your mouth and my mouth meet
> All my round shall be complete
> Imagining all its circles run;
> And there shall be oblivion
> Even to quench Cuchulain's drouth,
> Even to still that heart. (CP 191–92)

The event is deferred, but its significance is implied; it inheres in the oblivion of a stilled heart, in death. Cuchulain's mystical union is an example of "that eternal instant where the antinomy [between life and death] is resolved" (AV 214). It is fleeting, complete, perfect—and deadly. In subsequent plays, the tension between natural and supernatural increasingly becomes figured as that between the life and death of the body, as Yeats works closer and closer to the violent core of ritual action.

In *A Full Moon in March* (1935) and *The King of the Great Clock Tower* (1935), a variation on the same story, Yeats's drama follows the logic of ritual to its completion in blood sacrifice, becoming truly tragic.[12] The interpenetration and union of opposites posited by the earlier dance plays is now realized through ritual action; the question, "What marvel is / Where the dead and living kiss?" is answered, ostensibly if not rhetorically (CP 402). Both plays concern the ritual union of a virgin queen and a filthy vagrant through that ultimate kiss at which the earlier dance plays hinted, the kiss uniting all oppositions, life and death above all. In both plays the vagrant comes to woo the queen with singing but is beheaded for his insolence before he can perform. In *A Full Moon*, the queen actually wears the blood of the swineherd on her hands and clothes. This ritual union contains no half measures; only in death is it truly fulfilled. The head sings, the queen dances, their lips meet, and the attendants end the play with a song.

As Richard Taylor indicates, *A Full Moon in March* is characterized by "the extreme simplicity of its character relationships and the near abstraction of its elements" (139). This simplicity allows Yeats to depict the "[s]omething new and terrible" that he felt "had come in Ireland, the mood of the mystic victim," without specifying the Irishness of the victimization (qtd. in Dorn 87). That he would save for his final two plays. Likewise, the characters in *The King of the Great Clock Tower* are "symbols or representations of universal principles who ultimately complete their being in a world of time" (Richard Taylor 147). In this pair of plays, Yeats involves the audience in the play not through their shared Irishness but through the invocation of an essential "dialectic opposition on which the ritual [of murder, dance, and communion] is based" (Richard Taylor 152). The stage action is supported by the production methods ritualizing the theatrical experience itself. Like the earlier dance plays, these can be played in locations associated with "the reality of everyday life," making living rooms the space of strange masked rites (Richard Taylor 152). All of which, according to Taylor, is "designed to challenge the audience into a recognition of the truth which lies behind the ritualised stage reality" (152). Yeats, however, is not Brecht, and challenging an audience into a recognition of anything is perhaps too dryly rational an exercise to have truly interested him. It seems more likely, given the direction Yeats's

---

[12] The two plays are so similar as almost to be two versions of one play. *The King of the Great Clock Tower* was written as a prose play in 1934 and versified in 1935. *A Full Moon in March* was also written, in verse, in 1934, its main difference being that in it the Queen is a speaking part. See Richard Taylor 146.

political thought was taking at this point, that the only recognition he sought was that manifested during and within the ritual itself, an irrational reality that invited no rationalization.

What has tended to alarm critics about Yeats's final two plays, *Purgatory* (1939) and *The Death of Cuchulain* (1939), is that in them the deadly ritual action of the earlier plays *is* rationalized. Murder is legitimized along very specific, and rather disappointing, lines. The justifications for the Old Man's murder of his son in *Purgatory* are the very ideas that have turned so many critics away from (or against) the Yeats of the late 1930s. There is the cosmology of *A Vision* dealing with cycles of history, to end one of which the Boy must die. There is Yeats's and the Old Man's disgust at Ireland's decay, of which the Boy is a product, since the glorious era of her landed Protestant gentry:

> Men that had fought at Aughrim and the Boyne.
> Some that had gone on to Government work
> To London or to India came home to die,
> Or came from London every spring
> To look at the may-blossom in the park.
> ....
> ... to kill a house
> Where great men grew up, married, died,
> I here declare a capital offence. (CP 432)[13]

Finally, there are Yeats's increasingly clear eugenic ideas ("I killed that lad because had he grown up / He would have struck a woman's fancy, / Begot, and passed pollution on" (CP 435)) and his growing appreciation for violence as an organizational tool, both of which he expressed in no uncertain terms in *On the Boiler* (1939).[14] The Old Man possesses "an intimate relationship with the past" and with the dead "which his degraded son does not share" (Richard Taylor 169). He stabs his son to death in an attempt to "Appease / The misery of the living and the remorse of the dead" (CP 436). Unfortunately, these are the lines with which the play ends; the hoped-for result of the Old Man's action is never realized. In fact, the cycle from which he sought release seems destined to repeat itself: "Twice a murderer and all for nothing" (CP 436). His mother's ghost "must animate that

---

[13]   The Ascendancy house in this play, like the Post Office elsewhere in Yeats and in much other Irish literature, is an example of the construction of ordinary, secular places as the sacred spaces required by ritual. Jan Koster identifies the tendency to ritualize territory outside the ordinary boundaries of traditional sacred spaces as "ritual overflow" (218). It is one of the hallmarks, he argues, of political movements such as fascism. "The aggressive potential of ritual frameworks is at its most dangerous," he writes, "when the symbols and rituals break out of their confinements of a 'sacred space' and are taken to the battlefields and to the streets" (218).

[14]   Regarding the former, one quotation will hopefully suffice: "Sooner or later we must limit the families of the unintelligent classes, and if our Government cannot send them doctor and clinic it must, till it gets tired of it, send monk and confession box" (E 426).

dead night / Not once but many times!". Taylor asserts that in this play "there is no need for any kind of distancing technique or anti-illusionistic device to call attention to symbolic meaning for in this play surface level and symbolic meaning are one" (169). It is doubtful he had in mind anything quite so grim as the final image of the play suggests, though. As in *The King of the Great Clock Tower* and *A Full Moon in March*, the answer to the question of what happens when all oppositions are reconciled is ostended: a dead body. The Old Man's final words only ask the question again, even with the answer lying at his feet.

The evolution of Yeats's drama indicates at the very least a fascination with death, and, in light of some of his later prose writings, even a kind of love, which is itself not far from the fascination of violent action and the ideal of the supreme moment. His verse plays after 1916 move ever closer to the depiction of sacrificial death, culminating in the plays of the 1930s in which ritual death is treated as an end in itself. Even as he begins to subvert the notion of ritual death in *Purgatory* and *The Death of Cuchulain*, though, he elsewhere affirms it in language as remarkable as it is chilling. "No tragedy is legitimate," he writes in *On the Boiler*, "unless it leads some great character to his final joy" (E 448). In "Tomorrow's Revolution," he reiterates what he had "made Michael Robartes say in *A Vision*: 'Love war because of its horror, that belief may be changed, civilisation renewed'" (E 425). Here his thought seems to be utterly in sync with what Walter Benjamin identifies as one of the driving impulses of fascism, the love of death, even of the self, in war. Benjamin wrote in the famous Epilogue to "The Work of Art in the Age of Mechanical Reproduction" that fascism typifies the extreme "self-alienation" of humankind, which has enabled it to "experience its own destruction as an aesthetic pleasure of the first order" (242). The Italian Futurist Filippo Tommaso Marinetti wrote that "War is beautiful" for a number of aesthetic reasons, which, it must be said, are not the same thing as Yeats's spiritual-social ones (qtd. in Benjamin 241).

The appreciation for the technology-based "aesthetics of war" clearly distinguishes the fascist death fascination from Yeats's. Although Yeats was eager, late in life, for death to become both a part of public policy and the basis of ritual theatre, it must be inferred that Marinetti's "symphony" created by "machine guns ... cannonades, the cease-fire, the scents, and the stench of putrefaction" held little appeal for him.[15] Rather, his late appreciation for violence, death, and war emphasizes the ability of these things to refine and protect the identity of a people:

---

[15] One similarity between Marinetti's language and Yeats's dramatic aesthetic, though, is worth noting. Marinetti writes that "[w]ar is beautiful because it initiates the dreamt-of metalization of the human body" (qtd. in Benjamin 241). Yeats writes, in the stage directions to *The Only Jealousy of Emer*, that the Woman of the Sidhe's "mask and clothes must suggest gold or bronze or brass or silver, so that she seems more an idol than a human being. This suggestion may be repeated in her movements. Her hair, too, must keep the metallic suggestion" (CP 191). For Marinetti, metal seems to suggest machinery; for Yeats, sculpture.

> Armament comes next to education ... The formation of military families should
> be encouraged ... If human violence is not embodied in our institutions the
> young will not give them their affection, nor the young and old their loyalty. A
> government is legitimate because some instinct has compelled us to give it the
> right to take life ... (E 441)

That fascist regimes in Italy and Germany were modeled on the experience of a
war in which they had been soundly beaten is an indication of the central place
of death in the fascist imagination. Constant memorialization, the celebration of
martyrs and ruins, the political invocation of dead heroes, an overall "propaganda
of the corpse," located death close to the heart of the aesthetic strategy of fascism
(Eksteins 316). Needless to say, Yeats and countless other Irish artists utilized the
Easter Rising in precisely the same way: "I write it out in verse—/ MacDonagh and
MacBride / And Connolly and Pearse / Now and in time to be, / Wherever green
is worn, / Are changed, changed utterly: / A terrible beauty is born" (CPO 182).
Considering, though, that in the late 1930s the Foreign Legionnaires fighting
for Franco in Spain were crying, "Long live death!", Yeats's own imaginative
engagement with death appears, if not innocuous, certainly measured.

Like *The Only Jealousy of Emer*, the final two *Plays for Dancers* stage the
dangerous interplay of life and death within the insulating frame of dream. *The
Dreaming of the Bones* (1919) and *Calvary* (1920) have as setting and theme the
purgatorial region where the dead dream themselves imperfectly back into life. In
Yeats's mystical system, this is the region where the living are likely to encounter
ghosts. "In *The Dreaming Back*," he writes in *A Vision*, "the *Spirit* is compelled
to live over and over again the events that had most moved it" (226). The living
are implicated in this process because "[t]he *Spirit* finds the concrete events in
the *Passionate Body*, but the names and words of the drama it must obtain ...
from some incarnate Mind, and this it is able to do because all spirits inhabit
our unconsciousness or, as Swedenborg said, are the Dramatis Personae of our
dreams" (AV 226–27). He continues: "One thinks of those apparitions haunting
the places where they have lived that fill the literature of all countries and are the
theme of the Japanese Nō drama" (AV 227). This symbiotic relationship of living
and dead is clarified still further: "It is from the *Dreaming Back* of the dead ...
that we get the imagery of ordinary sleep. Much of a dream's confusion comes
from the fact that the image belongs to some unknown person, whereas emotion,
names, language, belong to us alone" (AV 229). The space in which these plays
take place, then, might be thought of as the common ground shared by the dreams
of the living and the purgatorial dreaming-back of the dead.

The Dreaming of the Bones gives the dreaming relation between the living
and the dead an almost concrete immediacy. The shift is based on an additional
component of Yeats's theory of dreaming-back explained in *A Vision*, namely, that
"[s]ometimes the *Spirit* ... may not merely dream through the consequences of its
acts but amend them, bringing this or that to the attention of the living" (228). This
arrangement allows Yeats to bring the dead and the living even closer together
than in the previous two plays. For the first time in the post-1916 plays, recorded

history becomes important and helps to concretize the relationship of the dead to the living, the past to the present. The play's subject combines the Irish legend of Diarmuid and Dervorgilla, "that most miserable and accursed pair" "Who brought the Norman in" and "sold their country into slavery," with the story of the 1916 Easter Rising (CP 282).[16] Diarmuid and Dervorgilla, "though seven centuries have run" since their deaths, have come, in the form of A Stranger and A Young Girl, to find forgiveness for their crime, which plunged Ireland into the destructive course culminating in the deaths at Easter 1916 (CP 281).

The Young Man, though, who has fought at the Post Office, is too mired in his country's historical bitterness to forgive. His nearsightedness is not only a shortcoming of Irish patriotism; it also betrays what Yeats saw as Ireland's "crucial, redemptive role ... in the recovery of European civilization from barbarism" (Deane, *Celtic* 46). In 1919 Yeats could see the concern for ritual and the spiritual life all but disappearing from the Irish independence movement, just as they had been largely obliterated by the "despiritualized carnage" of the Great War (Deane, *Celtic* 46). The play ends with the Musicians singing, their song having little necessary connection to the events that have just taken place. With no plot action left onstage for the audience to observe, there is only the song and the refolding of the cloth, as if to give "the rhythmical movements that seem to flow up into the imagination from some deeper life than that of the individual soul" the unchallenged attention of the audience (E 109). The play, as such, is over, and ritual has the last word.

The effect of the final song is oblique, its most striking effects its regular rhyme and meter and a strangely suggestive imagery. Alongside the "Music of a lost kingdom" and "Dry bones that dream," the red cock that has been sung in the play's previous two songs reappears: "The strong March birds a-crow. / Stretch neck and clap the wing, / Red cocks, and crow!" The violence of the imperative resounds after the sober refinement of the song (and indeed of the play). As for the red cock, beyond being a "universal harbinger of a new dawn," it is also "a ready symbol of sexuality and combat" and is associated with both "the spiritual cycle of Christ's death and rebirth, and ... that of Mars, god of war" (Richard Taylor 110). On the heels of this eerie performance, something big, it would seem, is coming.

In the next and last play in *Four Plays for Dancers*, Yeats advances another step down the path the Easter Rising and his new form of drama have laid out. *Calvary* acts as a thematic bridge between the comparatively indirect treatment

---

[16] It is worth noting that the play's Irish political content may have been responsible for the long delay in its production (Liam Miller 240). First published in 1919, it was not produced until 1931 at the Abbey's Peacock Theatre. As Karen Dorn notes, one of the circumstances that aligned favorably for a renewed interest in Yeats's Noh plays was the "growth of interest in nonnaturalistic drama" in the 1920s (91). The political circumstances were somewhat more complex but likewise conducive to Yeats's dramatic ideas. Certainly the claustrophobic social atmosphere produced in Ireland by the Easter Rising and the Irish Civil War had relaxed somewhat by 1931, at least enough to afford some breathing room around the play's subject.

of death in the previous three plays and the sacrificial action of the plays of the 1930s. As might be expected where Christ and Lazarus are central characters, the boundaries between death and life in this short play are highly unstable. The appearance of Lazarus confounds the narrating Musicians, who observe, "He has a deathly face, and yet he moves …", a "face that seems / Death-stricken and death-hungry still" (CP 289–91). The "man that died and was raised up," who "Lay in the tomb four days," has come to rebuke Christ for raising him and for the sacrifice bringing eternal life Christ is about to make. The two men face one another again to argue over the terms of the new order:

> *Lazarus.*   For four whole days
> I had been dead and I was lying still
> In an old comfortable mountain cavern
> When you came climbing there with a great crowd
> And dragged me to the light …
> You took my death, give me your death instead.
>
> *Christ.*   I gave you life.
>
> *Lazarus.*   But death is what I ask …
> You travel towards the death I am denied.
> And that is why I have hurried to this road
> And claimed your death. (CP 290)

Although the figure of Christ would seem to present Yeats with an ideal image of sacrificial death, the play questions its value on quite specific grounds and, suggestive of this doubt, ends with Christ hanging on the cross, near death but alive, his self-sacrifice unfulfilled.

Lazarus feels robbed of the death that was his right ("I was free four days, four days being dead."), and Judas insists that he betrayed Christ because doing so restored his free will ("I could not bear to think that you had but to whistle / And I must do") (CP 290, 291). He willingly chooses death ("now / You cannot save me") over eternal life, a gift Lazarus's complaints have shown it perhaps better to refuse:

> I thought to die
> When my allotted years ran out again;
> And that, being done, you could not hinder it;
> But now …
> ………………………………
> … you will disturb that corner
> Where I had thought I might lie safe for ever. (CP 290)

Once again, the doctrine of dreaming back is crucial to the meaning of the play, and again it insulates the depiction of death. The First Musician informs the audience that the stage action is actually that wherein "Christ dreams His passion through … / He climbs up hither but as a dreamer climbs. / The cross … but exists because He dreams it" (CP 289). As Richard Taylor points out, the "subjective reality of Christ's passion as reinterpreted by Yeats" is the play's real subject (115). The action, therefore, is "removed from direct association with the truth of either historical fact or orthodox tradition" (Richard Taylor 115). This knowledge makes it all the more clear that Yeats was still groping toward a complete image of the ritual reconciliation of life and death, and that the Christ story as he inherited it failed to satisfy.

Between 1920 and 1934, Yeats turned his attention increasingly to non-Irish subject-matter and wrote six plays, all of them predominantly in prose. His greatest achievements in this period are two prose translations of Sophocles, *King Oedipus* (1928) and *Oedipus at Colonus* (1934); and *The Resurrection* (1931). Although Richard Taylor believes that the first two have only "secondary relevance to [Yeats's] own creative work" (1), all three are integral to the development of Yeats's dramatic vision and to his evolving idea of Europe. In them Yeats demonstrates the expanding reach of his dramatic project by moving beyond local Irish mythology to engage directly with the foundational myths of Western civilization. Oedipus and Christ are at the center of Yeats's drama in this period, just as, in *A Vision*, they constitute "the two scales of a balance" in which all European history is contained (AV 28–29).[17]

In dramatic terms, as Karen Dorn notes, the Oedipus plays and *The Resurrection* connect Yeats to a "Greek theatre movement" begun in Great Britain "in the 1880s with rediscoveries of Elizabethan and Greek theatre architecture" and prompting new production methods based on "theories of the ritual origin of drama" (64, 63). His final plays, she argues, represent "the culmination of Yeats's long involvement in two aspects of nonnaturalistic theatre—the relation between stage performance and audience in the Greek theatre, and the nature of the poetic and dramatic image produced in that type of theatre" (63). Some of the principles drawn from Greek theatre shored up the ritual principles that had guided Yeats's drama as early as *Four Plays for Dancers*. For instance, Dorn writes:

> With an audience of only a hundred, closely connected with the stage by a long, low step, the Peacock could be used for a miniature version of the kind of production developed by the Greek theatre movement. Yeats devised [*The Resurrection*] so that the spectators, like the disciples and the revellers, would become part of the performance. (70)

This kind of interaction, of course, also typifies Yeats's previous plays, written in the Noh mode. In this later part of his career, though, Yeats took his plays not only back to the theatre but also back to the Western code of sacrifice exemplified in the Christ myth, Greek mystery-religions, and Classical drama (Arkins 101–02). He increasingly looked to Greece for the ideal form not only of drama but also of society. In addition to enjoying the best audiences, he wrote in 1939, Greek

---

[17] Elsewhere in *A Vision*, he substitutes Caesar for Oedipus, without altering the nature of the dyad: "Caesar and Christ always stand face to face in our imagination" (244).

drama possessed the most "elaborate unity" and an "intensity" unmatched by even Elizabethan drama (EI 439). And this dramatic perfection corresponded to the perfection of European civilization, which, he wrote, "rose to its highest mark in Greece" (EI 439). When Yeats returned to writing plays in verse, it was after a productive period spent contemplating the technical aspects of Greek drama but also the relationship of Greek tragedy, the most "noble" form of drama, to the health of a society (EI 449). The effects of his engagement with Greek mythology and drama are immediately apparent in his next and final group of plays, in which the earlier dalliance with themes of life and death becomes cruelly embodied, tragic. His final three plays represent the point at which Yeats's interest in "nonnaturalistic" theatre combined with the tragic impulse toward sacrificial death.

In *The Death of Cuchulain* (1939), the Old Man who introduces the play offers this rationale for the ostensive use of bodies: "I promise a dance. I wanted a dance because where there are no words there is less to spoil. Emer must dance, there must be severed heads—I am old, I belong to mythology—severed heads for her to dance before" (CP 439). The play follows the tragic pattern of the rest of Yeats's 1930s verse plays and culminates in the death of a hero. Indeed, it is the Irish hero of heroes who succumbs in this final play, suggesting, on one level, the culminating sacrifice implied by Yeats's entire career as metaphysician, political revolutionary, and ritualist. Moses suggests how thoroughly Cuchulain's death fulfills the requirements of meaningful sacrifice (and implied by the philosophy of Yeats's dramatic program), "by performing the sacrifice of its own heroic demigod. The god must die in order to be reborn; the cult must will the destruction of its own sacred figure in order that he might be transformed into a nationalist icon that serves the 'mundane' aims of modern Irish politics …" (575–76).

Cuchulain's death, transmuted into national life—as a statue in the Post Office—would seem, then, to close the book on the great question of Yeats's dramatic career—What is created at the intersection of death and life?—and to answer the play's own: "What stood in the Post Office / With Pearse and Connolly?" (CP 446). However, as Moses does not fail to notice, the whole business is thrown into question by the wildly disruptive scenes that frame the central action of the play and that produce an unavoidably ironic effect. From the opening lines, the seriousness of the sacrificial enterprise is undercut by the Old Man's admission of his own—and thus the play's—irrelevance: "I have been asked to produce a play called *The Death of Cuchulain* … I have been selected because I am out of fashion and out of date like the antiquated romantic stuff the thing is made of" (CP 438). When, in the course of describing his ideal theatre, he starts "getting excited" for the first time, he is signaled from offstage to calm down (CP 438). The second time, he is simply cut off, and the play begins: "'I spit! I spit! I spit!' *The stage is darkened, the curtain falls* … ," and Eithne Inguba enters (CP 439). The Old Man's silliness balances the gravity of Cuchulain's death as its antithesis, in the manner of the Blind Man who does the killing for a mere twelve pennies. The last lines of Yeats's last play on his greatest theme, the life and death of Cuchulain—"So ends the tale that the harlot / Sang to the beggar-man"—give irony the last word in this play and the last word in Yeats's dramatic career.

A Conflagration of the Past

Yeats's verse drama and European fascism are consonant in the desire to arrest and reverse what both see as the decay of Western civilization due to liberalism, and in the affinity for so intimately linking politics and aesthetics that the two become all but indistinguishable. Benjamin's famous definition of fascism as "the introduction of aesthetics into political life" remains the most useful because by reducing fascism to what is essentially a formal proposition, a formula, it helps to situate the phenomenon of fascism proper within other recognizable discourses and forms of mind—Yeats's verse drama among them—which, though they may aestheticize politics, are not fascist (241). Benjamin's further claim that "Communism responds by politicizing art," rather than clarifying the divide between extremes of right- and left-wing politics, obscures that divide and illustrates instead how thoroughly any number of politico-aesthetic gestures, of ostensibly opposed ideologies, partake of a common impulse. To concretize the problem, one might consider perhaps the most iconic visual image of 1930s politics—masses of people proclaiming their political allegiance with an arm theatrically raised, hand-open or hand-closed: which faction is aestheticizing politics and which politicizing aesthetics?

As Chadwick argues, Benjamin's definition of fascism comes tantalizingly close to defining Yeats's work of the interwar years. One assertion in particular, which Chadwick does not emphasize, helps illuminate this close but imperfect fit. "All efforts to render politics aesthetic," writes Benjamin, "culminate in one thing: war" (241). Yeats's late prose writings certainly seem to suggest that his thought was leading on to war.[18] His plays similarly trace a path from indirect to direct treatment of death by violence, culminating in Cuchulain's murder. Indeed, had he wished to start a war in Ireland (and had Cuchulain retained for Irish audiences in 1939 the same symbolic intensity the Irish peasant held for them in the early Abbey years), Yeats's final play would seem to provide enough of a spark. However, Yeats understood that by 1939 no Irish audience would rage very violently against the seemingly flippant depiction of the murder of their national icon by a degenerate beggar, their ancient hero's saga reduced to a "tale that the harlot / Sang to the beggar-man." The almost bitterly ironic tone of *The Death of Cuchulain* may be taken to indicate Yeats's displeasure at the decay of the heroic ideal in Ireland, and his identification with the romantic old man relegated to the sidelines of national passion. At the same time, it may also suggest that, unlike fascism as understood by Benjamin, Yeats's effort at aestheticizing politics was not designed to culminate in violence.

The coincidence of Yeats's final play and the beginning of the Second World War is too provocative to neglect. The song that closes *The Death of Cuchulain* describes the arc of aestheticized politics from myth to action to death and

---

18   Joseph Chadwick justifiably uses "violence" as a synonym for "war" in comparing Yeats's late work to Benjamin's discussion of fascism. There is also, however, enough of "war" proper in Yeats's late prose to all but eliminate the need for distinction.

memorialization, then by its own irony subverts the logic it has constructed. Might it not portray Yeats hesitating at precisely the threshold Europe crossed in 1939, its closing irony show Yeats refusing to go where his dramatic project had seemed to lead?

Chadwick suggests that the fascist element in Yeats's late poetry is undercut by Yeats's implicit and simultaneous commitment to elements of "the democratic-individualist order" (883). If violent death, then, is the ostended object of Yeats's ritual drama, it is the plays' formal elements that serve to destabilize the finality of that object. The play ends up pointing, rather than at Cuchulain's sacrificial death, at the ironic whole that is the play itself. Yeats's entire philosophy was based on the notion that "each situation contains its own undoing" (Dorn 69). At the end of his career (and indeed his life), he allows the ritual structure he has so painstakingly elaborated to be, in a few impertinent lines, undone. Moses concludes that as early as *The Only Jealousy of Emer* Yeats realized that "his powers to summon up an Irish national identity out of his imagination, to impose that vision by virtue of his creative will on the people of Ireland, to define in real terms the political culture of a new and independent Irish state, has [*sic*] ebbed away" (575). Perhaps this is so, but in light of the conflagration that engulfed Europe soon after he wrote *The Death of Cuchulain*, Yeats's hesitancy has the aspect not only of doubt but also of wisdom. In any case, in the year of his death, Europe was forced to take note of the destructive consequences of imposing "in real political terms" an imaginative vision on a people by virtue of the will, creative or otherwise.

The two interwar decades, while propitious for fascism, never fully embraced Yeatsian verse drama. The ghost of fascism, as it were, became fully embodied, effectual, and public, while the ghost of Yeats's ritual theatre dreamed itself only part way into reality, achieving some contact with life but never able to enter fully into it. Its complete realization was likely undercut by the playwright's own lurking mistrust of ritual as a political tool. As he wrote in 1930:

> I would found literature on the three things which Kant thought we must postulate to make life livable—Freedom, God, Immortality ... The first nation that can affirm [these] convictions ... as free powers—i.e., without associations of language, dogma, and ritual—will be able to control the moral energies of the soul. (E 332–34)

Ultimately, Yeats could not do without such associations, as a playwright or a political thinker. Those associations make abstractions political by striving to make them material, and as Yeats began to visualize what the material manifestations of his spiritual ideas might be, his thought approached the territory of fascism, which is itself the concretization of a handful of abstractions. For instance, his choice of fire as an image for his vision of history more than coincidentally resembles the fascist affinity for fire as symbol and tool:

> Free power is not the denial of that past but such a conflagration or integration of that past that it can be grasped in a single thought ... We ... are certain that

nothing can give dignity to human nature but the character and energy of its expression. We do not even ask that it shall have dignity so long as it can burn away all that is not itself. (E 335–40)

Surely this is what it means to aestheticize not just politics but all experience—to condense history into one flaming thought, one image, to care only for the "energy" of expression, not what it expresses. Fascism, obsessed both with change for its own sake and with eliminating perceived decay, gravitates naturally toward fire imagery.[19] The important thing about fire is what it does; it contains nothing, it only burns. It is, in short, a form without content, significant in its action not its object; thus it is natural that Yeats should equate fire with the kind of pure expression that need not have even dignity, so long as it burns. As Chadwick says of Yeats's late poetry, "[i]t is violence itself, rather than any coherent system of ideals that violence might serve as a means to realize, that forms the ground of value" (873–74). If nothing else, fire is the very image of violence and, along with expression, one of the badges of fascism. One need hardly be reminded of Benjamin's claim that "Fascism sees its salvation in giving these masses not their right, but instead a chance to express themselves" (241).

It is fairly well known that much of the aesthetic base of fascism is traceable to ancient Greece by way of Nietzsche and Richard Wagner. Virtually the same linkage, as Dorn expertly records, lies behind Yeats's late drama, but so does a great deal else, most importantly the philosophical, spiritual, aesthetic, and political material "hammered into unity" as *A Vision*. There is much in this "inherently dramatic" book (Dorn 68) that seems to place Yeats in the same imaginative current as European fascism, or rather to define the imaginative territory in which both fascism and Yeatsian drama found sustenance. The book, like the late verse plays, reveals Yeats attempting to come to terms with European history and thought, to fashion a unified image of European identity that might account even for the "discords" simultaneously tearing it apart and promising to be resolved in at best an "artificial unity" (AV 301–02). Fascism was engaged in the same project, but whereas fascism marched into the 1940s in pursuit of its image, Yeats sacrificed both Cuchulain and his vision of a mythologized national life on the threshold where heroic aestheticization threatened to overwhelm individual freedom, offering only death in return.

The ghosts and half-ghosts that populate Yeats's plays after 1916 are the figures of Yeats's desire to restore the past to the living present. As David Jones and J.M. Synge found the ancient heart of Europe on the very fringe of European geography, Yeats tried to uncover it in Ireland's small sacred particulars, her holy wells, houses, and hills. The form of the plays themselves is not the artificial resurrection of a dead European past but an attempt to remind Europe of itself by

---

[19] As witnessed, for instance, in the frequent Nazi nighttime ceremonies illuminated by torches, in the symbol of a phoenix clutching a swastika (also known as the "fire cross") in Nazi insignia, and, it should be added, in the Holocaust. See Sontag, "Fascinating Fascism."

mobilizing the ancient hieratic forms that once had and might still retain the power to give modern experience a sense of meaningful integration—with art, with the past, and with the exterior influences, such as the antithetical East, that complete what is native and local. The uncomfortable and paradoxical reality, though, is that such attempts to reconcile death and life, past and present, the particular and the universal, through ritual must end in death in the world of time, whatever they may promise on another plane. The only certainty toward which Yeats's interwar verse plays point is death by violence, but it is equally certain that, in *Purgatory* and *The Death of Cuchulain*, where Yeats found himself face-to-face with the object of his dramatic imagination, he chose not to press forward. His plays are an image of the unconscious of interwar Europe, whose furious attempts to reconcile its own basic oppositions seemed to point ineluctably to war. Their paths diverge, though, precisely on the brink of World War II, where Yeats finally drew up. The year of his and Cuchulain's deaths, 1939, was the same in which the two other most important verse dramatists of the era, Eliot and Auden, were forced to reconsider the place of ritual in modern Europe.

Chapter 3
Auden (and Company): A Taste for Ritual

Biographer Richard Davenport-Hines speaks of the "taste for ritual" behind W.H. Auden's dramatic project. Auden began his short career as a poetic dramatist with some very Eliotic ideas about the ritual roots of drama. In 1929, with a dogmatism reminiscent of Yeats and likely under the influence of Eliot's 1923 essay "Dramatis Personae," he wrote:

> Dramatic action is ritual. 'Real' action is directed towards the satisfaction of an instinctive need of the actor who passes thereby from a state of excitement to a state of rest. Ritual is directed towards the stimulation of the spectator who passes thereby from a state of indifference to a state of acute awareness. (P 159)

This ritual quality, according to Auden, is replicated in dramatic characters, which, in the manner of Yeats, "are always abstractions," and in dramatic speech, which "should have the same compressed, significant, and un-documentary character, as dramatic movement" (P 459, 497). In the program for the Group Theatre's performance of Eliot's *Sweeney Agonistes*, Auden went even further than Eliot in advocating the power of ritual drama to form community. "Drama began as an act of the whole community," he declared. "Ideally there would be no spectators. In practice every member of the audience should feel like an understudy" (P 497).[1]

However, the comparison with Eliot also suggests the key difference between the uses of ritual by the two poets, as well as suggesting why Auden's own verse drama project may have burned out so quickly and completely, reduced to merely a "distant episode" in his career (Hogg ii), while Eliot's, though at best a qualified success, could at least carry steadily on over several decades of cultural change. It might be argued that Auden shared all of Eliot's views about ritual drama except one. While he was convinced of its power to form community, it was not until much later in life, when he had long since stopped writing plays, that he came

---

[1]   Auden was, of course, prone to extreme shifts of attitude about artistic matters, but never to diffidence about expressing his opinion. In a 1971 panel discussion, Auden had this exchange with Marshall McLuhan:

> McLuhan— "The role of the audience as actor is worth watching ... I suppose the Mass is the greatest form of theatre possible and the one in which the audience is necessarily participant—in which there is no audience."
> Auden—"I must say, Mr. McLuhan, I profoundly disapprove of audience participation ... The whole point when I go to the theatre is that I look. I don't take part in the action. I observe" (Jeffares 129).

to share Eliot's conviction that no ritual can function in the absence of a living tradition and belief. In 1971, shortly before his death but well after his conversion to Anglicanism, he stated as much, citing, of all people, Chesterton, the arch-Catholic conservative whose views could not have been further from Auden's mind during his playwriting years:

> What I've decided is—the whole point about a rite is that it is the link between the dead and the unborn. It means that you need a timeless language which in practice means a dead language. In sermons they may do as they like, but liturgy must be static ... Do you know that marvellous remark which I quote to students often now when they think the past isn't interesting, that marvellous thing of Chesterton's about tradition? He says tradition means giving a vote to that obscurist [*sic*] class, our ancestors. It is the democracy of the dead. Tradition refuses surrender to the small arrogant oligarchy of those who merely happen to be walking around. (Jeffares 138)

It is the lack of this sense of tradition that destabilized and undermined Auden's verse-drama project.

Taken as a whole, his plays, including those written in collaboration with Christopher Isherwood, describe the impossibility of their own objective, which was to rejuvenate ritual drama within a European cultural context that had lost its spiritual identity and was in the process of losing its material one. In 1939, that year of endings, Auden gave up both ghosts, verse drama and Europe, relocating to the United States, leaving Europe "l[ying] in the dark" (P 417). The trajectory that culminated in these departures is visible throughout his work of the 1920s and 1930s. It is mapped in the form of his plays themselves—in their textual indeterminacy, the precarious and increasingly marginal role of poetic language, and the declining enthusiasm for the kind of popular forms that the earliest plays enthusiastically embraced—as well as the anxiety of their cultural point of view, seeking to reconcile English and European life to one another, but in the absence of a concrete shared tradition. The plays are frequently brilliant drama—perceptibly more, overall, than Eliot's—but Auden's own cultural and dramatic ideals provide the measure of his plays' shortcomings. This chapter finds Auden, like Eliot and Yeats, in pursuit of a dramatic ideal that, in the twentieth century, has been lost as often and almost as quickly as it has been found. The trajectory of this pursuit reveals as much about the cultural memories and desires of Europe as it does about the appeal and the difficulty of restoring ritual to the modern theatre. Auden's gifts and disposition—as well as his limitations—render his plays uniquely capable of bringing the British version of interwar European anxiety vividly before one's eyes.

On the Fringe of Europe: Early Plays

Auden's most important statement on the connection between modern verse drama and the culture of Europe is his lecture, given on December 8, 1938, "The Future of English Poetic Drama."[2] His introductory remarks make clear that he had a sense of a common European identity based on mutual influence and "the presence of the great dead":

> I am an Englishman, and I cannot but be aware when I come to your city of Paris that I am in some degree a provincial, belonging to a fringe of that European culture of which Paris is the centre. As I walk your streets, I am constantly reminded of the presence of the great dead to whom Paris was a spiritual home, and by great dead I do not only mean Frenchmen, but all Europeans. I think particularly, for example, of Baudelaire, Rimbaud, Heine, etc., names but for whom the history of the poetry of my own country would be very different ... I have reason to feel humble before France, which is the landmark, the continued centre, and the guardian of European culture ... ("Future" 513)

Eliot, of course, was more sanguine about England's role as a guardian of European culture, but what is striking about this passage, beyond the acuteness of Auden's feeling for a spiritual European essence, is his inability to specify the nature of that essence. The view expressed is moving, but it is also vague; at this stage, Auden can not articulate or concretize a European tradition beyond a felt sense of commonality. On what basis is France "the guardian of European culture"? For Eliot, of course, the essential framework interpreting and nourishing European culture was the Church, but until his own conversion, Auden did not endorse any such objective structure—though he keenly felt its necessity—and thus his plays create a general sense of restless search and multiplicity. It was the early events of the Second World War that solidified Auden's sense of "the desperate need for objective criteria from which to oppose Hitler," criteria he found, like Eliot, in organized Christianity (Carpenter 283). He had already shared Eliot's belief in a link between dramatic and cultural form, but his pre-conversion formulations on the subject could recur to nothing very solid. "[T]he search for a dramatic form," he insisted, "is very closely bound up with something much wider and more important, which is the search for a society which is both free and unified" ("Future" 522). Like the abstract concept of unity in diversity, the notion of a society both free and unified is noble, but, absent any objective justification, it can neither withstand much resistance nor support the kind of art that nourishes European culture.

In 1938, Auden's friend and sometime collaborator Louis MacNeice diagnosed the problem with modern British drama along precisely these lines. "The European theatre began in religion," he wrote, and, although some "compromise" is necessary "between the view that drama is an act of worship and the view that it is mere entertainment," the problem remains that "[i]n the British Isles to-day we lack a mythology and, further, we lack a community creed" (*Selected* 93). Shortly afterward, he would praise Eliot's *The Family Reunion* for its "embodi[ment of] a

---

[2]   This lecture was published, as interpreted by a French reporter, in *France-Grande Bretagne* July-August 1939, as "The Outlook for Poetic Drama" (Mendelson 510).

sincere belief" (110), the primary absence frustrating Auden's attempt at restoring to Europe the cultural utility of poetic drama.

It is certainly possible that Auden's 1938 remark about "the presence of the great dead" reveals him on his way to the "sincere belief" to which he committed himself shortly afterwards, in October 1940. It was made after his last verse play was written, but it does seem a logical point through which to pass on the way from questioning to commitment. Auden's earliest plays make important, though tentative, overtures toward the need for tradition, the need to reconcile death and the past with the living present, but each such gesture is ultimately inconclusive because it cannot suggest an ordering frame, much less a solution. The hesitancy of these forays into the theme of the presence of death is one characteristic of Auden's dramatic practice that reveals its underlying uncertainty about the ritual function of drama. He sees a problem but is as yet too much within the British mindset obsessed with "those who merely happen to be walking around," and lacking any unifying creed or myth to represent dramatically something like "the presence of the great dead." *Paid on Both Sides* (1928) is a small-scale meditation on the theme of the presence of the past, the role of memory in the construction (or, rather, destruction) of the present. Its abrupt shifts between different temporalities make the simultaneity of past and present visually explicit, as does the incorporation of the audience into the dramatic action. The plot concerns a feud between two English country families. In this context, death and the past are always associated with the perpetuation of enmity; it is tradition, in other words, that keeps the two houses locked in their destructive rivalry. "We cannot betray the dead," exhorts the character John Nower. "As we pass their graves can we be deaf to the simple eloquence of their inscriptions, those who in the glory of their early manhood gave up their lives for us? No, we must fight to the finish" (P 22). Here the invocation of tradition, in Chesterton's sense of a "democracy of the dead," points not to any renewal but only to a deadly stasis. When Bernard counters, "By loss of memory we are reborn, / For memory is death," the theme is reinforced. In this narrow setting, personal and family memories constitute the tradition that organizes the present, and renewal depends on relinquishing those memories, on a democracy of the living only (P 22).[3] A passage in Auden's next play, *The Enemies of a Bishop* (1929), written with Isherwood, likens the dead to a drag on life, over which the living must assert their precedence: "The song, the varied movement of the blood / Would drown the warning from the iron wood, / Would cancel the inertia of the buried" (P 42). Auden's ideas about tradition, however, even at this early stage, were not simple, and each of the plays allows for plenty of ambiguity in these matters. The same Spectre who speaks the above lines later announces, sounding a good deal like Yeats:

---

[3]   MacNeice treats the same idea in his verse play, *Out of the Picture* (1937). "When we are dead what shall we remember? / Shall we remember the jingles of the morning, / The pipers and the pedlars and the brass farthings," and so on? "No, we shall *not* remember." (120). And of course, Eliot's *The Family Reunion* is explicitly about the effect of memory on present experience.

The strings' excitement, the applauding drum
Are but the initiating ceremony
That out of cloud the ancestral face may come ...
....
And all emotions to expressions come
Recovering the archaic imagery. (71)

The combined effect is to suggest a desire to validate death as a productive part of the present, a desire thwarted by its inability to call up a positive model for doing so.

The Dance of Death (1933) stages a contest between the figure of Death and the "walking around," those who seek to infuse their lives with meaning by any means besides acknowledging death's presence. While there are echoes of the medieval *danses macabres*, in which Death stalks the living as a threat, Auden's play is more concerned with highlighting the triviality of a modern middle class existence which denies death a place. In other words, death in this context does not mean only the end of life; it represents part of a deeper existence than the purely apparent present can give. The people in the play merrily delude themselves that they might find true meaning by one or another of the various means the modern world recommends. They alternately try physical fitness, interwar-style nationalism, money, introspection, hyper-masculinity, country living, asceticism, theatre, and drink. In each case, their efforts come to nothing, and the real end of their search is no more apparent to them. The Announcer affirms:

In the face of death however violent their self-assertion
There comes at last an end to every exertion.
Nothing they desire now but to return to earth
To live for ever in the peace that preceded their birth. (P 102)

In the end, Marxism has the final word, having finally "liquidated" death, and the people are no-end grateful:

O Mr. Marx, you've gathered
All the material facts
You know the economic
Reasons for our acts. (P 107)

However, it is hard to read the closing scene as ingenuous. As Valentine Cunningham observes, the play presents only "an oddly jokey version" of Marxism, a symptom perhaps of the refusal (or inability) of the young playwright "to come to terms with the adult world other than frivolously" (*British* 142). Further, the play's construction as a series of "cabaret absurdities ... undoes any sense of *The Dance of Death* as a Marxist tract" (*British* 291). At this early stage, Auden, for all his perceptiveness, could mobilize nothing more consequential than a snicker at Europe's self-delusion. The playwright's talent is obvious, but the play's cultural critique is of the adolescent kind that must undercut every assertion it makes for fear of seeming too earnest, a tactic that always risks canceling out the seriousness of the situation, which Auden is capable of bringing home at times:

> The condition of these people is so drastic
> Any prophet can make them enthusiastic.
> It is pleasant to march about and all shout "glory"
> But the after results are another story. (P 94)

The play is chillingly full of anticipations of the political crisis that was about to envelop Europe.[4] At one point, the naked bathers, handed a basket of clothes, protest, "But these aren't ours. We've never seen them before. Why, they're uniforms. But this isn't the war," the implication being that, in a very real way, it is (P 88). The Announcer later offers that people like this "ruined each other for they didn't know how / They were making the conditions that are killing them now" (P 105). Such revelations, though, are always insulated by the noncommittal note of irony.

The end of the play is indicative of the instability that characterizes Auden's vision of poetic drama as much as it does his idea of Europe. Irony, for all its power to evoke awareness, to question, is finally a negative, not a positive statement. *The Dance of Death* is representative because it eloquently and enthusiastically points up a problem but ultimately offers no solution or alternative. Poetry, Marx, Freud, entertainment, family are so many perspectives on an issue, showing the shape of an absence by surrounding it on all sides. The same is more or less true of all of Auden's plays. They are expert at demonstrating how wrong socio-cultural circumstances are, but they refuse to show how the ship might be righted. Owen Brady argues that the "intellectual stance" of a later Auden play, *The Dog Beneath the Skin* (1935), is "best described as skeptical and consciousness-raising rather than ideological" (152 n.1). In a *Criterion* review of the same play, John Garrett notes:

> It has long been accepted that the artist who reveals abuses is under no obligation to indicate possible ways of escape. He has done his job when he kindles the indignation of 'Justice.' He gives the data, declares the urgency, and leaves to us the decision. How far this self-denying ordinance should obtain in work which belongs to the new political Marxist order of writing, is another question. Diagnosis without suggested cure seems like providing a cart without a horse. Mr. Auden has shown that the wheels are shaky, the shafts worm-eaten, and that given a few more years of decay no horse-power will avail to drag it out of the rut. (689)

---

[4]   Of course, the expectation of a great European calamity was all over the 1930s; Auden's auguries are simply among the most articulate. As Cunningham notes, "[i]t took little imagination to see the Second World War coming from a long way off" (*British Writers* 40).

It would be a stretch to say that any of Auden's plays is unequivocally of the "political Marxist order," but Garrett's observation does suggest why the end of *The Dance of Death* has to be read ironically. Since the problem the play poses is essentially a metaphysical one, Marxism is necessarily of no avail in correcting it. The idea of a "spiritual" European identity is as foreign to Marxist thinking as it is to Auden's verse plays. And *The Dance of Death* is a play about Europe. It is framed by the first two of what would become a regular feature of Auden's subsequent plays, the litany of European place names:

> Gents from Norway
> Ladies from Sweden
> Don't stand in the doorway
> Come, this is what you've been needing.
> Boys from France
> Join in our dance;
> Italian belles, valiant belles
> And anyone else
> With profs. from Germany
> All sing in harmony
> Come out into the sun. (P 83)

The appearance of such lists shows that Auden's thought was becoming more occupied with an idea of Europe, but the style simultaneously forecloses the possibility of that idea's being anything more than fragmentary. Each list creates a dual effect. First, the invocation of any group of European place names or nationalities tends to suggest some notion of European spiritual unity, and perhaps the tantalizing unity in diversity. The second effect, though, is to undermine any such unity by the sheer multiplication of parts. Auden's European litanies leave one with the same sterile feeling famously expressed in Eliot's *The Waste Land*: "Jerusalem Athens Alexandria / Vienna London / Unreal" (68). Just as Eliot's lines suggest there is no centripetal force (nor even punctuation) binding the ancient or modern centers of Western civilization together, Auden's technique paints a picture of trivial multiplicity as opposed to significant identity. It hardly requires an overt indicator like "Europe's in a hole" to make the impression clearly felt (P 84). In one remarkable passage, Auden weaves together the whole spiritual history of Europe from the Greeks to the modern day with the litany of popular palliatives from class consciousness to theatre, then chucks the whole thing with these lines in which the Announcer finishes summarizing Death's will:

> He asks for free drinks for the company here.
> To make their lives not so hard to bear
> So drink to his funeral in claret and beer
> For he wishes you all a very happy new year. (P 105)

Europe as a meaningful tradition, a pattern in history or language or culture, is just as flimsy as the modern European miscellany of societies and activities. Just before Marx's ironic finale, a group of Boys proclaims:

The French are mean and Germans lazy,
Dutchmen will leave you in the end.
Only the Englishman though he's crazy,
He will keep you for a friend. (P 106)

The preoccupation with Europe would grow more intense in the next group of plays Auden wrote with Isherwood, although it never found expression in anything so near to commitment as "the presence of the great dead." At the same time, the amount and range of the poetry would decrease in each play, a pattern tied to the authors' waning confidence in ritualistic means for evoking cultural order.

The Uses of Collaboration

Critics have frequently commented on Auden's almost compulsive need to collaborate, particularly on dramatic projects. Most agree that his collaborative works were infrequently more than the sum of their parts, that the potential rewards of collaborative writing were more often than not hampered by the plays' difficulty cohering as wholes. Auden himself seems not to have had a very clear sense of his own artistic reasons for so often joining forces with Isherwood, who, for the most part, wrote the prose sections of their hybrid plays, while Auden wrote the verse and songs. [5] In the 1938 lecture, he could offer only that "if ... I suggest to you that a possible form of drama for the future is one that combines verse and prose, that is partly dictated by the fact that my collaboration has been one between verse and prose;" and that "[t]he problem of writing a play in which verse and prose are combined is difficult and I think not yet solved" ("Future" 514, 521). Even his most thoughtful justification, while stimulating, sounds more evasive than positive: "Again, poetry unalloyed tends, if one is not very careful, to introduce a rather holy note. You cannot have poetry unless you have a certain amount of faith in something; but faith is never unalloyed with doubts and requires prose to act as an ironic antidote" ("Future" 521). In the final interview of his life, when asked "in some detail" about collaborating with Isherwood, Auden responded: "Well, we'd say, 'Well, you take that part and I'll take this part'; then we'd talk about it a bit and then go off and write it" (Wahl 104).[6] As Alan Jacobs suggests, Auden's recruitment of dramatic collaborators may have been an implicit acknowledgment of his own limitations as a dramatist (101). Cunningham sees obsessively collaborative and "mutually dedicated" work by not only Auden

---

[5]   This is a fair generalization, but it is still a generalization. There is also a significant amount of crossover, always difficult to quantify, between the two writers, not just on a structural but a "textural" level (Kerr 277). For a detailed account of Auden and Isherwood's collaborative practice, see Mendelson, "Auden-Isherwood," and Kerr.

[6]   The interviewer, William B. Wahl, subsequently recorded: "Auden had said that if anything important was said, the interviewer should remember it. I'm not at all sure that anything at all important was said that afternoon" (104).

but also his generation as symptomatic of their immaturity and cliquishness (136), both of which enabled Auden's circle to perpetuate "the old private references, the ingrained mythologies, the shared assumptions and jokes and beliefs of people whose sensibilities had all been honed at the same educational mills" (*British* 136, 138). Isherwood, for one, acknowledged that *Enemies of a Bishop* was "no more than a charade ... and full of private jokes" (qtd. in P xviii). This kind of practice, says Cunningham, "was all very well for the reader inside the magic social circle," but presented a real obstacle to more general appreciation (*British* 138). Even MacNeice, who was not exactly outside the circle, was dubious about the effectiveness of Auden and Isherwood's play *The Ascent of F6* and found *On the Frontier* "to fall between two stools" and to "[lack] cohesion" (*Selected* 101).

There is, however, a sense in which collaboration, though artistically unsatisfactory, fulfilled a crucial requirement in Auden's conception of verse drama, specifically with regard to ritual. Edward Mendelson describes the collaborative function in positive terms:

> Collaboration is a civil act. When two writers join forces to create a single work they cannot hold to an aesthetic theory that would trace the origins of art to the privacy of the individual vision or emotion. On the whole, collaboration is a public act in a public context, and it occurs when writers address an audience that is wide but well-defined, when literature enjoys the responsibility of a public role. ("Auden-Isherwood" 276)

In a similar vein, Lucy McDiarmid writes that, "[i]n a way, the community the poets wanted to engender in performance was already present in the collaboration that occurred during composition" (71). Auden's plays are all "composite texts, communal efforts to re-create the community" (McDiarmid 73). Collaborative work does not necessarily translate, though, to a broad community of appreciation. The classical situation Mendelson describes, and of which Eliot dreamed, cannot be willed into being. It requires "a viable public culture" to give rise to it (Jacobs 102).[7] Collaboration may create a kind of community, but without a living tradition it cannot create communion.

That both audiences and critics in the 1930s had mixed feelings about the success of the Auden-Isherwood dramatic collaboration underscores the fact that this literature, even as drama, did not truly enjoy "the responsibility of a public role," no matter how much the authors might wish otherwise. Certainly, Auden and Isherwood's audience was much more "well-defined" than "wide." That

---

[7]   There is always the difficult chicken-and-egg question of why and when an artistic impulse comes into being. To his French audience, Auden offered an approximately Marxist justification for his own dramatic program: "I am really talking about something which I myself feel I must do. But, after all, thought does not occur in a vacuum. What happens to occur to people as their own private belief has a curious habit of turning up when history requires it, just as is the same case with inventions. They do not appear until there is an economic necessity for them" ("Future" 515).

Auden considered the country-house charade among the forms of "living drama'" through which society could be renewed is, Valentine Cunningham points out, "a claim that helps measure Auden's and his London clubmates' distance from most of the population they purported to serve" (*British* 323–24). The profuse collaboration among a small group of British writers in the 1930s no doubt sprang from a real sense of commitment to notions of a public, but the context for the success of such efforts may have been much narrower than the authors imagined. Collaboration with another author may perform some of the same work of community formation that ritual is capable of accomplishing. In the absence of an appropriate public context, however, it may become a kind of substitute for the truly public communion the authors desire.

Another kind of collaboration, between audience and players, likewise plays a central part in Auden's dramatic writing, although it gradually fades from the plays written with Isherwood. *Paid on Both Sides*, perhaps Auden's most unalloyed dramatic effort, is "so essentially social that its audience and its actors were the same. He conceived the play as a 'charade' to be performed by the guests and hosts at a house party given by the family of one of his Oxford friends" (Mendelson, Introduction xv). The stage, in the manner of Yeats, can easily be got up in a living room. The characters/audience members, between their active turns, simply seat themselves in chairs on either side of the stage. Unfortunately for Auden, the family in question refused the performance, an indication that his ideal of a communal theatre had a limited appeal even within the narrow social parameters he envisioned. Thus, the device of audience participation, like authorial collaboration, comes to seem a substitute for true community rather than an adjunct of it. Similarly, *Enemies of a Bishop*, that exercise in "private jokes," ends with a direct appeal to the audience by the play's hero, Robert:

> You who have come to watch us play and go
> Openly to face the outer sky, you may
> As guests or as possessor enter in
> To the mysterious joy of a lighted house.
> But never think our thoughts are strange to yours;
> ....
> Although our anguish seem but summer lightning,
> Sudden, soon over, in another place,
> Although immune then, do not say of us,
> "It was nothing, their loss." It was all. (P 78–79)

Although excellent poetry, this rhetorical appeal to community is ultimately subjective, as opposed to the appeal of ritual, which is based on at least the residue of shared belief. One wants to believe the plea of the final two lines, but in a performance with such narrow accessibility, which has demonstrated no objective basis for commonality, no tradition, it is too much to expect the audience to accept the psychological premise that the subjectivity of the performance is somehow "all." By comparison, the Knights' direct appeal to the audience in

Eliot's *Murder in the Cathedral* seems a good deal more credible, based as it is in a careful construction of continuity between past and present, stage action and audience. Auden's later plays, *The Ascent of F6* (1936) and *On the Frontier* (1938), earn something like that credibility with the audience by fulfilling more of the expectations of realism. The increased appeal, though, is gained at the expense of the ritual-poetic elements of the early plays.

The Dance of Death tries another technical device to make the social character of drama manifest. Certain cast members are placed in the audience and respond, as audience members might, to the onstage action. Some have cockney accents— "And I don't blame him. 'E wants his girl friend. Did you see 'im making eyes at that little bit over there on the right?"—as though patently to democratize the play, to transcend the rarified Oxford air the play might otherwise be thought to breathe (P 98). One wonders how many of the cockney type actually attended performances at The Group Theatre.[8] The insertion of cast members into the audience is a fascinating contrivance, one that paid off in some of the most interesting British drama after World War II, but in Auden's 1930s, it seems rather a gimmick, a striking but ultimately superficial attempt to get as much of ritual as possible into drama while eschewing the fraught but potentially crucial element of belief. The alternative to shared belief is self-consciousness, and Michael Sidnell proposes that this may have been the fatal flaw in Auden's (and the Group Theatre's) dramatic vision. "If such a 'total theatre' is impossible to achieve," he says, "it may be because—as theorists from Aristotle to Brecht have explained— the consuming reality of ritual actions is incompatible with a thoroughly self-conscious art" (257). In the end, Auden chose the path of self-consciousness, not to the exclusion of social concerns but at the expense of the ritual ideal of theatre.

As though growing into the belief he would express decades later about the absurdity of audience participation in dramatic performance, the final three plays Auden wrote, all with Isherwood, forego such experimental means of simulating community. Instead, the immediate problem of demonstrating continuity between performance and audience is addressed in *The Dog Beneath the Skin* by borrowing from such forms as cabaret, music-hall, and pantomime to bring the drama into the more familiar world of popular entertainment, and vice-versa, and in *The Ascent of F6* and *On the Frontier* by a return to realism.[9] Auden outdid even Eliot, who held up music hall as a dramatic ideal, in extolling the utility for poetic drama of popular forms. A poetic dramatist, wrote Auden, ought "to start ... from the dramatic forms already in use. These are the variety-show, the pantomime, the musical comedy and revue ... to accept what he finds to his hand and develop its latent possibilities" ("Rev." 70). Contemporary entertainment, though, was not the

---

8   Michael Sidnell suggests not many. See p. 179 in his *Dances of Death.*

9   That Auden and Isherwood had sided with realism over ritual in *On the Frontier* is made immediately apparent by the play's increased prefatory matter, in which characters are described in terms of age, dress, attitude, political inclination, accent, and more, and the narrative is mapped out by place and time.

only device he found to hand. *Dogskin* (as it became generally known to Auden and his friends) and the next two plays also include choruses. Those of *F6* and *Frontier* are composed, along the lines of what Eliot tried in *Murder in the Cathedral* and *The Family Reunion*, of persons from within the world of the dramatic action. The choruses also afford Auden a handy place to put poetry, but the choruses in all of his plays skirt the issue raised by Eliot of how to make poetry integral to the advancement of plot rather than ornamental. In the case of *The Dog Beneath the Skin*, the Chorus, in addition to setting the scenes, adds a gravity otherwise foreign to the play's idiom, which is either in the popular modes mentioned above or in approximately naturalistic prose. The poetry in these choruses is generally regarded as among Auden's best, but it is thoroughly guilty of interrupting the dramatic action as opposed to emerging out of it.[10] The following lines begin a chorus that is, typically, sandwiched between two comic scenes written in the language of everyday conversation:

> So, under the local images your blood has conjured,
> We show you man caught in the trap of his terror, destroying himself.
> From his favourite pool between the yew-hedge and the roses, it is no
>   fairy-tale his line catches
> But grey-white and horrid, the monster of his childhood raises its huge
>   domed forehead
> And death moves in to take his inner luck,
> Lands on the beaches of his love, like Coghlan's coffin. (P 279)

This marginalization of poetry as a dramatic exception is repeated in *The Ascent of F6* and finalized in *On the Frontier*. In these two plays, the contest is no longer, as in *Dogskin* and the plays Auden wrote alone, between serious poetry and the banter of the music hall, but between verse and prose, and verse all but unequivocally surrenders.

Crooked Europe

The Dog Beneath the Skin also records Auden and Isherwood's increasing commitment to exploring themes of European identity. Philip Larkin would later recall that "Europe and the fear of war" were Auden's "key subject and emotion" in the 1930s (qtd. in Kerr 276). The scene is set first in a provincial English town, Pressan Ambo, but quickly becomes a tour of continental "post-war Europe" (P 206). Throughout the play, the English characters, like Auden in his 1938 Paris address, try to reconcile themselves to an idea of Europe of which they feel themselves on the fringes. Indeed, the central plot concerns the hero's search for an Englishman in continental Europe, part of the play's intention "to undermine

---

[10]   Such was precisely Eliot's assessment. For his comment on the chorus in *The Dog Beneath the Skin*, see Carpenter 194 n.1. Even Auden came to see the choruses as "a piece of self-indulgence that damage the play as drama" (Carpenter 192).

and explode ... bourgeois illusions about England that seem to insulate it from the madness afflicting 1930s continental Europe" (Brady 153). The play's opening chorus establishes the European theme in rich poetic language, tracing a narrowing line from Europe down to Pressan Ambo:

> The Summer holds: upon its glittering lake
> Lie Europe and the islands; many rivers
> Wrinkling its surface like a ploughman's palm.
> Under the bellies of the grazing horses
> On the far side of posts and bridges
> The vigorous shadows dwindle; nothing wavers,
> Calm at this moment the Dutch sea so shallow
> That sunk St Paul's would ever show its golden cross
> And still the deep water that divides us from Norway.
> We would show you at first an English village: You shall choose its location ...
> (P 191)

Outside of the choruses, the play treats Europe in far less committed terms. There are several of the rapid-fire inventories of place names—"There's lots of places I want to see: / Paris, Vienna, Berlin, Rome" (196); "All change for Malaga, Reykjavik, and Omsk!" (P 239)—and questions of European unity and diversity are generally put into the mouths of the most ridiculous characters. First, there is narrow Mildred Luce, wildly embittered against Germany for World War I. When Alan Norman, the hero, is given his task of going abroad to find the missing heir, she bursts out:

> Yes!
> Set off for Germany and shoot them all!
> Poison the wells, till her people drink the sea
> And perish howling. Strew all her fields
> With arsenic ... (P 204)

She is readily dismissed by the townspeople, whose easy cultural generosity renders Mildred little more than a straw figure. That the authors have nothing so simple in mind as to condemn European bigotry, however, is illustrated by another ridiculous figure, the flamboyantly polyglot Poet who resides in Paradise Park. To each of Alan's simple questions (in English), the Poet responds in a different European language:

> ALAN [*to* POET]. Excuse me, sir. Is this Paradise Park?
>
> POET. ἐστιν θάλασσ, τίς δέ νιν χατασβέσει.
>
> ALAN. I beg your pardon?
>
> POET. Nil nimium studeo, Caesar, tibi velle placere nec scire utrum sis al-bus an ater homo. (P 242)

He continues in modern Italian, French, and, finally, English. His behavior is at least as ludicrous as Mildred's; the son of a "famous financier," he spends his time in a tree, frustrates Alan's every attempt to have a normal conversation, and spews such philosophical nonsense as, "I'm the only real person in the whole world" (P 243). His outlandish cosmopolitanism is satirized as thoroughly as Mildred's provincialism, but then, so is almost every response, between the choruses, to the question of European order.

On his crossing to the Continent, Alan meets two Journalists, who assure him that they "have got the lowdown / On all European affairs" (P 211). Their complacency is a sharp contrast to the choruses, which must painstakingly construct an image of "European affairs":

> Night. And crooked Europe hidden in shadow:
> The Rhine catching the moonlight for hundreds of miles, watched by lovers:
> Night in England: Over Lincolnshire and the great churches:
> Glimpses of the constellations between their pinnacles and flying buttresses ...
> (P 253)

On the contrary, the play's action, with the Journalists' occasional guidance, leads Alan at a trot through a burlesque of fictional European locales, dwelling on any one only long enough to mock it. The first of these, Ostnia, is "loosely modeled on Austria before 1914," and the second, Westland, on "Germany after 1933" (Mendelson, Introduction xxiv). One has to assume that Westland is also intended to recall *Waste Land*, an appropriate criticism of a Nazi Germany Auden and Isherwood felt to have utterly shattered the fabric of European understanding. The effect of the pacing is one of random multiplicity, with the theme supported by the form. As Carpenter notes, the play is more a collection of "individual episodes ... like a pantomime, in which a thin and not very important plot could act as a vehicle for a series of virtually independent items" (171). Characters and regimes who would presume to restore some kind of order to the confusion are uniformly, and again very easily, ridiculed. The King and Queen of Ostnia, for instance, try to uphold the imagined ritual dignity of a bygone era by offering refreshments (indeed, champagne) to the widows of men who have just been royally executed (in their wives' presence) in a travesty of meaningful ceremony. "By the way," the King asks Alan and his companions, "are you sure you didn't see anything in the least bit out of taste in our ceremony? I always think the English have such good taste in matters of ritual. You didn't? That's very encouraging" (P 217). The second scene of European misrule is "lunatic, fascistic Westland, where the Leader has a loudspeaker for a face" (Mendelson, Introduction xxiv). This Leader, in an address heard in a literal lunatic asylum, proclaims that "Westland is the guardian of Europe," but his only justification is a vague national essentialism and a boldfaced appeal to fear: "Picture the scene, Oh mothers! Your baby's face, pinched and puckered: Not by hunger, no. Sated with poison from the air it breathes, its tender little mouth agape, choking up froth and green bile" (P 230). Finally, after royalism and fascism, the model of meaning that is not confined to any national regime but is general to Western civilization, medical science, comes under attack. The medical students in Paradise Park dutifully respond to the Surgeon's call, "I believe," by reciting in unison, "… in the physical causation of all phenomena, material or mental: and in the germ theory of disease. And in Hippocrates, the father of Medicine," and so on, and the pseudo-liturgy continues for some score of lines more (P 249). The satire is even more heavy handed than in the previous episodes, and again satirization is the end, for the scene ends and Alan and company move on. By grotesquing the tendency to treat medicine as a religious creed, the scene, like the play, points out the cultural hole but posits no legitimate way to fill it, not even the relative solidity of ritual, which the play parodies in turn.

The Dog Beneath the Skin is so hyper-self-conscious that in at least two cases even the smug tendency to satirize becomes the subject of criticism. The bizarre interlude at the end of Act 2, containing a debate (the political tenor of which goes without saying) between Alan's Right and Left Foot, is grossly caricaturized, but it contains this suggestive exchange:

> LEFT F. You and yer Public School edjerkytion! Ort ter 'ave bin a sky pilot, you art.
>
> RIGHT F. It's very easy to sneer. But the fact remains that without some kind of standards a fellow just goes to pieces. One saw enough of that in the War …
>
> LEFT F. Ow. lay orf it! Yer mikes me sick! … (P 255)

These lines, in the light spirit of the play's dialogue, momentarily call into question the use of satire without objective standards ("It's very easy to sneer"), but both Feet are equally absurd—never mind the fact that they are feet—so the passage is inconclusive on the point it raises. In the Chorus that follows, however, the self-criticism is more poignant, and it is unrelieved by farce:

> Writer, be glib; please them with scenes of theatrical bliss and horror,
> Whose own slight gestures tell their doom with a subtlety quite foreign to the
>   stage.
> For who dare patiently tell, tell of their sorrow
> Without let or variation of season, streaming up in parallel from the little houses
> And unabsorbed by their ironic treasures
> Exerts on the rigid dome of the unpierced sky its enormous pressures? (P 257)

In the only place for sober reflection the play's structure affords, Auden hints at a self-conscious dissatisfaction with the play's approach. Just as his own serious poetry is "foreign to the stage" of this play—hence its relegation to choral interludes—even the "slight gestures" of ordinary life are closer to the pith of experience than the play's restless activity. Although the choruses create a sense of true searching for the still point at the middle of all the play's whirling, the one finally suggested is little more than an abstraction: "another country / Where grace may grow and be given praise / Beauty and virtue be vivid there" (P 289). Far more likely to be remembered by the audience is the refrain of a tipsy shipboard song, on which the play seems finally to settle: "All countries are the same. Everywhere you go, it's the same: nothing but a racket!" (P 210).

Of all his plays, *The Dog Beneath the Skin* is perhaps the most complete example of Auden's unique dramatic vision, its peculiar triumphs and beauties as well as its inherent shortcomings and insecurities. An early line reads, "He tosses at night who at noonday found no truth," and this play seems to toss uncomfortably in pursuit, like its protagonist, of the illusory truth that would complete it. For both hero and play, that object includes an integrated European identity, and for Auden it includes a viable solution to the problem of getting poetic drama to do the work of rejuvenating European culture. Ultimately, though, the play is too miscellaneous and flippant to achieve goals such as these. Brady insists that in the sharpness of its social criticism, "The play is playing for keeps," but he is quite mistaken (161). It would be more accurate to say that it plays at playing for keeps. Like Auden and Isherwood's "Preliminary Statement" on modern drama, which plays at the dogmatism and solidity of a manifesto but is finally too fragmentary and idiosyncratic to have much public utility (and almost all of the principles enumerated therein the authors soon disavowed), *Dogskin* makes no very severe demands on either cultural or dramatic form. The moments of community formation it stages, in, for instance, the spontaneous group songs, are deliberately made as superficial as the popular forms from which they derive. Like the prose passages, these turns are a relief from the "certain amount of faith in something" the choral verse implies ("Future" 521). Ritual plays for keeps; *Dogskin* plays at ritual.

Carpenter writes that *The Dog Beneath the Skin*, by its own nature, "was a play entirely incapable of any satisfactory conclusion," as was the next one, *The Ascent of F6* (217). The latter, although a far more "straight" play than *Dogskin*, still struggles with the uncomfortable marriage of verse and prose, seriousness and satire. From the outset, *F6* establishes that it is going after big game, the meaninglessness of modern life. The search centers around the mountaineering expedition of Michael Ransom (inspired by T.E. Lawrence), and his psychological relationship to his mother and to the ordinary people of England. The English Mr. and Mrs. A., who function as the play's chorus, cry: "And everything is emphatically provided: / The Dial Exchange and the voice of the lift. / We must accept them all and there is no one to thank … Give us something to be thankful for … Give us something to live for. We have waited too long" (P 299). They find momentary hope in the prospect of a grand-tour style "spree," but, as is always the case in these plays with an inventory of European place names, multiplicity and the exoticism of foreign locales do not equal meaning:

> From the first-class gilt saloon of channel-steamer we'll peer,
> While the cliffs of Dover vanish and the Calais flats appear,
> Land there, take the fastest train, have dinner in the dining-car,
> Through the evening rush to Paris, where the ladies' dresses are.
> ………………………………………………………………

Rome and Munich for the opera; Mürren for the winter sports;
See the relics of crusaders in the grey Dalmatian ports;
Climb the pyramids of Egypt; walk in Versailles' ordered parks;
Sail in gondolas at Venice; feed the pigeons at St Mark's ... (305)

Although they do not end up making this trip, opting instead for Hove, it is understood that it would not have availed to restore purpose to their lives, given how little they feel this amusement-park picture of Europe had to do with their daily round of work, wireless, and want, "Papers, lunches, tube-fares, teas, / Toothpaste, stamps and doctor's fees" (331).[11] Just as they eventually tire of Ransom's exploits, preferring "the fears and ... achievements sufficient to our day," they decide "the shop-fronts at Christmas [are] a greater marvel than Greece" (P 343). Given the chaotic and meaningless picture of Europe this play, like the previous ones, paints, it is small wonder that the A's would find little in it worth leaving home for.

F6 marks a long step in the direction of realistic as opposed to ritual drama, but, like *Dogskin*, it does deal with ritual as a thematic element. As in the previous play, ritual action is presented through the eyes of its English observers. Contrasting with the ludicrous execution scene in Ostnia, however, the ritual enactments in *F6* are received with far greater sobriety. Ransom and his assistants observe the monks on the mountain performing a ceremony of spiritual protection: "I've read about these rites, somewhere. They're supposed to propitiate the spirits which guard the house of the dead" (P 323). Ransom's companions are more frightened than reflective, but the Abbot monk recognizes Ransom's special sensitivity:

ABBOT. You know the legend?

RANSOM. I have read the Book of the Dead.

ABBOT. Such interest, Mr. Ransom, is uncommon in one of your race. In that case, you will have comprehended the meaning of the ceremony that was performed this evening out in the courtyard: the office for the souls of the dead and the placation of the Demon. I am afraid that you, with your western civilization, must consider us here excessively superstitious ... No, you need not contradict me out of politeness. I understand. You see the painted mask and the horns and the eyes of fire and you think: "This Demon is only a bogey that nurses use to frighten their children: I have outgrown such nonsense. It is fit only for ignorant Monks and peasants. With our factory chimneys and our furnaces and our locomotives we have banished these fairy-tales. I shall climb the mountain and I shall see nothing." But you would be wrong. (P 323)

---

[11]   MacNeice gets a similar effect in his *Out of the Picture* by setting one scene in a tourist agency and parodying the idiom of travel brochures. By piling up a list of cities and sites, from Yellowstone Park to the Sistine Chapel, he makes even the oldest and holiest of them seem "Unreal" (See MacNeice, *Out of the Picture* 50, 88).

Unlike the King of Ostnia, the Abbot does not think so highly of Englishmen's ritual appreciation. Throughout the play, the mystery-less West appears grasping and trivial next to the richness of the monks' and mountain people's "fairy-tales." The juxtaposition to the Ostnian execution scene, plus the fact that the Demon does in fact become real at the end of the play, suggests that, although Auden and Isherwood were clearly gravitating away from the attempt to ritualize drama, their sense of ritual's power (with its roots in tradition and shared belief) to invest experience with meaning had not yet vanished.[12]

At the same time, the utility of ritual action and some of its attendant features—poetic language, heightened awareness, sacred space—is increasingly associated with the individual as opposed to the collective, and it loses its power to unify in the process. Ransom's introspection in the face of mystery serves to distinguish him from the group, rather than to unite him to it. His personal quest for meaning drowns out everything around him; nor does the play seem to criticize him for it. This is perhaps the strongest argument against Mendelson's claim that Auden, in his quest for a communal and collaborative drama, successfully "[broke] free from the whole set of assumptions and methods that informed the romantic tradition" ("Auden-Isherwood" 276).[13] As the later plays retreat from the radical actor-audience collaboration of the early ones, they increasingly focus on the spiritual adventures of the individual. Indeed, the last play, *On the Frontier*, shifts poetry back into the emotional-personal realm to which romanticism found it best suited. Poetry in this play is confined almost entirely to the "mystical love scenes of Eric and Anna" which made even sympathetic MacNeice "long for a sack to put one's head in" (*Selected* 101). While not unvaryingly abhorrent, they do illustrate how much of the ground he had tried to gain for dramatic poetry Auden had surrendered: "The place of love, the good place. / O hold me in your arms. / The darkness closes in" (P 417).[14] This is not the choral verse of *Dogskin*, positing a rich fabric of meaning behind the surface confusion in Europe. Yet the play places any hope of European reconciliation in the relationship of these two young lovers from the opposed nations of Ostnia and Westland. The model of European identity is reduced to the secret assignations of two individuals, and any suggestion of order that falls outside the purview of their subjectivity is rendered meaningless. Thus, Valerian, the mighty industrialist, labors under the delusion that his commercial empire is the true heir and guardian of what holds civilization together: power.

---

[12]   Rather, they may have been beginning to look for it farther from home. Two years later, Auden and Isherwood would go to China for the writing of *Journey to a War*, and Isherwood eventually became a Buddhist. For that matter, Auden did not return to Christianity until he came to the United States.

[13]   Not surprisingly, the hero-fixation of *F6* also got the authors accused of having fascist sympathies. See Ostrem.

[14]   Anna and Eric's exchanges are presumably among those situations "in which the characters are not their normal, everyday selves," and in which, according to Auden, flights into poetry in a mixed prose-verse play might be justified ("Future" 522).

The Valerian Works ... How beautiful they look from here! Much nicer than the cathedral next door ... A few people still go there to pray, I suppose—peasants who have only been in the city a generation, middle-class women who can't get husbands ... Curious to think that it was once the centre of popular life. If I had been born in the thirteenth century, I suppose I should have wanted to be a bishop. [*Factory sirens, off, sound the lunch-hour.*] Now my sirens have supplanted his bells. But the crowd down there haven't changed much. The Dole is as terrifying as Hell-Fire—probably worse ... (P 364)

The revolt of his workers later makes him out to be a fool, but neither is the church he imagines himself to have supplanted redeemed in the space of the play. It is only included among the ineffectual voices clamoring from a remote past for a say in Europe's present. When Anna's mother speaks of tradition, she sounds merely silly: "The trouble [with Westlanders] is, they've no traditions. That's why they're jealous of us. They always have been. They're spoilt children, really ... You may say what you like; tradition and breeding count" (P 377). Her devotion to institutional religion is included among her delusions: "Did you read Father Ambrose's article on the consequences of heresy? We must defend the Church. The Church is in danger!" (P 384). Sensitive and idealistic Eric provides a convenient counterpoint to the narrow rhetoric of the play's other characters, locked in the obviously ridiculous biases ignorance and habit have bred in them. His family chides him for writing about "'The chances of European peace,'" which, they believe, are nil and probably not even desirable (P 377).

On the Frontier focuses even more explicitly on the idea of Europe than any of the previous plays. Its conclusions, though, do not extend much beyond those of *Paid on Both Sides*, *The Dance of Death*, even *Dog Beneath the Skin*. The familiar questions are raised and insinuations made. One is the implication of the local in the corruption of the international: "The country is in danger / But not from any stranger. / Your enemies are here / Whom you should fight, not fear" (P 392).[15] Underscoring this claim, the confrontation between Ostnia and Westland is rapidly obscured by internal revolutions, mutinies, and civil war. The web of complicity and similarity between England and the supposed extremes of corrupt Europe is sketched, as in *Dogskin*, and the whole still appears little more than a "racket." England is in Europe, and Europe is in England, but not by virtue of a common tradition, only common disorder.

The political conflict in the play, which is based on nothing more substantial than prejudice and misinformation, deteriorates into a confusion even the authors seem unable to see through, so that they are forced to take refuge within the story of Anna and Eric. Dr. Thorvald speaks for all of them when he asks, "What are we really fighting for? I feel so muddled!" (P 398). It is a question the play never answers, at least outside of Anna and Eric's charmed circle. As usual, *On the Frontier* seems fairly sure what the solution is *not*: it offers commerce, religion,

---

15   A *Dogskin* chorus similarly advises the audience: "Do not comfort yourself with the reflection: 'How very unEnglish'" (P 212).

family, tradition, patriotism, the glory of war, and proletarian revolt (with the support of "a handful of intellectuals, who, for the last twenty years, have signed letters of protest against everything from bi-metallism in Ecuador to the treatment of yaks in Thibet") (P 408). The pseudo-cultures hiding behind the farcical Frontier are no more worth fighting for than the ones *Dogskin* mocked in rapid succession, and Auden seems to have conceded that neither is the ideal of a poetic drama. This last play's poetic voice is much more a whimper than a bang, and, in a closing addendum, it is given the last grim word: "Europe lies in the dark" (P 417).

From the narrow confines of rural English family life (and private jokes), Auden's drama steadily expands in scope out into Europe. Usually this expansion is traceable to Isherwood's influence. The evolution of *The Dog Beneath the Skin* is instructive. As William Ostrem notes, "With Isherwood's help ... the revised version of *The Chase*—which would soon receive the title *The Dog Beneath the Skin*—became a tour of the entire European political landscape" (166). *The Chase*, written by Auden alone, is concerned almost entirely with the English scene: It includes no Ostnia and no Westland; its central episodes are a local mine strike and a boys' reformatory rebellion. It also differs from *Dogskin* in two important ways: It is written almost entirely in verse, and it is often far more personal than public in emphasis. An example of the latter is one chorus in *The Chase* containing the refrain, "Repent ... Repent ... Repent" (P 179–80). In *The Dog Beneath the Skin*, this becomes "Repent ... Unite ... Act," a dramatic shift from introspection to engagement matching the movement from England out into Europe (P 280–81). In the Auden-Isherwood machine, though, with Europe comes prose, and, as Auden himself believed, prose is most useful for the expression of doubt. Predictably, then, the scattered idea of Europe present in Auden's earliest plays gains not at all in order or coherence in the collaborative works. On the contrary, it is presented with even greater uncertainty. Form and content keeping step, the order and coherence implied by poetry give way to prose, the language of doubt. The tiny flame of "belief in something" that presumably led Auden to write plays in verse in the first place, and is a necessary component of any vision of European order, is methodically obscured by doubt and dismay until it yields to darkness at the end of *On the Frontier*. By the time he rediscovered it, the hour may have seemed too late to visualize any spiritual communion for Europe.

The Poet of Anxiety

The case of Auden's plays is one in which textual history provides a clue to meaning. Brady mentions the "indeterminacy" that inheres, for instance, in talking about *Dog Beneath the Skin*, owing to its collaborative construction and revision and to the several versions in which it survives (153 n.4). There is an indeterminacy about all of the plays; each appeared in more than one incarnation, and many of them were published and produced with different endings (Brady 153). Auden and Isherwood wrote several endings to *The Ascent of F6*, none of which satisfied the authors. Many of the plays pick up and reuse or rework bits of previous ones. *Dogskin* contains pieces of *Enemies of a Bishop*, *The Chase*, and an unpublished piece called *The Fronny*. This instability is compounded by Auden's own well-known tendency to suppress and/or disavow his own work, what James Stewart describes as "Auden's willingness to see jettisoned whatever he no longer thought appropriate, or no longer liked" (204). Stewart cites one case in which Auden inscribed a copy of *The Dance of Death*, "This is rubbish." The plays, the texts, and the man all tend to confound impressions of certainty, confidence, and objectivity. As Richard and Janis Londraville observe:

> Auden, then, seemed to be a struggling student doing an algebra problem, and his incompleteness as a dramatist is that he didn't understand that a closed system can only be defined in terms of itself. His plays are replete with the sense that people can be taught and can be helped through the maze that is the twentieth century. But he isn't sure how that will happen; he hasn't quite gotten the answer and realizes it by the end of most of his dramas. So he tries another external force, and another. There must be *something* that we are not doing that would help us refrain from killing one another, so let's try love—or socialism— or … what? (176)

One might add collaboration, audience participation, or choral verse, all in the end insufficient and disposable. The texts, then, frequently reflect the temperament of their creator, who, particularly in the 1920s and 1930s, was on a hectic search for permanence, for the great *something*. Biographer George Wright considers Auden "fundamentally a poet of doubt, of uncertainty, of insecurity, of hesitations, second thoughts, qualifications—in short, of anxiety" (155). This anxiety comes through in all of his plays, not only in the political and cultural turmoil they portray but also in the fitful attempt to make drama into ritual, without the proper equipment for doing so.

In addition to suggesting his "stringency of self-criticism," disavowals of the kind mentioned above indicate the radical alterations of which Auden's thought was capable. Most prominent and permanent among these was his 1940 conversion, or rather recommitment, to Christianity in the form of the Anglican (Episcopalian) Church (Wright 204). As with Eliot, conversion was the expression of extant desires and patterns of thought, and it did not result in a complete disavowal of his pre-conversion efforts to find meaning through dramatic art. It did, however, enable him to see some of the shortcomings of those efforts for what they were. Shortly afterwards, he came to see in his plays of the 1920s and 1930s an unsatisfactory fumbling toward order that no amount of collaboration or technical innovation could complete. In 1942 he inscribed a copy of *The Ascent of F6*: "The end of this play is all wrong, because, as I now see, it required, and I refused it, a Christian solution" (P xxvii). Along with artistic solutions came cultural ones. Not long before his conversion, Christianity had already begun to present itself to Auden's mind as of more than sentimental importance:

... I visited Spain during the Civil War. On arriving in Barcelona, I found as I walked through the city that all the churches were closed and there was not a priest to be seen. To my astonishment, this discovery left me profoundly shocked and disturbed. The feeling was far too intense to be the result of a mere liberal dislike of intolerance ... I could not escape acknowledging that, however I have consciously ignored and rejected the Church for sixteen years, the existence of churches and what went on in them had all the time been very important to me. If that was the case, what then? (Cunningham, *Spanish* 306)

Besides beginning his personal journey of faith, Auden's question, or one like it, marks the beginning of the end of his pseudo-ritualistic verse drama. A taste for ritual, it appears, was no longer enough to sustain it. Once he had found an objective and historical ritual community—one, besides, with a personal appeal— the urgency behind constructing a substitute for it in the theatre began quickly to fade.[16]

---

[16] Auden was not quite done writing for the stage, however, as his move to the United States also heralded his turn toward libretto writing. Matthew Paul Carlson picks up Auden's "quest for a theatrically viable form of dramatic verse" precisely where I leave it and argues compellingly that the opera may, in fact, have provided Auden with his most "lasting solution to this problem" (409). That the opera for which he wrote his first libretto was Benjamin Britten's *Paul Bunyan* is some indication, at least, that the European question would no longer be uppermost in Auden's mind as he pursued such a solution.

Interchapter:
Los Toros no Hablan Inglés

In a sense, the idea of Europe begins with the bull. In the myth, Zeus, disguised as a bull, abducts the Phoenician princess Europa and takes her to Crete. In Ovid's version of the story, "Agenor's daughter wondered at the bull's beauty, amazed that he did not threaten to attack" (Morford 354). She is even bold enough to sit on the bull's back, and then he carries her across the sea, not revealing himself as Zeus until they have reached Crete.[1] There are so many bull myths and rituals behind ancient Europe that the question of the origins of the modern Spanish *corrida de toros* remains open to debate.[2] Hypotheses involving Persian, Roman, Arabic, and Cretan rituals, and Spanish folk practices and prehistoric rites all retain some credibility, if varying degrees of evidence. What is certain is that each possibility, like the modern *corrida* itself, has the dual effect of tethering modern Spain to an imagined European essence and distinguishing Spain as alien to Europe. All of the theories of origins emphasize a continuity between the shadowy nativity of Europe and modern Spanish custom. At the same time, depending on who is interpreting, all suggest Spain's distinction from the rest of Europe. Explaining his sequence of drawings, "*El rapto de Europa,*" Salvador Dalí explained:

> It seems like a paradox to me. It is Europe that has to ingress into Spain. It was the Iberian toro that held onto Europe … The bull, which is Spain, did not take away Europe, he held on to her with his determination, with all his bravery, and kept her where she is. Europe owes to Spain her very being. We are the bull that ravished Europe for ourselves. (qtd. in Carrie Douglass 110. Trans. Douglass)

However, other views have often exerted greater influence. Joaquín Costa, for one, proclaimed: "We want to breathe the air of Europe, so that Spain ceases to be African and becomes European … The bullfights are the greatest evil that harm us more than many believe … from the perversion of public feeling to lowering us in the eyes of foreigners, there is a dismal series of comparisons that degrade us" (qtd. in Shubert 2). "Africa begins on the other side of the Pyrenees," wrote Alexandre Dumas, and this notion of Spanish exceptionalism has always influenced interpretations of the bullfight by the rest of Europe.

---

[1] For a vivid and multifaceted discussion of the Europa-and-bull myth, see Michael Wintle, *The Image of Europe*, Chapter 3. Also see Carlos Fuentes, *The Buried Mirror* 17-20.

[2] *Corrida de toros* is the full name for the ritual that takes place inside a ring (*plaza de toros*) involving horses, matadors, and the killing of bulls (or *toros bravos*). It includes *picadores* on horseback equipped with long spears, the placing of barbed sticks (*banderillas*) in the bull's back, the matador's capework (*faena*), and the death of the bull by a sword thrust. *Corrida* can also refer to the group of six bulls in one bullfight.

The Spain-as-bull image, invoked above by Dalí, was one of the most popular among British writers of the Spanish Civil War era. It is precisely the tension surrounding the bullfight as a symbol of Spanish identity, whether shared or exclusive, which provides the ritual's utility for discussing an idea of Europe. The discomfort with which the *corrida* frequently strikes the British (or American) observer is frequently due to two misgivings: first, that such a contest is not governed by the rules of fair play, and, second, that it is cruel to animals. As Ernest Hemingway explained in *Death in the Afternoon* (1932), "The bullfight is not a sport in the Anglo-Saxon sense of the word, that is, it is not an equal contest or an attempt at an equal contest between a bull and a man. Rather it is a tragedy; the death of the bull, which is played, more or less well, by the bull and the man involved and in which there is danger for the man but certain death for the animal" (16).[3] There is a way in which the tragic impulse seems especially at home in Spain, where the rites and symbols of Catholicism are more violent and go deeper than in perhaps any other European country. The bullfight is not a Catholic event, but its codes and those of the Mass seem, to recall Eliot, to flourish in the same hedgerow (A Spanish law, notably, dictates that all bullrings must have a chapel for the toreros (Lewine 85)).

In the same way that, as Julian Pitt-Rivers stated in a 1992 study for the European Parliament, "the bullfight is 'inherent in the Spanish mentality,'" the code of sport has often appeared to be inherent in the British mentality (qtd. in Shubert 4). So, too, has the love of animals. The distance between these two conceptual systems is pithily stated in the Spanish saying, *Los toros no hablan inglés*: The bulls do not speak English. Yet Adrian Shubert is quick to point out that "the famous British 'love of animals' is not a transcendent feature of English character and society but historically contingent and class specific" (13). Just so, there are times when the bulls have spoken English of a kind. Great Britain, after all, does understand tragedy as an art form, and, if nothing else, the Spanish Civil War, often under the sign of the bullfight, lent itself to that mode of interpretation.

John McCormick argues that literature predominantly about bullfighting is almost invariably poor because it involves a double abstraction. As a ritual, the bullfight places unusual demands on literature, and McCormick suggests why this is so: "The result of one afternoon's work cannot be known generations later in print or on canvas. The result is the act itself" (6). Whatever spiritual dogmas or interpretations with which it is overlain, the result of a ritual is ultimately the act itself, the unanswerable moment of its performance. Seen in another way, the bullfight, as an art form, is an abstraction from reality, and writing about art requires a further abstraction. "The novelist of toreo," McCormick writes, "is required to transpose the matter of one art into another, one of the most difficult things in the world to bring off" (231).[4] Taurine fiction, he argues, works much better when, if

---

    [3]   See also McCormick 1–4 and Lewine 24 for more on the important distinction between bullfighting and sport.

    [4]   *Toreo* is the term for the whole art of the *corrida de toros*. It is a noun that comes from *toro*, the word for bull. English has no precise translation. The one most often used, and which I will use throughout, is "bullfighting," a notoriously inadequate term for an art form

"[t]oreo is at the center of the work, … it is not the central subject; it is related to the novel as an architectural plan is related to the finished building" (241). Such is the case in Lawrence's short story "None of That!" but not, as I will argue, in his novel *The Plumed Serpent*. Although most of the works discussed in this section involve bullfighting, very few take it as their "central subject." They invoke bulls, matadors, and other elements of the corrida as the images and symbols of other, less local concerns, whether these be "those relationships which are at the root of all art: life and death, sensibility and intelligence, human failings and the seed of tragedy implicit in all human activity" (McCormick 250), or the political tensions of a Europe at war with itself. What is more, most of the texts in this section are poems, and there is reason to believe that poetry is better equipped than fiction to handle a ritual art form like bullfighting.

Literature of the Spanish Civil War seems to suggest that this war's reality also was best accessed through synchronic or nearly synchronic art forms such as photography, poetry, and toreo, and most often through a combination of these forms. Many Spanish Civil War poems are based on or inspired by photographs. This war, captured to a greater degree than any previous one by film and photography, made itself known to Europe and the world through the mediation of the visual image, so much so that even its writers gravitated toward that material that is best understood visually, synchronically, and sculpturally—and the bullfight certainly qualified.

Much if not most of contemporary Europe sees the bullfight, as it did in the 1920s and 1930s, as an archaic survival from a culture, better left behind, of brutality, bloodlust, and fear. Edward Lewine, however, proposes that in another way, "the bullfight is the essence of civilization, if by civilization we mean humanity's subjugation of the natural world and the development of custom and ritual to replace violence as the governing principle of human interaction" (227). And just as Europe's cathedrals did not disappear when Christendom reportedly did, more bullfights are held annually in Spain (and southern France) today than at any other time, despite increasingly vocal opposition from various quarters (Lewine 89, 146).[5] This section attempts to show that the appeal of the bullfight for British writers during a period of uncertainty over European identity reveals more than simply the quaintly benign attraction of a local peculiarity. Whether Europe begins with the bull or not, interwar British writing demonstrates that the Spanish bullfight provided a unique arena for the expression of a modern idea of Europe often obscured by the most powerful accepted definitions.

---

that is not truly a fight in any obvious sense. To *torear* is literally to "bull." "Bullfighting" (and "bullfight" for *corrida*) will suffice here, though, because I am primarily concerned with English interpretations, including linguistic ones, of the Spanish form.

[5]   Although the animal-rights movement represents the most visible challenge to bullfighting in Spain, a necessarily invisible one—increasing indifference among Spanish young people—will likely have more impact on the fate of the bullfight in the coming years. See Shubert as well as Lewine 90.

Chapter 4
We Are One Blood:
Lawrence and the Bullfight

One of the most frequent, and valid, criticisms of Lawrence's 1926 novel *The Plumed Serpent* is that it does not hang together. I will show that it does not hang together because it demands a tragic resolution but cannot find one. The novel abandons its object in the first chapter, then sends its heroine, Kate Leslie, on a furious quest trying to find it. The object is a symbolic reconciliation of the opposites that tear at individual and European cultural identity, a reconciliation uniquely figured in a ritual, the bullfight, which actually and symbolically links Europe to its imagined opposite, "native" Mexico. Catherine Bell writes that "ritual is a type of critical juncture wherein some pair of opposing social or cultural forces comes together"—for example, "belief and behavior, tradition and change, order and chaos, the individual and the group, subjectivity and objectivity, nature and culture, the real and the imaginative ideal" (16). To this preliminary list I would add the oppositional pairs elite and masses, and, in the particular context of a Mexican bullfight, European and non-European. The utility of "ritual as … a medium of integration or synthesis for opposing sociocultural forces" (Bell 23) is particularly strong where the ritual bridges two historically opposed cultures, here the "old" world and the "new." *The Plumed Serpent* climaxes with an invented ritual intended to do what the complete *corrida de toros* is capable of doing, but this invention provides its heroine, Kate, no satisfaction; nor has it satisfied many critics. The narrative is incomplete because Kate, like Lawrence himself, runs away from the bullfight before she can see where it is leading, to the tragic climax fusing the pairs that, unreconciled, keep her and the novel in a state of constant agitation.

Lawrence's previous novel, *Kangaroo* (1923), suggested that, while British people habitually travel to faraway climes and continents in search of the missing "dark" parts of themselves their home culture seems to deny, they need not go very far at all in order to have their seasons inverted. For *Kangaroo*'s hero, R.L. Somers, Cornwall had been far enough to make his "dark, blood-consciousness tingle," to transport him "back, back into the blood-sacrificial pre-world" (*Kangaroo* 243). Even so, after Italy, India, and Australia, Lawrence, like his characters, continued his centrifugal journey, and he chose Mexico for his next destination and the setting of his next novel, *The Plumed Serpent*. Kenneth Rexroth argued in 1947 that "Lawrence did not make any very definite contact with the ancient Mexico, but he could see and sense it" (Rexroth 129). This observation, while coming close to positing an "essential" idea of Mexico, remains instructive. Rexroth was well aware that what Lawrence saw and sensed in Mexico was a function of his

European mind and might as productively have been sought out closer to home—say, in Cornwall or Wales.[1] Whatever Lawrence sought, and found or did not find, in Mexico, the writing that grew out of his experience there describes his ideal image of Europe far more than it does ancient Mexico. It is a paradoxical ideal, arising from a desire for the basic oppositions of culture to be reconciled once and for all in an aesthetically satisfying way. It led Lawrence to try to represent it in *The Plumed Serpent* through invented rituals. His other primary Mexican writings, *Mornings in Mexico* and "None of That!", however, suggest that the need to invent such a ritual in that novel is based on an initial inability to recognize the reconciliatory potential of the bullfight. "None of That!" recuperates the ritual value of the bullfight lost in *The Plumed Serpent* and is itself infused with the bullfight's ritual structure. It is by restoring that value to the sociopolitical context of *The Plumed Serpent*, and by using that structure to define the novel's narrative lacuna, that one arrives at the fullest picture of the relationship between the bullfight, Lawrence's writing, and his idea of Europe.

Lawrence attended a bullfight in Mexico City on Easter Sunday, 1923 (Nehls 212). Like his heroine, Kate, he was revolted and left almost immediately; Lawrence biographer Jeffrey Meyers records that Lawrence "ran away from the terrible bullfight on April 1 after only ten minutes" (294). Yet, Meyers also notes, "he was sufficiently interested in the spectacle to see another bullfight six months later, in Tepic, in October 1923" (294), which he apparently "sat through" (Sagar 156). His reaction to this one is unclear; Lawrence does not mention it in his letters.[2] Yet a change in his apprehension of the rhythm and order of the bullfight is apparent, as we will see, in "None of That!", a short story he wrote in 1927. From the juxtaposition of these two works emerges an intertextual pattern describing the role of sacrificial ritual in Lawrence's imagination of Europe. I will first examine some of the ways critics have understood the cultural and political implications

---

[1]   Paul Fussell echoes this argument in *Abroad: British Literary Traveling Between the Wars* (1980). "Of course," he writes, "[Lawrence] never found what he sought, or, if he thought he had found it, soon discovered that he himself had manufactured the ecstasy and laid it over the actuality of a place. He thus repeatedly took off again, embittered and disillusioned. He is always both escaping and seeking" (147).

[2]   His traveling companion Kai Gótzsche, however, was sickened: "I felt sick to my stomach, qualmish ... But how loathsome ... I get provoked and furious just to think of the yellow and dumb performance" (Nehls 263). He notes also that there were no horses involved. Thus it was likely a *novillada sin picadores*, a bullfight featuring younger, smaller bulls and no picadors. The absence of the equine component, which has long been identified as the one most likely to upset non-aficionados, may conceivably have lessened Lawrence's indignation at the spectacle's brutality. As Barnaby Conrad writes, "No one—except Hemingway's little Old Lady [in *Death in the Afternoon*]—derives pleasure from watching this act [with the horses], but it is necessary ... 'I like everything but the horses' is the most common statement by Americans about La Fiesta Brava" (69). This remains true even though horses have long been required to be protected by a thick layer of padding, a rule enacted in the early 1930s, too late, alas, for Lawrence.

of Lawrence's imagined Mexico. In the process, I will highlight those features of the criticism that imply the relation of this Mexico to European politics and that suggest where a more thorough understanding of ritual could clarify this relation. The bulk of the chapter is then given to a detailed analysis of the bullfight in *The Plumed Serpent*, drawing on important bullfighting criticism and biographical information about Lawrence to show precisely where Lawrence's needs and the bullfight's strengths failed to meet. It concludes with a reading of "None of That!" which attempts to show how the later bullfighting story closes some of the ritual loops opened by the earlier novel.

Fiction, Politics, and the Uses of Mexico

Postcolonial criticism knows that opening up the critical understanding of intercultural exchange has implications not only for the culture of the formerly colonized but also for that of the former colonizers. "Who in Britain or France," asks Edward Said, "can draw a clear circle around British London or French Paris that would exclude the impact of India and Algeria upon those imperial cities?" (15). Still, the model of postcolonial inquiry that continues to predominate, particularly in transatlantic studies, is that which emphasizes the impact of the "old" world on the "new." If Algeria and India have left their mark on Europe's capitals, then surely the Americas have done the same, yet the question of how Mexico, for instance, figures in the mind of Europe is asked only infrequently. Yet during the interwar years, one British writer after another traveled to Mexico, where a version of the European identity crisis was being enacted and where, indeed, the buzzwords *socialist* and *fascist* were on everyone's lips.[3] Theresa Mae Thompson, borrowing Said's metaphor, asks:

> But what do we find when we examine interactions between indigenous populations and invading Europeans and Americans of European descent? Of course, it would also be impossible to draw a circle around Mexico City and isolate that which is only Spanish, but the balances of power there were different from those in London or Paris. (221)

The question of Lawrence's relationship, as an English author, to the cultural forms and practices of Mexico has received more critical attention than perhaps any other raised by *The Plumed Serpent*, and it has provided the basis for some of the harshest criticisms both of the novel and of Lawrence's political views. Joyce Wexler summarizes these criticisms in her essay "Realism and Modernists' Bad Reputation." The two common threads uniting most of them, she argues, are an

---

[3]   In addition to Lawrence, interwar writers who went to Mexico and wrote books based on their experiences included Greene (*The Lawless Roads, The Power and the Glory*), Waugh (*Robbery Under Law*), Aldous Huxley (*Beyond the Mexique Bay*), and Malcolm Lowry (*Under the Volcano*).

insistence on a realist-political reading of the novel despite the obvious indicators Lawrence provides that symbolism is at work, and a sweeping objection to the use of "extreme acts and foreign cultures as raw material for Western fantasies" (60).[4] The combination leads many critics to label the novel irresponsible and a failure, and Lawrence a proto-fascist or worse. It leads others, such as Theresa Mae Thompson, to praise Lawrence on the grounds of being both a realist and *not* a fascist:

> Despite the strong presence of European religions, languages, economic structures, and social practices in the area, the novel Lawrence wrote while living there ... asserts a position completely antithetical to the white-supremacist eugenics discourses gaining power in Europe and the United States during the same period. (222)

This easy association of European religion, language, economics, and "social practices" with "white-supremacist eugenics discourses" is baffling, but it allows Thompson to situate Lawrence neatly outside of fascism as she conceives of it. By the time of the novel's revision, she writes, "[s]omething in Lawrence has altered regarding ethnic and racial relations—an alteration unlikely in the fascist context of European thought during the 1920s" (224). In the early 1920s, when Lawrence wrote and revised *The Plumed Serpent*, fascism was a nascent political movement and hardly widespread enough to describe the whole "context of European thought." The ideas of race and ethnicity in Lawrence's novel of Mexico do more than challenge a simplified notion of fascism-as-white-supremacy. They situate fascism within a pattern of thought, gaining currency in 1920s Europe, that finds sustenance in what Europe imagines to be its cultural and spiritual opposite but is in fact an extension of itself.

Wexler makes a strong case for a symbolic, as opposed to realist, reading of the novel's key scenes, arguing that the "vague, contradictory, allusive, figurative, or repetitious" language of those scenes—that is, their obvious "rhetorical exaggeration"—signals the presence of symbolism (61). Larry Gates's Jungian argument amplifies Wexler's. The prose of *The Plumed Serpent*, he writes, "has nothing to do with rational and linear thinking. This novel is imagistic and rhythmic; its images are not external or literal. Like Jung, Lawrence circumambulates images, amplifying and associating" (281). In his attempt to redeem those elements of the novel that other critics have found so strange and distasteful, Gates presses a bit too far in the direction of the psychological. Even Wexler's reading, which is far

---

[4]   A parallel debate centers on the liberties Lawrence routinely takes with empirical reality in his travel writing. (See Fussell, *Abroad* 141–64). Fussell suggests a way around this issue, though, arguing that Lawrence, "[l]ike all literary travelers worth reading ... played a spume of imagination upon empirical phenomena, generating subtle emotional states and devising unique psychological forms and structures to contain them" (155). "[T]here is no way, ultimately," Fussell concludes, "to distinguish his travel writing from his fiction" (156).

more sophisticated and productive than those which tend to "substitute realistic or political readings for symbolic interpretation" (63), occludes something important about this novel. "Lawrence depicts sex and murder," she argues, "as symbols of psychic states, not as models of behavior. Political readings of these scenes treat them as realism: they end interpretation at the immediate referent. In contrast, symbolic readings explore additional possibilities" (63). While this view is true, one of the possibilities for which it does not seem to allow is the *combination* of symbolism and politics.[5] For it cannot be said that the kinds of socio-political questions on which the realism-inclined critics focus were not present to Lawrence's mind at this stage of his career, or that they are not present in those scenes of extremity. On the contrary, Lawrence was very much occupied in the 1920s with "the question of how a mass society should be organized and governed," writes Meyers (247). Even more specifically, his "political ideas" in this period were "influenced by the war in Europe, his persecution in England and his direct experience with the rise of Fascism in Italy" (Meyers 247). This circumstance invites a politico-symbolic reading of *The Plumed Serpent* because these very events are both the originators and the expressions of the unique aesthetic-symbolic politics of Europe in the 1920s. Thompson's "fascist context of European thought in the 1920s" is too reductive to be of much use in interpreting either *The Plumed Serpent* or the cultural relations between Europe and the Americas in that era. It is not enough to say either that Lawrence works within that perceived context or outside it. Rather, Lawrence's strange novel, like fascism, and like much contemporaneous left-wing praxis, makes sense within a broader context of European thought in the 1920s: aesthetic, symbolic, political, ritual.

Those who would label Lawrence's views fascist on the basis of a purely realist reading of *The Plumed Serpent* are as mistaken as those who would excuse him on the same basis and those who would insist that the novel implies no politics but only symbols of consciousness. A great deal is indeed "lost if we refuse to read modernist texts symbolically," but, as Wexler acknowledges, "ignoring history" is no solution (61). Rather, like the bird-and-serpent symbology of Quetzalcoatl, symbolism and realism, myth and history, complete one another. This is especially true in the case of an era—and a writer's imagination—in which symbolic ritual frequently played a central role in the demonstration and exercise of political power. It is further true in the ritual, imported from Europe, which Lawrence chose to open his novel of Mexico.[6]

---

[5]   Wexler does, however, argue against the realist critical tendency to "undo the modernist conjunction of *myth and history*" (61, my emphasis).

[6]   Bullfights have taken place in Mexico nearly as long as in Spain. Adrian Shubert names Manuel Dominguez y Campos, an early nineteenth-century matador, as "perhaps the first Spanish bullfighter to cross the Atlantic" (74). At times Latin America has been a kind of "minor league" (74) for Spanish bullfighters. Contemporary bullfighters regularly perform in Latin America during the Spanish off-season months (October to February), when the Latin American bullfighting season is in full swing.

The bullfight is a richly symbolic act, but it is also a "real" act, materially and historically present, witnessed by some thousands (or, in Mexico City, tens of thousands) of spectators, and fully engaged in the kind of material politics—of gender, of race, of class, of culture—that a purely private or internal symbolism denies.[7] The *plaza de toros* is the site of a symbolic action, but it is also, as a ritual space, a place where abstract politics become actual in the gathering of real people. Even though its treatment of the bullfight is abbreviated, Lawrence's novel extends the meaning of the bullfight along what Wexler calls symbolism's "vertical axis of substitution" (61). At the same time, it affirms a political reading of the bullfight through its clear attempt at realism and references to historical reality. The scene simultaneously illuminates and is illuminated by the specific European cultural context out of which the most extreme modern instances of political symbolism arose.

"Beginnings of a Bull-fight"

By the time he wrote "None of That!", Lawrence demonstrated that he could imagine the bullfight as a ritual capable of symbolically reconciling the most pressing dichotomies of both identity and culture. Prior to this recognition, though, the corrida first functions, in *The Plumed Serpent*, as merely a demonstration of those oppositions, a site of contest but not of reconciliation. This corrida, which is formally incomplete, is based on the essential dichotomy of culture as opposed to its dialectic, the opposition of culture's parts as opposed to their interaction. Although it is a European form, the corrida seems to encompass all of what mesmerizes and shocks Lawrence about Mexico. By the end of *The Plumed Serpent*, he molds this mesmerism and shock into what has occasionally passed as an authentically native Mexican form, the Quetzalcoatl cult organized by Don Ramón Carrasco. Even here, though, Lawrence has not abolished Europe from his imagination of indigenous Mexico, nor has he smothered Mexican reality with European fantasy. Rather, he has simply renamed the cultural banner under which the basic oppositions appear. As Thompson helpfully points out, "[t]he depictions of native spirituality in this novel reveal more than a simple appropriation of native culture or the inscription of European beliefs on indigenous beliefs and practices; they reveal the inescapable entanglements between cultural narratives that occur in twentieth-century literature" (225). The bullfight in this novel is one site in which those entanglements—cultural, political, symbolic—are truly inescapable.

The relationship between the bullfight and the sacrificial rituals of the Quetzalcoal cult provides a key to understanding the complex cultural interplay that is one of the primary themes of *The Plumed Serpent* as well as of this stage of Lawrence's career. Yet, conspicuously and inexplicably absent from critical discussions of the novel is the bullfight that, equally conspicuously but far more

---

[7]   This is the basis of Shubert's argument in *Death and Money in the Afternoon*.

explicably, introduces it. Of all the chapters in *The Plumed Serpent*, "Beginnings of a Bull-fight" is crucial for several reasons. First, as Neil Roberts argues, "[f]rom Kate's point of view, the story can be seen as a quest" (136). The starting point of Kate's quest narrative establishes the terms according to which her search will progress, including the place of violence and/or blood sacrifice in the formation of a people's identity; the sometimes rigid, sometimes permeable boundaries between two models of "consciousness;" and the integrity of the individual in relation to the "mass." In the second chapter, Lawrence writes: "The world is made up of a mass of people and a few individuals," underscoring one of the novel's basic oppositions (38). David Kertzer writes that "[r]itual dramatizes and energizes collective representations that mediate between society and the individual" (63), and the Mexico City bullfight does so with more drama and energy than Kate can comfortably tolerate. The chapter is organized around a ritual, the bullfight, which encapsulates the chaos of impressions that defined Mexico City for Lawrence and that pitch Kate into near hysteria. It sets images of "Europe" and "America" into a vivid and violent motion that will fuel the subsequent narrative. Finally, the way the bullfight is depicted inverts a number of its accepted political associations. Despite his obvious philosophical differences from, for example, Wyndham Lewis and Ezra Pound, Lawrence is consistently included among the modernists with fascist inclinations, and, as the following chapter will show, fascism is supposed to have kept rituals such as the bullfight in its hip pocket. Yet Lawrence, like Kate Leslie, hardly took to the bullfight easily or naturally.

Criticism that does treat the bullfight often situates it as a convenient counterpoint to more attractive "native" ritual practices. Such arguments emphasize Lawrence's depiction of the bullfight, like the Catholic Church, as an unwelcome European imposition in the Americas. Cheng Lok Chua returns repeatedly to the comparison of "the obscene imported European bullfight" to native rituals and "idyll[s]" in order to point up Lawrence's apparent judgment in favor of indigenous Mexico (104). Thus, for instance, the birth of an ass-foal, late in the novel, is "a dialectical opposite of the slaughter in the bullring," signifying indigenous peace and order-defying European wantonness and violence (105).[8] This logic overlooks how thoroughly Europe is implicated in those parts of Mexico supposedly representative of indigenous life as well as how much of "native" Mexico inheres in the supposedly alien European forms. It is, after all, Ramón, "an intellectual with a European education" who becomes "obsessed with returning the old gods to Mexico" (Gates 275), and his ideal of a ritualistic military dictatorship is hardly alien to European thought of the time.

Just how easily this cultural interaction is missed is evident from Chua's next observation. "This obscene European ritual killing of five bulls," he writes, "contrasts with the more meaningful native rite of Huitzilopochtli later on when

---

[8]   Here Chua is using *dialectic* as I use *dichotomy*, implying not exchange but opposition. The difference is important to my argument about Lawrence's treatment of Europe vis-à-vis Mexico.

General Viedma cleanly executes the five would-be assassins to demonstrate religious power and justice" (105). The latter murders certainly seem more meaningful insofar as they are interpreted to their audience and the reader through accompanying text—General Viedma's liturgical poetry and staged explanation to the Guards—but the basis on which they constitute a "native rite" is ambiguous at best, as is how stabbing five people in the heart can be "cleanly" done. The executions are couched in the language of a European (even an English-language) reinterpretation of Aztec mythology and are overseen by Don Ramón, whose Europeanness is largely responsible for his vision of the renewed Quetzalcoatl cult. Lawrence himself seems to have been well aware of this. In *Mornings in Mexico*, the travelogue written contemporaneously with *The Plumed Serpent*, he observed, "The Aztec gods and goddesses are, as far as we have known anything about them, an unlovely and unlovable lot. In their myths there is no grace or charm, no poetry" (45). Thus it is difficult to dispute John Middleton Murry, who writes, "The well-head of the new gospel is the essentially European soul of Ramón Carrasco ... [T]he conditions of its manifestation, Mexico, Cipriano, Kate herself, are accidental" (290). Perhaps not accidental, but at least not essential. As Rexroth argues, "[t]he re-awakening of mystery, the revival of the old Aztec religion, the political 'Indianism'—even if it all came true, one knows it would be a fraud, a politician's device, as Indianism is in Latin America today. Lawrence knew that, of course" (129).[9] Indeed, there can be little doubt that Lawrence was not truly taken in by the allure of the "primitive." It is merely a "mental trick," he wrote, to

> fool yourself and others into believing that the befeathered and bedaubed darling is nearer to the true ideal gods than we [Europeans] are. This last is just bunk, and a lie ... The sooner we realise, and accept this, the better, and leave off trying, with fulsome sentimentalism, to render the Indian in our own terms. (MM 87)

Further, the rationale Cipriano gives for the executions—"If men that are men will live, men that are less than men must be put away, lest they multiply too much. Men that are more than men have the judgment of men that are less than men" (PS 394)—recalls too well a strain of European social philosophy typified, for instance, by Nietzsche, Yeats, Shaw, and the leaders of fascism too to be classed as purely "native." The novel's characters, Rexroth writes, "seem to become secretly aware that all this gorgeous parading in primitive millinery, this Mystery, and Fire, and Blood, and Darkness, has been thought up. There is something Western European, British Museum, about it" (130). The Quetzalcoatl mysticism they practice, like Theosophy, "is the creation of over-civilized Hellenistic intellectuals; ... and the Aztecs were not mystics, they were just Aztecs" (Rexroth 130). Lawrence's depiction of this created mysticism is not quite as skeptical as Rexroth would have it, but it is not without its deep ambivalences.

---

9   Rexroth's essay was written some fifty years ago. What he means by "political Indianism" is likely something quite different, more performative and superficial, than the aims of post- and anti-colonial theorists influenced by Said, Frantz Fanon, and others.

The Plumed Serpent does not embrace any imagined native Indian blood-consciousness entirely. Just so, disapprove as he might of the bullfight as, according to Charles Rossman, "cruel, repulsive, and hateful, an especially bloody European intrusion on native culture" (190), *The Plumed Serpent* does not condemn Europe for it. The novel's true enemy is not Europeanness but, rather, the sterile offspring of European liberalism, Americanism. American-style democracy is roundly mocked throughout the novel, and especially in the bullfight chapter. Kate's companions, Owen and Villiers, struggle to protect their personal space in the seats of the Mexico City plaza de toros, framed by the narrative comment: "Oh, home of liberty! Oh, land of the free! Which of these two men was to win in the struggle for conflicting liberty? Was the fat fellow free to sit between Villiers' feet, or was Villiers free to keep his foot space?" (PS 17). Owen and Villiers are repeatedly identified as Americans. Their Americanness is, for instance, why they, unlike Kate, are so "keen" on the bullfight idea (PS 12). As the bullfight develops, this "Americanism" appears to Kate increasingly alien and dangerous (PS 21). The fact that Villiers "would not even feel sick" strikes Kate as typical of the "Americanism which is coldly and unscrupulously sensational" (PS 21).[10] She is no prude, though. Much later she comes to understand "the old, terrible bond of the blood-unison of man, which made blood-sacrifice so potent a factor of life" (PS 434). For the time being, her European sensibility keeps her from taking pleasure in mere spectacle, but it also prepares her to appreciate the deeper aspects of the ritual that, though they may see it through to the end, Owen and Villiers will never grasp.

More specifically, it is Kate's Irishness that grants her this special receptivity. "'Mrs. Leslie is English—or rather Irish,'" says Owen (PS 39). Considering the kinds of cultural problems that so concerned Lawrence during the latter part of his career, his choice of an Irish heroine seems not to be coincidental. On the one hand, she is European, and so possessed of all the enlightened, rational, individualistic qualities that the more "primitive" parts of the world treat so roughly in Lawrence's fiction. On the other, her Irishness makes her not quite European, a condition the narrative probes in terms of her potential identification with Mexico's mysterious side:

> Ireland would not and could not forget that other old, dark, sumptuous living. The Tuatha de Danaan might be under the western sea. But they are under the living blood, too, never quite to be silenced. Now they have to come forth again, to a new connection. And the scientific, fair-and-square Europe has to mate once more with the old giants. (PS 432)

---

10 Lawrence's other traveling companion, the American Witter Bynner, chooses instead to conflate Europe and the United States, as against their common opposite, Mexico: "And we did stay [at the bullfight]," he writes, "though we were as revolted by the performance as are most Europeans and Americans. I supposed the audience had more than once seen outraged foreigners bolt away, and learned to ignore them as barbarians" (51–52).

The mating of the halves of Europe in Ireland is a primal scene from which white Americans like Owen and Villiers are excluded. Their "old giants" are buried even deeper than the Tuatha and, although geographically closer than Kate to the Mexican Indians, they are spiritually more distant. In the same way, Owen and Villiers can enjoy the bullfight as spectacle, but they cannot see its meaning.

Kate is a European, yet, like Lawrence, she detests the ritual of the bullfight more than the Americans do. At the same time, though she has come from across an ocean, she shares with the Mexicans Ramón, Cipriano, and the ancient Aztecs the awareness that eventually enables her to accept blood sacrifice as a necessary social and spiritual force. So something besides geographical proximity must account for the way characters in the novel are located in relation to the dark blood-consciousness all but welling up out of the Mexican soil, and to the blood rites into which it crystallizes. In a round-about way, John Xiros Cooper provides the framework for seeing that something as an apprehension of ritual inevitability and wholeness based on the negation of liberal humanist ideals. His use of the bullfight to interpret *The Waste Land* is based on a sound apprehension of ritual logic:

> The situation of the reader in *The Waste Land* is slightly more complex than that of a spectator at a football match. If we need an analogy for the reader in the poem, then we would do well to think of a spectator at a bullfight. The bullfight is not a competition between man and animal; it is a ritual sacrifice, and we take the same pleasure in it as we might take in the celebration of a Mass, not as an isolated spectator on the sidelines, but as a kind of participant. We let the primal form of the event be the framework in which the inevitable death of the bull is simply the culminating episode in a ritual narrative. The pleasure we are meant to take derives from the satisfaction of a properly completed rite and in the final, unambiguous affirmation of the values, embodied as myth, that underlie the visible celebration. The death of the beast is not an act of cruelty, but an act of closure to which the myth assigns a kind of redemptive force. To hope that the bull at the end might somehow escape the sword in his heart is analogous to the hope that Pontius Pilate might be able to talk Christ into getting himself a good lawyer. (47)

This passage appears rather unexpectedly halfway through *The Politics of Voice*, Cooper's monograph on *The Waste Land*, although its description of the tragic necessity of the bullfight is entirely consistent with Cooper's argument about the construction of a strategic inevitability in *The Waste Land*. "Ophelia and Philomel die," Cooper writes, "because they must ... Their deaths complete the rites to which they belong and in which they play a part" (47). Eliot uses this tragic insight not only to deflate the liberal-humanist belief in "the personal integrity of individuals, the redemptive potential of intimacy, free choice, and instrumental rationality" but also to "knock liberal-humanist sentimentality and weakness, the inner voice, right out of his readers' heads" (Cooper 48). The bullfight metaphor provides a provocative reading of the poem which enables a bold cross-cultural interpretive leap. What is more, Cooper's careful comparison of *The Waste Land* to a bullfight indirectly constructs a political lens through which to view other modernist artists' *actual* use of bullfights. It suggests that the bullfight, too, insofar as it shares *The Waste Land*'s ritual inevitability and violence, contradicts the assumptions of liberal humanism, an implication that provides a political point of entry into literary bullfights such as Lawrence's.[11]

Cooper's ritual logic illuminates the experience of Kate Leslie. Her journey through revolutionary Mexico begins at a bullfight and climaxes with her participation in the bloody sacrificial rites of a new Quetzalcoatl cult. At each stage, argues Chua, Kate's "distinctively European values are put into question," the "most distinctive" of which is "an ontology of individualism ... a psychology of personal uniqueness as well as an ethic of action" (101). The development of her character, Chua writes, reflects Lawrence's sense that "this individualism ... developing in the third world ... is dangerously over-developed in Europe" (101); Lawrence uses her "to dramatize the perils of the European individualist" (110). *The Plumed Serpent*, however, is not Cooper's *Waste Land*. It hardly traces a uniform trajectory toward any philosophical certainty. Rather, its thematic movement is one of wild oscillation between extremes of individual and community, body and mind, emotion and intellect, "Europe" and "Mexico." Lawrence's own "pendulum swing of attitudes" about Mexico, resulting from his "effort to accommodate his long-held—and cherished—ideal of the New World" with its "mundane reality," provide the pattern for Kate's thoughts (Rossman 208). Her European individualism is certainly battered along the way, but it does not finally succumb to its opposite, a merging of the self into a communal blood-consciousness. As Gates argues, "Kate can't decide whether or not to allow the horror of Mexico into her soul" (278). After her formal acquiescence and marriage to the Mexican Cipriano, she still knows "all the time it is I who don't altogether want them. I want myself to myself" (PS 461). She has accepted "the primeval assertion: *The blood is one blood. We are one blood* ... the assertion that swept away all individualism," including the "English-Germanic" individualism that divides people into social hierarchies (PS 433). Yet she maintains the egoism of the cat, whose "lifelong lustful enjoyment of its own isolated, isolated individuality" makes it powerful in and apart from moments of contact (PS 455). In this tension she is like Lawrence himself, who, according to Wyndham Lewis, advocated that "we should allow our [European] 'consciousness' to be overpowered by the alien 'consciousness' of the Indian," but who also wrote, "The Indian way of consciousness is different from and fatal to our way of consciousness ... We can never recover an old vision, once it has been supplanted" (qtd. in Meyers 318). Gates argues, again in Jungian

---

[11]   Although I will not be dealing with them here, other occurrences of the bullfight in modernist literature more broadly are also illuminated by Cooper's insight. Some examples are parts of Ezra Pound's Cantos XXVIII and CIII, Molly Bloom's torero in *Ulysses*, Wyndham Lewis's *Snooty Baronet*, Denis Devlin's "Meditation at Avila," "Mother Superior in the City of Mexico," and "Communication from the Eiffel Tower," and, of course, Ernest Hemingway's bullfighting works.

terms, that while "Lawrence does, indeed, over-romanticize the dark forces of the psyche, ... Kate, the voice of his soul, never ceases to criticize the dark, reptilian, oppressive, half-created forces she has discovered and can no longer live without" (278). Meyers agrees, concluding that Lawrence "did not, as Lewis claimed, want to surrender his European to an archaic consciousness" (318). The bullfight that opens *The Plumed Serpent* places this contest between supposedly modern "Europe" and the archaic "Indian" in vivid relief, even as it confounds and compounds those categories at every turn.

Kate's reaction to this bullfight is full of complex cultural and political implications. "Kate's disgust with the bullfight," Chua argues, "is significant, for the sport is not native to Mexico but imported from Europe" (105).[12] The very first lines of the chapter and the novel tether the spectacle Kate, Owen, and Villiers are about to witness to the Europe from which it originates: "It was the Sunday after Easter, and the last bull-fight of the season" (PS 11).[13] The crowd of Mexicans are made to look ridiculous for their European accouterments, their "sky-blue chiffon with brown chiffon hats and faces powdered to look like white marshmallows," their "black Sunday suits" (PS 14–16). The sense of incongruity becomes especially cruel when one Mexican man sits too close to the white trio. "'Don't you wonder who was his tailor?'" asks Kate, "with a flicker in her voice. Villiers looked at the femalish black coat of this Mexican, and made an arch grimace at Kate. 'I should say he hadn't one. Perhaps he did it himself'" (PS 18). In every part of the stadium, Europe and Mexico are violently juxtaposed, creating a tension that is unrelieved not just throughout the chapter but throughout the novel. Even the bulls themselves are European: "Four special bulls had been brought over from Spain for the occasion" (PS 11). The toreros, in contrast, are Mexican, so the ordinary colonial power dynamics are inverted, at least insofar as one feels the bull to be at a disadvantage in the bullfight. Certainly Kate feels this way, so vehemently that she does not wait to see even one Mexican matador kill a Spanish bull.

Lawrence's nonfiction account of his travels in Mexico reveals that he shared an unease between the poles of individual and community not only with Kate but also with the Mexican peasants. In *Mornings in Mexico*, he describes it as the essential condition of rural Mexican market days:

---

[12]   Chua's use of the term *sport* here seems careless rather than indicative of a fundamental misunderstanding of the corrida because in the same passage he refers to the bullfight as a "ritual killing" (105).

[13]   While bullfights were long used symbolically to shore up Spain's imperial rule in the new world, they have even more frequently been used to honor colonial liberation. For example, bullfights were "held to celebrate the restoration of Ferdinand VII and the abolition of the Constitution of 1812," Shubert writes, but also to celebrate Mexico's independence in 1821 (194). Indeed, "[f]or the lower classes in particular the bullfight was a vehicle of Mexican nationalism, a nationalism that included a strong dose of anti-Spanish sentiment" (212). See Shubert 193–95 and 211–14.

It is fulfilled, what they came to market for. They have sold and bought. But more than that, they have had their moment of contact and centripetal flow. They have been part of a great stream of men flowing to a centre, to the vortex of the market-place. And here they have felt life concentrate upon them, they have been jammed between the soft hot bodies of strange men come from afar, they have had the sound of stranger's [*sic*] voices in their ears ... [T]he natives curved in a strong swirl, towards the vortex of the market. Then on a strong swerve of repulsion, curved out and away again, into space. (79)

The same pendulum energy, frequently in the form of a furious attraction-repulsion response to the country itself, motivates Lawrence's Mexican travels and suggests a logic of travel that provides the novel with its quest motif. Both Lawrence and his fictional protagonist begin their journey in Mexico City and move farther and farther afield, motivated alternately by love and hate, desire for contact and desire for isolation, in search of an imagined ideal. For both, it is the bullfight that spurs them to flee the city, to seek Mexico's essential spirit elsewhere. In light of the "ontology of individualism" Kate brings to the bullfight, it is little surprise that it did not sit well with her, for the bullfight is a ritual. As such, it "appeals to ... the ... experience of collective unity at the cost of one's individual and more rational self. In fact," writes Jan Koster, "all otherness and distinctiveness, individual or external, is the natural enemy of the ritual mode" (217). The corrida as seen from Kate's point of view in "Beginnings of a Bull-fight" is uniformly loathsome. Chua writes that Kate finds the spectacle "offensive," which is to understate the profundity of her repulsion (105). Her entire being recoils in disgust from the ritual, which to her is a travesty of the noble ideals under which it is advertised: "Human cowardice and beastliness, a smell of blood, a nauseous whiff of bursten bowels!" (PS 20). She feels "crushed by a sense of human indecency, cowardice of two-legged humanity. In this 'brave' show she felt nothing but reeking cowardice" (PS 21). Even after she has left the plaza and had a cup of calming tea, "She could not get the bull-ring out of her mind, and something felt damaged in her inside ... [s]he felt as if she had eaten something which was giving her ptomaine poisoning" (PS 31). Offended indeed.

Ernest Hemingway posits that not only bullfighting audiences but, in fact, all people may be divided into "those who, to use one of the terms of the jargon of psychology, identify themselves with, that is, place themselves in the position of, animals, and those who identify themselves with human beings" (5). Given these choices, which, even in Hemingway's scheme, are more nuanced than the simple dualism might suggest, Kate is clearly among the former, the animal group, as was Lawrence. His traveling companion Witter Bynner observed that "Lawrence's head rose and sank with the bull's," that he became "as tense as the animal, with whom he was almost identifying himself" (49–50). When Kate's exasperation with the cape-work peaks, she exhorts the bull, "'Run at the *men*, idiot! ... Run at the men, not at the cloaks'" (PS 22). Afterwards, she allows that "'if I knew that some of those toreadors were going to be tossed by the bull, I'd go to see another bull-fight.[14] Ugh, how I detest them! The longer I live the more loathsome the human species becomes to me. *How* much nicer the bulls are!'" (30). Meyers argues that "the novel charts the *degeneration* of Kate from a woman who is revolted by the cruelty of the bullfight to one who is indifferent to Cipriano's bloody executions," but this is not quite accurate (322, my emphasis). The image of her later indifference is, rather, contained in her early hostility. Hemingway proposes that animal-lovers "are capable of greater cruelty to human beings than those who do not identify themselves readily with animals" (5). Lawrence, venting his own frustration, declared, "[the bull]'s the only one among them with heart or brain ... He's not the brute; they're the brutes. He abhors them and so do I" (Bynner 50). Certainly Kate hovers on the brink of violence throughout her bullfight experience, and a palpable cruelty toward humans pervades the chapter as a whole. In a twist on Hemingway's formula, the Kate-dominated narrative voice consistently animalizes humans, particularly Mexicans, but without encouraging identification or sympathy. The stadium is "a big concrete beetle trap" surrounded by and full of "lousy men" (PS 12). Mexican men looking for their parties are "lost mongrels" that "prowled back and forth" disconcertingly near Kate's feet (PS 16). The one who does invade the personal space of Kate's group is a "beetle-like intruder" whom she and Owen are "tense with will to annihilate" (PS 18). Owen looks at the man "as he might glance at a dog with rabies, when it had its back to him" (PS 18). The bullfighters and ring attendants, too, are "mongrel men" whom Kate enjoys watching "skipping for safety" (PS 22).

She seems less an animal-lover than a human-hater. Not even her companions Owen and Villiers or their Polish acquaintance escape her scorn. Indeed, Kate alone among the humans in the chapter is not made the object of categorical derision. In light of the symmetry between her views and those of the narration, as well as the biographical information about Lawrence, she appears to be invested with full moral authority in judging the bullfight, and her disgust at the human elements of the corrida is even further cast in terms of class, gender, and nationality. Kate and company begin their bullfight adventure with ideas of mixing with the people. They choose seats in the Sun rather than the Shade both "to economize" and owing to Owen's desire "to sit among the people" (PS 11). Any hint of fellow feeling, though, is immediately squelched. Well before the bullfight even begins, Kate declares, "I really hate common people ... How I detest them!" (PS 14). Not for Kate Henri de Montherlant's bullfight as "the great unifier of all the social classes" (*Les Bestiaires*, qtd. in *Los Toros* 46). She finds the absence of a truly noble element a great disappointment:

> So this was a bull-fight! Kate already felt a chill of disgust. In the seats of
> the Authorities were very few people, and certainly no sparkling ladies in

---

[14]   The word *toreador* does not exist in Spanish, where a bullfighter is always a *torero* (or a *picador*, a *banderillero*, or a *matador*, more specifically). The generally attributed source of the adulteration *toreador* is Bizet's nineteenth-century opera *Carmen*. It is, nevertheless, the term Lawrence and his characters use.

high tortoise-shell combs and lace mantillas. A few common-looking people, bourgeois with not much taste, and a couple of officers in uniform. The President had not come. There was no glamour, no charm. A few commonplace people in an expanse of concrete. (PS 18–19)

Bynner noted the presence at the Easter bullfight of several "dignitaries" in the presidential box, including "three or four bright-fluttering women who wore flowered mantillas and high combs" (48).[15] Even the real-life President, Álvero Obregón, had been a revolutionary leader, so that, in revolutionary Mexico, his presence would likely have signified something more like solidarity than class stratification. Lawrence has deviated from his real-life experience to emphasize Kate's social views. The novel uses the President's absence to suggest the missing elements of nobility and authority: "The newspapers had said that the President would attend. But the Presidents are scarce at bull-fights in Mexico, nowadays" (PS 15). As the bullfight progresses, Kate's "breeding and her natural pride were outraged," and it becomes apparent that this is as much due to feeling herself part of a mass of commoners as to the incomprehensible, to her, violence of the spectacle itself (PS 21). Even Owen, the socialist, is prone to a kind of elitism. The first lines of the chapter explain that "Owen, who was a great socialist, disapproved of bull-fights," but they do not explain the connection between the politics and the form (PS 11). Presumably, it has to do with the commercial aspects of bullfighting, the formation of the toreros into a small cultural elite, or the intuitive, though unexamined, connection between the political right wing and rituals like the bullfight. In any event, the grounds on which he disapproves of the corrida are anything but socialist ones. "As a socialist, Owen disapproved" of Kate's social snobbery prior to the bullfight, but "his own real self, as far as he had any left, hated common rowdiness just as much as Kate did" (PS 14). The association of bullfighting with wealth or the political right (or, rather, of disapproval of the bullfight with the political left) is further undercut by the fact that, although Kate, Owen, and Villiers take in their bullfight during the heat of Mexican proletarian revolution, there is no shortage of enthusiastic Mexican workers to fill Mexico City's plaza de toros, even in 1923 the largest in the world.

Middle-class snobbery is one thing, but Kate's sentiments take on a harder political edge as the corrida approaches:

A diversion was created by the entrance, opposite, of the military bands, with their silver and brass instruments under their arms. There were three sets. The chief band climbed and sat on the right, in the big bare tract of concrete reserved

---

[15] The seating arrangements in bullfighting arenas, particularly in Latin America, had long been fraught with questions of class, including after the war of 1812 when controversy arose as to whether the Mexican nobility, greatly enlarged, would enjoy the same privileges of balcony seating as they had previously. "Questions of who got what balcony," writes Shubert, "now also spoke to something much more serious: the very legitimacy of Spanish rule" (194).

for the Authorities. These musicians wore dark grey uniforms trimmed with rose colour, and made Kate feel almost reassured, as if it were Italy and not Mexico City. (PS 15)

That Kate takes comfort in the martial presence, even of a band of musicians, confirms at once her displeasure with "mob authority" and her positive disposition toward symbols of official power. That this heartening martial presence reminds her, in 1923, of Italy encourages her association with a specific strain of power politics concurrently on the rise in Europe under the name of fascism. Lawrence's trip to Mexico in 1923 followed upon a period spent in Italy during the civil war, just prior to Mussolini's takeover of power.[16] Lawrence, like Kate, was far too skeptical and independent to countenance fascism as such, but this episode in "Beginnings of a Bull-fight" is certainly written so as to foreground the kinds of social disorder to which fascism addressed itself in the 1920s, and the appeal (but also the futility) of certain military and symbolic means of doing so, means with which fascism soon became popularly synonymous. Lawrence uses the presence of the bands to stage a contest between competing political forces, Authority and the People, even within a supposedly united popular front. "'*La musica! La musica!*' shouted the mob, with the voice of mob authority. They were the People, and the revolutions had been their revolutions, and they had won them all. The bands were their bands, present for their amusement" (PS 15). The musicians, however, view things quite differently. They sit "in as much pomp as they could muster ... in lordly authority," refusing, for the time being, to play. They

> were military bands, and it was the army which had won all the revolutions. So the revolutions were *their* revolutions, and they were present for their own glory alone ... *La musica!* The shout became brutal and violent. Kate always remembered it. *La musica!* The band peacocked its nonchalance. The shouting was a great yell: the degenerate mob of Mexico City! (PS 15)

Finally the band does strike up, but only briefly. When the music stops, the mob atmosphere returns with a vengeance, as "the masses in the middle, unreserved seats suddenly burst and rushed down on to the lowest, reserved seats ... round and about our frightened trio" (PS 16). The band, symbolic of order and authority, could not protect them from the "People," and "Kate now sat among the crowd" (PS 16). It is an experience she cannot bear for long, not even to the conclusion of the first bull's turn in the ring. Here she seems to embody Lawrence's own aversion to mobs. In *Mornings in Mexico*, he describes the type of people, "like myself, who have a horror of serving in a mass of men, or even of being mixed up with a mass of men" (62). That horror no doubt also diminished whatever appeal fascism held for him.

---

[16] "By the time he returned" to Italy, writes Meyers, "in November 1925, the opposition had been destroyed, the dictatorship was absolute and civil order had been restored" (248). *The Plumed Serpent* had been completed in February 1925 and was published in 1926.

Upon the arrival of the toreros in the arena, the "last of Kate's illusions concerning bull-fights came down with a flop," that is, before the bullfight even begins (PS 19). The bullfighters are described as "four grotesque and effeminate-looking fellows in tight, ornate clothes ... With their rather fat posteriors and their squiffs of pigtails and their clean-shaven faces, they looked like eunuchs, or women in tight pants, these precious toreadors" (PS 15).[17] The first (and only) bull Kate sees is similarly unimpressive. He is "a smallish, dun-coloured bull" who finds himself "utterly at a loss" in the middle of the ring (PS 19). He is not the *toro bravo* who seeks out a fight; rather, "the little bull trotted on round the ring, looking for a way to get out" (PS 19). Rather improbably, he leaps the barrier surrounding the ring four times in his attempt to escape.[18] He gores the first horse not maliciously but "rather vaguely, as if not quite knowing what he ought to do" (PS 20). Before long,

> a bull seemed to her a fool. She had always been afraid of bulls, fear tempered with reverence of the great Mithraic beast. And now she saw how stupid he was, in spite of his long horns and his massive maleness. Blindly and stupidly he ran at the rag ... Blindly and foolishly the bull ran ducking its horns each time at the rag, just because the rag fluttered. (PS 21–22)

Although Owen and Villiers know a very little about how the bullfight works, and share their knowledge with Kate, she seems unaware that a fighting bull has never faced a man on foot before. Thus it has no idea that the man, not the cape, is the real threat, although a smart bull begins to learn.

It is crucial that, since she leaves before the cape- and sword-work, the *faena*, of even one matador, Kate misses the best opportunity to improve her estimation of the torero's craft as well as of the bull itself. In the *faena*, the matador and the bull are alone in the ring. The man uses a much smaller cape than the magenta-and-gold ones employed in the early stages of the corrida, thus deliberately placing himself in much closer proximity to the bull and to injury or death. The picadors on horseback and other assistants are gone, and the bullfight is reduced to its core image: a lone man and a bull dancing, so to speak, each carrying the other's death and his own in the movements of his body. As the corrida progresses, the bull grows weaker but more dangerous. He begins to suspect that the man, not the cape, is his true enemy, and, though his body is tiring, his horns have lost none of

---

[17] Here again Bynner's account differs notably from Lawrence's fictional rendering: "On the exact moment advertised ... a square colorful procession strutted with music into the arena toward the President's box to make bows, with waists and trim buttock held tautly, shoulders back; two groups of fine-stepping *toreros* ... " (49). Lawrence was apparently unimpressed. "'The right symbol!' muttered Lawrence" upon the arrival of the mule teams, "'They're all jackasses'" (49).

[18] Improbable because a bull jumping the barrier is seen as a sign of cowardice, not bravery. He would almost certainly have been removed from the ring for a substitute bull, especially on such an important occasion. Lawrence's account of the bullfight is factually erroneous in only a few minor details. Kate's bull also paws the ground, which, contrary to the popular notion, is also seen is a sign of cowardice, not bravery.

their killing power. His movements become less frantic and more deliberate, and the small space, containing death, between himself and the man grows continually narrower. Had she stayed, Kate's chances of seeing a matador gored would have greatly improved.

Since Kate misses the *faena*, the bullfight's *raison d'etre*, her responses are truly to the "beginnings of a bull-fight," the name Lawrence chose for his correspondingly truncated chapter. It seems a perfect demonstration of the rightness of Hemingway's view that "[t]he aficionado, or lover of the bullfight, may be said, broadly, then, to be one who has this sense of the tragedy and ritual of the fight so that the minor aspects are not important except as they relate to the whole" (9). Kate, like Lawrence in Mexico City, cannot see past the "minor aspects" or preliminaries to the whole, nor did Lawrence see much need to try to do so. He categorically refused Bynner's argument for seeing it through. In the latter's account, Lawrence rises to leave but is temporarily dissuaded: "'It sickens me too, Lorenzo,' I agreed. 'But hadn't we better see at least one round of it through, to know what we're talking about when we say we don't like it?'" To which Lawrence responds bitterly, "'I don't need to see a round through, as you call it. The trouble is that you're as bloodthirsty as the rest of them'" (50). There is no whole, in other words, that could redeem the violence of the preliminary *tercios* for Lawrence. According to Hemingway's logic, Lawrence, while possessing a great deal of ritual enthusiasm and curiosity, was short on the ritual "sense" required to appreciate the bullfight.

In a full corrida, six bulls are killed (in the novel it is five), and each death unfolds in three parts or acts (*tercios* in Spanish): *picadores*, *banderillas*, and *faena*. When Lawrence wrote *The Plumed Serpent*, in May and June of 1923, he, too, had never seen a *faena*. Thus the impressions of the bullfight he is able to convey are limited to less than two-thirds of the entire progression, and to only one sixth of the progressions that together constitute a bullfight. Bynner suggests that Lawrence did not stay even for the *tercio* of the *banderillas*, although it is approximated in the novel. "Lawrence might have enjoyed the birdlike poise" of the banderillero, he writes (52). He further suggests that seeing a *faena* might partly have redeemed the bullfight for Lawrence, describing the first *faena* of that Easter Sunday this way:

> Then came the matador, his scarlet cape hung athwart a long sword. Here came a sudden, sure, personal authority. Lawrence would have liked this presence, this sureness, this motion of a bird with wings slow, then swift. This was different. Directly facing the bull, choosing a moment when the horns hung toward him at precisely the right slant, this lordly authority, this death-dealer, thrust the *espada*[19] half to its hilt in the vulnerable spot exposed between the lowered shoulder blades. There with the banderillos [*sic*] the sword joined a halo like a section of the nimbus around Our Lady of Guadalupe; I would tell that to Lawrence. (52)

---

[19]   *Espada* is the curved sword the matador uses to kill the bull.

He enthusiastically describes a later *faena* of Juan Silveti (along with Rodolfo Gaona one of the headlining matadors of the Easter corrida), again noting the impact that seeing it might have had on Lawrence:

> Silveti kneeled to let the clumsy beast attack, as ever, the cloak instead of the man. By adroit passes, he attracted two or three charges in the customary time of one, then walked nonchalantly away with his back to the bull, dragging his cape at his heels. Finally he placed a handkerchief on the ground and succeeded in so directing the victim's attack that he could thrust the *espada* without budging from his small white foothold. The game needed these variations, these graces, this ballet precision; Johnson and I reluctantly confessed to each other that the crowd's enjoyment was not altogether blood lust, and wished that the Lawrences might have seen the artistry ... (53)

What is perhaps most important about Bynner's observations is that, although he had been able to see the bullfight through and appreciated something of its purpose and beauty, he leaves the stadium vowing, with Willard Johnson, "that it was our last bullfight" (54). Whether or not he has enjoyed the ritual, he has understood it because he has seen it through, acquiring in the process some sense of the ritual's tragic inevitability.

It cannot be said, however, that Lawrence had less ritual sense than Bynner. "Audience participation," writes Eileen Fischer, "persists as a standard performance value in bullfighting," and Lawrence's flight from the ring betrays his recognition that his own presence constituted a kind of participation (248).[20] Also, when his "nerves exploded" (Bynner 51) and he could take no more, he rebuked the crowd, not the bullfighters, implicitly acknowledging the continuity between audience and performance that characterizes ritual. "Fortunately," writes Bynner, "people were too intent on the ring to notice him, and only a few of them heard a red-bearded Englishman, risen from his seat, excoriating cowards and madmen ... denouncing the crowd in Spanish" (51). Lawrence's awareness of the bullfight spectators' implication in the action, which drove him from the plaza, is of the very ritual stuff that so appealed to dramatists such as Yeats, Eliot, and Auden. He did not distinguish between what happens on the arena's sand and in its seats, thereby demonstrating some sense of the corrida as a ritual whole from which the spectator-as-part cannot be dissociated.

Kate follows Lawrence almost exactly in her reaction to the bullfight and, as has been noted, in her subsequent Mexican odyssey. While a wounded matador might have soothed her pragmatic indignation at the corrida's injustice, staying

---

[20] Taken to an extreme, but not unrepresentative, length, this audience participation in the bullfight may take the form of an *espontáneo*, "the over-zealous spectator" who leaps into the arena in an attempt to insert himself into the action of the bullfight (Fischer 248). Such an (illegal) entrance has provided more than one torero with his first public exposure, even his first bullfighting experience. See, for instance, the story of Manuel Benítez, "El Cordobés," in *Or I'll Dress You in Mourning* by Larry Collins and Dominique Lapierre.

for at least one *faena* might also have symbolically satisfied some of the longings that prompt her flight from the plaza and the city into remote Mexico and Ramón's Quetzalcoatl cult. For the ultimate purpose of this cult, all but irresistible to Kate, is to "to bring the great opposites into contact and into unison again … bringing together the two great human impulses to a point of fusion" (PS 435). In a sufficiently "transporting *faena*," writes Fischer, opposites, as well as "the dancers, the dance, and the audience converge" (253). The contest between Kate's desire for communal contact and her fear of massification is only one of those motivating her quest but also symbolically resolved in the bullfight. An equally urgent division between archetypes of masculinity and femininity keeps Kate in a state of anxiety throughout the novel but is likewise repaired in the symbolic action of the corrida. There is no agreed-upon gender signification in the various elements of the bullfight, but a residue of gender nonetheless clings to them. It was certainly not lost on Bynner, who wrote of the horse's goring: "There had been something phallic, Lawrence might have noted, in this fierce penetration, this rape of entrails, this bloody glut" (51). "Beginnings of a Bull-fight" makes plain that Lawrence had not failed to appreciate the phallic, or at least sexual, resonance of such scenes:

> [T]he bull lowered his head and pushed his sharp, flourishing horns in the horse's belly, working them up and down inside there with a sort of vague satisfaction …
>
> Kate knew what was coming. Before she could look away, the bull had charged on the limping horse from behind, the attendants had fled, the horse was up-ended absurdly, one of the bull's horns between his hind legs and deep in his inside. Down went the horse, collapsing in front, but his rear was still heaved up, with the bull's horn working vigorously up and down inside him. (PS 20–23)

Kate's revulsion is so thorough, and her viewpoint so dominates the novel's presentation of the bullfight, that there is little chance of the reader being other than sympathetically disgusted by this sexual(ized) violence. But if in this context figurative rape appalls Kate, it later appears to her quite differently in the context of her marriage, after which she concludes, "'Without Cipriano to touch me and limit me and submerge my will, I shall become a horrible, elderly female'" (PS 457). Her "sexual apotheosis," writes Meyers, "is merely her sexual degradation" (323).

Again, Meyers makes a strong point, but he makes it a bit too simply. His reading of Kate is limited by the realist-political interpretive mode that Wexler identifies as too often stripping Lawrence's fiction of its complex symbolic resonance. In the same passage, Kate affirms "'I must have both'" limitation and freedom, and she is not speaking merely of sex (PS 457). She desires to be dominated, yes, but she also desires to dominate, sexually but not only sexually, a paradoxical aspiration the bullfight renders concrete, if only Kate had brought her psychic angst to bear on one *faena*. In his observation above about "something phallic,"

Bynner was speaking of the goring of a horse during the first *tercio* of the bullfight, but the same description applies equally well to the corrida's other penetrations, that of the bull by the matador's sword and that of the unlucky matador by the bull's horn. There is indeed "something phallic" in all of these, but the attempt to identify that "something" is invariably short-circuited by the intervention of its opposite, something soft, open, receptive. Thus, Bynner's imprecision, by allowing for "the proliferation of meanings that symbolism requires" (Wexler 60–61), is surprisingly well suited to the description of the sexual signification of the corrida, a symbolic event. As Wexler argues, the "extreme acts modernists used as symbols" (60), no doubt including this bullfight, are chosen not for the clarity of their association with a given historical or political referent but for their capacity to push interpretation beyond the reach of everyday categories.

Each of the principal actors in the bullfight alternately (and sometimes simultaneously) wears the sign of both male and female. Both bull and man are supremely phallic in their weaponry, yet each is as much recipient as deliverer.[21] The bullfight critic Carlos Luis Alvarez insists upon "the essential womanliness of the bullfighter" in rather Lawrentian terms:

> [In] the enticing and fleeting grace of his curvilinear and morbid play, in addition to power [*sic*] the 'eternal feminine,' like the ornamental passes and the showing off, as against the rectilinear agitation of the bull and the elementary power of its blood … [W]e see the divine genesial virility—the 'young bull from Heaven'—and the recondite mysteries of the waters in perpetual motion—like the bullfighter—because the moon moves them; starting the march toward integration. (42)

Alvarez also likens the dressing of the matador prior to the fight to that of a bride before marriage. "Bride and bullfighter already are on the threshold of drama: the moment has come when they will have to be locked up alone with what is their definitive 'opposite'" (42). Fischer, however, argues that it is the bull's entrance into the arena that "signifies a virgin's ritual debut" and that the "inevitable *peripeteia* occurs when both the matador and bull, along with the audience *aficionados*, 'know' that the man will soon 'have' and control the virgin bull" (249–52). The tenability of both views is a testament to how "mysteriously" the sexual "'signifiers' … shift and float" in the corrida (Fischer 249). The "march toward integration" of shifting signs is completed, Alvarez and Fischer agree, in the moment of truth, the killing of the bull. In what Alvarez, like most taurine critics, calls "the most perfect form for killing a bull," the matador does not move, does not take the sword to the bull, but rather allows the bull to run itself onto the sword while he remains stationary. It is "to receive and kill at the same time."

---

[21] Lawrence's gored horse unintentionally echoes another instance of this sexualized reciprocity. The majority of bullfighting deaths, owing to the usual level of the bull's horns, are caused by gorings in the area that includes the matador's groin and rectum. Many matadors, that is, have died in the manner of Lawrence's unfortunate horse.

In this form, called killing *recibiendo*, Alvarez sees the supreme fulfillment of ritual (42). "In this," he writes, "is something more than mere terminology. In this is the deepest secret of love and death, the final cataclysm, the great confusion of opposites" (42).[22] At the end of the novel, as Kate struggles to reconcile her contending impulses within the rigid gender codes of the Quetzalcoatl cult, she momentarily rests on the idea that a "*positive* passivity" is her power (PS 438). By that point, her capacity to embrace paradox has begun to develop, whereas, at the beginning of her quest, it is no help to her in understanding what little she sees of a bullfight.

In addition to being more dangerous than the ordinary form, killing *recibiendo*, explains Alvarez, "today is not in vogue because nowadays the bullfighter does not want to fulfill his role of female, which is precisely what would make him a great bullfighter" (42). We do not see Kate's toreros do any killing, but they are nonetheless relentlessly feminized, and not to the advantage of their stature as bullfighters. Just as their European costume strikes Kate as ludicrously incongruous, she sees their appearance as a grotesque inversion of a farcical masculinity ("they looked like eunuchs or women in tight pants"), and Owen compares the "chief toreador" after the bullfight to "a male Venus who is never undressed ... lying on his bed like Venus with a fat cigar, listening to her lovers" (PS 32). This easy yet comical androgyny both anticipates and counters the symbology of absolute gender that Kate is to encounter in her experiences with Ramón and Cipriano. Its appeal, though, in the context of ritual violence, is as yet nonexistent for her.

The Plumed Serpent ends on a note of utter uncertainty. Kate, Ramón, and Cipriano argue around and around about the necessity of her going, encompassing a return not just to Europe but to resolute individualism and a life of the mind, versus her desire to stay, implying a full embrace of the blood-consciousness "primitive" Mexico has awakened in her: "'I don't really want to go away from you ... 'You don't really want me' ... 'Yes, I want you!' ... 'I want myself to myself,' ... 'Then go! Oh certainly go!' ... 'I knew you didn't really want me' ... 'You don't want me to go, do you?'" and finally, "'You won't let me go!' she said to him" (PS 461–62). It is the point to which the logic of her journey and of the novel has brought her, a point at which no closure is possible, only perpetual vacillation over the same questions she brought to the bullfight, condensed into her relationship with Cipriano. Absent the closure of tragedy, the search for the reconciliation of all oppositions must end in this way.

---

[22]   A more common form of killing, *volapié*, achieves a different kind of metaphorical fusion, not so much of genders as of life and death. "If performed ideally," writes Fischer, "the final stroke enables the matador to levitate, like Grotowski's actors, over the bull's horns. This entrancing thrust ... unites the flying man and the dying bull. The penetrating sword connects the sacrificer and his victim: the double. One ascends when the other falls" (253).

End of a Bullfight

The next piece Lawrence wrote about Mexican bullfighting, though, has that tragic ending. As a result, "None of That!" holds together in a way that *The Plumed Serpent* does not. The change is in no small part due to Lawrence's developing sense of the bullfight as a ritual tragedy, so that "None of That!" proceeds with the ordering inevitability he could not build into *The Plumed Serpent*, try as he might. In Wexler's terms, it might be said that Lawrence's early reading of the bullfight, as far as can be inferred from the novel and Bynner's account, was predominantly realistic, not symbolic, whereas the treatment he gives of it in "None of That!" is clearly intended to foreground its symbolic value. Symbolism, as Kertzer and Koster have demonstrated, is but a small step from ritual. At the same time, among the oppositions that ritual reconciles is that of real and symbolic meaning.

"None of That!", written in Italy in 1927, is, as Conchita Díez-Medrano claims, "first and foremost an embedded narrative" (304). First, it is a story of Mexico embedded in a story of Europe. It is more specifically the story of Ethel Cane as told by the "Mexican exile," Colmenares, to an unnamed first-person narrator in a Venetian café ("None of That!" 211). Beyond embedding the narrative in these framing devices, "None of That!" differs from "Beginnings of a Bull-fight" in its treatment of the corrida. While none of the characters in "None of That!" is to be equated with Lawrence himself, of course (although the "I" seems a good deal like him), one can easily feel the difference having seen a bullfight to its conclusion makes on Lawrence as a writer of bullfight stories. The later story has a composure quite unlike the extreme agitation of "Beginnings of a Bull-fight," a difference which might be attributed not only to the structural devices insulating Lawrence from his subject but also to the comfort afforded by his physical distance from unsettling Mexico. The ending of "None of That!" is enormously unsettling, but it is not, as *The Plumed Serpent* is, unsettled.

At the center of the story is the relationship between Ethel Cane and the famous Mexican bullfighter, Cuesta. Cuesta's friend, Luis Colmenares, tells the tale of their romance, such as it was, to the "I" narrator as they sit together in Venice. Although Colmenares is transported by his recollections of Cuesta's brilliance as a torero, the narrator, like Kate, is initially skeptical: "'But he wasn't interesting, was he?' I said. 'Wasn't he just a—a bull-fighter—a brute?'" ("None of That!" 211) Colmenares, though, is emphatic about Cuesta's artistry:

> '[I]n the bull-ring, he mesmerised everybody. He could draw the natural magnetism of everybody to him—everybody. And then he was marvellous, he played with death as if it were a kitten, so quick, quick as a star, and calm as a flower, and all the time, laughing at death. It is marvellous he was never killed … And then suddenly it was he who killed the bull, with one hand, one stroke. He was very strong. And the bull sank down at his feet, heavy with death. The people went mad! And he just glanced at them, with his yellow eyes, in a cool, beautiful contempt, as if he were an animal that wrapped the skin of death round him.' ("None of That!" 213)

As Colmenares's story unfolds, the parallel between Cuesta's work with a bull and his work with Ethel Cane becomes more and more pronounced. "'At first I think he took many women. But later,'" says Colmenares, "'I think he would have liked to whip them, or kill them, for pursuing him.'"

> 'Only he must enchant them when he was in the bull-ring,' said I.

> 'Yes! But that was like sharpening his knife on them' ("None of That!" 214)

And enchant them he does. Colmenares describes Cuesta's performance with a bull:

> And Cuesta opened his arms to him with a little smile, but endearing, lovingly endearing, as a man might open his arms to a little maiden he really loves, but really, for her to come to his body, his warm, open body, to come so softly. So he held his arms out to the bull with love. And that was what fascinated the women. They screamed and they fainted, longing to go into the arms of Cuesta, against his soft, round body, that was more yearning than a fico. ("None of That!" 221–22)

Like her predecessor Kate, Ethel is a woman of powerfully conflicting impulses of body and mind, contact and isolation, sex and what she calls "the life of the imagination" ("None of That!" 217). Unlike Kate's, Ethel's development is all but explicitly depicted for the reader as corresponding to a tragic code, figured here as the bullfight. It is Colmenares, of course, an aficionado, who is responsible for creating this correspondence.

Indeed, he seems driven by the same emotional patterns in and outside of the plaza de toros, and the analogy of the *faena* begins to color his depictions of his relationships with both Cuesta and Ethel. "'He fascinated me,'" he says of Cuesta, "'but I always hated him. I would have liked to stick him as he stuck the bulls'" ("None of That!" 221). He describes Ethel in virtually the same terms, as though she were the matador and he the bull:

> '[S]he would draw me out, draw me out … Sometimes I stayed till after midnight … And I think some part of her wanted me to make love to her. But I didn't. I couldn't! I was there, under her influence, in her power. She could draw me out … marvellously … But … I couldn't even touch her. I couldn't even take her hand in mine. It was a physical impossibility. When I was away from her, I could think of her and of her white, healthy body with a voluptuous shiver. I could even run to her apartment, intending to kiss her and make her my mistress that very night. But the moment I was in her presence, it left me. I could not touch her.' ("None of That!" 219)

Here is the ambiguity of the *faena* missing from *The Plumed Serpent*. The matador kills what he loves, woos women by coaxing a bull, playing, as Colmenares says, with death. The logic of tragedy dictates that this dance of attraction and repellence ends only in death, and so it does here. It is largely Ethel herself, Colmenares is convinced, who keeps him away. "'She too had a lot of power. She could send out of her body a repelling energy, to compel people to submit to her will'" ("None of That!" 217). Nor can she tolerate the thought of giving her body to a man absent an "imaginative" connection between them: ""'I'm afraid my body has fallen—not fallen in love with him, but fallen *for* him,'"" she says of Cuesta. ""'It's abject! And if I can't get my body on its feet again, and either forget him, or else get him to make it an imaginative act with me—I—I shall kill myself—'"" ("None of That!" 227). The tragedy is completed when she does just that, having been gang-raped by members of Cuesta's *cuadrilla*: "'She actually went to Cuesta's house that night ... And there in his bedroom he handed her over to half-a-dozen of his bull-ring gang'" ("None of That!" 229). Placing the final stamp of inevitability on the story, the note she leaves Colmenares reads, ""'It is as I told you!'"" ("None of That!" 229)

It is not easy to redeem such brutality through the consolations of fictional structure. However, Díez-Medrano has provided an intriguing analysis of the way the narrative of "None of That!" implicates the reader in the rape of its heroine. Díez-Medrano probes the gender signification of the story and, to a lesser extent, of the corrida itself, with real insight, highlighting, for instance, the intense homoeroticism underlying Colmenares's obvious sexism, and the strain placed on his masculinity by the competing gender codes of Mexico, America, and Europe. As a meditation on the relationship of sexual politics and narrative structure, Díez-Medrano's argument is formidable. Still, the endpoint, the referent, of her reading is the rape, beyond which her realist approach does not avail. She does not trace the kinds of ambiguities the frame story creates to the ritual at the heart of the story, although they are clearly present there. The corrida is more than a conveniently colorful backdrop to the description of Ethel's plight; it is an integral part of the way that plight takes on narrative shape. As such, it dictates that one read the associated violences of narrative, toreo, and rape-suicide as more than equivalents in a gender-political cipher. That Ethel's death is the fulfillment of what the story's form itself sets in motion is indeed a frightening realization, as is the fact that her being American makes her a more easily disposable victim in Lawrence's fictional scheme. The danger, though, is not so much that one will miss the fact of her victimization by Cuesta or even Colmenares, the narrator, Lawrence, or the reader. Far more likely is that one will miss the ambiguities inherent in Ethel's own imaginative patterns and in her and Cuesta's pursuit of one another. The danger is, rather, that one will not see that her predicament has been figured all along in the ritual of the bullfight, where the "imaginative" dance always ends in death. Told in only a slightly different way, the story might have ended with Cuesta dead. Stories abound of bullfighters who die after sacrificing an imaginative ideal on the altar of sex. What redeems the bullfight in all of these cases is that it figures in comparative safety the elusive reconciliation of opposites which, pursued beyond the boundaries of ritual space, kills not as symbolic action but in vile earnest.

In an early stage of his Mexican journey, Lawrence offered to Bynner his wholesale judgment of Mexico as "'a land of death'" (Bynner 40). "It's all of one piece,'" he said, what the Aztecs did, what Cortes did, what Diaz did—the wholesale, endless cruelty. The land itself does it to whoever [*sic*] lives here. The heart has been cut out of the land. That's why hearts had to be cut out of its people. It goes on and on and will always go on ... Look at this dead soil all around us—the dagger-fingered cactus—the knife-edged sun! It's all death. (Bynner 40)

Here, instead of recognizing his observation as a demonstration of the "inescapable entanglements between cultural narratives" (Thompson 225), Lawrence loads all this death and darkness upon an imaginary Mexican identity. Although Cortes was a European and Diaz was the leader of Mexico under a Europe-derived system of government, the death they dealt was not, in Lawrence's view, a product of the mind of Europe but, rather, of a Mexican essence. Perhaps most surprisingly, although the clearest and, to Lawrence, most despicable picture of death and "'wholesale, endless cruelty'" he found in Mexico was the Spanish bullfight, and although he emphasized its Europeanness at every opportunity in his fiction, he nonetheless insisted on seeing Mexico not as the receptacle but as the origin of the violence. His writing about Mexico, particularly in *The Plumed Serpent*, suggests that such either-or propositions about culture as this dictate that the pointless cruelty go "on and on and will always go on." It also suggests, in spite of itself, that the ritual structure of the bullfight modeled the integration and confusion of categories—political as well as symbolic—that might rescue Europe from perpetually chasing its own hidden face to the ends of the earth.

Chapter 5
The European Wound:
Bullfighting and the Spanish Civil War

In the interwar years, the most compelling theories of the corrida's origins were those positing prehistoric roots. The discovery, early in the twentieth century, of paleolithic and neolithic bull paintings on the walls of Spanish caves, followed by their exhibition (as reproductions) in 1918, gave momentum to the thesis that bullfighting was native to the Iberian peninsula and preceded Roman or Arabic influence (McCormick 10). In the 1930s Sir Arthur Evans's research on Crete gave rise to the argument that the modern bullfight derived from ancient Minoan bull practices, though many nationalistic Spaniards resisted this possibility (Shubert 6; McCormick 11). While both of these theories sparked the imaginations of some modern observers, rarely do they obtrude upon Spanish Civil War poetry, which almost invariably treats the corrida in its present immediacy as a modern ritual— one perhaps with vague ancient roots but whose current form is the product of only some two hundred years' refinement. Conjectures about its historical roots have their place, but for the vast majority of bullfighting spectators, Spanish and otherwise, these simply do not obtain in the experience of watching a *corrida de toros*. What does obtain is the sense that "the bull is the thread that ties all of [Spain's] regions together" (Douglass 7). "The bullfights," wrote León de Arroyal, "are the sinews of our society, the fuel of our patriotism, and the workshops of our political customs" (qtd. in Shubert 150). One British poem after another shows that just as the bullfight was Spain's political workshop, the Spanish Civil War was the political workshop for Europe, the arena in which the increasingly urgent questions of tradition and modernity, continuity and difference, order and freedom were contested on the ground, as well as in literature.

Auden was one among countless British writers in the interwar period to have been moved by the Spanish Civil War and drawn toward it for the way it seemed to concretize personal concerns. Like so many others, he found that,

> On that arid square, that fragment nipped off from hot
> Africa, soldered so crudely to inventive Europe;
>> On that tableland scored by rivers,
> Our thoughts have bodies; the menacing shapes of our fever
> Are precise and alive. ("Spain" 53–54)

George Orwell, who fought and was shot in the war, took issue with the implication of involvement from an Auden whose sojourn in Spain was brief and fairly insulated. A related, more common, criticism is that Auden's poem itself maintains a secure distance from the messy details of the firsthand. Both kinds of censure, though, ignore how important artistic mediation was to the "reality" of Spain. One need not resurrect the old "Poet's War" cliché to appreciate that the better part of what Spain meant for and in 1930s Europe was a function, as Orwell understood only too well, not of frontline actualities but of the imaginative processing of Spain as a symbol. John Lehmann, editor of the magazine *New Writing*, described the phenomenon of the Spanish Civil War in terms that suggest how reality can become myth without becoming an untruth. In Spain, he writes, "everything, all our fears, our confused hopes and beliefs, our half-formulated theories and imaginings, veered and converged towards its testing and its opportunity, like steel filings that slide towards a magnet suddenly put near them" (273). In many cases the bodies, too, of Lehmann's generation were pulled as though magnetically to Spain, but their "imaginings" did at least as much of the work of manifesting Spain to the rest of Europe.

The English poetry that came out of the war is shot through with an imaginative identification with Spain, a translation of Spain's symbols into the expression of personal, British, and European preoccupations. One illustrative example is the favorite rhyme of Spanish War poets writing in English: *Spain-pain*. The frequency with which it occurs suggests that it held an appeal beyond simple convenience. *Spain* itself contains *pain* within it, and British poets tended to use the rhyme as the indicator of a fundamental consonance between place and concept. W.B. Keal warned, in "To the Fallen," "Think of their travail, their suffering, pain! / ... Lest we see in England what happened in Spain!" (196). "Oh, watch the map of Spain / and you can see the sodden earth of pain," Jack Lindsay wrote in "Looking at a Map of Spain on the Devon Coast (August, 1937)" (398). In an early version of "To a Spanish Poet," Stephen Spender condensed the thought even further into "the map of pain" (Valentine Cunningham, *Penguin* 472). George Barker was particularly good at getting Spanish place names to seem to contain the images or ideas they occasioned. For instance: "the grave of a nation with human pain. / Spain like a sleeping beauty finds her kiss ..." (101). Barker was generally fond of alliteration and assonance, but his poetic use of the names of Spanish towns goes beyond the aurally pleasant. "I heard three women weeping in Irun's ruins," he writes in *Calamiterror* (52). *Ruins*, of course, is an anagram for *Irun's*, and the preposition *in* balances the three word chain, so that the whole structure seems one indissoluble concept. The same technique drives a remarkable line from Barker's "Elegy on Spain": "The pall of the hero who by the Ebro bleeding" (99). Here *Ebro* draws *hero* (as well as parts of *who*, *by*, and *the*) into itself and translates it into *bleeding* as a kind of evolution. The hero's suffering becomes inseparable from the setting, as though each were integral to the other. R. Vernon Beste recalls how Lindsay's poem for public recitation, "On Guard for Spain!", mined Spanish place names for similar effects:

> 'Badajoz!!' The word ... expressed hurt surprise and anger, anger so quick that it scarcely preceded the action it stimulated ... 'Malaga!!' It was a deep growl of fury rather than a name, not just a place in Southern Spain, but a word to give vengeance a sharper meaning ... 'Teruel.' ... Infinitely slowly the drawn-out

vowels went beating down the smoke-filled hall gripping every stomach with sorrow, the awful sorrow that comes with the first realization of loss, irretrievable and irreplaceable, that is death. (Cunningham, *Penguin* 45–46)

I begin with this brief analysis of language to suggest how integral the signs and symbols of Spain became to British writers' reinterpretation of the Spanish War itself as a symbol of their own anxieties, including anxieties about the places of Spain and Britain in an idea of Europe.

For English-speaking poets trying to show what the Spanish Civil War meant to themselves, to Britain, and to the rest of Europe, Spanish particulars, in this case place names, not generalities, provided the most effective delivery system. Suspended between "hot," bodily, irrational "Africa" and enlightened, ordered, "inventive Europe," Spain presented northern Europeans like Auden with an interpretive puzzle. The literature of the war shows that because of, rather than in spite of, the perceived ambiguity of its position relative to modern Europe, Spain also provided a microcosm of interwar Europe's ideological war with itself, its struggle to reconcile tradition and modernity, parts and imagined whole, culture and politics, a sheltered inside and a threatening outside. The English poet Rex Warner writes in "The Tourist Looks at Spain":

> Say clearly: Spain has torn the veil of Europe.
> ....
> 'In Spain the veil is torn.
> In Spain is Europe. England also is in Spain.
> There the sea recedes and there the mirror is no longer blurred.' (393–95)

Lindsay also thought of the sea as joining Britain and Spain, rather than dividing them, as the image of a basic commonality beyond politics or even culture. "Looking at a Map of Spain" begins: "The waves that break and rumble on the sands / gleaming outside my window, break on Spain" (396). And in "Requiem Mass: for the Englishmen fallen in the International Brigade," he asks of Spain, "Is this a strange country / ... ?" and answers, "No. I have recognized it" (181). From 1936–1939, Spain's civil war made the feeling of likeness even more acute. "If there is one decisive event," writes Valentine Cunningham, "which focuses the hopes and fears of the literary 1930s, a moment that seems to summarize and test the period's myths and dreams, to enact and encapsulate its dominant themes and images, the Spanish Civil War is it" (*British* 418). The identification of Spain with Europe and, specifically, with Great Britain on numerous levels repeats itself throughout British writing about the Civil War. Miles Tomalin's warning in "Down the Road" is a political one: "'Another hair's breadth, it'll be the same / To walk in England as to walk in Spain'" (384). "[T]he Spanish quarrel," wrote Vita Sackville-West, "... is really a quarrel between Communism and Fascism in Europe, not only in Spain" (*Authors* 229). Although the political standoff in Spain between, broadly, right and left, fascism and communism, was general throughout Europe, the feeling of identification rarely confined itself to political solidarity. In civil-war literature, it often took on a cultural caste. In "Fata Morgana," Kathleen Raine reflects: "There was a village with no people left / It was like England, but it was in Spain" (403). Pearl Binder's belief that "[t]o-day the future of European Culture is being decided on Spanish soil" (*Authors* 226) was widespread, and this feeling of cultural kinship continued to assert itself despite the obvious, though sometimes superficial, cultural differences between Spain and Britain.

So it is that the bullfight, "the very mirror of Spain's social and historical traumas in the modern period" (Mitchell 158), frequently provided a crystallization of the Civil War, even for British writers to whom bullfighting might have been (and sometimes was) the glaring signal of Spain's otherness. A significant part of the British literature of the Spanish Civil War traces and retraces the linkage between the bullfight, Spain, and Europe. Although this literature remains incompletely collected, more than enough is available, particularly in two anthologies edited by Valentine Cunningham, *The Penguin Book of Spanish Civil War Verse* and *Spanish Front*, to enable a reasonably broad intertextual analysis of the role of bullfighting in the writing of the war.[1] This chapter will examine several works, especially poems, in which British writers use the bullfight as an image of war, of Spain, of Europe, and of themselves. Like Lawrence, these writers come to the corrida as outsiders, and the sense they are able to make of it is as much the product of their own preoccupations as of the form of the ritual itself. However, the unfamiliar demands placed on their perception by the bullfight lead some of these writers into the ambiguous territory in which the richest idea of Europe often resides.

"Images of our Grovelling Spirits"

For poets trying to make sense of violent death, to situate it within an ordering pattern, the bullfight afforded ready-to-hand images.[2] Hemingway explained his initial attraction to bullfighting in this way: "The only place where you could see life and death, i.e., violent death now that the wars were over, was in the bull ring" (2). Only the bullfight could provide that "certain definite action which would

---

[1]   These remain the primary collections of Spanish-Civil-War writing, even though the most recent, *Spanish Front*, was published in 1986, and although both are regretfully out of print. Other useful collections exist, such as John Miller's *Voices Against Tyranny* (also 1986), but many more are either out of print or, as with Alvah Bessie's *Heart of Spain*, so politically partisan as to diminish the reader's sense of the war's literary breadth. The obvious absence in the available literature is the writing of Franco's supporters. It is regrettable that Roy Campbell's remains virtually the only poetry in English that one associates with the Nationalist movement in Spain.

[2]   Some readers will notice the conspicuous absence from this chapter of John Cornford, perhaps the best known British poet of the Spanish Civil War. His poems, notably "A Letter from Aragon," often deal poignantly with violence and death, but I could not find any that treated the bullfight. Nor could I find much in his political poems that demanded inclusion.

give me the feeling of life and death that I was working for" (3). Now that war was back, however, the bullfight did not lose its literary appeal. As themes of courage, heroism, freedom, and civilization, but also of tragedy, sacrifice, fear, and barbarism came exploding back into the consciousness of a generation most of which had missed out on the First World War, and as the poets of that generation struggled to hammer that material into art, the bullfight provided an instructive local model. The corrida de toros had for centuries been a fulcrum on which the idea of "Spanishness" balanced. For British writers drawn to Spain by the civil war, the corrida quickly became a fulcrum and a test for an idea of Europe as well.

Whether they went there physically or only imaginatively, many British writers saw Spain as their great opportunity to reclaim what they had been denied during the previous war, as much by the general disillusion the war had occasioned as by the simple fact of their having been too young to fight. "Spain held out the possibility," writes Cunningham, "of real action to writers who had long envisaged action, the prospect of journeying to a war whose cause looked good and brave and just enough at least to expunge those collective bad memories of the journey to fight in an inglorious, unheroic, soured First World War" (*British* 450). Spain made it clear that, whatever Great War poets like Wilfred Owen and Siegfried Sassoon had done to disabuse poets of their notions of war's glory, the impulse toward the "Bigness Heroic" was alive and well in Britain in the late 1930s (Cunningham, *British* 453). For a generation of poets coming of age in the highly charged political climate of the interwar years, Spain also seemed to promise a chance to make one's politics precise and alive by backing them up with positive action, whether through military service or by using committed poetry as a kind of public action for the cause. Spain provided a theatre in which the dream of the writer as "man of action," of "the poem born in action," might find its body (Cunningham, *British* 452). It also, however, provided a test for that dream, as Orwell and countless others learned firsthand. The Civil War's mechanization and impersonality—Spain was the first war in which large civilian populations were bombed from the air—surpassed even the Great War, and this modern kind of fighting used the poetic-heroic ideals of young men and women roughly, to say the least. Whatever "military virtues" (Cunningham, *British* 454) debunked by the First World War returned to Spain did so at the safe remove from the front lines Orwell detested. Few survived the reality of combat. Bracing as the 1930s "revived cult of the heroic body" (Cunningham, *British* 458) may have been, it was no match for the trenches and massive aerial bombing campaigns. Death in Spain proved, as it does all too often in war, to have little of the "Bigness Heroic" about it.

It might also be said that the 1930s were, in a sense, obsessed with death. As Cunningham puts it: "The period's writers address death, they sing about it, they offer it overtures, they dance with it, they visit funerals, they make journeys to wars, they watch dying and killing" (*British* 57). It is little wonder, then, given a powerful inclination toward themes of both heroism and death, that the idea of a war for the freedom of Spain seemed just what the era ordered. Moreover, Spain itself afforded British writers pursuing those themes a vivid resident tradition in the bullfight. "Spain's bracing combination of poetry, action, and a mass audience" (Cunningham, *British* 452) already had a local habitation and a name in the corrida de toros, one which had not been bled of its heroic code by the brutality of the Great War. Cunningham notes that the 1930s "caged you in violence" and that "Spain caught up and extended the thirties crisis rhetoric of violence" (*British* 430–31). More specifically still, Spanish culture itself, and especially the cultural form of the bullfight, organized, refined, and redefined the terms of this rhetoric of violence for many British poets. The "Spanish acceptance of violence" (Cunningham, *British* 431), exemplified by the bullfight, is completed and given structure by a ritual logic that contains, manages, and aestheticizes violence, making it tragic. If the era presented Europe with a cage of violence, Spain presented it with an arena.

Whether still under the spell of the "Bigness Heroic" or despairing of the possibility of heroism, meaningful action, and the efficacious body, writers of the Spanish war regularly take up the bullfight as the image of both their own and the era's obsessions, and their choice has to do with more than local color. Whether in support of the heroic ideal or as a refuge from war's brutality and confusion, a model of the dignified dying the war refused, the bullfight's ritualized form of heroism and violent death stiffens many poetic representations of wartime Spain.

For the British in particular, the question of sympathy is paramount in the construction of the bullfight as a metaphor for the war.[3] At times, Spain is the bull, overmatched by the clever matador, who is fascism. At other times, Spain is the matador, small and vulnerable next to the ruthless killing machine of fascism, or bravely fending off the bull's charges.[4] However, such simplistic associations, while politically expedient, are rarely as moving or as truthful as the poetry that recognizes and draws upon the bullfight's inherent ambivalence. The way British poets read the war often determines, or at least anticipates, the way they read the bullfight. It is not only a question of *afición*, of approval or expert knowledge of the bullfight; it is also a question of ritual sensibility in general. As Catherine Bell notes, ritual is where sociocultural forces are synthesized in action (23). It is a "dialectical" as opposed to dichotomous process (23). Ritual confuses categories, so its terms are not well suited to the expression of strictly partisan or oppositional rhetorics, what Paul Fussell, speaking of the First World War, calls "adversary proceedings" (*Great War* 75). The experience of the Spanish Civil War often confounded attempts to keep oppositional categories distinct, even as propaganda

---

[3]   The tradition in Spain and in her former colonies of using the bullfight as a political metaphor, into which the British writers inserted themselves, is long and varied. Adrian Shubert highlights some of the most notable such uses relating, for instance, to the French invasion of 1808, the Napoleonic wars, and the Spanish-American War of 1898. See Shubert 205–11.

[4]   The "fascist" forces also included armies of Muslim Africans, whom leftist poets were particularly fond of animalizing. In the context of the bullfight, though, the effect could be ambiguous. "And the rebellious Moors go down," wrote the Spanish poet Plá y Beltran, "Stricken like badly wounded bulls" (278, trans. Rolfe Humphries).

on both sides relentlessly constructed the war as a clear division between two Spains, two Europes, two visions of the future of Western civilization. After the war, Lindsay, who had tried hard to believe in the war's bracing polarities, could not even hate those he thought had been his enemies:

> [T]o blame them is no answer. Strip the mask.
> They were but images of our grovelling spirits.
> Citrine is only my cowardice in a discreet mask,
> Bevin is only my bull-smugness behind a desk. ("Two Days" [1939] 450)

The movement of the bullfight, a contest in which a man loves what he kills and fights not so much a bull as himself, is uniquely suited to these kinds of reflections. The individual actors of the bullfight shift, blend, and reposition—dancing as much as fighting, but with death the only certainty. In the literature of this war, opposed parties contend and are confused, personal anxieties are externalized as other, and the whole event often resolves itself into an aesthetic figure. Which is not to say that British writers internalized the Spanish cultural form of the corrida without difficulty. Rather, their imperfect understanding illuminates their attraction. Their idiosyncratic use of a form so foreign to their own culture yet, in the context of a civil war, so familiar, situates the corrida in an environment broader than Spain and helps to identify the features of the ritual that do *hablan inglés*. That sliver of commonality provides the first term in a symbolic European language pulsing beneath the 1930s rhetoric of ideological opposition.

The propaganda and poetry of the war, on both sides, routinely relied on one of the modern West's cherished concepts and terms, *freedom*. In Spanish culture, the fighting bull is traditionally associated with freedom, but a freedom of a paradoxical sort. Like humans viewed existentially, the toro bravo is born to die. It has been bred for centuries for the sole purpose of performing and dying in the arena. It is free in the sense that it lives its life in vast open spaces and is virtually untroubled by humans until its fourth or fifth year, when it goes to the plaza de toros to be killed. The freedom it signifies derives from its function within the ritual structure of the corrida, not from the absolute liberty one attributes to, say, a hawk. The bull's is freedom within form. As Carrie Douglass explains:

> According to Spaniards, the toro bravo is ... wild, but in a cultural rather than natural sense. They have been raised on ranches in Spain since at least the mid-eighteenth century. The word *bravo* when applied to animals means 'wild and untamed.' 'Tame' (*manso*) is not a positive characteristic in Spain. Mansos are those animals used for meat, milk, or labor, and for a Spaniard there is nothing particularly admirable about an animal that lets itself be yoked to a cart or plow, or walks obligingly to its death in the slaughterhouse. (17–18)[5]

---

5 In bullfighting, *mansos* are also the castrated bulls, or steers, who lead a defective or pardoned toro bravo out of the arena. *Manso* is also used as a derogatory term for a bull who is perceived to lack courage.

Although its fate is all but settled from birth, the fighting bull is thought of as free for the way it lives and the way it dies. Oxen, in contrast, hold a very low place in the Spanish imagination, and during the civil war the bull-ox comparison proved a handy one for poets, Spanish and British alike, looking for images of freedom and its opposite. It is the driving theme of Miguel Hernández's "The Winds of the People," here translated by A.L. Lloyd:

> Oxen may bow their heads
> gentle and impotent
> before their punishment;
> ....
> I come not from a people of oxen,
> my people are they who enthuse
> over the lion's leap,
> the eagle's rigid swoop,
> and the strong charge of the bull
> whose pride is in his horns.
> ....
> The agony of the oxen
> is of little countenance.
> That of the virile animal
> travels the universe. (285–86)

Or more succinctly still: "Oxen were never bred / On the bleak uplands of Spain. / Who speaks of setting a yoke / on the shoulders of such a race?" (285). The Englishman Herbert Read echoed Hernández in "A Song for the Spanish Anarchists":

> The oxen pass under the yoke
>   and the blind are led at will:
> But a man born free has a path of his own
>   and a house on the hill. (248)

Roy Campbell's poem "Toril" takes the form of a dialogue between a toro bravo and an ox. Having heard the Ox's reasoned justification of its own life of quiet and reflection, the Bull, facing his turn in the arena, demands, "But tell me what is blacker than this Death?" "My impotence," answers the Ox. "It was your soul that spoke! —/ More hideous than this martyrdom?" asks the Bull, to which the Ox: "The Yoke!" (147). In this sequence Campbell, a South African supporter of Franco notorious for building up his adopted Spanishness, fairly easily adopts the Spanish idea of the bull, but some British poets found it more difficult to embrace the kind of freedom that is only freedom to die. Apart from Orwell and John Cornford, many poets anxious to unite their own lives of creative introspection to bold, public action hesitated at the Spanish war's toril gate.[6] Auden, for all

---

[6]   Cornford represents as dramatic an exception as Orwell. He was killed in action fighting for the Republic in December 1936.

the apparent resolve of "Spain," did not so much as drive an ambulance for the Republic, much less fire a weapon. His counterpart Spender, though also a non-soldier, saw that fighting to the death, no matter for what cause, ran unproductively contrary to the inborn impulse toward the freedom of peace common to so-called Nationalists and Republicans, as well as bulls. Spender's poem "Two Armies" touches the bull to suggest the fundamental sameness of the warring armies:

> … No one is given leave
> On either side, except the dead, and wounded.
> ………………………………………
> All have become so nervous and so cold
> That each man hates the cause and distant words
> That brought him here, more terribly than bullets.
> ………………………………………
> From their numb harvest, all would flee, except
> For discipline drilled once in an iron school
> Which holds them at the point of the revolver.
> ………………………………………
> … who can connect
> The inexhaustible anger of the guns
> With the dumb patience of those tormented animals? (151)

Spender's is not a poetry enamored of decisive violent action, no matter how noble. At the same time, it does not privilege the contemplative response to crisis—the poet's response—over the active one. "My mind is paper on which dust and words sift," he writes in "Port Bou," "I assure myself the shooting is only for practice / But I am the coward of cowards" (160). Although it does not suggest approval of the bullfight, Spender's poetry about the war displays a sensibility akin to bullfighting afición, which holds that the true battle is between man and death, not between any two material actors. Accordingly, Spender dismantles the ostensible divide between the life of action and the life of reflection that, as Campbell would have it, defines not only the bullfight but also the possible responses to war.

"Was What We Saw the Thing, or Do We See It Now?"

Orwell seems, almost in spite of himself, to have been enamored, if not with bullfighting itself, at least with the idea of bullfighting as a handle with which to hold onto traditional Spain. In *Homage to Catalonia* he laments the bulls' absence in civil-war Republican Spain:

> Barbastro, though a long way from the front line, looked bleak and chipped. Swarms of militiamen in shabby uniforms wandered up and down the streets, trying to keep warm. On a ruinous wall I came upon a poster dating from the previous year and announcing that 'six handsome bulls' would be killed in the arena on such and such a date. How forlorn its faded colours looked! Where were the handsome bulls and the handsome bullfighters now? It appeared that

even in Barcelona there were hardly any bullfights nowadays; for some reason
all the best matadors were Fascists.[7] (*Homage* 15)

While it is true that, for a number of economic and cultural reasons, many of the
best matadors supported General Franco and his nominally fascist rebellion, it is
doubtful that many of them were legitimate "Fascists," just as there were relatively
few orthodox Marxists among the broadly left-wing supporters of the Republic.[8]
There is no question that Franco gave bullfights an especially prominent place
in the public demonstration of his power. His military uprising commenced at
five o'clock in the afternoon because that was the traditional hour for bullfights
to begin. Adrian Shubert describes the "Liberation or Victory Bullfights" that
commemorated Franco's civil-war victories even into the 1950s (214). Certainly
the moneyed landowners who raised fighting bulls sided overwhelmingly with the
rebels, and the bullfight seems to satisfy many of fascism's obsessions—with, for
example, action, death, and symbols of national character. The French writer Jean
Cau wrote:

> Bullfighting, I have been told time and time again, is an essentially 'rightist'
> spectacle. It is asserted that blood, virility, death, sexuality, in short, all the
> ingredients which enter in the composition, when examined through the potent
> microscope of the left, reveal the perverse nature of bullfighting … The fiesta
> was brutality and rite, death and past; that is to say, of the rightist party since the
> left was all progress and life. (35)

Yet, as Shubert points out: "During the Spanish Civil War both sides held
bullfights as fund-raisers" (213). And Douglass notes that "this institution that had
been intimately tied to the dictatorship … continued to thrive in democracy" (5).
How, then, should one read the anti-fascist Orwell's statement, with its association

---

[7]   González Tuñon's poem, "Long live the Revolution" begins, in A.L. Lloyd's
translation, "The bullfighters are monarchists," which, in civil-war Spain, amounted to
the same thing. In his autobiography, *I Wonder as I Wander*, Langston Hughes recalls a
conversation he had with a young African in Valencia during the Spanish war, in which
the African says that "'all the famous matadors have run away to Franco where the money
is. They are not as brave at fighting fascists as they are at facing bulls.'" Hughes adds, "A
common saying in Valencia was, 'All the best bullfighters and all the best whores have
gone over to the enemy—but we'll get along without them.' That summer I did not see any
bullfighters, but the few remaining prostitutes were making a fortune" (329–30).

[8]   Indeed, the stated intention of Orwell's narrative is to sift out the internal conflicts
and disruptions among the heterogeneous members of the left, "the kaleidoscope of political
parties and trade unions"—communist, socialist, anarchist, liberal, and so on—"with
their tiresome names—P.S.U.C., P.O.U.M., F.A.I., C.N.T., U.G.T., J.C.I., J.S.U., A.I.T."
(47). Peter Stansky and William Abrahams write that "such labels as 'Trotskyist' and
'Communist' did not have deep roots in Spain, but were really in large part foreign names
for native movements" (320). John Cornford, however, consistently identified himself as a
Communist.

of bullfighting with fascism, and his palpable longing not only for bullfights but also, as illustrated in a later comment, for the whole apparatus of symbols that traditionally defined Spain and that Franco and the forces of the right had committed themselves to defending?

At this early point in his narrative, Orwell is quite comfortable differentiating absolutely between supporters of the Republic, like himself, and "Fascists," those opposed to it, but the distinction regularly breaks down. Speaking of an early encounter with fascist deserters, he notes, "It struck me that they were indistinguishable from ourselves, except that they wore khaki overalls" (*Homage* 17). At the Huesca front, he describes the unintelligibility of opposing forces "if every position had not flown a flag" (*Homage* 24).[9] The Spaniards, fighting as they were against their countrymen, were even more prone to identification with the enemy. Orwell records that the opposed armies were given to shouting slogans at one another in an attempt to incite desertion, a practice he finds "scandal[ous]": "The idea of trying to convert your enemy instead of shooting him!" (*Homage* 42). Still later, when his gaze shifts from political to cultural questions, the note of identification truly shows itself, and the result is to throw the whole notion of strict opposition into question. In Christopher Hitchens's view, "It suited Authority in the West, and some of the men-in-the-street too, to maintain that the war was what it seemed—Catholic nationalist Spain on one side and 'Red' anti-clerical Spain on the other" (69). Yet Orwell "knew that the whole picture was false and the whole story was a lie," and his book is devoted to debunking them (Hitchens 69).

The gestures he makes when he is not consciously interrogating political misinformation, however, frequently do more debunking than the political passages. At the other end of *Homage to Catalonia*, Orwell, back in Barbastro, again gives himself up to the romance of Spain's traditional symbols:

> I seemed to catch a momentary glimpse, a sort of far-off rumour of the Spain that dwells in everyone's imagination. White sierras, goatherds, dungeons of the Inquisition, Moorish palaces, black winding trains of mules, grey olive trees and groves of lemons, girls in black mantillas, the wines of Málaga and Alicante, cathedrals, cardinals, bull-fights, gypsies, serenades—in short, Spain. Of all Europe it was the country that had had most hold upon my imagination. (203)

There is telling irony in the juxtaposition of this unapologetic flight of admiration with Orwell's earlier declaration that Franco's "military mutiny ... was an attempt not so much to impose Fascism as to restore feudalism" (*Homage* 48). For almost all of the examples Orwell cites here are vestiges of medieval Spain. Just so, he remarks his fondness for the symbols of the Church (cathedrals and cardinals), but earlier he has sneered, "It seemed that the Fascists always heard mass before going

---

9   Even then, all the flags looked vaguely alike: "The P.O.U.M. and P.S.U.C. flags were red, those of the Anarchists red and black; the Facists [*sic*] generally flew the monarchist flag (red-yellow-red), but occasionally they flew the flag of the Republic (red-yellow-purple)" (24).

into action" (*Homage* 73). This disconnect between Orwell's political dogmatism, which is unquestionable, and his cultural affinities, which he seems incapable of camouflaging, periodically surfaces in *Homage to Catalonia*, revealing what is to some extent a feature of all war but particularly of civil war: the impracticability of maintaining a clear sense of opposition given the persuasive evidence on behalf of identification.

In Spain's ongoing struggle to define itself as a modern European nation, inventories like Orwell's—cathedrals, mantillas, and bulls—are regularly made the object of scorn. The perpetuation of this arcane symbology, the argument goes, keeps Spain locked in a backward, romantic, dimly lit stasis, cut off from progressive, enlightened, industrialized Europe (McCormick 3–4, 34). In "The Tourist Looks at Spain," Warner was particularly intolerant about traditional cultural symbols, Spanish or English:

> All cupolas, all storks, all holy virgins,
>   curious uniforms, oranges,
> what every tourist knows, both the flowers and the dancing,
> pompous processions ...
> ……………………………..
> Was what we saw the thing, or do we see it now?
> ……………………………..
> It is rather around us that the mist is clinging,
> and our oldest landmarks that have become a veil.
> See in the mirror rather our most holy buildings,
>   our smoothest kindest words,
> our most successful pageantry, our parades
> as trash and blots and blurs on the moving truth. (393–95)

Here culture's inherited markers are presented not as the containers and preservers of collective identity but as hindrances to its full realization, or as lies. Much of visible Spanish culture, of course, comes from the presence of the Roman Catholic Church, and during the war the Church and its objects were subject to fierce attack, figurative as well as actual, by the progress-minded. Lindsay snarls that "There is ... a smell of powder / in draped sacristies," and "The muddy light drowning in cathedral-aisles / favours conspirators" ("On Guard" 255). He notes happily that in Barcelona "The noticeboard of the People's University / is nailed above the church's door of stone / over the face of the Virgin in the shrine" ("Looking at a Map of Spain" 397).[10]

---

[10] The degree to which the forces of the left actually persecuted the Church during the war remains a contentious question. Estimates of the number of priests and nuns executed by the Government side range from a handful to many thousands. Valentine Cunningham rather cagily admits that "Nationalist clerics were bumped off, to be sure, but peasants and soldiers were taught to read ..." (*Spanish Front* xxii). Auden, Orwell, Lindsay, and many other Republican sympathizers acknowledged the presence of burnt-out churches.

Its opponents in particular have always cited the bullfight as the symbol of all that is wrong with Spain: primitiveness, barbarism, obsession with death and blood, and so on. Douglass writes:

> Another adjective used to describe los toros is 'primitive.' Again, this poses the fiestas against 'modernity,' 'civilization,' and 'Europe.' It is not only the format that is primitive, but also the emotions elicited. The themes of life and death are primitive in a primordial way. Furthermore, this controlled celebration of aggression and the bloody rite are more savage (in the evolutionary sense) than civilized, thus more primitive than modern. (100)

Spain has been divided as deeply as it has been unified by the bullfight. Since at least the Generation of 1898, the corrida has symbolized the divide between the "two Spains," one eager for contact and continuity with Europe, the other pleased to maintain Spanish exceptionality.[11] Douglass argues that, in effect, "[t]he 1936–1939 Civil War was fought over these two visions of Spain's future" (109). While this may be true up to a point, we have seen that the Spanish Civil War was always already a European war, that its divisions matched those of the rest of Europe, and that Orwell, for one, had difficulty maintaining a clear separation between the romantic Spain he loved and the rational one he was ostensibly fighting for. The closer one approaches to Spain, the image of all Europe's anxiety in the 1930s, the more clouded the ostensible ideological divisions of Europe become. In the literature of the Spanish Civil War, as in the corrida as a cultural form, ambivalence trumps any suggestion of certain difference.

While it was routine for international volunteers on the left to disavow publicly their romantic visions of Spain, it is hard to see Orwell's feelings for Spanish landscape and custom as atypical in light of the regularity with which affection for traditional Spain shows itself in civil-war literature by other British writers. Perhaps surprisingly, the corrida rarely appears uncivilized in the leftist poetry of the war. More often, it figures as a symbolic corrective to war's senseless violence. It is arguable that the opposite of Douglass's summary of bullfighting's primitivism above is also true. A "controlled celebration" is itself the civilizing of those "primitive" themes of life and death.[12] The corrida is actually a "modern" representation of what had once been "savage" or "primordial," just as the poetic ordering of war's life-and-death themes is a civilizing act. As war forced primordial themes and emotions to consciousness, the European civilizing impulse looked for patterns, and it frequently found them in the blood ritual of the bullfight, a primitive practice with suddenly very modern applications.

The primitive-modern debate at the center of which the bullfight is so often situated was certainly part of the rhetoric of the Spanish Civil War, but the

---

[11] At the end of *Death in the Afternoon*, Hemingway decries "the great wish of [Spain's] European-minded politicians to see [the bullfight] abolished so that they will have no intellectual embarrassments at being different from their European colleagues that they meet at the League of Nations, and at the foreign embassies and courts" (268).

[12] And see Lewine's case for bullfighting, already quoted in the Interchapter, as "the essence of civilization" (227).

available political associations matched up rather uncomfortably with it. Each side accused the other of seeking to return Spain to a state of barbarism. Franco advertised himself as a defender of European culture; his opponents saw in his nationalist movement the death of civilized society. They pointed particularly to Franco's employment of mercenary Moorish forces as evidence of the Nationalists' barbarism. Back in Great Britain, left-wing authors announced their certainty about where the salvation of civilization lie. The famous "Authors Take Sides on the Spanish War" questionnaire, printed in the *Left Review* in 1937, goaded British writers with: "But there are some who ... aver that it is possible that Fascism may be what it proclaims it is: 'the saviour of civilisation'" and asked "Are you for, or against, the legal Government and the People of Republican Spain? Are you for, or against, Franco and Fascism?" (*Authors* 51). The respondents picked up the rhetorical ball and ran with it, sticking close to the terms of debate suggested by the questionnaire's drafters. Many emphasized the past-future divide. Edgell Rickword asserted that "Fascism is all the power of the past striving to throttle the future" (*Authors* 55). Lehmann wrote that "No writer who is trying to create for the future, and not merely dabbling in outworn forms and sentiments, can be on any other side [than the Republican]" (*Authors* 54). "I am opposed to Franco," wrote Spender, "firstly because Franco and his supporters represent the attempt of the aristocracy and clergy of Spain to prevent the history of Spain from developing beyond the Middle Ages" (*Authors* 56). Others, such as Louis MacNeice, focused on civilization and culture versus barbarism: "if this cause is lost, nobody with civilised values may be able to get anything out of anything" (*Authors* 55). Added Randall Swingler, "I believe that culture has always been the directive force of man's progress toward freedom: that Fascism is destructive alike to culture and to human progress" (*Authors* 56). And Warner declared, "the Republican Government ... represents the forward movement of humanity and civilisation" (*Authors* 56). Unsurprisingly, very few writers spoke up in support of Franco at this time. Those who did said virtually nothing positive about "fascism." And after the war, those sympathetic to the Nationalist cause used language familiar from the leftist responses to "Authors Take Sides." In 1942, Hilaire Belloc applauded Franco's fidelity to "the mission of Europe—which mission, I take it, has been to found and perpetuate the highest culture, and, happily, the enduring culture, of our race" (Cunningham, *Spanish* 373). Arnold Lunn, too, saw the Nationalists as a friend of civilization, not a threat to it: "It was interesting to contrast the carefully cultivated fields in territory which had been under Nationalist control since the outbreak of the war with the ill-kempt disorder and neglect of the territory captured from the Republicans" (Cunningham, *Spanish* 370). A host of loyalties, of course—religious, political, sexual, racial, class-based—informed individual Britons' choice of allegiances during the Spanish War. Neither the question of civilization nor of progress, however, did much in the way of delimiting the sides.[13]

---

[13]   The "Authors Take Sides" questionnaire, in its supreme confidence in solidarity, was blind to one set of differences in particular. Addressed "To the Writers and Poets of England, Scotland, Ireland and Wales," its obvious presumption was of a front more or

Orwell found all of this survey business "bloody rot" (*Collected* 312). Next to sending food or enlisting, he had no use whatever for "that damned rubbish of signing manifestos to say how wicked it all is." No one has written with more clarity than Orwell about either the idealism or the practical muddle of the Spanish Civil War. His transparency, his disdain for pretense, is what allows the touching ambivalences into the narrative of *Homage to Catalonia*. Just as when faced with the pressing but prosaic realities of the trenches he could not insist on the reality or importance of political allegiances, when faced with "romantic" Spain and all its supposedly reactionary apparatus—cathedrals, mantillas, dungeons, palaces, and bullfights—he could not make fascism stick to it.

Grief and Bloodshed in War and Toreo

Through a resonant alignment of circumstances, the Spanish bullfight taught British poets how to mourn. One of the earliest and most jarring events of the war was the execution of Spanish poet Federico García Lorca by a rebel firing squad.[14] Easily the most famous poet in 1930s Spain, Lorca immediately became a symbol of what was at stake in the Spanish conflict, and his death resolved many British writers to become involved in the war, physically or creatively. Not long before he died, Lorca wrote perhaps the most important bullfighting poem ever, "Lament for Ignacio Sánchez Mejías." Lorca had been a bullfighting aficionado as well as a close friend of the bullfighter Sánchez, who was gored by a bull in the Manzanares

---

less unified along Great-British lines. There is telling, if subtle, dissent, though, visible in the responses. Neither Yeats nor Joyce participated. Hugh MacDiarmid used his reply, which was unequivocally pro-Spanish Government, to highlight Scotland's unease in the questionnaire's equation. "But for the connection with England," he wrote, "Fascism would never be able to raise its head in Scotland itself" (*Authors* 54). It is little surprise that the questionnaire also entirely elided the question of Spanish regionalism, the loyalties associated with which were and are notoriously stronger than national ones. In Tom Wintringham's poem "Monument," Catalonia is, for instance, "Catalonia, Spain and not Spain, and our gateway" (306). As for bullfighting, "Los toros," according to Douglass, "serve as a vehicle to talk about two historical Spanish debates about identity. The first is the place of 'Spain' in Europe ... The second debate concerns *regional identity and the place of the various regions in the construction of the Spanish state*" (6–7, my emphasis). The bull may be "the thread that ties all of the regions together," but it has also been the symbol of regional dissent. Two Spanish regions currently pushing for European Union recognition of their local languages, Galicia and Catalonia, point to the (relative) absence of bullfighting as evidence of their cultural autonomy.

[14] The facts of this death remain subject to some question. One Peter Kemp, "an Irishman fighting for Franco," wrote that "The Nationalists...strongly denied any responsibility for Lorca's death, attributing it to the vengeance of his private enemies, of which he had a large number; certainly he had many good friends on the Nationalist side who would have saved him if they could. His murder was a crime that robbed the world of one of its greatest living lyric poets" (In Payne 162).

bullring on August 11, 1934 and died two days later In addition to being an elegy, the poem is a sustained meditation on the corrida's strange brew of bravery, beauty, and death. It has also been adopted as a proto-Spanish-Civil-War poem, notably by Spender in the Introduction to *Poems Against Tyranny: Writing of the Spanish Civil War* (1986). The "Lament," he writes, "so prophetic of the tragedy to come," "can be taken almost as a prelude to the drama of the war, taking death and violence, in the context of the bullfight, as its themes" (Spender, Introduction 14–15). He does not specify how "the context of the bullfight" anticipates the drama of this war, but he might have begun with the pained response in the poem to the fact of a man's spilled blood:

> I will not see it!
> Tell the moon to come
> for I do not want to see the blood
> of Ignacio on the sand. (García Lorca 56)[15]

So long as the blood is visible, the poem is nearly hysterical. Blood agitates the second section, irregular stanzas of short lines bristling with exclamations and cries between flashes of gore. Only when the blood is gone does the poetry regain its balance. The body laid out on cool stone occasions a calmer reflection on the ritual of death. Even in the grip of grief, the speaker never blames the bull for the death of the matador. Instead, Ignacio dies of "the death he carries" within himself into "the round bull ring of the moon" (García Lorca 61). The stone that restores tranquility to the scene "yields not sounds nor crystals nor fire, / only bull rings and bull rings and more bull rings without walls" (García Lorca 59). The torero and the bull are never set up as adversaries. There are only life, blood, death, and the poem, intimately rotating within "the grey bull ring of dreams" (García Lorca 56).

Lorca, in turn, became the subject of elegies by several British poets, his own lament for Sánchez providing the model for poetic remembrances of himself.[16] Although Lorca was not himself a bullfighter, the association was so natural that elegies for him habitually render his death tragic through reference to the bullfight. While these poems convey plenty of hatred for the Francoist firing squad that ended Lorca's life, they generally do not transfer this hatred into vilification of one or another of the actors in the bullfight. As though in homage to the aficionado-poet, wartime elegies for Lorca tend to conflate bull and man, as in that "grey bull ring of dreams," emphasizing his calm defiance and stolidity in the face of certain death, but also his vulnerability and pure victimization. Jacob Bronowski's "The Death of Garcia Lorca" suggests the tragic inevitability of Lorca's death as akin to the bull's:

---

[15]   The translation is by Stephen Spender and J.L. Gili.

[16]   Peter Kemp wrote plainly that "In [Lorca's] lines on the death of his friend, Sánchez Mejías, it seems, lies Lorca's own epitaph: "*Díle a la luna que venga, / Que no quiero ver la sangre / De Ignacio sobre la arena*" (In Payne 163).

Walking, did you see the cape and the dancers
flutter and fall still, the falling lances?
The picador is Don Quixote,
the gipsy [*sic*] begs, and the poet's
mouth is bloody. (208)

Although the firing squad is responsible for the poet's death, the executioners are in a sense outside of the true contest in these poems, which is between Lorca and death itself. "You joked with the dead," writes Bronowski:

… did you not hear
their voices lower year by year?
their dumb trumpets? and the word Doom
when the gun's echo answered the drum?
You walked with ghosts, and their time is done. (208)

Here the doomed poet dies as the toro bravo, whose moment of truth in the bullfight is signaled by a final trumpet phrase. He is identified with both matador *and* bull, though, in the implication that he "joked with death" while death in earnest crept closer. In "The Death of Garcia Lorca," Bronowski associates this dying with the loss of a romantic Spanish past, "the loss / of the gipsy's glory and the matador's" (208). Like Orwell, he mourns its disappearance. In Geoffrey Parsons's elegy, Lorca dies, whether as a bull or as a man, heroically. His executioners measure his steps precisely:

… They would let him take all but the last one,
Hoping that he would run for it, hoping for fear.
But the bullfighter's friend was not afraid of their hate. (207)

Lorca's death, like the bull's, is inevitable. Like the toro bravo, he does not shy from death. Like the brave matador, his feet remain still. Like other British poets of the war, Parsons is a bit heavy-handed with his political metaphors:

And he stopped and turned and faced them, standing still;
He stared at their aiming eyes, his imminent murder;
He was one with the people of Spain and he stood as they stand. (207)

Here Parsons relies on the people-versus-power model of the war so attractive to leftist writers of the time but so awkwardly attached to the bullfight, de Montherlant's "great unifier of all the social classes" (In *Los Toros* 46). Parsons clearly wants his elegized Lorca to partake of the best elements of both toro and torero, but that ritual fluidity abandons him when partisan politics creep back into the poem.

In its true form, the bullfight regularly confounds the attempt to conceive of the war in purely adversarial political terms. "[I]f bullfighting," wrote Cau, "does not decay in Spain it is because [it] exceed[s] all political boundaries" (35). The utility the bullfight had for writers of the left seems to provide support for this claim. Given those "ingredients" of "blood, virility, death, sexuality ... which enter in [the bullfight's] composition," one would have been hard pressed to avoid looking to the bullfight for wartime metaphors. Blood is the most resonant and emblematic substance of both war and toreo, the one that most explicitly sets these events off from ordinary life, and the one, by being common to both Nationalists and Republicans, men and bulls, that insists most relentlessly on identification as opposed to adversary proceedings. José Ortega y Gasset explained the power of visible blood in elemental terms: "When blood is shed and the essential 'inside' goes out, the whole of nature shrinks up with nausea and terror, as if the most radical nonsense had been perpetrated: to make external what is purely internal" (qtd. in Alvarez 41). In both bullfighting and war, blood is the signal that the stakes have been raised. In poetry about these subjects, the image of visible blood carries the symbolic weight and delivers the emotional stimulus more efficiently than any other object.

This remains true even in a literature fairly dripping with blood. One notices at a glance that the poetry of the Spanish Civil War is particularly bloody. Lindsay's "On Guard for Spain!" cries "O dip the flag in my heart's blood" (259). In "Passionaria," a poem praising Dolores Ibarruri, Charlotte Haldane writes, "iron is in your blood. / ... You have stood / ... / above this sea / Of hatred and blood" (252). Even "the friendly streets run blood" in Margot Heinemann's "On a Lost Battle in the Spanish War" (252). Spender links taurine and human blood explicitly in "The Bombed Happiness":

> Children ...
> ....
> Are forced in the mould of the groaning bull
> And engraved with lines on the face.
> Their harlequin-striped flesh,
> Their blood twisted in rivers of song ... (163)

These examples are among the less graphic treatments of blood to come out of the Civil War. There are also Lindsay's "cobbles slippery with blood" ("On Guard" 255) and the "burnt blood" in J.T. Roderick's "Memory" (452). "Certainly no war literature," Cunningham argues, "flows redder with blood than the Spanish War's" (*British* 425). He is likely correct, but he is typically nonchalant about the special resonance of blood in the Spanish context:

> And images of that blood shed so freely merged naturally with the traditional rednesses of Spain: the blood of bull-fights, matadors' red capes, Goya's scenes, the blood of the thousands of effigies of the crucified Christ worshipped with such fierceness in the peculiarly sado-masochistic adorations of Spanish Catholicism. (*British* 425)

The Spanish War's is indeed a bright red poetry. "Red is the bed of Poland, Spain, / And thy mother's breast," wrote Edith Sitwell in her 1940 poem "Lullaby"

(269). However, in establishing the confluence of "rednesses" in civil-war writing, Cunningham skips over the ritual significance that more sturdily unites all these figures of bloodshed. The bullfight and the crucifix are representations of a hermeneutic of sacrifice, not merely a convenient color palette, and it is on this precedent that so much sanguineous civil-war poetry draws. Even Spender's analogy above, far less sustained than Barker's in "Elegy on Spain," suggests a more purposeful "merging" of images than one based on their shared redness. Herbert Read's "Bombing Casualties in Spain," which Cunningham cites in passing, treats blood in Ortega y Gasset's terms:

> ... These blench'd lips
> were warm once and bright with blood
> but blood
> held in a moist blob of flesh
> not spilt and spatter'd in tousled hair.
> In these shadowy tresses
> red petals did not always
> thus clot and blacken to a scar. (165–66)

Here is the "nausea" with which nature greets bloodshed. However, Ortega y Gasset did find one important exception to the rule of blood-made-visible. "There is a case," he wrote, "in which blood does not provoke that nausea: when it springs up from the nape of the neck of a bull well worked by the picador and runs down both sides of the beast. Under the sun, the crimson of the shining liquid acquires a splendor that turns blood into a jewel" (qtd. in Alvarez 41). Ortega was not a bullfighting advocate, but his interpretation does ring with the insight of the initiate. That Ortega, a supporter of the Republic, could find such beauty in a spectacle he did not particularly approve of suggests again that the aesthetic logic of the bullfight extends not only beyond the bullfighting afición but also beyond the extreme right wing.

Even so, his enthusiastic and concise formulation is not quite sufficient. Alvarez offers a corrective that is especially helpful in accounting for the use of bullfighting in British poetry of the Spanish war:

> The blood shed in the arena does not provoke the nausea it would provoke if, for example, the bull were killed with a poniard inside a cage, because this blood publicly shed has a lustral and expiatory character. Let us say once and for all that the bull dies in the place of the entire public, consummating thus its tragedy and ours, liberating us, by its dying, of the feeling that 'someone has to die.' (41)

This reading of the bullfight as a sacrificial rite is widely accepted, naturally among Girardians, but especially among those well versed in the history and mystery of toreo and taurine literature. Although few if any British poets of the civil war were so well attuned, the evidence that some version of Alvarez's view was present to their minds is written into many of their poems. Searching for an image of meaningful blood sacrifice to redeem poetically the deaths of friends, poet after poet insisted on the bullfight's "expiatory character." There are two key differences, however, between the way they read the bull ritual and the way Alvarez does. The first is that for most of these poets the blood of the bullfight *does* still nauseate, only it does more than nauseate. Writers sickened and terrified by the shedding of their friends' blood see the stricken bull not as a substitute but as a kind of analog with a difference. The utility of bullfighting in British war poetry is most often based not on its lack of horror but on its *use* of horror. The corrida's aesthetic control over terror, violence, and bloodshed, and its suggestion of meaning provided a frame through which to view war's violence. No British poets rhapsodize like Ortega y Gasset about the beauty of blood in the bull ring, but invoking the bullfight does help them to do the necessary work of organizing sensation that must accompany its translation into art. The second difference is suggested by the saying, *Los toros no hablan inglés*. It might better be said that for British poets of the Spanish Civil War the bulls speak only a rudimentary English, that much of the bullfight's apparent power to encapsulate British poets' wartime meditations is lost in its translation into a poetry attracted to the bullfight but only vaguely familiar with the logic of ritual (whatever Auden's King of Ostnia might think).

A good example is Barker's "Elegy on Spain," dedicated "to the photograph of a child killed in an air-raid on Barcelona." The poem constructs the child's death as a martyrdom leading the way to future peace and life. Likewise, it presents the bull as the noble victim of an injustice and its death as a righteous gesture of self-sacrifice. Thus the poem encourages both child and bull to go ahead with dying. To the former: "So close for a moment that long open eye," and to the latter: "Go down, my red bull, proud as a hero," "Drop, drop that heavy head, my less and more than dead" (100; 101). Their dying is redeemed, the poem argues, by virtue of its restorative promise, its simultaneous transcendence of death:

> This flower Freedom needs blood at the roots,
> Its shoots spring from your wounds, and the bomb
> Booming among the ruins of your houses, arouses
> Generation after generation from the grave
> To slave at your side for future liberation. (100)

The problem with rhetoric like this is that it diminishes the horror of death, particularly that of the child, by swaddling it in impersonal political slogans, insulating the poet and the reader from the plain horror of spilled blood. The poetry and the politics are much more powerful when the language hews close to the painful particulars, however nauseating, of the moment contained in the photograph. Yet Barker is reluctant to let the gore of the first and last stanzas— "dead as meat / Slapped on a negative plate ... ," "the child's remains / Staining the wall and cluttering the drains"—speak for itself (98; 103). Instead, the poem ends: "All this builds a bigger plinth for glory, / Story on story, on which triumph shall be found" (103). To reduce the individual child's death to "all this" and to bandage such horror up in the vague promise of future "glory" is to commit the rhetorical sin against which Owen and the First World War poets said so much. Barker, however deeply he felt Spain in his bones, was not a combatant. For those who have been close to violent death themselves, the consolation, if any, offered by such a technique is almost always transient at best. Indeed, one feels that the poem, for all its political gusto, may be intended to console only one person, the poet.

The poem's juxtaposition of two modes, although ultimately unsatisfying, betrays an anxiety common to much Spanish Civil War writing about how to be true to the darkness of violent death while holding onto the light and life of political progress. Its attempt to reconcile the opposites of death and life in the service of an overarching purpose, though, might have been better served by a more discerning attention to the ritual at the heart of the poem. Like so many other observers during the war, Barker is not content to take the corrida on its own terms. Instead, the bull in the poem dies as the result of a corruption of the corrida form:

> Laid let that head be, low, my bull, stunned,
> Gunned from the royal box by a trigger pull.
> Bigger no courage is than the blood it can spill. (101)[17]

It is difficult to see what the bull's courage is, killed in this manner. Certainly the killer is pictured as cowardly and the death as unfair, but how is being gunned down from a distance more courageous than charging a sword at close range, as the bull must in the corrida proper? In *Calamiterror*, Barker's long poem written in the year of the war's outset, the play of opposites is much more intricate and the poem's emotional reach much greater. Although it is concerned partly with Spain and with politics, *Calamiterror*'s Lawrence-style mysticism locates all such topical questions in a fluid poetic imagery that has not yet given way to the rigidity imposed by political imperatives:

> Here on the lunar rocks the female vulture seizes
> The skeleton of love, and the rocking of their interlock
> Confuses categories, convulses shape, rocks the rocks. (34)

Much of the poem concerns the state of being "Suspended like a world between pull of opposed forces, / The downward demon pull, the upward angel," rather than that of having arrived at a clearly demarcated zone of possibility. Even the fact of war has not ossified the poem's ambiguity into opposition: "The weeping shell propelled from war / Drops in a chaos of life *and* death" (39, my emphasis). Male and female, war and peace, animal and human, life and death are all intertwined

---

[17]   The American poet Edna St. Vincent Millay does something similar in "Say That We Saw Spain Die" by multiplying, rather than changing, the bull's adversary: "the enemy indeed ... A thousand of him, interminably into the ring released" (221). Her bull, like Barker's, suffers from a corruption of the corrida ritual: "Say that we saw the shoulders more than the mind confused, so profusely / Bleeding from so many more than the accustomed barbs, the game gone vulgar, the rules abused" (221–22).

in the poem as in the bullfight.[18] Although *Calamiterror* does not treat bullfighting specifically, it is much closer to the ritual logic of the bullfight than is "Elegy on Spain," which abandons the provocative but ideologically ambiguous confusion of categories the corrida presents in favor of a politically simplified portrayal of injustice.

Even thus perverted, the bullfight holds out to Barker the image he seeks of a death that is somehow "less and more than dead." One does not present the bull and the innocent victims of the Spanish war as analogues absent the conviction that both deaths are similarly redemptive. By passing over the richer commingling of opposites the bullfight ritual offers, however, the argument (and it is most emphatically an argument) of "Elegy on Spain" and poems like it is limited to the confines of ordinary dualistic political rhetoric. In "On Guard for Spain!" Lindsay tells the audience in the same stanza that Spain is "the arena where a weaponless man / takes the charge of a bull of havoc" and "where the workers, going to battle, / go as to a fiesta" (254). At no point in the bullfight does a weaponless man have to face a bull; or, if he should drop his weapon, he quickly retrieves it or flees over the barrier to safety. As Barker places a gun in the royal box, Lindsay disarms the torero in order to heighten the rhetorical effect but in doing so loses more than he gains. Moreover, "fiesta" in Spain is all but inseparable from the bullfight, and vice-versa, bullfights occurring almost exclusively within the context of a town's or city's fiesta, and fiestas almost invariably culminating in a bullfight (Douglass 21). Lindsay seems to mean "fiesta" as *party* in the English sense, but the Spanish term implies the ritual celebration with the corrida, the ritual of death, at its center. Nor are workers, as suggested above, the only class who go happily to bullfights. In "Looking at a Map of Spain," Lindsay speaks of the bodies lying around a city square "after death's careless fiesta" (397). In Spain, death and fiestas are often messy, but neither is careless. Lindsay's bullfight and fiesta seem rather hollowed of their local content—which, preserved, might have provided richer and more accurate metaphors—and refilled with a content of political expedience.

Portraying evil as a perversion of the bullfight ritual has the indirect effect of ennobling the corrida in its true form, of suggesting that the unadulterated corrida is somehow just. However, the justification of the corrida form, as already noted,

---

[18]   Interestingly, "Elegy on Spain" was written shortly after "Poem on Ireland," in which Barker meditates on his ancestral country's persistence in himself: "I wore the shape of Ireland in my mind" (97). The poem seems in a way to have prepared him for Spain. Ireland is "Europe's sore that will not heal" as well as the vehicle for the poet's own introspection: "Having no nearer Hesperides, I create / Ireland my Hesperides near at hand ... / I mean my own Ireland which no latitude / Can categorize and no map show—/ Because only I possess the plenitude / Of passion it has—only I know / The lonely inhabitant, whose home is / Imagination." (97). Such flexibility undoubtedly prepared many British and Irish writers to "create" Spain in turn, but it likely also led to some of the problematic liberties they took in writing about Spain.

is not its creation of an equal contest.[19] It is a sacrifice, not a sport, and the need to recast it in terms of ideals of "fair play" and their violation helps explain why poets might misread the war in the process of misreading the bullfight. Taking away the judge's rifle or returning the matador's sword restores an order and a kind of justice, but only those dictated by the ritual form, not by an abstract ideal of sportsmanship. The sporting ethic, as Modris Eksteins and many others have noted, runs deep in "British social discourse" and "social intercourse as a whole" (Eksteins 120). In the First World War, the British notion that "the sporting spirit was the essence of civilization" helped clarify the terms of cultural debate, providing Britons with perhaps the key measure of difference between British and German worldviews (123). "As the war dragged on," of course, "such sentiments would fade" (124).[20] In Spain, however, they resurfaced, particularly in those cases in which a British writer attempted to come to terms with a game, as it were, a form—of fighting, of art, of ethics—organized by another code, one alien yet not entirely unfamiliar, disturbing yet attractive. On one level, the bullfight seemed to represent everything against which the British worldview defined itself. On another, it held out the possibility of a model in which competition, war, death, art and action might be contained and needfully reconceived.

"On Guard for Spain!" illustrates how a rhetoric that reduces the war, and the bullfight, to simple oppositions fails to hit on the complex interrelation and overlap of parts that characterizes both. Just as Orwell is constantly confronted by the absurdity of his attempt to maintain strict oppositional categories in Spain, British poets are often confounded by the bullfight's ambiguity. In order to represent clear-cut political oppositions, they must change and distort the terms of the corrida, and the result is frequently the furious, one-sided politics of poems such as "On Guard for Spain!" This strategic poetic adulteration of the bullfight often coincides with the reduction of the war along dialectical lines of class. "On Guard for Spain!" offers no middle term between "Spain" and "the world" except the universal proletariat. It is all "fascists" versus "the people of Spain" or the "workers of the world" (255–62). The poem's sweeping condemnation of the Catholic Church (one such possible middle term) all but forecloses the possibility of an audience identifying with Catholic workers and Republicans on religious grounds. Neither does the word *Europe* appear anywhere in the poem, as though even this secular, but a-material, concept represented a surrender to the kind of aesthetic mystification on which fascism relied so heavily. R. Vernon Beste's reflection (cited earlier in this chapter) on the sonority of Spanish place names ("Badajoz!" "Málaga!" "Teruel"), however, shows that at least one Englishman found the appeal of "On Guard for Spain!" to be aesthetic, not ideological. Certainly he says nothing about class solidarity in his description of the poem's

---

[19] Measures are taken to ensure that the bullfight stays relatively dangerous for the matador, however, such as prohibitions against horn shaving or weakening the bull prior to the corrida. (See McCormick 34 and 215 n.10).

[20] See Eksteins 120–28.

emotional impact. All too often, such class-based appeals fell flat, as though the speakers misjudged the basis on which non-Spaniards might identify with the Spanish situation. Jan Koster argues, indeed, that before Stalin, European "socialism was handicapped by its internationalism and roots in Enlightenment universalism," and that ordinary nationalism and then fascism "offer[ed] a more seductive experience of *communitas* among large segments of the labor forces than the international solidarity of class" (238). In the essay "Looking Back on the Spanish War" (1943), Orwell acknowledges that class solidarity had not been nearly enough to mobilize sufficient foreign involvement in Spain:

> Time after time, in country after country, the organised working-class movements
> have been crushed by open, illegal violence, and their comrades abroad, linked
> to them in theoretical solidarity, have simply looked on and done nothing; ...
> To the British working class, the massacre of their comrades in Vienna, Berlin,
> Madrid, or wherever it might be, seemed less interesting and less important than
> yesterday's football match. (*Collected* 60–61)

Orwell's disgust at such indifference is profound. It does not, however, lead him here to consider possible structures for European solidarity other than Marxist ones.[21] He knows that proletarian poems such as "On Guard" miss their mark in modern Britain, but, even though he thinks in European cultural terms ("Vienna, Berlin, Madrid"), he cannot see in those terms a more influential pattern than the "theoretical solidarity" of class. Even more stubbornly, "On Guard for Spain!" distorts or obscures a good deal of cultural material, including the fiesta and the bullfight, that might otherwise have pricked up more ears like Beste's.

Nabara to the Rescue

Perhaps surprisingly, a civil-war poem by a leftist, indeed a Communist, poet who may never have been to Spain makes more effective use of the corrida's structure to make a political statement. Cecil Day Lewis's *The Nabara* is based on the account of the attack on the Basque town of Guernica in G.L. Steer's book, *The Tree of Gernika* (1938). It uses bullfighting imagery in order to ennoble Basque sailors' deaths without resorting to political flag waving. In its second stanza, the poem hits on the kind of primary feeling, present to both war and bullfighting, that Barker misses:

> I see man's heart two-edged, keen both for death and creation.
> As a sculptor rejoices, stabbing and mutilating the stone
> Into a shapelier life, and the two joys make one—

---

[21]   There is one exception. Orwell does allow that, "underneath this, secret cause of many betrayals, has lain the fact that between white and coloured workers there is not even lip-service to solidarity" (260). It is difficult to see how the racial divide, though, applies to the Spanish situation.

So man is wrought in his hour of agony and elation
To efface the flesh to reveal the crying need of his bone. (236)

When Hemingway referred to "the sculptural art of modern bullfighting," he meant not just the plastic beauty of the figure created by man and bull during a series of well executed passes; he meant also this quality of creation out of destruction (13). Day Lewis has the tragic sense of which Hemingway spoke, whereby the fact of death countenances no rhetorical consolations. The action of Day Lewis's poem takes place against the backdrop of "the unimpassioned / Face of a day where nothing certain but death remained" (238). The death of a bull shot from above by a rifle is not inevitable, not tragic, not even noble in the Spanish sense. The death from wounds endured in conflict, Day Lewis's poem suggests, from blood lost in the creation of something more—a nation, a ritual, an aesthetic object—is. Day Lewis's epigraph is "They preferred, because of the rudeness of their heart, to die rather than to surrender," and he compares the heroes of his poem, ships and men alike, to the bull that dies of its wounds in the corrida. The sea is the plaza de toros, and the battle progresses according to the rhythm of the bullfight. The Bizkaya executes "a bold manoeuvre," "Her signal-flags soon to flutter like banderillas, straight / Towards the Estonian speeding, a young bull over the spacious / And foam-distraught arena" (240).[22] The Basques who await relief are "grown sick with … the drain of their country's wounds" (240). The fire that consumes the Guipuzkoa "gushed from her gashes and seeped" like blood (241). Finally, "gallant Nabara was left in the ring alone, / The sky hollow around her," and "The battle's tempo slowed" as the moment of truth approached: "Slower now battle's tempo, irregular the beat / Of gunfire in the heart / Of the afternoon, the distempered sky sank to crisis" (241–42). The ships and the crews slowly pulse away their life: "filthy with grime / And … blood, weary with wounds," "a bloody skein reeled out in their wake … so weak / From wounds," "They fought in pain / And the instant knowledge of death," "half-killed / With wounds" (242–44). In bullfighting, the bravest bull is one who charges well to the end and never opens his mouth; at the climax of this battle the "Nabara's tongue was stilled" (244). The honor of her fight, "satisfied long since," is that of the bull, having "held out and harried" a better-equipped enemy, here "A ship ten times their size; they could have called it a day" but did not (242). Just as the bull does not enter the ring with a legitimate chance to defeat his enemy, these sailors "went into battle foreseeing / Probable loss, and they lost" (244). This is the truly tragic death, the inevitable death war and toreo bring achingly to consciousness which cannot be redeemed by anything outside itself, but by which much more than simply one poet's grief is redeemed.

Day Lewis's political sympathies are the same as Barker's and Lindsay's, but Day Lewis's poem has a ritual sensitivity the more doctrinaire leftist poems lack,

---

[22] The names of the Spanish ships in the poem—*Bizkaya, Guipuzkoa, Nabara*—are all those of places in or near the Basque country in northern Spain and southern France. This allows Day Lewis to heighten the correspondence between the *toro bravo* and Spain itself.

allowing it to mine the corrida, and the war, to maximum effect. In comparison, Barker and Lindsay attempt to employ the bullfight as a political expedient, and the effect is more superficial. All of which suggests that, beneath the visible, though not unambiguous, conflicts between Fascism and Communism or between Catholicism and atheism, an underlying crisis of the Spanish Civil War may have centered on the divide, illuminated by the corrida de toros, between those with ritual sense and those without it.

In a January, 1937 *Criterion* Commentary, Eliot referred to the Spanish Civil War as "an international civil war of opposed ideas" (289). His phrase, while paradoxical, is apt. By the strictest definition, a civil war concerns the internal division of a single nation and thus cannot be "international." The Spanish Civil War, however, became almost immediately an international affair, not merely because of foreign involvement—aid from Italy, Germany, and Russia, volunteers from Britain, Ireland, France, and America—but because of the war's character as the microcosm of a European crisis. Those things that attracted writers about Spain, the things they tried so earnestly to avoid glamorizing in their writing but which often remained long after the "theoretical solidarity" of class had fizzled, are the very things of which Europe may have stood most desperately in need. Romantic Spain, the Spain of bullfights, did not jibe with class solidarity and thus was often mistrusted, but, beyond rescuing at least one great civil-war poem—*The Nabara*—from the literary pitfalls of explicit political commitment, attending to Romantic Spain's reality often redeemed more of the war's violence and bloodshed than could the orthodoxies of class. In the poem "Postscript for Spain," J.C. Hall called Spain "the European wound" (457). As Spain bled, most of liberal Europe responded with nausea and terror, as though the essential insides of Europe were suddenly made visible. The most audible voice offering to make sense of the nonsense was the voice urging a reasoned identification based on ideals of progress, the future, and light. A more articulate voice, though less well understood, may have been the one speaking from the old workshop of Spain's political culture, the bullfight.

Interchapter:
A Trinity of Converts

All three of the authors covered in this final section are converts to Roman Catholicism, which is unsurprising, considering that the majority of British Catholic literary voices of the first half of the twentieth century are those of converts: Greene, Waugh, Jones, G.K. Chesterton, Siegfried Sassoon, Edith Sitwell, and Christopher Dawson, to name only the most prominent. One thinks also of Eliot, a convert to Anglo-Catholicism. The evidence of their writings, particularly those of Greene, Waugh, and Jones, suggests that the fact of conversion played a formative part in their perception not only of Catholicism but also of the European culture with which Catholicism had been associated for many centuries. Greene, Waugh, and Jones bring the convert's insight and perceptiveness to Catholicism, and the relative outsider's point of view to the idea of Europe. Auden, the Englishman (and later the American), felt himself to be on the fringe of European culture, a feeling supported in part by Great Britain's separation from the traditional religion of Europe, one of the most profound and longstanding schisms in the European surface. The decision by the group of writers including Greene, Waugh, and Jones to return to Rome represents at once reunification with a European tradition and alienation from the local culture of Britain. Being Catholic made all three outsiders of a kind in their own country, even as it strengthened, in a way, their ties to Europe.

There is instructive irony in the differing circumstances of their conversions. Of the three, only Jones, the first to convert (in 1921), admitted having been captivated by Catholic ritual. In a late letter, he describes his "first sight of a Mass" (DGC 248). Gathering firewood at some point after the battle of the Somme, he happened upon a damaged farm building. Peeking inside through a crack in the wall, he saw "the back of a sacerdos in a gilt-hued *planeta*, two points of flickering candlelight … , white altar cloths and the white linen of the celebrant's alb and amice and maniple … and kneeling in the hay beneath the improvised *mensa* were a few huddled figures in khaki" (DGC 249). He did not linger, "as it seemed rather like an uninitiated bloke prying on the Mysteries of a Cult. But," he acknowledges, "it made a big impression on me" (DGC 249). Jones's approach to Catholicism is, from that moment, usually of the local, microcosmic kind that one finds in professional students of ritual, such as Kertzer, who writes: "Symbols provide the content of ritual; hence, the nature of these symbols and the ways they are used tell us much about the nature and influence of ritual" (11). Jones is ever concerned with ritual as Emile Durkheim defines it: "the rules of conduct which prescribe how a man should comport himself in the presence of these sacred objects" (41). His attention is always directed towards that physical part of Catholicism that one can glimpse through a crack in the wall.

Waugh, in contrast, downplayed the role that ritual played in attracting him to the Catholic Church, which he joined in 1930. "[T]he purely aesthetic appeal," he writes, "is, on the whole, rather against the Roman Church" in Great Britain (EAR 103). He goes on to note that "the first discovery" that made his choice inevitable was that European civilization depends for its life on Christianity, which "exists in its most complete and vital form in the Roman Catholic Church" (which was the "second discovery") (EAR 104). He has a true appreciation for the Church's tangible symbols and rituals, but these are often dwarfed in his writing by the great system of social organization into which these small signs have opened up over the centuries.

After his 1926 conversion, Greene would go on to elaborate his religion, and his doubts, with unparalleled seriousness both in fiction and nonfiction. Initially, though, and rather more prosaically, he became Catholic in order to marry his Catholic girlfriend, Vivien Dayrell-Browning (Sherry 192–93).[1] Also, over the course of his career, Greene would distance himself from the institutional Church, personally and creatively, far more than Jones or Waugh, so much so that Greene's novels written after the 1930s and 1940s have at times been called his post-Catholic works.[2] However, even during his periods of greatest commitment to his religion, Greene always treats Catholicism as a way and as a tool of resistance, a means of carving meaning out of the face of a world slipping into apathy and spiritual lethargy, particularly in Great Britain. "So many years have passed in England," he laments, "since the war between faith and anarchy: we live in an ugly indifference" (LR 34). The Catholicism in Greene's writing, early and late, is portable, flexible, and potent even where it is without the visible support of the official Church, its dogmas and infrastructure. Rather than being a function of the Church's leaders, documents, and history, it is, to use a phrase of Greene's from *The Lawless Roads*, more a "religion of the earth" (171).

In the juxtaposition of these three accounts, then, three of the potential faces of Catholicism come into focus. The Church as the site of ritual action, the Church as the framework for a civilization, and the Church as an oppositional instrument form the bases for Jones's, Waugh's, and Greene's respective writings on Catholicism. That three writers so differently disposed regarding the nature of their religion—and, as will be seen, regarding its political implications—may with equal validity be classed as exemplars of the same church suggests a measure of unity in diversity within Catholicism. However, while there seems to be a vast space between these three visions of the Church, these authors seem to agree

---

[1]   Some argue that Greene's interest in the themes of cultural order and tradition that concerned his convert peers was more influential in his decision than his need to satisfy his future wife. See, for instance, Adam Schwartz's *The Third Spring*, Chapter 2.

[2]   Refuting this logic is the object of Mark Bosco's book, *Graham Greene's Catholic Imagination*. Bosco argues that Greene's supposedly post-Catholic work is in fact an accurate reflection of his continuing engagement with a changing Catholic church, in the context, for instance, of Vatican II.

that two things which cannot be accommodated there are indifference and what Eliot in 1939 called the "negative" solution of liberalism, which, "in meaning too many things," means nothing (CC 11). Despite the diversity of their political positions, all of these authors have consciously rejected one key part of "what the Western world has stood for" (CC 11) and chosen another. Waugh and Jones, in the Eliot mold, would have been far more likely to become Communists, strange as that may sound, than liberals. Greene, who savages the atheistic materialism of the socialist Mexican government, reserves his harshest criticism for the nothingness represented by American liberalism with its Monopoly, Coca-Cola, and entertainment magazines. For all the sociopolitical distance between them, Waugh's classical, Jones's cultish, and Greene's revolutionary Church squeeze out nearly all that might be called liberal, bourgeois, or secular. In combination, though, their writings demarcate a zone within which unity is possible and which simultaneously supports real, though not unlimited, diversity.

More than either verse drama or bullfighting—whose imaginative utility, I hope to have demonstrated, is not absolutely circumscribed by national boundaries but is nonetheless and necessarily limited by virtue of being tethered to very specific national cultures—Catholicism, which is essentially supranational, overlaps demonstrably with Europe's imagination of itself, in conceptual as well as historical ways. The European Union, whose motto is "United in Diversity," has generally minimized, for understandable reasons, the Catholic component of its inheritance. It is worth noting, however, that the concept of European unity in diversity itself may have far more to do with Roman Catholicism than is immediately apparent at this late date when, after all, the United States, far more a liberal than a Catholic country, stamps "*e pluribus unum*" on its coins. Gonzague de Reynold identifies "two sources of European federalism." The first is "Germanism, which recognizes the rights of 'folk' communities" (qtd. in de Rougemont 380). The second is "the trinitarian doctrine formulated by the earliest Councils of the Church." It seems perhaps a tenuous connection until one considers the ways in which the paradox of the trinity—three in one, one in three—actually served as the model for European identification. According to Friedrich Heer: "From 800–1815 all the European peace treaties concluded *in nomine sanctae et individuae Trinitatis*" (16). There is, then, a legitimate precedent for associating Europe's modern idea of itself with its Catholic heritage.

However, Europe has never been entirely Catholic. Peace treaties invoking the Christian Trinitarian God plainly minimize the claims of Europe's Jewish, Muslim, liberal, and secular peoples to a stake in the European project of unity in diversity. Although European Catholicism has, of course, historically exercised a far broader power of social organization than the ritual traditions covered in the preceding two sections, it shares with verse drama and the bullfight, especially in the twentieth century, the limitation of incompleteness as a paradigm for comprehensive European unity. Catholicism is not Europe, but, as the English language does in the mind of Eliot, the ritual framework of Catholicism gathers in some of Greene's, Waugh's, and Jones's most important preoccupations regarding

Europe's nature and purpose. Catholic ritual enables these writers to articulate a notion of European identity that is partly spiritual, partly political, partly cultural, partly historical, but that always finds its sustenance in the tension between these categories, not in the reduction of the meaning of Europe or ritual to any one of them.

Chapter 6
Like Going Home:
Greene and Waugh in Mexico

In the chapter on D.H. Lawrence, I attempted to show how an English literary appropriation of Mexican ritual could outstrip the interpretive possibilities afforded by standard post-colonial paradigms. In the current chapter, I take up two more Englishmen, Graham Greene and Evelyn Waugh, who traveled to Mexico, ostensibly to report on the Mexican socio-political situation but whose reflections tend consistently back toward contemporary Europe. As with Lawrence, the meditations of Greene and Waugh are Europe-centered but are not particularly well illuminated by the well-worn notion of Eurocentrism. Even more than Lawrence, Greene and Waugh traveled to Mexico at a moment—the height of the Spanish Civil War—and with a set of preoccupations—Roman Catholic—that reinforce the European connection. In Mexico a socialist and secular nationalism had asserted itself positively against the Catholic religious element, while in Europe the Spanish Civil War had signaled a contest between communism and fascism, and between atheism and Catholicism. For Greene and Waugh, Catholicism underscored the European implications of the Mexican situation. The kinds of conclusions reached in both writers' Mexican books suggest that English ideas of Mexico had important nuances to add to the idea of Europe being contested in Spain and about to swell into a world war.

Greene traveled to Mexico in the spring and Waugh in the fall of 1938. Greene had wanted to visit Mexico for some time, and he secured a deal with Longman's to write a nonfiction account of the Mexican government's persecution of Catholics. Waugh was enlisted by Clive Pearson "to advertise the injustice" of the expropriation of British oil interests by the Mexican government (Stannard, *Early Years* 478–79). Although the religious question was not specifically part of his assignment, his attention almost immediately gravitated in that direction. In the late 1930s, Mexico was at the end of two decades of sharp conflict between the state and the Catholic Church.[1] Following the Mexican Revolution, the 1917

---

[1]   The major stages of anti-clericalism in Mexico in the early twentieth century, according to Roderic Ai Camp, were the Mexican Revolution of 1910, the Constitution of 1917, and the Cristero War of 1926–1929. (26–27). The period from 1929–1940, he writes, was characterized by a series of quiet, unofficial compromises between the church and the state. Not all historians agree on this sequence, though. Derek Davis, for one, dates the period of church-state cooperation "from approximately 1937–38 through the late 1940s or early 1950s" (9). In any case, Greene and Waugh both went to Mexico at the end of the worst antagonisms between religious and secular elements, but their attention was focused on those areas where government persecution remained strongest.

Constitution, designed on broadly Marxist class-struggle lines, included several articles intended to curb the influence of the Church in society. These prohibited, for example, religious education, religious orders, and public religious ceremonies. It was not until 1926, though, under President Plutarco Elías Calles, that these provisions were strictly enforced on a national level.[2] The result was the Cristero Rebellion of 1926–1929, after which the Church gained minor concessions from the government, but violent army retribution against Cristeros and their sympathizers continued. After a six-year period in which three presidents held office, General Lázaro Cárdenas came to power and implemented several measures designed to keep the revolution moving leftward. Leader of the Partido de la Revolución Mexicana (PRM), General Cárdenas presided over the nationalization, which Waugh was sent to criticize, of the Mexican oil industry. During this period, the severity of government repression varied considerably among the Mexican regions and states, according to the inclination of the local governor. Michoacán, for instance, where Cárdenas had been governor from 1928–1932, was particularly hard hit, and, Greene writes, in Mexico City "four hundred and eighty Catholic churches, schools, orphanages, hospitals were closed by the Government or converted to other uses" from 1931–1936 (LR 66). By 1938, however, the PRM had begun to temper its anti-clericalism, though in states such as Tabasco and Chiapas, to which Greene made haste, persecution was still the rule.[3] Mexico City, the hub of Waugh's three-month journey, was comparatively peaceable.

Waugh and Greene were two very different kinds of travelers. Waugh might best be described as a centripetal traveler; Europe is the axis toward which all of his impressions bend. By his own admission, his Mexican journey never takes him far from recognizably Western comforts. Greene, in contrast, travels and interprets centrifugally, content to let his experiences abroad spin him out into unexplored areas of mind. He, too, measures his impressions against a European standard, but his travel writing does give the sense of a man swimming out as far from land as he can and still make it back. Thus, the two authors use the Mexican scene to articulate very different ideas about the relation of Catholic ritual to political power, to explore from an objective distance the ways in which their religion had been and might be of use to a Europe searching for its own sense of identity in the late 1930s.

In neither Spain nor Mexico was the alliance of Catholicism and political commitment clear cut, but Catholicism's conservative social function was

---

[2]   For some time after the ratification of the Constitution, Brian Hamnett writes, truly representative government remained an impossibility. "Instead, localised boss-rule [the *caudillo* system], private networks of power, and armed political factions competed for power within or against the Revolution" (226). It was not until the 1930s that the Mexican political structure had matured to the point that a Cárdenas, for instance, could emerge as the legitimate leader of a widely recognized political party.

[3]   Owen Chadwick correctly notes that Greene "went to Tabasco because it was one of the last two states where religion was still banned" (265).

broadly assumed, owing to the widely perceived conflict between Christianity and Marxism,[4] and to such highly visible alliances as that between General Franco's Nationalist uprising and the Catholic Church in Spain.[5] But Waugh, writing after Greene, did not condemn or discount Greene's leftist political conclusions, nor is his own account devoid of appreciation for the liberatory component of Catholicism. Waugh's Catholic Church, however, affirms a top-down and Europe-out vision of Christian civilization. In addition to ordering and ennobling Mexican culture, this Church anchors it to a European tradition and core which sustains it. Greene's version, in contrast, mobilizes the sacraments, as it were, detaches them from institutional sources of power, and uses them as a spade with which to burrow under and subvert even a proletarian social ideal. Although great difficulty, antagonism, and even violence attaches to the articulation and the working-out of these religious visions amidst the scenery of the socio-political world—in Mexico, in Spain, in Great Britain—such divergent ideologies do not appear conflictual, in Waugh and Greene's Mexican books, within the boundaries of Catholic ritual spaces.

The Case for Europe

In discussing Greene's *The Lawless Roads* (1939) and *The Power and the Glory* (1940) and Waugh's *Robbery Under Law: The Mexican Object-Lesson* (1939), there are at least three good reasons for shifting attention from the Mexican political situation in its own right to the ways in which both authors use Mexico to talk about Europe. The first, advanced by Latin American scholars Enrique Dussel and Carlos Fuentes and alluded to in the Introduction, is that Latin America is an indivisible part of modern European cultural identity. To occlude "the *first periphery* of modern Europe" from that identity, Dussel argues, is to ignore the defining feature of European modernity, the expansion that first enabled Europe to see itself from the outside (67).[6] Dussel's insistence on Latin America's importance to the formation of the modern European idea is a necessary counter to the northern-Eurocentric strain of thought, running from Hegel to Habermas, which

---

[4]   This perception was shared by Catholics as well as non-Catholics. See Donat Gallagher in Waugh, EAR 155.

[5]   Martin Conway writes: "Though there remained Christian democrats who sought a rapprochement with the political left, the weight of Catholic political engagement during the 1930s was predominantly on the right, and often on the anti-parliamentary right. This did not," he notes, "equate with support for fascism. Catholic opinion, particularly outside Italy and Germany, was predominantly hostile to the cult of the state and 'brown bolshevism' which they associated with the Fascist and more especially Nazi regimes" (167–68). On "the authoritarian drift in Catholic politics during the 1930s" and the role of publicly Catholic political leaders in it, see Conway 167.

[6]   The title of Carlos Fuentes's magnificent study of Spain and the Americas, *The Buried Mirror*, refers precisely to precisely this kind of self seeing.

sees not only Latin America but also the Iberian nations themselves as of secondary importance to the idea of Europe. Bernard Crick argues that non-geographically European places like Mexico may be "nonetheless in some undeniable sense European in culture, or clear modulations thereof" (xiii). A similar view underpins Greene's and Waugh's interpretations of Mexico, and neither writer shares the view, aphorized by Dumas and others, that Europe ends at the Pyrenees. Both Greene and Waugh, as will be seen, place Iberia near the center of their late-1930s meditations on the idea of Europe.

The second reason, almost uniformly agreed upon by critics, is that neither Greene nor Waugh does a particularly good job of objectively describing the Mexican situation during the latter stages of government persecution of the Catholic Church in its local, historical particularity.[7] Bernard Schweizer writes that Greene provides only "sketchy historical references" to account for what "was in fact a more complex and involved political situation" (76). Jeffrey Meyers's criticism of Greene's *The Lawless Roads* as a "didactic—and curiously insular—book, which reeks of propaganda and piety ... but does not provide a clear picture of the historical background" sounds like that normally reserved for Waugh's *Robbery Under Law* (62).[8] "[N]either writer," observes Michael Brennan, "expressed any significant level of personal interest in South American politics or religion before the mid-1930s" (15), and the contextual analysis in the books, he argues, is correspondingly thin.[9] Biographer Martin Stannard writes that "Waugh's smattering of the [Spanish] language was of the barest; his previous knowledge of Mexico negligible" (*Early Years* 480). Although Waugh was able to "absorb" an impressive amount of "political history" in a short time, "[t]he fact remains," Stannard continues, "that his book often reconstructs the information at his disposal" (480) to suit the expectations of the Cowdray Estate, which was

---

[7]   Waugh biographer Selina Hastings demurs somewhat. "Waugh's account is on the whole factual and dogmatic ... Where Greene treats his material in a manner both manipulative and melodramatic, Waugh mainly confines himself to a selective but sober statement of fact" (377–78).

[8]   Paul Fussell also disapproves of Greene's treatment of Mexican politics but, rather than for being too aloof from it, for being too passionately involved. Fussell categorically prefers travel writing in the subjective-interior mode of Greene's previous book, *Journey Without Maps*, whereby the author "conceive[s] the journey as a metaphor for something else" (*Abroad* 67). He naturally objects to Waugh's Mexican book as well, as another example of the era's tendency to politicize travel writing. See Fussell, *Abroad 159*, 222. Waugh, in contrast, believed that "Mr. Greene's cinematographic shots of present conditions provide ample evidence, the more damning because they are not linked by any political thesis" (EAR 250).

[9]   Somewhat ironically, Waugh's review of *The Lawless Roads* notes that Greene "makes little attempt, except by occasional implication, to give the historical background of the tragedy. His book is a day-to-day account of his movements" (EAR 249). That is, it is a travel book of the kind favored by Fussell.

paying Waugh to make its case against General Cardenas's expropriation of British oil (478).

Even without the financial incentive, Waugh was never known as the kind of traveler who approaches new places with an open mind. Rather, as Nicholas Shakespeare observes, "Waugh travels to have his biases confirmed" (xvi). Waugh himself was forthcoming about such insularity: "When we go abroad we take our opinions with us; it is useless to pretend, as many writers do, that they arrive with minds wholly innocent of other experience; are born anew into each new world" (Nicholas Shakespeare xvi). Regarding the books' trenchancy of cultural observation, insisting on the ethnographic shortcomings of either one thus seems redundant, even petty. Recuperating and delineating the books' European component seem more productive critical enterprises at this point. The texts themselves certainly suggest that Greene and Waugh had Europe squarely in mind.

That both authors conceive of the Mexican situation quite frankly in terms of its European relevance is the third reason for mitigating the critical demand for ethnographic objectivity. Both *The Lawless Roads* and *Robbery Under Law* end with chapters underscoring the European connection, and neither makes any absolute distinction between Mexican and European culture. Instead, Waugh, perhaps unexpectedly anticipating Said's formulation of Orientalism, describes Mexico as the "distorting mirror" of Europe, "in which objects are reflected in perverse and threatening forms" (RUL 912). It is, he suggests, what Africa was to the Romans and what Ireland has been to England (RUL 803; 912). Likewise, Greene's interest in "far-off places" like Mexico, Judith Adamson argues, was that in them "one's own culture was thrown into sharp relief" (xvi). Specifically, writes Sheryl Pearson, Greene defines Mexico "in terms of … a European, especially British, scheme of social history that is remote to Mexican realities" (282). He "habitually leaves behind the literal Mexican setting, establishing and reestablishing links between Mexican history and the Western mainstream" (282). Thus Greene writes that the Mexican government's anticlericalism represents "the fiercest persecution of religion anywhere since the reign of Elizabeth" (LR 19) and sees Mexico as "a Belgium fought over by friend and enemy alike," belonging to "the same subterranean struggle" as Russia and Spain (LR 33). Mexico City, he observes, has more to do with Europe than with Mexico's own outlying areas (LR 63). Waugh sees Mexico as the extremity, but still very much a part, of a civilization with Europe at its center; he remarks during his journey that "a European war would at any rate settle the Mexican question" (RUL 720; 833). The Spanish Civil War was not quite the "European war" he had in mind, although he does declare that its outcome is "vital" to the Mexican situation. At any rate, neither Spain nor the broader war of which Europe stood on the brink in 1938 "settled" Mexico any more than Mexico, however much light it seemed to throw back across the Atlantic, settled the European question.

Political events at home were in no small way responsible for the European outlook Greene and Waugh brought to Mexico. The Spanish Civil War, then at its peak, frames both authors' reflections on Mexican culture and politics. Surprisingly for two such prolific writers, both, as Dan Kostopulos notes, are "fairly mute on the subject of the Spanish Civil War" outside their Mexican books (125).[10] Indeed, biographer Christopher Sykes states flatly that "*Robbery Under Law* was Evelyn's Spanish War book" (255).[11] For Greene, explains Norman Sherry, "Mexico ... offered the same conflict as in Spain—religion versus atheism" (655). On his return voyage, any distinctions Greene may have retained between Mexico and Europe fall away in light of the Spanish Civil War: "The shadow of the Spanish war stretched across the South Atlantic and the Gulf; it cropped up in Las Casas of an evening round the radio—one couldn't expect to escape it in a German ship calling at Lisbon" (LR 215). That both used Mexico for their most sustained written reflections on the Spanish war suggests a subtler linkage between Europe and the Americas than any narrow Eurocentrism can explain.

In the following pages I hope to show how the common ritual framework of Catholicism clarifies as well as expands that linkage. Of the guiding characteristics of ritual outlined in the Introduction, two are especially important in analyzing the treatment of Mexican Catholicism by Greene and Waugh. The first is ritual's creation of and dependence on sacred spaces. George Mosse writes that "the idea of the 'sacred space,' a place that could be filled only with symbolic activity ... was considered a prerequisite to liturgical action" well before Christianity (208), but Christianity did more than uphold the idea. In the Mexico of the 1920s and 1930s, the sacred spaces of the Church were virtually synonymous with its identity. The second is the quality of ritual of being both revolutionary and conservative. Catherine Bell, echoing Kertzer and Koster, writes that "ritual attends conservative politics of 'reaction' as well as the potentially transformative politics of 'revolution'" (169). The Church's rituals have been the tools of both political control and political resistance. Indeed, Greene's and Waugh's depictions of Mexican Catholicism suggest that ritual's ideological flexibility is often demonstrated in one place and at one time.

---

[10]   Of Waugh's political journalism from 1935–1945, Gallagher notes two significant "silences, about Spain by choice, and about Mexico because newspapers showed absolute non-interest in the subject ... The Spanish Civil War drew from Waugh neither article, nor review, nor letter, but only an answer to a questionnaire" (Waugh, EAR 156–58). Thus *Robbery Under Law* is doubly important as the fullest explication of Waugh's views on both fronts. He would clearly have published more on Mexico if he were able: "Though Waugh tried very hard to sell articles about Mexico, going to the extent, unusual for him, of circulating summaries of his proposals, no editor could be induced to show interest" (159).

[11]   Waugh finds considerable justification in the views of the Mexicans themselves. The Spanish Civil War, he writes, was "more real to them than any other piece of contemporary history ... They understood the Spanish issue in Spanish terms ... It was like part of their own lives" (RUL 748).

Catholic Ritual and Politics

Catholicism, of course, is more than a ritual or even a collection of rituals. In 1930s Mexico, however, the presence of Catholicism and the enactment of its rituals were almost entirely coextensive. There are two primary reasons for this circumstance. The first is that the Mexican government's campaign against the Church aimed not so much at a faith as at a religious praxis: a faith is much more difficult to censor than its public enactment. Moreover, the utility of illegalizing the *practice* of a religion is considerably greater where the religion in question is essentially a "sacramental system," as Waugh puts it (EAR 377), relying on dedicated places and communal practices such as ritual. Waugh enumerates the features that make a public faith like Catholicism such an effective target for suppression:

> What is not reasonable is the attitude … that religion is a purely private business; that if a man is disposed that way he can sit at home and be religious by himself; that he needs no special class to minister to him, no special association with sympathisers, no place to associate and no means of conveying his belief to his descendants. Either his religion will die or it will find concrete expression in these ways.
>
> The Church for her life, has to have a priesthood, an order of men peculiarly educated and consecrated for a specific work; she has to have property where she can preserve her sacred things from outrage; she has to have the opportunity of conveying her teaching to children whose parents desire it. Deny her those elementary claims and you deny her life. Each one of these is still being denied in Mexico. (RUL 891–92)

Greene's and Waugh's Mexican texts show that the government met Catholicism on precisely the ground of concrete expression and ritual space. Civil servants, Waugh writes, "are liable to expulsion if … they are seen to practise their religion" (RUL 769). In schools, "religious instruction or practice of any kind is forbidden … the girls may not even say grace after meals" (RUL 854).[12] For Greene, too, with his sacramental way of thinking, the enactment of the most concrete and communal rituals of Catholicism—illegally, in secret, in improvised ritual spaces—constitutes virtually the whole preservation of the faith in Mexico. Certainly the whisky-priest hero of *The Power and the Glory* feels the internal element of his religion as nothing compared to its tangible manifestations. Praying over a dead child, "He could feel no meaning any longer in prayers like these. The Host was different: to lay that between a dying man's lips was to lay God.

---

12   See Davis 8–9: "The new policies severely limited the number of priests in a region, banned all foreign priests from holding ecclesiastical offices, prevented religious rights [*sic*] and instruction in private schools and even homes, and made all violations subject to severe penalties under criminal law." Owen Chadwick reports that by 1933, "there were fewer than 200 priests in Mexico; in 1810 there had been 7341" (265). See also Abel 186–87.

That was a fact—something you could touch, but this was no more than a pious aspiration" (PG 151). This conviction is primarily spiritual—"Why should anyone listen to *his* prayers? Sin was a constriction which prevented their escape" (PG 151)—yet in political terms, too, the Host was a different matter from the prayers of an individual.

The second reason for this preponderance of ritual—in the texts as in the culture—is, as Mark Bosco explains, that Catholic theology and sensibility of the period (that is, prior to the Second Vatican Council of the early 1960s) stressed the centrality of rituals presided over by priests as against the diffusion of divine revelation outside the institutional church. In writing about Mexico, both Greene and Waugh reflect what Bosco calls the "traditional Catholic sensibility of the early twentieth century" ("From" 64). Waugh's sense of the indispensability of ritual—and of symbol, one of its constituent elements—to the Church, particularly in Mexico, is explicit. He observes that Catholic resistance to government suppression necessarily took on a physical form, including not only the secret Masses of rebellious priests but also "courageous malcontents who give secret religious instruction to their pupils" (RUL 769). Through local acts of religious defiance, he writes,

> the Church is being re-established in Mexico. A European is tempted to write 'Faith' instead of Church. I had, indeed, done so and struck it out, for the Faith has never been lost to the vast majority of the country. But the Faith cannot exist for ever without its tangible expression; it is not a mere system of philosophic propositions and historical facts; though it may sometimes appear as this, in certain intellectual types living in a sympathetic atmosphere. It is a habit of life and a social organisation. The simpler a people, the ruder their living conditions and the more limited their information, so much the more do they need to symbolise their ideas in concrete shapes. They must have buildings in which they consort for worship, statues and pictures to make the ideas of their creed intelligible and memorable; above all they—equally with the most arid theologian—must have the sacraments. (RUL 891)

More expansively still, referring to the Virgin of Guadalupe, he writes, "it is only in material symbols that man is capable of recognising the truth by which he lives" (RUL 876). Although, as we will see, Greene's novel traces matters of salvation well beyond the boundaries of the institutional Church and its official ritual tradition, the priest's essential and central role as the administrator of sacraments remains. "When he was gone," the whisky priest reflects, "it would be as if God in all this space between the sea and the mountains ceased to exist" (PG 65). It is a position a priest, and certainly Greene, would have been less likely to defend after the adjustments of Vatican II.

Jan Koster's theoretical characterization of ritual performance as "the spatial marking of a territory ... by filling a designated space with the prescribed ritual actions [and] symbols" (216) is especially apt in light of the crucial role of ritual spaces in both the suppression of Mexican Catholicism and its resistance to suppression. No matter how many churches the government closed or burned, it seems, the landscape remained "littered with churches, like pieces of rock," in Greene's words (LR 201), or, in Waugh's, "graced, every few miles, by the domes and facades of the conquerors' churches" (RUL 731). The way the Mexican government dealt with churches underscores the inseparability of ritual and ritual space from a political perspective.[13] Of one church "converted into a public library" Waugh observes, "It is a curious thing, but churches never seem suitable for any other purpose than the one for which they were built" (RUL 889). Whereas one year earlier every church in the state had been closed, Catholicism was making something of a comeback in Vera Cruz. Waugh compares the secularized church at Vera Cruz with another nearby still serving its original purpose. Here,

> the decorations were shoddy and shabby; plaster statues had taken the place of the rich colonial sculpture, but at every altar there were people making their devotions, not old women only but quite young men, and in the nave a young catechist was giving instruction to a large class of school-children. They were learning the responses of the Mass, repeating them in unison … The Church was being allowed to compete with the State on equal terms for support of the new generation. (RUL 889)

In some cases churches were permitted to remain open "but," writes Greene, "no priest allowed inside" (LR 173). In such instances, though art and ornament still suggested a sacred space, the fundamental connection was broken. "It gave an effect of fullness—and of emptiness, like a meeting when the leader has gone. Nothing meant anything any more" (LR 173). Even thus under siege, the churches, because of the rituals with which they were associated, remained a focal point of the battle between politics and religion in the towns where they were left standing. Greene notes an incident in Villahermosa in which the peasants, though "[t]hey had no churches to open … set up a rough altar against the back wall of the one ruined church and prayed amongst the rubble. The soldiers came and opened fire and a few were killed—men, women, and children" (LR 183). This underground Catholicism so impressive to Greene, although officially denied the physical apparatus on which a sacramental religion depends, relentlessly carved out, reclaimed, and improvised ritual spaces in which the faith could be sustained. Without these, both Greene's and Waugh's Mexican texts seem to argue, the Church's battle against government suppression would have been practically meaningless.

The diverse political applicability of ritual is likely a function of one of the inherent features of ritual not shared by politics proper: the indissoluble tension

---

13   Waugh highlighted the special social integration of Catholicism in "Converted to Rome: Why It Has Happened to Me" in 1930: "No one visiting a Roman Catholic country can fail to be struck by the fact that the people do use their churches. It is not a matter of going to a service on Sunday; all classes at all hours of the day can be seen dropping in on their way to and from their work" (EAR 105).

between oppositions. "[T]he efficacy of ritualization as a power strategy," Bell argues, "lies not only in the domination it affords, but in the resistance as well ... The circularity of this phenomenon is intrinsic to it" (215). This circularity and simultaneity establish a space where ideals can coexist which in political life can only conflict. As we have seen in the case of the bullfight and the modern verse drama, the rituals themselves seem to dictate that every step in the direction of control is countered by one in the direction of subversion, and vice-versa. Although they share the same religion, its rituals and ritual spaces, Greene and Waugh could not have made political sense of Catholicism's ritual framework in ways more different. Greene's reading of the Church's presence and activity in Mexico is most often intensely leftist. His is a Catholicism of the people, a revolutionary force working from below on the institutions of oppression. In a 1941 essay, "Eric Gill," he wrote that "Conservatism and Catholicism should be as impossible bedfellows as Catholicism and National-Socialism" (133–34). Waugh's interpretation of Mexican Catholicism, in contrast, is often conservative in the extreme. It looks unapologetically back toward Spain and sees in the places and practices of Catholicism in Mexico a continuity with Europe, Christendom, and classical civilization. What he calls "the monarchical, feudal, hierarchic, baroque culture of Mexico" (RUL 791–92) is a direct product of Mexico's close ties, through the Church, to Spain. He rather audaciously claims that Americans "are in love with Europe; they are nostalgic for the Classical-Christian culture from which they remotely spring, which they find transplanted, transformed in part, but still recognisable in Mexico" (RUL 725). Likewise, the decline of the Church in Mexico is synonymous with the decline of cultural order, so that by the late 1930s "[d]isorder is grossly rampant" (RUL 861). Whereas Mexico, "a huge country with a long and proud history, taking precedence in its national unity of half the states of Europe," once "rich and cultured and orderly" and the parent of "sons illustrious in every walk of life" is now with each year of secular rule "becoming hungrier, wickeder, and more hopeless; the great buildings of the past are falling in ruins; the jungle is closing in," and so on (RUL 862).

The case of the Virgin of Guadalupe is illustrative of the distance between Greene's and Waugh's views of Catholic ritual's political function. *La Virgen* is at the heart of Mexican Catholic devotion, and Greene and Waugh give entirely different political inflections to this sacred object and its attendant myth and ritual practices.[14] Greene stresses the revolutionary elements of the Virgin's miraculous apparition to Indian peasant Juan Diego and the subsequent establishment of a holy shrine containing her image. "The legend," he writes, "gave the Indian self-

---

[14]   I am indebted to James Levernier and his paper "Including Catholic Texts in the Re-Formation of the Early American Canon: The Case of the Virgin of Guadalupe" for stimulating and clarifying my understanding of *La Virgen*. For commentary on the function of the Virgin of Guadalupe in Mexico (and elsewhere), see Deborah Boehm, "Our Lady of Resistance" (2002); Linda Craft, "Goddesses at the Borderlands" (1999); and William Taylor, "The Virgin of Guadalupe in New Spain" (1987)

respect; it gave him a hold over his conqueror; it was a liberating, not an enslaving legend" (LR 87). Waugh sees the same legend, no less approvingly, as an extension of the international order of Catholicism, proof that "the religion of the Spaniard was equally the religion of the Indian" (RUL 878). Both men's fondness for the Guadalupe myth and shrine and for the role of these in Mexican peasant life are unmistakable, but the difference in their interpretations reveals the wide, even contradictory, political commitments Catholic ritual structure may support.

That their shared religion allows for great diversity of political leaning is further evident from the fact that Greene and Waugh based almost diametrically opposed positions on the Spanish Civil War on their common Catholic allegiance. For both of them, the war presented an opportunity to make the religion precise and alive and politically relevant. Faced with this opportunity, and from a shared Catholic commitment, Greene leaned toward the Republic, Waugh toward Franco and the Nationalists. Waugh's response to the *Left Review*'s "Authors Take Sides on the Spanish War" questionnaire was grouped among those few "Against the Government." He refused, however, to be drawn into what he saw as the fatuous polarity encouraged by the questionnaire's framers:

> … I am no more impressed by the 'legality' of the Valencia Government than are English Communists by the legality of the Crown, Lords and Commons. I believe it was a bad government, rapidly deteriorating. If I were a Spaniard I should be fighting for General Franco. As an Englishman I am not in the predicament of choosing between two evils. I am not a Fascist nor shall I become one unless it were the only alternative to Marxism. It is mischievous to suggest that such a choice is imminent. (qtd. in Patey 146)

Nothing from Greene appears in "Authors Take Sides," but Sherry explains that Greene's views on the war, like Waugh's, were complex. "[A]lthough he was against Franco," Sherry writes, "he was not 100 percent for the Republicans, chiefly because of their brutality and the murder of nuns. But he did side with the Basques" because "while they were on the side of the Republicans they were not fighting for a Communist or anarchist state, for they were Catholics and their army was attended by 82 priests who would celebrate Mass and be present at the last moments of the dying" (612). The commitments behind this nuanced outlook form the basis of his treatment of contemporaneous Mexico. In his autobiography *Ways of Escape*, Greene remarks, without going into particulars, that Spain, Mexico, and Catholicism coalesced imaginatively in the late 1930s. Prior to the Spanish Civil War, he writes,

> My professional life and my religion were contained in quite separate compartments, and I had no ambition to bring them together. It was 'clumsy life at her stupid work' which did that; on the one hand the socialist persecution of religion in Mexico, and on the other General Franco's attack on Republican Spain, inextricably involved religion in contemporary life. I think it was under those two influences—and the backward and forward sway of my sympathies— that I began to examine more closely the effect of faith on action. (*Ways* 78–79)

Greene's first idea for addressing the "restlessness" this new perspective produced in him was to get to civil-war Spain. His attempt to reach Bilbao, though, ended at Toulouse, where, despite carrying "a letter of recommendation from the Basque Delegation," he could not convince the local pilot to risk once again Franco's anti-aircraft guns (*Ways* 79). Still seeking the refining fire for his nascent faith of political action, he turned next to Mexico, and here he was more successful. Like Waugh, he struck a deal that sent him to Mexico with a mission, in this case "'to study the present conditions of the country with a special eye to the religious situation for a book which Longman's will publish'" (qtd. in Sherry 663). As a Catholic with leftist political leanings, his eye would come to rest on aspects of the Mexican religious situation quite different from those occupying the attention of Waugh and the institutional Church.

Waugh and Catholic Order

As suggested above, although the shortcomings of both *The Lawless Roads* and *Robbery Under Law* have been thoroughly enumerated over the years, Waugh's book has been the object of the most vitriolic criticism. Strange, though, is the fact that Waugh himself censured *Robbery Under Law* in the same terms as critics often have. In the preface to *When the Going Was Good*, a 1946 collection of his travel writing, Waugh referred to his Mexican book, not represented in the volume, as one "which I am content to leave in oblivion, for it dealt little with travel and much with political questions" (ix). The book has never been of much interest as a "travel" book, and its usefulness regarding "political questions" is consistently dismissed because of the Eurocentrism, political bias, and religious sympathy the author makes no attempt to hide.[15] Waugh made no bones about the kind of book he was writing. He begins *Robbery Under Law* with the declaration: "This is a political book" (719). He repeats the warning on the following page and ends the book explaining: "Every marked step in [Mexico's] decline ... has corresponded with an experiment towards 'the Left'" (916). "A conservative," he continues, "is not merely an obstructionist who wishes to resist the introduction of novelties; nor is he, as was assumed by most nineteenth-century parliamentarians, a brake to frivolous experiment. He has positive work to do, whose value is particularly emphasised by the plight of Mexico" (917). To say the very least, Waugh did not share Greene's awkwardness over the affiliation of conservatism and Catholicism. In the 1930s, the classical-conservative vision of Catholicism was far more

---

15   For a representative, if not particularly nuanced, example of this critical position, see Kostopulos. *Robbery* has also received the usual accusations of snobbery (see Stannard *Early Years* 487 and *Later Years* 198 n.52), despite its winning attempt at humility: "It is interesting to read the travel books of fifty years ago," Waugh writes in the first chapter, "and notice their air of tolerant or intolerant superiority. Perhaps at the time there was some justification for it; now there is very little ... No, we must leave our superiority in bond when we cross the frontier; it is no longer for exportation to foreign countries" (RUL 728–29).

prevalent, even assumed, than Greene's radical one; there was as yet, for instance, no Liberation Theology as such.[16] Because of this cultural atmosphere, the specific implications of Waugh's argument in *Robbery Under Law* as it applies to Europe have often been taken for granted instead of properly interrogated. However it may disappoint as a travel book about Mexico, *Robbery Under Law* retains real value as a meditation on the idea of Europe in the 1930s.

Waugh deviates early and often from the straight travelogue mode because he appears to be formulating not so much Mexico as civilization itself. In doing so he is developing a thesis he had initially expressed in 1930 upon his conversion to Catholicism: "[Western] civilization ... the whole moral and artistic organization of Europe—has not in itself the power of survival. It came into being through Christianity, and without it has no significance or power to command allegiance ... Christianity is essential to civilization and ... is in greater need of combative strength than it has been for centuries" (EAR 104).[17] Applied to Mexico, the thesis becomes that cultural and political deterioration reveals the role that religion must play in the maintenance of civilization and, specifically, that Catholicism has played in that of the West. "It is not land or oil or race or political organisation but religion," he writes, "which is the single, essential question of the nation" (RUL 864).[18] Only by permitting the Church to safeguard and nurture the values and infrastructure on which that culture is based could Europe avoid falling into decay in its turn. Waugh returns again and again to the theme of Catholicism's unavoidable function as a source of social order, as "a habit of life and a social organisation" (RUL 891). The pattern of organization it fosters is visible on the lowest levels of underground practice, in which Waugh, like Greene, places a good deal of hope, and in widening circles from the parish and the village to the

---

[16] See EAR 155–56. Gallagher, however, skillfully argues that, although "[c]onservative politics and Roman Catholicism seriously entered Waugh's journalism together in the mid-1930s ... he had been a conservative before he became a Roman Catholic, and his conservatism developed independently of his religion" (EAR 155–56). Thus it is incorrect "to treat his political attitudes ... as a simple extension of his Catholicism."

[17] His position anticipates substantially the one Eliot outlined in "The Idea of a Christian Society" (1939) and "Notes Toward the Definition of Culture" (1949). In the former, Eliot wrote that "the only hopeful course for a society which would thrive and continue its creative activity in the arts of civilization, is to become Christian" (CC 19). For both writers, the adoption of Christianity—Waugh's of Roman Catholicism and Eliot's of Anglicanism—shored up and filled out extant suppositions. The difference in their religious subscriptions made little difference to their views on the matter of Europe's fundamental religious identity.

[18] The decade that followed strengthened Waugh's beliefs about the decline of Europe. In 1949, he wrote that "[t]he tragic fate of Europe is witness to the failure of secular States" (EAR 380). His estimation of the ability of the "New World" to assume "the historic destiny long borne by Europe," though, improved (EAR 378). See "The American Epoch in the Catholic Church" (EAR 377–88).

nation and the extra-national Church. Waugh describes the effects of the Mexican government's assault on the Church at each of these levels.

From Waugh's point of view, the Church in Mexico historically has been synonymous with order, and its ordering function is particularly vivid in light of the national decline that has accompanied secularization. "[I]n Mexico nationality, colour and race are so confused, the divisions of class so artificially emphasised and embittered and the whole principle of government so disordered that only some extra-national force can bring relief. Such unity as the country ever enjoyed was the gift of the Church" (RUL 898). On a drive to Puebla, the sight of a nameless village allows him to reflect on the direct relationship between anti-Church laws and the disintegration of Mexican society. The village "had once been of some size but most of the houses seemed empty now, and the garden walls were mere heaps of stone; from above ... one could see that it had once been carefully planned with level terraces and symmetrical, transecting streets" (RUL 746). All of this ruin is traceable to the expulsion of the priests: "When the fathers had been sent away the village began to disappear." What he elsewhere calls "the tangible fabric of [the] parish church" (RUL 873) has been the primary organizing factor in Mexican life on this local level, and its attenuation destabilizes more than just the village.

In his review of *The Lawless Roads* Waugh once more celebrates, and laments, Mexico's bygone glory as a bastion of Western civilization. "In its colonial days it was prominent in culture in the New World; not only was it a land of magnificent architecture and prosperous industry, but of civil peace and high culture" (EAR 250). Mexico's achievements, the product of its Catholic order, often exceeded even those of the liberal democracies, new and old:

> [A] century before the first printing press was set up in British America, books were printed in Mexico, not only in Spanish, but in twelve Indian languages; there were three universities there a century before the foundation of Harvard; anatomy with dissection was taught ... eighty-six years before William Hunter opened the first school in England; the Academy of Fine Arts, under Tolsa, was in the last years of Spanish power illustrious even in Europe; examples can be multiplied almost indefinitely. (EAR 250)

During the height of Catholic order, this impressive Mexican culture grew directly out of the social framework of the Church. Fortunate monasteries "became in many cases horticultural and agricultural experimental farms as well as centres of learning" (RUL 842). Near the empty village, though, Waugh "walked round the garden where an elaborate system of irrigation was choked and dry and the monks' fruit-trees sprawled untended, full of dead wood" (RUL 745–46). An Indian informs him that a "great fortress-like building" across the square "had once been an important college" (RUL 746). The Indian himself had once been a student there. The order and security represented by the old system, imported from medieval Spain "into New Spain," extended even to the Indians, the lowest class in almost every other social respect (RUL 842). Not only had enslaving them been forbidden by the Pope and the Spanish King, "they were members of the Church which, as in mediaeval Europe, gave them the hope of advancement in the priesthood and in education, and ensured their right to marry and bring up their families" (RUL 842). For all its uncomfortably congratulatory nostalgia, Waugh's vision of Catholic power in Mexico does embrace, if not exactly the Indians' liberation or power over their conquerors (as Greene's does), at least the protection of the most vulnerable from the most dehumanizing kinds of abuse; "it was the Church who saved the Indians from slavery and established their fundamental equality and identity with their conquerors" (RUL 898–99). The dignity with which New Spain endowed the Indians endured "real distress," however, immediately upon Mexican independence and secularization. "From the middle of the nineteenth century until today," Waugh writes, "the living conditions of the Mexican Indian have been as degraded as can be found in any except notoriously savage countries" (RUL 843–44). The materialist philosophy of successive governments, he argues, has severed the least of Mexico's least from the only guarantee against their virtual abandonment.

If such dignity and stability did in fact characterize the place of Mexican Indians under Christian Spanish rule, Waugh understands it to be partly attributable to the fluidity with which the Catholic ritual system merged with the native one. For instance, following "the policy traditional to her, of accepting all that was assimilable in the existing order; the new churches were built, just as they had been in Europe, on the sites of the old temples" (RUL 875).[19] Nor was the "love of statues and holy places [which] plays an enormous part in the Indian's religion" difficult to assimilate in the Church framework (RUL 874–76). Indeed, the shrine of the Virgin of Guadalupe, as has been noted, became the linchpin of Mexican ritualism, anchoring the faith brought from Europe to an image and a ritual space of the native country.[20]

Few would today agree with Waugh's characterization of a benign, even benevolent, Spanish subjugation of Mexican Indian culture. Waugh's argument depends on a distinction, difficult to countenance, between the ruthlessness of the Spanish *Conquistadores* and the munificence of the Catholic Church that accompanied it, consoling the native population and sowing harmony and security. The distinction, though, is crucial to the way one understands what Waugh's book says about the place of Mexico in an idea of Europe. Mexico is European, Waugh argues, partly by political affiliation and history: "The traditions of Spain are still

---

[19] Of course, not all observers take such a happy view of this work of assimilation. "The royal government," Derek H. Davis notes, "routinely destroyed the old pagan temples and religious artefacts ... However, it was impossible to completely erase centuries of culture from the Native Americans, and some elements of their old religions and the new faith were merged. In some cases, old gods were given new names of Christian saints, and natives recycled old pagan temples into shrines to these various saints" (5).

[20] Owen Chadwick points out that Jesuits and other Catholic missionaries in Mexico "tried to use Indian words for some of [their] religious ideas" (187). They often used native music and dance and "allowed people to appear at services in the ritual garments of their older faiths" (187).

deep in Mexican character and I believe it is only by developing them that the country can ever grow happy ... the Mexicans, though they may sometimes *feel* like Aztecs or Tlaxcalans, *think* like Spaniards; their minds have been formed on the Aristotelian model" (764–65). Yet it is on Spanishness as Catholic, and Catholicism as ritualistic, that Waugh ultimately places his hope for Mexico. He observes that "to the great majority of Mexicans [the appearance of Our Lady of Guadalupe] is something far more real and personally significant than the coming of Cortes ... They believe that it was at Guadalupe that Mexico became a nation and that Our Lady took them in her keeping" (RUL 882–84). Thus, while no statue of Cortes exists in Mexico (766), most Mexicans visit the Shrine of Our Lady of Guadalupe "several times in their lives" (883).[21] Both the conquest and the alleged apparition have the effect of suturing the Americas to European civilization and thus to the idea of Europe. Yet Waugh insists throughout his book on Mexico and Europe on the efficacy of the ritual space and devotion over that of political conquest, on the ways that the small, peaceful sites and practices underpinning the Church do more to unite America and Europe than any coercive political or religious program.[22]

This kind of religious intervention may well be less an openhanded process of assimilation than a veiled imperial violence.[23] The question remains, however, whether, 500 years after conquest, Mexico is involved in the modern idea of Europe, and, if so, on what basis. Even if, against Waugh's (and Greene's) inclination, the religious aspect of the relationship is isolated, one would need to ascertain the level below which Catholicism does not do its political work. Waugh's book suggests that, just as European culture is nothing without its Christian history and structure, the idea of Europe can extend only so far as its religion, and that its religion's ritual framework is inseparable from its institutional function as a basis of culture. Waugh's idea of Europe recognizes a need for thoughtful conservatism. Waugh's description of cultural stability and order emerging naturally from Catholic ritualism—welcome or not—is a formidable and articulate interpretation of the conservative relation of ritual to political power.

---

[21]   Waugh also visits the shrine of Los Remedios, Our Lady of the Remedies, which he has been told is "'the Spanish Virgin.'" However, among those who come "to kiss the little statue which a soldier of Cortes's had brought with him in his saddle bag," Waugh writes, "we were the only whites" (RUL 883).

[22]   The quiet is perhaps Waugh's strongest impression of the shrine at Guadalupe. "Mexico," he had written, "is the most shrill and thunderous city in the world. Noise is the first, shattering greeting to the stranger, it is the constant companion of all his days, the abiding memory which he takes home with him to the nordic stillness of London or New York. Noise of every kind competing for predominance ... For Mexicans feast on sound, as the more ascetic nordics fast on stillness" (RUL 734–35). The Cathedral at Guadalupe, though, "was the only place in Mexico that never seemed noisy" (RUL 884).

[23]   Waugh is happy to point out, though, that the Indians "were exempt from the Inquisition (a fact constantly forgotten by the painters of Mexico's modern historical frescoes)" (RUL 842).

Greene's Ritual Revolution

The interrelationship of Catholicism and social order is pithily illustrated by Greene in *The Power and the Glory*: "One of the oddest things about these days was that there were no clocks—you could go a year without hearing one strike. They went with the churches, and you were left with the grey slow dawns and the precipitate nights as the only measurements of time" (PG 100). Rather than merely bemoaning this vertiginous new experience, however, Greene delves into it for the answers to his question of how to relate faith to action. It is in this clockless world that Greene encounters an aspect of the power of Catholicism that flourishes best far from fortress-like buildings, centers of learning, and the hope of advancement, where nearly bare ritual actions themselves constitute the truly meaningful measurements of time.

Compared to *The Lawless Roads*, which is Greene's nonfiction account of his travels in Mexico, *The Power and the Glory*, a novel, has received relatively little condemnation for the liberties it takes with the literal Mexican scene. Critics have tended to demand less verisimilitude as well as less political rigor from the fictional text (and to permit more spiritual exploration) than from its travelogue companion. The two books almost invariably appear together in criticism because of the added light the comparison sheds on Greene's practices of transposing reality into fiction. Sheryl Pearson argues:

> One has to begin with *Another Mexico* [the original American title of *The Lawless Roads*] to recognize the full reference of *The Power and the Glory*, because the novel impinges so closely upon the travelogue's matter. [*The Lawless Roads*] functions at once as a work independent of the novel and a sourcebook for it, although a knowledge of contemporary Mexican history *and Greene's political motives* provides a necessary context for both. (278, my emphasis)

Yet the weight of political responsibility routinely falls on *The Lawless Roads*, and, as we have seen, that text often fails to bear up. *The Power and the Glory* may deserve a more prominent place in discussions of Greene's political outlook. Pearson argues that in the novel, "Greene would eventually make Mexico a less literal landscape, but no less political" (278). The contours of that politics are not difficult to discern in the way Greene situates religious ritual in the novel relative to political power.

The practical political, as opposed to the theological, significance of Greene's choices is my primary subject, yet Bosco's astute analysis of the novel's Catholic theology provides a point of entry to those political concerns. Bosco argues that, in its depiction of the relation between the divine and the earthly, *The Power and the Glory* typifies the Catholic conception of sacramentality prior to Vatican II. Specifically, the text's focus on the priest as "the primary mediator of the presence of God through his sacramental service" and on "a vertical relationship to God … decidedly locate [Greene's] theological vision in the Catholic world before the Second Vatican Council" (Bosco, "From" 62–64). The Council's eventual "reorientation of the sacramentality of Catholicism" away from its isolation in "ritual actions stemming from the priest" and toward "a theological perspective from below" (Bosco, "From" 54) emphasized the horizontal, social, even secular elements of experience as potential vehicles of divine grace. As a result, the Church opened the way for its fuller engagement with "the political and social struggles of peoples" (Bosco, "From" 55). In contrast to Greene's later novels, then, which reflect this understanding of a horizontal diffusion of grace and the increased politicization of faith, Catholicism in *The Power and the Glory* "stands as a mythic and almost monologic voice, valorized in explicit ways in both style and structure" (Bosco, "From" 65).

There is little reason to doubt the validity of Bosco's argument on the theological level, which is its focus. However, because of the ritual emphasis of *The Power and the Glory*, there is considerable room to expand upon the political implications of the novel's depiction of Mexican Catholicism. Bosco acknowledges that Greene's "Catholic vision is always in dialogue with the cultural and political world in which he finds himself," and that "Greene's religious fusion of faith with political action marks all his works" ("From" 56; 68). Yet, while the theological mandate of Vatican II may have brought such engagement to fruition, there is a good deal more Catholicism-from-below in *The Power and the Glory* than Bosco indicates, as well as more political engagement and resistance.

Bosco attributes to Greene a more conservative outlook than *The Lawless Roads* and *The Power and the Glory* support in the context of political thought in the 1930s. Just as for Waugh the "distorting mirror" of Mexico throws into relief those features of the Church suggestive of tradition and order, the Mexican setting of *The Power and the Glory* enables Greene to foreground the revolutionary element of the ritual structure of Catholicism. One might say "proletarian" instead of revolutionary, were it not for the novel's depiction of Catholicism-from-below probing lower and still lower than any traditional peasantry or working class. The roots of the novel's secret church reach below the ordinary, generally noble, poverty of "workers" to the rootless destitution of a wandering "whisky priest," a fugitive murderer, beggars, exiles, and native Indians, who exist outside, or more specifically below, the conventional register of class hierarchy. Halfway through the novel, the priest himself realizes that the revolutionary character of the Church proceeds not from the top down but from the myriad of confusing, violent, even ignoble relations among ordinary persons, relations that transcend even the broadest understanding of a class system but that are not without political significance. If humans are made in God's image, then "God was the parent, but He was also the policeman, the criminal, the priest, the maniac, and the judge. Something resembling God dangled from the gibbet or went into odd attitudes before the bullets in a prison yard or contorted itself like a camel in the attitude of sex" (PG 101). These are the kinds of figures that perpetually challenge the priest's, and the reader's, acceptance of a purely magisterial or monologic Catholicism.

That the whisky priest continually runs up against—and embraces—instances of the diffusion of the Church, its sustenance from all-but-invisible sources below the surface of public life, seems the best reason to question the existence, in political terms, of a "monologic" Catholicism in the novel. Political, as opposed to theological, questions come sharply into focus less in the priest's internal spiritual life than in the occasions in the text wherein a revolutionary Catholicism is demonstrated materially. The centrality of ritual to the narrative is especially important in this regard because of the way ritual embeds belief, which may be purely internal, in the social and physical world, thus establishing an inevitable articulation with the political. "Ritual," in Watson Holloway's words, "exteriorizes unspoken religious concepts" (48). Besides this articulation, an even more basic feature of ritual performance may serve to challenge, or even render impossible, the acceptance of the novel's Catholic monologism. John Updike declares that the "unit" of the novel's politics "is the individual, not any class" (xi–xii), and Bosco seems to argue the same about the text's index of salvation. Yet ritual performance necessarily places individuality in a precarious position. Koster argues that the essential goal and requirement of ritual is the "temporary suspension of one's sense of individual identity" (219), and even its "replac[ement] ... by an awareness of collective identity" (216). It is, in other words, fundamentally incompatible with the notion of the primacy of individual over collective identity. Thus it is not unreasonable to expect to see the priest's ritual actions deflating his prior sense of self and leading him into an awareness of his place among others.

The whisky priest's first illegal Mass in the novel takes place under the immediate threat of discovery and retribution. In a forest village, home to his one-time lover and his illegitimate daughter, the attendees are restless: "He knew they were longing for the Mass to be over: they had woken him very early, because there were rumours of police ..." (PG 69). He is forced to cut his homily short when the news arrives that indeed "'the police are on the way. They are only a mile off, coming through the forest'" (70). Even thus under duress, the ritual does not admit of shortcuts, and the sequence illustrates with excruciating precision the inefficiency of this kind of religion:

> He turned his back on them and began very quickly to recite the Credo. [...] He kissed the top of the packing-case and turned to bless. [...] He began the prayer for the living: the long list of the Apostles and Martyrs fell like footsteps—Cornelii, Cypriani, Laurentii, Chrysogoni—soon the police would reach the clearing [...] He began the Consecration of the Host [...] He began the Consecration of the Wine [...] He knelt by the packing-case [...] Somebody opened the door: a voice whispered urgently, 'They're here.' (PG 70–71)

The scene also highlights the necessity, and the danger, of maintaining the bond between the ritual performance and the ritual space. Although this Mass takes place in a mud-floored hut, every possible measure is taken to approximate the atmosphere of a church. A packing case serves as altar; the candles on it—which might easily give the whole thing away—"smoked steadily upwards" (PG 69). After the Mass's hasty conclusion, Maria "nipped the candles, so that the wick would not leave a smell" (PG 72). The crate itself is even adorned with an altar cloth, which Maria similarly spirits away afterwards. Every adornment they add increases the risk to their lives, yet the villagers have insisted on creating the sacred space their ritual requires.

The tangible means through which this ritual is gotten up suggest the power, born out of necessity but born nonetheless, of a Catholicism-from-below. There are the hut itself and the packing crate. Whereas once the priest had had proper Eucharistic elements, the ones he must use now have never been stored in a church: "a piece of bread from Maria's oven," wine "in a chipped cup" (PG 71). Once he had had wafers and a chalice, and each necessary substitution represents "one more surrender" of the institutional faith, not only to the authorities but also to the poorest strata of the Church itself. The mud-hut Consecration "was in silence: no bell rang" (PG 72). Yet, his "ragged peon trousers and the torn shirt" signal his capacity to "talk of suffering to them now without hypocrisy—it is hard for a sleek and well-fed priest to praise poverty," and he is well pleased with the new relation (PG 71). The lieutenant pursuing him lectures the villagers on the evil of the Church, proclaiming of one little girl, "'This child is worth more than the Pope in Rome'" (PG 75), and the whisky priest is little inclined to disagree. Poverty is his new element, and the least of the least his new power. Encouraged to flee north to neighboring Las Casas where, a woman tells him, "'They've still got churches ... Nobody can go in them, of course—but they are there," and where "'there are priests too,'" even the possibility of a proper Mass "'in a house, with a proper altar, and the priest all dressed up like in the old days,'" the priest heads south instead.

In doing so he heads deeper still into those reaches of his church below the official recognition of the hierarchy and the secular authorities. Rather than cling to Church power in the form of its remaining institutional property, the priest makes a choice to do the reverse, to seek out those places where its ritual life is hanging on by unfamiliar threads. One such place is the grove of crosses to which he is led by an Indian woman carrying her dead son:

> At sunset on the second day they came out on to a wide plateau covered with short grass. A grove of crosses stood up blackly against the sky, leaning at different angles—some as high as twenty feet, some not much more than eight. They were like trees that had been left to seed. The priest stopped and stared at them. They were the first Christian symbols he had seen for more than five years publicly exposed—if you could call this empty plateau in the mountains a public place. No priest could have been concerned in the strange rough group; it was the work of Indians and had nothing in common with the tidy vestments of the Mass and the elaborately worked out symbols of the liturgy. It was like a short cut to the dark and magical heart of the faith. (PG 154)

Besides a bold political defiance, the passage emphasizes a revolutionary deviation within Catholicism's ritual structure itself. Although this stunning ritual space appears to have "nothing in common with" the Catholicism of Europe, it is at the same time integral to it, its "magical heart." In *The Lawless Roads*, Greene sees in the actual grove of crosses on which this scene is based "the Indian religion—a dark, tormented, magic cult" consistent with "the magic element of Christianity—the man raised from the dead, the devils cast out, the water turned into wine" that Europeans tend to be "too apt to minimize" (170–71). "One thought," writes Greene, "of the spittle mixed with the clay to heal the blind man, the resurrection of the body, the religion of the earth" (LR 171).

Like the whisky priest, Greene allows himself to consider the pervasive power of ritual supported by the institutional Church but not limited to it. In *Ways of Escape*, he traces the development of his own Catholicism from formal observance to living action. Upon conversion, he writes, "I had not been emotionally moved, but only intellectually convinced; I was in the habit of formally practicing my religion" (*Ways* 78). Ten years later, however, "Catholicism was no longer primarily symbolic, a ceremony at an altar with the correct canonical number of candles, with the women in my Chelsea congregation wearing their best hats, nor was it a philosophical page in Father D'Arcy's *Nature of Belief*. It was closer now to death in the afternoon" (*Ways* 79).[24] The trip to Mexico, in particular, fed his growing "emotional belief" (*Ways* 79–80). Such is the spiritual territory into which the whisky priest's wandering takes him in turn.

Later, the priest will even conclude that tidy whitewashed village churches "belonged to a dream. Life didn't contain churches" (PG 181). He seems, however, to mean that churches do not contain all of life. After all, even cut off from the tidy comfort of a legal church, he goes about creating ritual spaces in which to carry out the religion and observing those similarly exiled doing the same. The mother who accompanies the priest performs the same kind of devotion her fellows do in churches and outside them throughout the region. The action of lying her son at the foot of a cross is not far removed from those of the Indians Greene observes in Santo Domingo on Good Friday brushing the image of a crucified Christ with green branches, or in Las Casas, on their knees, carrying a cross to and from the local river (LR 182–85). Such practices are unconventional but not inconsistent with Greene's Catholicism of the earth, nor with the ritual pulse on which his church draws. A semblance of European tradition even attends the Mexican Indians' "bizarre services" Greene describes in *Ways of Escape* that are "celebrated by the Indians from the hills, who tried to remember what they had been taught—scraps of strangely pronounced Latin and odd uncanonical gestures" (88). All of these strange things may derive from "those secret minds" of Indians and peasants, but they are minds "with which only priests have ever made real contact" (LR 182). And at least one priest, the whisky priest himself, seems well suited to be "concerned in the strange rough group" of crosses. His former self, identified with "the tidy vestments ... and the elaborately worked out symbols" of Catholic liturgy, seems from another world, but the guerrilla priest he has become is less and less a stranger to the rough ritualism of the forest and the mountains.

---

[24] *Death in the Afternoon* is the title of Ernest Hemingway's famous 1932 nonfiction book about toreo.

A step back into the comfort of civilization brings home to the priest just how far he has traveled. The comparative luxury of the Lehrs' farmhouse, in a region where the practice of Catholicism is permitted (though not in churches), immediately puts him ill at ease. Even the rude site—a barn—he is given for the performance of his sacramental duties seems uncomfortably distant from "the religion of the earth" and certainly from death in the afternoon. Hearing confessions "sitting on a rocking-chair in a horse-box," he recalls "with an odd sense of homesickness ... the hostages in the prison yard, waiting at the water tap, not looking at him—the suffering and the endurance which went on everywhere the other side of the mountains" (PG 171–72). The annoying complacency which government toleration of the Church has bred in the faithful of this neighboring state prompts him to chide one penitent and to feel himself "back in the little stuffy wooden boxlike coffin" in which he had used to offer absolution (PG 172). The Mass that follows, packed with people, also takes him back to the old days. Although "he had no vestments, ... the masses in this village were nearer to the old parish days than any he had known in the last eight years—there was no fear of interruption, no hurried taking of the sacraments as the police approached. There was even an altar stone brought from the locked church" (PG 176). This approximation of normalcy, for which he and the rest of the novel's persecuted Catholics have yearned, now seems strangely disappointing: flat, safe, a poor substitute for the guerrilla sacramental life across the mountains. It prompts the whisky priest to turn once again toward the precincts where there is not even the consolation of a horse barn in which to say Mass, where danger and secrecy have forced Catholicism to recall and to draw upon its revolutionary potential.

The barn Mass occupies a peculiar place in the narrative arc of *The Power and the Glory*. The scene is striking for the absence at its center; it begins with the priest, filled with "expectant happiness," watching the Indians and townspeople "walking up from the village on the way to Mr. Lehr's barn" (PG 174). Once in the barn, he considers the unaccustomed safety and the borrowed altar stone, but then the action of the Mass itself goes almost unnoticed, save for a few snippets of liturgical speech, while the priest recalls a dream he once had. Then: "'... and we saw his glory, the glory as of the only-begotten of the Father, full of grace and truth.' Mass was over" (PG 176). The first full celebration of the ritual the absence and remembrance of which has provided the organizing problems of the novel slips past almost invisibly, as though one had been watching for an eclipse and blinked in the time it took to pass. The priest's point of view is partly responsible—his mind is clearly elsewhere—but Greene's political interpretation of Catholic ritual also informs this conspicuous elision. The Mass in Mr. Lehr's barn, although impoverished next to those of pre-persecution days, figures in the context of government toleration as a conservative force. Permitted this out-of-the-way space in which to act out their faith, the people come, are consoled, and return to their politically docile daily lives. The illicit rituals of the mud huts compete with the secular government on its own ground, whereas the Mass in Lehr's barn is situated unthreateningly apart. This stand-in church, besides lacking the social influence of a parish embedded in village life, lacks the insurrectionary energy of the secret church to which the whisky priest promptly returns as though going home.

The episode that follows this welcome but politically benign interlude places the priest finally where Catholic ritual cannot avoid public entanglement. Persuaded, but not fooled, by a treacherous *mestizo*[25] to give last rites to a dying American fugitive, the priest accepts the inevitability of his ritual function bringing him into the government's grasp. The Yankee lies either "just the other side" of the border or "just this side" ("A mile or two makes no difference," and "who knew where one state began or another ended?") (PG 178–80), and the authorities, too, lie in wait. Still, the priest has no choice but to follow the mestizo and try to perform his sacramental duty. His attempted absolution of the American in an Indian hut is messy and perhaps ineffectual—"only one criminal trying to aid the escape of another" (PG 190)—but, besides fulfilling a religious necessity, it closes the loop of power through which the priest has previously been able to slip. The last rites may help to free a man in the next life, but in this one they promptly get the priest arrested, and he would have it no other way.

Both the novel and *The Lawless Roads* make eminently clear that, owing to the anti-Church laws of the 1930s in states like Tabasco and Chiapas, every Mass, every baptism, every confession and last rite is already an act of political resistance, the assertion of an alternative model of social organization, what Updike calls "an ideal communism even more Christian than Communist" (xi). This ideal comes not from above but from below, in the vagrant and almost penniless improvisation of ritual that undermines secular political hegemony by refusing to cede the basic structure of rituals and ritual spaces that is its life. Severed from the tangible signs of Church power—the churches themselves, the clerical hierarchy, the display of Christian symbols—this revolutionary ritual practice carves a Church out of packing crates, contraband wine, mud huts, hidden groves of Indian crosses. Bosco concludes that the "triumph of faith" in *The Power and the Glory* is gained "at the expense of the political world" ("From" 65). I would propose, rather, that the religious triumph, which is undeniable, occurs below the radar, as it were, of the political world, but still within it and working upon it. The faith has spread itself so thin and so low as to be almost undetectable in the political world, yet the revolutionary spirit it represents outreaches even the Revolutionary spirit of the authorities.

---

[25] A *mestizo* is defined in the *OED* as "a Spanish or Portuguese half-caste; now chiefly, the offspring of a Spaniard and an American Indian." Although, as Waugh affirms, racial mixing is so prevalent in Mexico as to be almost moot, Greene chooses to identify his *mestizo* as such presumably to emphasize his function as one who moves between two worlds. This mestizo declares himself a Catholic, for instance, yet he betrays the priest into the hands of the secular authorities for money. Earlier, in prison, he has the opportunity to do the same but does not.

The Mexican Object-Lesson

Fairly early in his Mexican journey, but already sufficiently disoriented by the strangeness of Mexican (and American) culture, Greene is pushed almost beyond his limits by the sight of a cockfight: "That, I think, was the day I began to hate the Mexicans" (LR 48). Already in a mood of disappointment, he arrives at the bullring, in which the cockfight and then a rodeo are to take place: "One had the feeling that all the activities in San Luis were half-hearted—one eye was always fixed on the road to Las Palomas" (LR 47). He is predictably underwhelmed by each action leading up to the cockfight: the singing, the preparation of the birds, the marking of lines in the sand. Sherry makes virtually no sense of the episode, saying "Greene was aware of the significance of the ritual" despite his "impatience" with it (672). The impatience Greene feels is in fact the result of trying to see the cockfight *as* a ritual—encouraged by the ritualistic trappings of the event drawn from bullfighting: plaza, procession, costume, music—but finding it instead a ridiculous game, albeit one ending in death, "the scurry in the sand, pain in miniature, and death on a very small scale" (LR 47). His grand conclusion—"death dictates certain rites. Men make rules and hope in that way to tame death" (LR 47)—would be apt in other contexts but is ludicrous in this one of an entertainment in which man's death is not on the table, in which "the crowd hooted and jeered" at the birds "as if they had been cowardly or unsuccessful bull-fighters" (LR 48). Although this cockfight and the rodeo that follows are enacted in the town's bullring, Greene does not consider that the absurdity of the spectacle may have something to do with its failing to meet the demands of the ritual space it has appropriated for the afternoon. This silly sport, "all this mummery" (LR 48), is not the death in the afternoon animating Greene's new religious-political vision. "[W]ith death over," he writes, "it wasn't worth staying for all the rest" (LR 48), as though bullrings, like churches, seem unsuitable for any other purpose than the one for which they were built.

Immediately after this disappointment, Greene steps into a church, and Mexico no longer seems alien to him. "I went into the Templo del Carmen, as the dark dropped, for Benediction," he writes. "To a stranger like myself it was like going home—a language I could understand—'*Ora pro nobis*'" (LR 48). If the language of the ritual is familiar, the style of the space is not: "The Virgin sat on an extraordinary silver cloud like a cabbage with the Infant in her arms above the altar; all along the walls horrifying statues with musty purple robes stood in glass coffins; and yet," he insists, "it was home" (LR 48–49). Here men and women participate in an enactment of the taming of death, deeper and more explicit than either the cockfight or the English Catholicism with which Greene is familiar, by mortifying themselves in the presence of the central symbol of their religion, the sacrificial body and blood of Christ. "You would say that life itself for these was mortification enough," Greene writes, "but like saints they seek the only happiness in their lives and squeeze out from it a further pain" (LR 44). It is this Mexico that Greene takes back to Europe.

The vague notion of political Catholicism, of faith in action, that the Spanish Civil War had earlier engendered in him has been refined out on Europe's first periphery, and it promptly begins to alter his perception of the Church at home. "Mass in Chelsea," he writes on the last page of *The Lawless Roads*, "seemed curiously fictitious; no peon knelt with his arms outstretched in the attitude of the cross, no woman dragged herself up the aisle on her knees. It would have seemed shocking, like the Agony itself. We do not mortify ourselves. Perhaps we are in need of violence" (224). Writing as the Spanish Civil War comes to a close and the early stirrings of another world war are being felt in Great Britain, his choice of words suggests how much he felt had been at stake in the many violences of Mexico: not, to be sure, in the mummery of the cockfight, which only mocks this need for meaningful violence, but certainly in "the atmosphere of violence" (LR 80) the Church in Chiapas and Tabasco shared with fugitive criminals, "politicians and *pistoleros*" (LR 20), the atmosphere in which a group of "unarmed peasants attempting to pray in the ruins of a church" are shot by police (LR 117). Catholic ritual manages violence, but in Mexico, Greene knows, it also invites it, a dangerous situation still preferable to English "indifference" (LR 34). "Over here lay the grave of Pro, Tabasco with every church destroyed, and Chiapas, where the Mass was forbidden" (LR 34); Britain is perhaps not so fortunate, he reflects, to have been spared this kind of violence for so long. Like the rest of Europe, though, Britain had not long to wait for the kind of violence adhering to Mexican Catholicism to assert itself in earnest: "Violence came nearer—Mexico is a state of mind" (LR 224). In saying so, Greene comes a bit closer than Lawrence to recognizing that the violence and death Mexico makes visible to European writers have less to do with Mexico itself than with an unavoidable part of the mind of Europe. Indeed, at one point when he is irritated by the behavior of Mexicans on a train, Greene admits: "If Spain is like this, I can understand the temptation to massacre" (LR 199). Violence, it seems, is as near to Greene's mind as to Lawrence's.

Both Greene's and Waugh's nonfiction accounts conclude with the author bearing the lessons of Mexico back to Europe, where the Spanish Civil War is bringing close not only violence but also the question of the relation of Catholicism to politics. The lessons of the periphery, as might be expected, are not always clear from the point of view of the center. "From the beginning of the Spanish war," writes Waugh, "the Mexican governing party expressed the belief that the Spanish republicans were fighting the battle which they themselves had already won" (RUL 907).[26] However, he continues, "[t]here were some Mexicans on both

---

[26] Hugh Thomas corroborates this view, noting: "The Mexican government was from the start an ardent supporter of the Spanish Republic, as might be expected from a country whose Constitution had itself derived from a rising against clerical and aristocratic privilege" (232–33). Indeed, in the earliest days of the war, when military aid to Spain was a highly fraught topic, "Mexico ... alone of all the Governments of the world, openly began to send arms ... to the Republicans" (Thomas 260). The Mexican position was far from unanimous in the Americas, however. "Chile, Mexico, Argentina, Uruguay, Paraguay and Cuba, had received many recent immigrants from Spain. But all the countries of Latin

sides in the Spanish war, more I believe, on Franco's than the republic's" (907).[27] If this is true, it is likely because the appeal of European tradition was still strong among Mexicans. According to Waugh, "Franco's soldiers have fought under the inspiration of their past; they saw their country disintegrating, as their colonies had done, into a group of republics run by men whose policies were derived from abroad and were antagonistic to national tradition. They fought to prevent Spain becoming like Central America" (RUL 909). The feeling of national identity and pride associated with this project, *Hispanidad*, Waugh writes, "has been caught up outside Spain in South and Central America ... It is being taken up as the antithesis not only of communist rule but in the words of Cardinal Goma against 'Monroeism, Statism, Protestantism, Socialism and simple mercantilism" (910).[28] Insisting on its place in the trinity Mexico comprises along with nationalist Spain and the Catholic Church, Waugh suggests, is the soundest way for Mexico to arrest its slide into at least secular-liberal meaninglessness and at worst chaos.

Greene's observations on his homeward journey illustrate the strange logic according to which Catholicism makes political bedfellows. Momentarily challenged by a group of Spaniards traveling back to Spain to fight for Franco, Greene finds the common ground. Their sizing up of Greene is full of an irony that the diversity of Catholic political associations in the late 1930s permits:

> [T]hey blocked the door after I got in; they wore their berets like a uniform and each had a little gold chain round his neck with a holy medal dangling under the shirt. At first I couldn't understand their Castilian—they seemed perturbed, they wanted to know who I was. The word '*inglés*' didn't reassure them, but when I said '*Católico*' and showed *my* lucky charm they looked a little easier. The stranger was a stowaway, he was going to 'pay the Reds.' (LR 216)

---

and South America felt to some extent concerned by the events in Spain. There was strong feeling for the Nationalists in Brazil and the Canadian province of Quebec, where, as in Spain, there existed Fascist organisations in a Catholic background. Chile was also strongly pro-Nationalist" (Thomas 232).

[27]   This seems unlikely, but reliable figures of this kind are notoriously difficult to locate. In any case, Mexican intervention in the war was predominantly monetary and armorial. Thomas cites no Latin American countries among those from which volunteers came to fight, on either side, in Spain. He does note that "No Americans fought for the Nationalists. Not more than a dozen British subjects appear to have done so. Of these, most were at least half Irish" (635). Gabriel Jackson, who confirms Thomas's assessment of Mexico's official sympathy ("One country alone reacted without fear, and with great generosity, toward the plight of the Spanish Republic."), also adds an important qualifier: "At the same time, the Mexican embassy in Madrid, like those of the other Latin American states, sheltered priests and Spanish conservatives endangered by the revolutionary anarchy of the first weeks of the war" (260). On the ground, that is, grand political either-or propositions routinely broke down, especially where religion was concerned.

[28]   Waugh is wary, though, of the "close affinities" of *Hispanidad* "with the German race-myth. At present, since its opponents have been, in the main, atheists it has been strongly Christian in sentiment, but Christianity and the race-myth cannot long work together" (RUL 910–11).

Greene chooses not to use the opportunity to reveal his leftism or his Basque sympathies. Furthermore, the difference in their political views seems of small importance next to their shared religion. "There was something agreeably amateur, too, about their fascism" as opposed to that of their German allies on board (LR 216). When, after an impressive Mass attended by the novice Falangists, "every arm went up but mine" in the fascist salute, "no one minded at all. These were Spaniards, not Germans" (LR 217).[29] The real others on board seem to be the atheistic Germans, the un-amateurish fascists who jealously guard their ceremony and symbolic trappings, "who joined heartily in the right cries and hated Christianity" (LR 217).

In Mexico, Greene discovers an aspect of Catholicism that he has long suspected but that Europe had kept hidden from him: the capacity of the religion to mobilize a substantial power from the reaches where its most magisterial structures have little visible influence. The Basques, separated from the official stance of the Church on the war in Spain, but armed with a group of priests, are not far, in this respect, from the Mexicans of the mountains and mud huts.[30] So, too, however, is Waugh confirmed in his beliefs that European civilization's present decline is the result of its marginalization of the Church, and that its continued infatuation with secularism, materialism, and totalitarianism will hasten its further deterioration. "There is nothing," he writes, "except ourselves, to stop our own countries becoming like Mexico. That is the moral, for us, of her decay" (RUL 917). Both men return to fragile Europe suspecting that the future of Europe, reflected in the distorting mirror of Mexico, is visible too in the more local microcosm of Spain. Their writing of Catholicism's place in Mexican, Spanish, and European politics reveals that the same ritual structure would effectively support contending political views. However the Church aligned itself politically, these writings suggest, its ritual structures would play an instrumental role in the exercise of or resistance to power.

---

[29] "I think," writes Greene, "the Germans looked a little askance when the arms went up in salute for nothing at all, for a silly old man, for a joke. '*Arriba España's*' and '*Viva Franco's*' burst boisterously out for no reason on the hot unshaded deck, with a hint of mockery" (LR 216).

[30] The schism in Spain, during but not limited to the Civil War, "between the church hierarchy, which was usually loyal to the prevailing government, and the clergy at the local level, who often led movements for reform," also characterized Mexico from early in its own history, though not quite accurately during the persecutions of the 1920s and 1930s (Davis 5).

Chapter 7
Keep the Islands Adjacent:
David Jones and the "European Thing"

Of all the ways of writing and of thinking about Europe covered in this study, David Jones's are most intimately and explicitly connected to one another. Owing largely to Jones's 1955 essay "Art and Sacrament," the principle of sacramentalism, out of which all of Jones's poetry—and, indeed, all of his creative art—grows, has become a cornerstone of scholarship on Jones and his work. Less often remarked is the way in which a kind of sacramental thinking informs Jones's idea of Europe. That he is in a unique and very meaningful way a European writer has recently begun to become more apparent, and important, to scholars, most of whom have heretofore focused on the combination of characteristics Eliot identified in the introductory note to Jones's *In Parenthesis*. "As for the writer himself," Eliot wrote, "he is a Londoner of Welsh descent. He is decidedly a Briton. He is also a Roman Catholic, and he is a painter who has painted some beautiful pictures and designed some beautiful lettering. All of these facts about him are important" ("Note" vii). Jones himself emphasized these strands of his identity throughout his life and made them, unequivocally and unapologetically, the core of his work, creative and critical. That these same strands provide keys to Jones as a European and, specifically, to *In Parenthesis* as a poem of Europe, is the argument of this chapter. It may seem too limited a basis from which to begin, but limitation, Jones knew, is often the precondition to any doing or knowing. In "Art and Sacrament" he uses ligaments as a metaphor for the local binding that makes movement possible: "[I]t is the whole purpose of a ligament to bind in order to secure freedom of action; ... to sever a ligament is to make impossible any further action or freedom to act" (EA 160). The following pages will try to identify some of the ligaments that, in Jones's mind, keep Britain's islands adjacent, not only to one another but also to Europe.

Jones's idea of Europe is summed up in the same words the European Union has chosen as its motto: United in Diversity. The Union's difficulties in agreeing upon a constitution (among other basics) are evidence of the difficulty of making that abstraction a living reality among its member states. Jones, however, never reaches any conclusions by way of abstractions. Rather, his method is always to pick up a particular local thread and to follow it, without any "loppings off of meaning or emptying out, any lessening of the totality of connotation, any loss of recession or thickness through" (EA 120) to the larger whole, the cultural DNA of which is then seen to have been present in the thread.[1] It is a method

---

[1]   As with abstractions, so with generalizations. Jones writes, "there is a danger of generalizations, and they are useless, especially to the artist, who, of his nature, deals in the contactual and the particular" (DG 31).

Jones saw as the inevitable result of the sacramental nature of man—brought to consciousness in himself by the high Anglicanism of his mother and his own Roman Catholicism—which dictates that small objects, words, and actions are the available as well as the necessary vehicles for revelation of the greater truth of the divine. Jones was explicit in his belief that the sacramental model determined his process of artistic creation—in poetry, engraving, painting—and a version of sacramentalism underlies the idea of Europe that he shapes in his long poem *In Parenthesis*.[2] The major threads he follows to the text's final, culminating scene of ritual action are what he calls in various places—using an idiomatic phrasing reflective of his concrete habit of mind—"the Catholic thing" (DGC 223) and "the Welsh thing" (qtd. in Blissett 101). For all the richness of association into which these two threads lead, they are not, of course, complete; each leaves out important aspects of European history and culture. Jones, however, makes no apologies for either the limits imposed by his choice of traditions or for using them as the key with which to open Europe's gates. In a letter to René Hague, he writes:

> [F]or what little I know or have assimilated through this channel or that is all I have in my make-up—had I been nurtured in some other complex of tradition and belief the writing would necessarily have had to draw upon *materia* very other. But as the blasted thing was wholly conditioned both in form and content from what I had known as a child or from what I learned as an art-student or from—or Tiger Dawson or—and so on, how could it have been other in its ingredients than it is? (qtd. in Hague 65)

If his idiosyncratic approach recalls the parable of the blind men and the elephant, its justification is that knowing the tail, or trunk, or foot, is a far better indicator of an elephant's *haeccitas* than is any abstraction of elephant-ness. Jones's is a poetry of "contactual experience" (EA 144), to invoke another term preferred by Jones and his critics, in which "concretely realised particular details" (Hague 57–58)— heterogeneous, often humble, sometimes obscure—are mined and arranged for what they reveal of a perceived unity. The process is not quite mythologization, because the unity is never achieved at the cost of the particular object's diminution or abstraction. Rather, the European thing in *In Parenthesis* containing Catholicism and Celticism is a concrete approximation of the shape of true unity in diversity.

A sharpened sense of Jones's European-ness, or rather that of his aims in writing *In Parenthesis*, has the further benefit of putting two of the most durable criticisms of Jones, if not to rest, at least in perspective. The European point of view reveals the comparative narrowness of the ground from which Paul Fussell reaches his reluctant but firm conclusion that Jones is guilty of romanticizing and thereby

---

2   Although *In Parenthesis* has also been called a modernist novel and an epic, I am content to consider the book a long poem and to leave discussions of its mixed generic features alone for the time being. If nothing else, Jones was the consummate poet. Moreover, William Wootten has convincingly situated *In Parenthesis* in a tradition of the modern British long poem, wherein the poet "harness[es]" his own "vision to some wider historical, ethnic or national identity" (28).

tacitly excusing the violence of the First World War by swaddling it in the stuff of myth and legend.[3] Fussell's censure focuses on the injustice that Jones's mythical method does to the supposedly unprecedented human experience of the trenches. If "the state of the soldier is universal throughout history," Fussell asks, "what's wrong with it? And if there is nothing in the special conditions of the Great War to alter cases drastically, what's so terrible about it? Why the shock?" (150). For Jones "to keep hinting that this war is like others" is, for Fussell, utterly misguided on humanist grounds. Fussell is not content, to say the least, to take Jones's word for it that the accretions of meaning attaching to the firsthand soldier's experience are the legitimate result of the poet's attempt "to appreciate some things, which, at the time of suffering, the flesh was too weak to appraise" (IP x). The broader historical and moral perspective claimed by Jones, outreaching by far the intense and limited subjectivity so famously associated (due in no small part to Fussell's own work), with the Great-War poets, is, for Fussell, impossible to countenance.[4]

A critic who shares Fussell's admiration for Jones and for *In Parenthesis*, Neil Corcoran, also shares his condemnation of the book's mythical method.[5] Corcoran, however, emphasizes the way the poem's mythologizing apparatus undermines the good work it otherwise does in terms of working-class and colonial liberation. "Alert to … caste and class," Corcoran writes, the poem "witnesses [after Brecht] that it was not kings" but working men who built Thebes (223). Overlaying this kernel of truth with myth, ritual, and romance, Corcoran argues, amounts not only to a falsehood but also to an implicit leaning toward the most objectionable rightwing politics of the 1930s.

Thinking in terms of Europe alters the way one receives the less popular though not forgotten suggestion that Jones was a proto-fascist, that his cultural views as expressed in his art were reactionary at a time when that was inexcusable. Corcoran accuses *In Parenthesis* of attempting to "blanch out and sentimentalize those political realities" which characterized Europe in the 1930s, the time of its composition and publication (215). Those realities, for Corcoran, are dominated by

---

[3]   A critic who shares, but chooses not to pursue, my objection to Fussell's argument is Allen Frantzen, who identifies a "fundamental disagreement" with the "premise that the war savaged and ended reverence for 'great traditions,' replacing them with ironic commentary that juxtaposed the horrors of war to the high culture of the Victorians" (298 n.23). Frantzen cites a soldier's letter which "shows that such juxtapositions were not always ironic." Jones escapes irony in many instances by appealing to an objective literary tradition.

[4]   In a late letter, Jones specifically addresses the difference between his own war poetry and that of Fussell's representative war poet, Wilfred Owen. "[H]ad he not himself become one with those fallen," Jones writes, "but had survived to consider 'in tranquillity' he *might* have hesitated and seen that there was no 'old lie', but something more akin to Isaias' *non est species ei neque décor, et vidimus eum et non erat aspectus*" (DGC 246).

[5]   See Fussell 144–54. Corcoran complicates Fussell's argument by arguing that Jones eventually became aware that his attempt in *In Parenthesis* "to wash the war's dirty linen ... in the waters of Camelot" was "a bloody lie," and that such was his tacit admission in the later fragment, "The Book of Balaam's Ass" (209–10).

the growing Nazi menace and the irresponsibility of a Briton doing anything other than seeking Germany's destruction. He does not go quite so far as to call Jones a Nazi, but he does condemn Jones's (admittedly brief and tenuous) political views of the period as "inexcusable and disgusting" (211). Corcoran argues, rightly, that *In Parenthesis* is "a poem of the moment of its own publication—1937—rather than a poem definable by the period (1915–16) which it describes" (214). Thus, Jones's "desire for peace between English and Germans" at a moment "when 'peace' was likely to undergo a sullying slippage into 'appeasement' ... was not, unfortunately, a neutral or innocent desire" (Corcoran 215). Corcoran chastises Jones for such conciliatory gestures as dedicating *In Parenthesis* in part "to the enemy front-fighters who shared our pains against whom we found ourselves by misadventure" (IP overleaf); for tacitly suggesting that another war between Great Britain and Germany, "under whatever provocation" (Corcoran 216) would likewise be "misadventure"; and for concluding *In Parenthesis* with a scene of reconciliation between English and German soldiers (215).[6]

Although his chapter raises some excellent points, Corcoran may fairly be grouped with those critics—some of whom, including Valentine Cunningham and Dan Kostopulos, have been cited in earlier chapters—for whom all that is not historically political is mystification. Such a view, as I argued in the Auden chapter, leaves little or no room for a nuanced idea of Europe. Corcoran, for example, is on his most comfortable ground in suggesting Jones's later recognition of "the complicity of the allusive and mythologizing strategies of *In Parenthesis* in the maintenance of an English ruling class ideology" (212), and condemning myth, "tradition" (when not dutifully "stripped of its Eliotic grandeur"), even the idea of Europe itself as "a bloody lie" (210–11).

Such a view demonstrates how much of Jones's meaning is lost in a critical approach blind to (or intolerant of) all that extends beyond the narrowest modern nationalisms, a criticism in which an idea of Europe appealing to more than historical materialism is as nothing compared to "unaccommodated and irreducible historical fact" (Corcoran 225). In fairness, Corcoran's view leaves out no more than that of critics who see in *In Parenthesis* nothing more than Jones's Welshness. The European perspective, though, recovers much of what falls away in both approaches. A.M. Allchin eloquently commends Jones's ability to hold disparate cultural parts together "in a way which if it were more common would make our whole situation, political and social, no less than cultural and spiritual, substantially less despairing, substantially more hopeful than at present it is" (82). *In Parenthesis* may well be a timely poem for the present; in the ensuing pages I

---

6   The proto-fascist argument was put forth at length by Elizabeth Ward in *David Jones Mythmaker* (1983). Thomas Dilworth, in "David Jones and Fascism," refutes many of her claims on the evidence of an unpublished Jones essay, "Hitler" (Matthias 143–59). He cites Kathleen Henderson Staudt as having also effectively countered Ward's claims. I have chosen to use Corcoran's piece, slightly more recent and, to my mind, more nuanced than Ward's, because it has not received the same public attention.

hope to show only that its timeliness for the late 1930s, still clearly not accepted by all readers, is in large part a function of its European scope and culmination in ritual.

Christine Pagnoulle argues that "Jones strangely (yet compellingly) associates" the "Celtic soul ... with the fire of the Roman faith" (70). Even a cursory reading of Jones's poetry and his writings on art and culture reveals that his idea of Catholicism and his idea of Welsh tradition are intimately joined and interdependent. In one letter, Jones writes that "in an obscure way and at a deep level the more Welsh the *numen* is, so much the more will there be found to be Catholic affinities" (DG 119). While this association makes obvious sense with relation to Ireland, Wales has not been a predominantly Catholic country for several centuries. Still, Catholic sacramentalism and Welsh tradition, writes Allchin, are "two things which, in David Jones's mind, were closely connected" (75), their congruence evident, for example, in Celtic art forms. Jones sees Wales's Celtic identity as ineluctably securing a Catholic identity in Wales, whatever the changes in religious demographics. Jeremy Hooker correctly observes that Jones's Wales is "made in a far older image, as part of Catholic Europe" and that Jones is always "thinking about Wales in relation to the Catholic West" (12). Specifically, that relation has to do with Jones's hope of the essential—as opposed to official—Catholic-ness of Wales preserving and eventually restoring the cultural and spiritual cohesion of Europe.

So thorough and so un-obscure does Jones make the joining of Welsh and Catholic tradition that it appears quite natural in a poem such as *In Parenthesis*, but it does raise some questions regarding principles of selection for the critic. On the one hand, sacramentalism and the notion of Wales as a part (a sign?) of Europe pair well in the appreciation they encourage for the integrity of the local and concrete. On the other hand, as a Catholic, Jones sees sacrament as so revelatory of essential human nature, as well as so ineluctably tied to the "Redemption of the World ... once and for all" (EA 167) prefigured at the Last Supper and completed on Calvary, that one is hard pressed to avoid following Jones into territory well beyond the scope of a reading of a given British poet in a given historical moment. Hooker, for instance, moves easily from "issues concerning ... national identity in twentieth-century Britain" to "human identity in the modern world." *In Parenthesis*, he writes, "is a celebration of humanity" (12–13). Similarly, David Blamires argues that Jones's "loving attention paid to the particular has as its aim a depiction of the universal and ... the tangible world points beyond itself to the transcendental" (1–2). The present chapter will thus limit itself to an investigation of how Jones's religious ideas can be seen to interact with his idea of European identity. As in the previous chapters, the method will be to use Europe as a middle term between the local and the universal, as well as a kind of ceiling on the investigation of one author's cultural ideas. The threads of Jones's Welshness and Catholicism will be followed into the European maze only to the point that it threatens to open onto something much broader.

The Welsh Thing

A discussion of Jones's idea of Europe must begin with an understanding of his "Welsh affinities" (DG 30) because, with his abhorrence of abstraction, Jones uses Wales as a major example of the "hard material" (EA 244) that is the only evidence of such an idea existing at all. His life's work, in Blamires's words, represents an attempt "to distil the essence of civilization as manifested in the historical, cultural, and spiritual deposits of the British Isles" (10). Like Eliot with his notion that the English language is the best indicator of the mind of Europe,[7] Jones might be accused of choosing too small a handle with which to hold onto the European whole. Yet for him, just as the reality of the supernatural is fully present in the local particulars of sacrament, Europe is substantively present in Welsh Britain. Early in *In Parenthesis*, Private Ball rebukes himself: "Keys of Stondon Park. His father has its twin in the office in Knightryder Street. Keys of Stondon Park in French farmyard. Stupid Ball, it's no use here, so far from its complying lock" (IP 23). The rest of the poem, however, reveals that keys from Britain do have real utility in France.

Jacques Darras, a Frenchman forthcoming about his difficulty in accepting Eliot's English-language idea, classes Jones, along with Eliot and Pound, as "the best European poets of this century" (126). That Pound and Eliot were Americans, he writes, is "extremely significant ... More than anyone in Europe at the time, they picture Europe to themselves as a whole, not as a collection of segments" (126–27). Yet, like Jones's sense of the unity of Europe, theirs is initially anchored to "a deep, scholarly interest in a remote corner of the European mind" (Darras 127). Sanskrit and Provençal are for Eliot and Pound, respectively, the early signs of the greater cultural reality they can sense but seek ways to demonstrate. Being "totally out of love with their country, the United States" (Darras 127), both go on to follow their respective threads into that reality, meanwhile making themselves European in ways scarcely less idiosyncratic than the one chosen by Jones. In his 1937 review essay "The Roland Epic and Ourselves," Jones notes the momentary recurrence of "that dream [of a united Europe] which has been, on and off, for many centuries, with variations of time and place, the half-waking, half-sleeping preoccupation of the European mind" (DG 103). Perhaps it is by virtue of being, like Eliot and Pound, "of the western fringes" of European civilization (DG 103), where "variations of time and place" seem temporarily to have brought the dream, that Jones is able to give it concrete expression in poetry.

---

[7]   See Chapter 1 of this book and Eliot's "The Unity of European Culture" in *Christianity and Culture* 187–202. Although Jones made no such argument for the English language, Hilary Davies sees his prosody as a demonstration of the diversity and density of which the language is capable, and which Eliot clearly had in mind. Jones's "muscular line," Davies writes, the product of his assimilation of Shakespeare, Welsh, Cockney, Latin, and much more, enables Jones to access "the richness of all the different ways in which English can express itself: in the differences of vocabulary that indicate class, regions, dialects, educated and uneducated, men and women, colonial and colonised" (23).

The problem, as well as the opportunity, presented by Jones's Welshness begins with the fact that he was not entirely Welsh. His father was Welsh, but his mother was English of half-Italian descent. David Jones was born and raised in "an entirely English atmosphere" in London and made only infrequent visits to family in North Wales (DG 23). Yet, writes Jones, "[f]rom about the age of six, I felt I belonged to my father's people and their land" (DG 23). His "initial visit made an indelible mark, not to be erased" (DG 23). Although he used Welsh words frequently and well in his writing, "he never learned to read Welsh fluently," writes Allchin, "let alone speak it or understand it when spoken" (76).[8] Thus there is always an invented quality about Jones's Welshness, an imaginative ordering of the elements of his history and environment that best correspond to a sense of his own place within a cultural complex. In Hooker's words, "Jones's imagination fed on his *hiraeth* for Wales" (12), where *hiraeth* translates as longing, nostalgia, or homesickness. Jones knew that he was on one level Welsh "by 'desire' only, and not by 'water'" (EA 108), that is, deliberately and with difficulty, not automatically.

Welsh blood is part of the picture, but one not nearly so large as Jones's gift of identifying what Welsh particularities reveal of the larger cultural unity of which he feels himself a part. Critics have in general accepted this invented Welshness as part of Jones's pattern of making art. Pagnoulle writes that "Wales was part of his personal history ... in an indirect and literary way" enabling him to treat place as "mythical reference" and landscape as sign (63–65). "The layering of the immediate and the imaginary, the present and the already reechoed or divined," writes W.S. Merwin in the Foreword to *In Parenthesis*, "would characterize his work all his life" (ii). The perception is individual, and Jones tolerates the way, as he wrote in *In Parenthesis*, "The memory lets escape what is over and above" (153). However, it is not quite accurate to say, as Pagnoulle does, that Jones's Wales is also a "mere figment of his personal imagination" (63). For all its idiosyncrasy, Jones's thought is too consistently rooted in the tangible "deposits" of culture and tradition to be classed as purely subjective. He uses the word "deposits" frequently in his prose to refer to "the monuments, both great and small, left to us from bygone cultures" (Wootten 48). As he writes in the essay "Some Notes on the Difficulties of One Writer of Welsh Affinity Whose Language is English": "All works, whether of written poetry or of the visual arts, but especially of written poetry, depend to some extent upon the images used being drawn from the deposits of a common tradition, by virtue of which their validity is to be recognized by reader or beholder" (DG 30).

Jones prefers to express the "acute imaginative awareness of his mixed heritage—Welsh, English, Latin" (Hooker 11) in the objectivity of "hard material" and with recourse to objective tradition, a very different thing indeed from the

---

8   See also Blamires 10: "David Jones has not spent very much of his life in Wales: the longest period was what he spent with the Gill family at Capel-y-ffin in the mid 1920s. Nor does he speak or read Welsh, but manages to puzzle out the meaning of words and phrases with extreme difficulty."

dominant modern feeling, identified by Hilary Davies, "that the minutiae of the chronological self are *ipso facto* of poetic value" (25).[9] Blamires shares this view. In *David Jones: Artist and Writer*, he argues that "[Jones's] material, indeed his whole concern as a poet, is non-subjective" (12). Jones's "scale of reference" may be miscellaneous, he writes, but, bridging particular and tradition, past and present, it all but precludes his writing the purely "personal poetry" (13) preferred, for instance, by Fussell.[10] In the end this scale of reference always comes down to the "hard material" equally available to a poet and a people. "The imagination," writes Jones, "must work through what is known and known by a kind of touch ... [T]he roots must be in hard material though the leaves be conceptual and in the clouds; otherwise we can have fancy but hardly imagination" (EA 244). The ways in which Wales most resonates in Jones's mind are thus presented in *In Parenthesis* under the form of concrete detail and always with reference to objective tradition.

The two main Welsh literary traditions underpinning and illuminating *In Parenthesis* are the sixth-century elegiac sequence *Y Gododdin* and the roughly contemporaneous legend of King Arthur by way of Sir Thomas Malory's fifteenth-century interpretation. Although only the first is attributed to a Welsh author (Aneirin), Jones chooses both for what they reveal of Welsh cultural identity, most notably, in the context of *In Parenthesis*, the Celtic "defeat-tradition" (DG 53), the commitment to unity in diversity among the peoples of Britain, and the essential Catholic-ness of medieval Welsh culture. In Jones's sacramental economy, the Welsh peculiarity of both stories is inseparable from the European unity they recall and enact. Their European implications, though, must correspond to the local particulars of the legends themselves as Jones finds them.

In the Preface to *In Parenthesis*, Jones quotes Christopher Dawson on Arthur's place in the local tradition of defeat. "And if Professor Collingwood is correct," Dawson writes, "and it is the conservatism and loyalty to lost causes of Western Britain that has given our national tradition its distinctive character, then perhaps the middle ages were not far wrong in choosing Arthur, rather than Alfred or Edmund or Harold, as the central figure of the national heroic legend" (IP xiii). In the Celtic defeat tradition as Jones interprets it, a lost cause is never a total loss; Arthur sleeps, like the memory of Rome, below the surface of the Welsh imagination, infusing it with life out of seeming death. The *Y Gododdin* sequence

---

[9]   Long ago, Kathleen Raine identified the problem, for Jones and others, of trying to be objective in a resolutely subjective age. "Such is the paradox of our time," she wrote, "that the more a poet draws on an objective tradition, the less on subjective experiences, the more obscure he will seem. It is important to realise that neither *The Waste Land*, the *Cantos*, nor even *Finnegan's Wake* is obscure to us chiefly because its author refers to some subjective and private world, but for the opposite reason. All these works assume a knowledge of a common fund of traditional culture, that few any longer in fact do possess" ("Sacred and Profane" 19). This reasoning has obviously not deterred critics (see Corcoran, Pagnoulle) from labeling Jones excessively subjective.

[10]   Here again, Jones's thought is highly consonant with Eliot's. Indeed, Louis Bonnerot argues that "'Historical thinking' as defined by T.S. Eliot [in "Ulysses, Order and Myth" (SE 16)] ... is the root principle of David Jones's writings" (126).

is concerned, firstly and irrevocably, with death and defeat. In the first substantive Note to *In Parenthesis*, Jones writes that *Y Gododdin*

> commemorates raid of 300 Welsh of Gododdin … into English kingdom of Deira. Describes the ruin of this 300 in battle at Catraeth … Three men alone escaped death including the poet, who laments his friends. 'Though they may have gone to Churches to do penance their march has for its goal the sure meeting place of death.' (IP 191)

Jones uses lines from *Y Gododdin* as epigraphs to each of the seven sections of *In Parenthesis* and, indeed, as a subtitle to the whole work: "*Seinnyessit e gledyf ym penn mameu*": "His sword rang in mothers' heads" (IP 191). The saga provides a perfectly apposite framework for Jones's poetic account of the deaths of a group Royal Welch Fusiliers at the Somme, the kind of "sure meeting place of death" in which the First World War seemed to specialize. That *Y Gododdin* is also, as Jones writes later in "The Dying Gaul," "celebrative of … the birth time of the Welsh nation" (DG 53), provides a clue to the intimate relationship between defeat and identity in the "Welsh thing." *Y Gododdin*, Jones argues, is an early part of the Celtic defeat tradition, immortalized in the Roman statue the Dying Gaul, which Jones first encountered in 1909 and which "would condition my feelings in all sorts of contexts, both personal and impersonal, from then" onward.[11] It is a tradition, he writes,

> with newer calamities piling up in plenty to give the old saws their modern instances and to intensify the feeling in differing localities of the Celtic West, developed, centuries later still and under the influence of a European-wide movement, a romantic conception of Celtdom, whereby, as we all know, if you want a minstrel boy it is 'In the ranks of death you'll find him.' (DG 53–54)

The Dying Gaul, that is, continually dies but is never quite dead, embodying the rich paradox of this tradition, in which death is not final and a defeated people draw life from their defeats. Jones points to James Joyce, in whose writing "the Celtic demands with regard to place, site, identity, are a hundred-fold fulfilled," as the best evidence that "the Dying Gaul is not dead yet" (DG 58). Just as "the birth-poetry of Wales makes continuous anamnesis of the Dying Gaul," so "[t]he Gaul dies daily" in, among other places, a poetry like Jones's, making a thing and a way, even a kind of aesthetic, where purely materialist thinking sees only an end.

This aspect of the "Celtic thing" (DG 57; EA 198)—obviously consonant with the Christian tradition of life from death—encourages a reading of *In Parenthesis*, and particularly of the climactic scene of ritual benediction of the dead, that some critics have been loath to accept. They see the piled-up deaths of the Great War as the endpoint, if not the negation, of possible literary meanings. Fussell's refusal to reconcile the war's ostensibly unprecedented dying with what he sees as Jones's

---

[11]   That the Gaul depicted in the statue is a Celt is clear from his nakedness and his Celtic torque, shield, and war-trumpet (DG 50). For more on the Celtic associations of the Dying Gaul statue, see Thomas Cahill 82, 97, and 131.

attempt to redeem it through the perpetuation of literary tradition, and Corcoran's denunciation of *In Parenthesis*'s "final images ... of an Anglo-German fraternity in death" (215) as pseudo-fascistic, mark a point at which Jones's "Celtic thing," like the mythical method, pushes *In Parenthesis* beyond the preferred limits of historical materialist criticism.

Two passages from *In Parenthesis* dealing with the resurrection of soldiers suggest the subtler demarcation between life and death (common, Fussell argues, to many soldiers in the trenches) in Jones's scheme. The first depicts soldiers rising who have been not dead but only sleeping:

> Morning sergeant—kiss me sergeant.[12]
> Whose toe porrects the ritual instrument to
> break the spell to
> resurrect the traverses.

> Fog refracted, losing articulation in the cloying damp, the word of command unmade in its passage, mischiefed of the opaque air, mutated, bereaved of content, become an incoherent uttering, a curious bent cry out of the smarting drift, lost altogether—yet making rise again the grey bundles where they lie. Sodden night bones vivify, wet bones live. (IP 60)

Darras notes the centrality of stories of sleeping lords and warriors, Arthur among them, to Celtic mythology, connoting a "sleeping power" in the culture (126).[13] A similar theme pervades Jones's poetry. In an earlier passage, he has written of "his mess-mates sleeping like long-barrow sleepers, their / dark arms at reach. / Spell-sleepers, thrown about anyhow under the night. / And this one's bright brow turned against your boot leather, tranquil as a fer sidhe sleeper, under fairy tumuli, fair as Mac Og sleeping" (IP 51). In the note to these lines, Jones names several instances of "the persistent Celtic theme of armed sleepers under the mounds" and notes that the landscape and disposition of "the Forward Zone, called up easily this abiding myth of our people" (IP 199).[14] The myth and Jones's writing move easily

---

12   The homoeroticism of this line is often remarked, not unjustly, by critics. There is a great deal of such male intimacy throughout *In Parenthesis*. There is equal justification for reading the line, however, as merely a soldier's joke. "Kiss Me Sergeant" was the title of a 1932 film, and phrases such as "kiss me goodnight sergeant-major," for instance, recur in First-World-War songs. In immediate context, it also evokes the legend of the Sleeping Beauty, the spell of whose sleep is broken by a kiss.

13   In a brilliant turn, Darras also identifies the motif of sleep as central to Jones's (and Eliot's and Pound's) imagination of Europe, and argues that present-day Europe is awakening from a kind of sleep. "Nobody knows for sure," he writes, "what sleep Europe is to be ravished from" (126).

14   The legend of Arthur is, of course, no small part of this "abiding myth." In "The Myth of Arthur," Jones quotes Caxton's preface to *Le Morte d'Arthur*: "Yet some men say in many parts of England that King Arthur is not dead, but had by the will of our Lord Jesu into another place" (EA 213).

between death and sleep because they picture all of life as a kind of sleep before the ultimate awakening, and thus death as no ending, indeed, as a power. Sleeping soldiers and dead soldiers on earth, then, are little different from one another. The second passage involves stretcher bearers and their burden of wounded, or possibly dead, soldiers:

> Carrying-parties,
> runners who hasten singly,
> burdened bearers walk with careful feet
> to jolt him as little as possible,
> bearers of burdens to and from
> stumble oftener, notice the lessening light,
> and feel their way with more sensitive feet—
> you mustn't spill the precious fragments, for perhaps these raw bones live.
> (175)[15]

Both passages, like the culminating battle scene in which the deaths are quite certain, treat death with a familiarity and an un-finality characteristic of the Celtic view. And both are designed to recall the foundational Christian myth with which the Celtic tradition of defeat is thoroughly intertwined.

The next important way in which *Y Gododdin* and the legend of King Arthur support "the Welsh thing" is their concrete demonstration, from Jones's point of view, of British unity in diversity and, by extension, of Britain's place in Europe. In his essay "The Myth of Arthur," Jones writes: "What makes the Arthurian thing so important to the Welsh is that there is no other tradition at all equally the common property of all the inhabitants of Britain (at all events those south of the Antonine Wall), and the Welsh, however separatist by historical, racial and geographical accidents, are devoted to the unity of this island" (EA 216). Their devotion to unity, however, works hand in hand with a commitment to difference, with what Jones in *The Sleeping Lord* called a love of "place, time, demarcation, hearth, kin, enclosure, site, differentiated cult" (59). It is this difficult synthesis of unity and diversity, of the feeling for the whole and the "advocacy of local culture and regional diversity" (Goldpaugh 132) that Jones believed defines the Welsh thing. He also felt it to have been materially alive in his First-World-War London-Welsh regiment, of the Royal Welch Fusiliers. In the Preface to *In Parenthesis*, he writes:

> My companions in the war were mostly Londoners with an admixture of Welshmen, so that the mind and folk-life of those two differing racial groups are an essential ingredient to my theme. Nothing could be more representative.

---

[15] The final line in particular, like that of the passage on the rising soldiers, recalls the parallel theme in *The Waste Land* and Eliot's use of the same passage from the Book of Ezra in *Ash Wednesday*: "And God said / Shall these bones live? shall these / Bones live?" (SPO 85). There is also a vivid likeness between Eliot's "veiled sister between the slender / Yew trees," the "Blessèd sister, holy mother, spirit of the fountain, spirit of the garden" (SPO 91–92) and Jones's Queen of the Woods.

> These came from London. Those from Wales. Together they bore in their bodies
> the genuine tradition of the Island of Britain, from Bendigeid Vran to Jingle and
> Marie Lloyd ... Every man's speech and habit of mind were a perpetual showing
> ... of the commons in arms. (IP x–xi)

The attempt to represent this combination of unity and diversity provides one of
the main rhythms of *In Parenthesis*, where Britain's regional dialects, deprived of
none of their peculiarity, mingle on equal terms as parts of a whole.

Passages such as the following, in which the voices of speakers are differentiated
only by the peculiarity of their speech, show forth in language the idea of unity in
diversity:

> Horses' tails are rather good—and the way this one springs from her groomed
> flanks.
>> He turns slightly in his saddle.
>> You may march at ease.
>> No one said march easy Private Ball, you're bleedin' quick at some things
> ain't yer.
> The Squire from the Rout of San Romano smokes Melachrino No. 9.
>> The men may march easy and smoke, Sergeant Snell. (4–5)

Employing what Chris Hopkins identifies as "a set of regional references" (319),
but eschewing the usual markers such as inquits ("he saids," for example) and
quotation marks, the language of the passage presents a mixture of registers
without establishing an apparent hierarchy between them. The result is something
approaching pure polyphony. Hopkins argues that such sequences "reduce the
clash between the different voices, while leaving them their distinctiveness"
(323). Not only do the identifiable characters' voices interact in this way, but the
narrative voice as well as voices from the near and distant past speak on equal
terms with them, suggesting a unity in diversity across not only geographical but
also temporal and literary regions.

For Jones, *Y Gododdin*, like the legend of King Arthur, is a deposit significant
of British unity, of which the Welsh are the special, if unlikely, guardians. "The
whole poem," he writes in a Note to *In Parenthesis*,

> has a special interest for all of us of this Island because it is a monument of
> that time of obscurity when north Britain was still in Celtic possession and the
> memory of Rome yet potent ... So that the choice of fragments of this poem as
> 'texts' is not altogether without point in that it connects us with a very ancient
> unity and mingling of races; with the Island as a corporate inheritance, and with
> the remembrance of Rome as a European unity. The drunken 300 at Catraeth fell
> as representatives of the Island of Britain. (IP 191–92)

In this explanation the notions of British unity and European unity slip almost
automatically into one another. This, Jones writes in "The Myth of Arthur," is a
long-standing tradition among Welsh writers. "The oral style," he explains, "easily
telescopes history and transposes geography ... ; the domestic bards [of Wales]

would describe the doings of the princes of Powys or even of the lord of a *cantref* as though their swords had been decisive in the fate or Europe" (EA 217). In a similar way, Jones's appreciation of the role of the Arthurian myth in unifying British culture is inseparable from his view of it as a European inheritance. He points out that Arthur is not only integral to the Welsh thing but also is "the pivotal figure of the most important cycle of romantic literature in Europe … the focal point of medieval romance in Britain, France, Germany, indeed all the West … the star figure in a vast body of literature spreading over many countries and centuries" (EA 213–14). Hague cites a diagram of Jones's detailing the European descent of the Arthur myth. It situates "1150–1250/French & German/Romance," Malory, Geoffrey of Monmouth, and the "Late English tradition, Drayton, Camden, Spenser, Milton, Blake, etc.," as well as Celtic and pre-Celtic Ireland and Wales within a system including sources from much earlier: "Greece, Rome, Byzantium, cults and literature" (qtd. in Hague 53). Arthur's particularization as (pre-)Welsh is the local deposit implying the European relationship. For all of Jones's careful attention to "the Welsh thing" and to matters of cultural identity in the British Isles and Ireland, the lines he draws around his subject invariably encompass Europe as well.

In this practice Jones is within a Welsh and, more broadly, Celtic artistic tradition of trying to fold all the world into a small space. Asked by his friend Aneirin Talfan Davies to account for "the passion for the intricate and complex" in Celtic works of art as seen, for instance, in a page from the Book of Kells or James Joyce's *Ulysses* or *Finnegan's Wake*, Jones follows a thread of thought leading from aesthetics to social order and to the Catholic dogma of the Incarnation. All art, but especially Celtic art, he writes, is driven by the desire to include everything, the whole "*mewn lle bychan* … I mean the entirety or totality in a little place or space" (qtd. in Allchin 82). Such a work of art containing the whole world in a small space is, he believes, analogous to the Incarnation itself, whereby all divinity and the natural world are enclosed in the smallest of spaces. He quotes this passage, which credits Mary's body with the qualities of a Celtic work of art, from the Mass of the Eve of the Assumption: *quem totus non capit orbis, in tua se clausit viscera factus homo*: "he whom the whole world cannot contain, made man lies enclosed in your womb." He continues:

> We want to say of this poem or that picture that that which the whole world cannot comprehend or hold has been enclosed within the strict confines of this or that *cerdd* (song or poem), *celfyddydwaith* (artefact), *cerfddelw* (sculpture), *ilun* (picture), or *delw* (image) or any of the 'carpentries of song' that chaps have done and do no matter what the *trai a llanw* (the ebb and flow) of the centuries. I've thought that the artist's best text or motto is found in that psalm (… CXXI in the Vulgate) about Jerusalem being builded as a city whose parts are united in one.

It is this impulse that Jones sees "in that inter-joining (which is what, I suppose, *chdgyssylltu* in the Welsh version of the psalms means) … of unparalleled ingenuity and complexity ... making a Celtic art work like a *dinas* (city) whose parts are united in one" (qtd. in Allchin 81–82).

Jones thus indirectly provides a frame for reading *In Parenthesis* (and his other works, plastic and poetic), situating it within the tradition of Celtic art, difficult, intricate, but unified, stretching at least as far back as the complex illuminations of the Book of Kells. In describing this local aesthetic, he recurs without hesitation to the central tenet of his religion and to a geographically distant model of cultural unity in diversity, and one begins to see the rightness of Hague's view that "we cannot isolate one strand in the complex hierarchy of [Jones's] concepts" (63). Rather, we must allow one to lead naturally to and join another where Jones seems to encourage the interaction.[16] In this case, the twin ideas of unity in diversity and enclosing the whole in a small space, which Jones finds everywhere in Welsh art and culture, lead quite readily into Jones's political idea of Europe and, crucially, back again. Hague describes Jones's treatment of all cultural material, whether the Arthur myth, Celtic art, or the mystery of the Incarnation, as "a circular process. We start from a particular fact, or as close as we can get to a fact, expand it to the universal concept in our mind, and then further and more accurately particularise it" (57). At present, however, the universe will not be larger than Europe, nor the particular much smaller than Wales.

Given Jones's Welsh affinities, indeed, his Welsh allegiance, it seems surprising that he was so thoroughly attracted to the idea of a powerful united Europe. Put another way, the appeal of a strong union would seem to conflict with Jones's concern for "the life and values of small cultures and nations" (Hooker 24), for what he calls in *The Anathemata* "the diversities by which we are" (15). In Jones's vision, though, this seemingly impossible union is nearly actual. Instead, Europe is the whole through which the Welsh part is more accurately particularized. In a highly pragmatic mode, he declined—prior to World War II—to condemn the German annexation of Moravia and Bohemia, writing in an unpublished essay, "we choose to apply different standards over this 'sacredness of small nationalities' principle according to how it suits us and according to all kinds of necessities and accidents" (qtd. in Dilworth, "Fascism" 151). He could even envision scenarios in which it would become legitimate for Wales to be pulled back within "the English sphere of control" (Dilworth, "Fascism" 151). It seems natural to him that Wales will always fall within the purview of English influence in the same way that Czechoslovakia, for instance, will always be a part of the German world. Jones is routinely unimpressed by the claims to sovereignty of modern nation-states, preferring instead to look for patterns—historical, cultural, spiritual—which suggest identity on other grounds. The operative principle seems to be

---

[16]   In his essay "The Heritage of Early Britain," Jones also writes, "the character of the Celtic liturgies shows a tendency towards the elaboration of forms, rather than towards simplicity; which is certainly what one would expect from the culture-complex that produced the intricate arabesques of Kells, the involved and exacting patterns of the Welsh bardic versification and of Celtic art-forms of every sort" (EA 198).

that a system of purely official political sovereignties is no guarantee of Europe maintaining its cultural diversity, just as more than independence is required to safeguard the individuality of a local culture. Wales's rich cultural deposits, despite its lack of political or religious autonomy, are for Jones the evidence that unity is not always a threat to diversity. Similarly, Britain's irrepressible variety has never fully dissolved its underlying unity.

Jones's friend Harman Grisewood saw a similar principle at work in Jones's treatment of the Roman Empire, particularly in later works such as *The Anathemata* and *The Sleeping Lord*. In a letter to Thomas Dilworth, Grisewood wrote that Jones's cultural views are well illuminated by considering

> his appreciation of the Roman Empire and of the imperial idea. Some would say he was inconsistent, sometimes presenting Rome as the provider of a culture of which we are the heirs; at other times Rome is the destroyer of local communities and of local loyalties. David was able to see the truth of both aspects. The truth of one did not invalidate the truth of the other. (qtd. in Dilworth, "Fascism" 155)[17]

It is a unique "strength and … delicacy of mind," Grisewood continues, "which enabled him to hold such a distinction." Jones's writings suggest that a fully realized Europe must be both Rome and Wales, both whole and heterogeneous localities. Hence his emphasis on Arthur, for instance, as both the common possession of Europe and the special property of the Welsh. Pagnoulle is correct that "[n]owhere in David Jones's writings are the paradox of … 'Catholic non-conformism' and the strange combination of a fascination for Romanitas with a clear antinomy between the requirements of the Roman Empire and the shifting nature of the Celts clearly articulated. But," she continues, "references to those concomitant though apparently mutually exclusive aspects are everywhere present" (67–68). Her observation underscores Jones's discomfort with generalizations and his fondness for the accretion and juxtaposition of concrete detail, through which hard material he can turn what seems mutually exclusive as idea into poetic images both consistent and inclusive. Part of Jones's project, Hooker argues, is "to put England in its place" on a number of levels, as part of "a diverse culture with roots in an ancient unity" (24). England has been the oppressor of Wales, Jones acknowledges, but it has also been instrumental in the formation of modern Welsh culture. Moreover, Wales is uniquely situated to recall England and the rest of Britain to the whole "*mewn lle bychan*" of which Wales is both container and

---

[17] In light of Jones's view of the Nazi annexations, the rest of Grisewood's comment is apropos. Jones's both-and thinking, Grisewood continues, is "relevant to his understanding of Nazi Germany in the thirties and of his view of the disastrous war which ensued. In the thirties he saw Hitler as a necessary rebuke to the debility of the Western world. His sympathy with that rebuke in no way diminished his eventual revulsion at the terrible chastisement which followed" (qtd. in Dilworth, "Fascism" 155).

sign.[18] *In Parenthesis* suggests that the British unity which, in Hooker's words, Jones believes to be "in the keeping of the Welsh" (19) is also a European unity.

At the center of *In Parenthesis* is the famous boast of Dai, a Welshman who "articulates his English with an alien care" (79), in which he recites an imaginative family history bristling with allusions reaching from Palestine, Greece, and Rome to Spain, Scandinavia, and, of course, the British Isles. The boast, writes Merwin, "reclaims the power of language to speak from, and with, the whole of its past" (vi). An example of one short passage suggests how dense Dai's speech is with European *materia*:

> and in the standing wheat in Cantium made some attempt to form—(between
> dun August oaks their pied bodies darting) And I the south air, tossed from high
> projections by his Olifant; (the arid marcher-slopes echoing—
> should they lose
> Clere Espaigne la bele).
>   I am '62 Socrates, my feet are colder than you think
> on this Potidaean duck-board.
>   I the adder in the little bush
> whose hibernation-end
> undid,
> unmade victorious toil. (IP 80)

These lines telescope Caesar in the *Gallic Wars*, Charlemagne in the *Chanson de Roland*, Socrates in Plato's *Symposium*, and Malory's Arthur (IP 208). If Arthur unites much of Europe in a romantic tradition, Charlemagne, whose conquests ranged from 768–814, does so in political terms. He is hailed in 799 by Angilbert as *Rex, pater Europae*, "the father of Europe" (de Rougemont 45–47). The Song of Roland is thus in part concerned with the formation of Europe as "a single Christian empire, born outside of Rome, under uncontested … Franco-Germanic domination," for the first time "an autonomous entity, endowed with spiritual virtues" (de Rougemont 46–47). Denis de Rougemont also points out that "[t]he first concrete attempt at a European federation in the twentieth century, that of the Six, was, not without reason, baptized 'the Europe of Charlemagne'" (379). As in the dialogic passages between soldiers and commanders, the persons Dai invokes are made to coexist, their peculiarities intact, with little or no suggestion of

---

[18] A passage from Jones's later long poem, *The Anathemata*, helps to illustrate this pattern of finding a united Britain and thus a united Europe in the small space of Wales. The passage ends, "His uncomforming bed, as yet / is by the muses kept. / And shall be, so these Welshmen say, till the thick / rotundities give . . ." (67–8). The final allusion is to what the Welshman of Pencader, as reported by Giraldus Cambrensis, said to Henry II: "Nor do I think, that any other nation than this of Wales, or any other language, whatever may hereafter come to pass, shall in the day of severe examination before the Supreme Judge, answer for this corner of the earth" (qtd. in Hooker 19). The consistency and ease with which Jones moves between Wales and Europe in his writing suggest that the "corner of the earth" for which he asks Wales to speak encompasses more than the British Isles.

hierarchy or estrangement. Indeed, the reference to the duck-board of the trenches gathers all the historical references unassumingly as one literary-historical-material unity in the present.[19]

Dai's long speech hinges on his cry to "keep the land, keep us / keep the islands adjacent" (IP 82). The words, Jones explains in a note, recall a "phrase common in Welsh legend … 'The Island of Britain and the three islands adjacent' (i.e., Wight, Anglesey and Man)" (IP 209). For Dai's regimental audience and for the attentive reader, the lines no doubt carry back to the islands. Yet the phrase is on precisely equal footing with the rest of the references to European myth and history, from Artaxerxes (IP 79) to the Roman "Loricated Legions" (IP 80), from Troy to William Dunbar's London (IP 81). Just as the Welsh Dai is the recipient and orderer of millennia of Western culture, so is the whole West intended to receive and assimilate what Dai has brought from the islands. For, it must be remembered, Dai is not standing in Wales as he speaks on the duck-board of a French trench. His plea will echo first in French soil and in close proximity to German soldiers. It is to these, too, that he wishes to stay adjacent. Just as the peoples of Britain are only separated from one another by various "accidents," Britain and Germany, the reader has been reminded, are now racially linked and against one another by "misadventure." Dai's plea, if it reaches Wales, will do so having enfolded a considerable portion of continental Europe.

The Catholic Thing or, "Why is Father Larkin talking to the dead?"

Dai's work of constructing an image of European unity amidst the scenery and proof of its disunity is painstaking, as is Jones's. It is based on the observation and discrimination of centuries of historical and mythical material, virtually all of it objective, but nonetheless requiring the influence of a perceptive and creative mind to give it meaningful shape. This need is particularly great in a world from which, as Merwin writes, "a shared frame of reference of any depth or perspective" has all but vanished (v). Without a living sense of the past, Merwin explains, "whole tracts of significance were beyond recall … Jones was well aware of how far from the surface" were the echoes of shared tradition even to English readers of his own day; hence his attempt to bring that tradition tangibly home through the evidence of hard material. The difficulty, Jones affirms, "is that all artists … are in fact 'showers forth' of things which tend to be impoverished, or misconceived, or altogether lost or wilfully set aside in the preoccupations of our present intense technological phase" (DG 17). Catholicism, to be sure, falls within this category of things. However, it is still "contactually" present enough to require rather less

---

[19] My theme is not the heroic per se, but Dai also achieves a unity across time, as William Wootten observes, by placing himself in the ranks of past heroes. Dai "escapes specificity," writes Wootten, "by opening a door into an Anglo-Welsh reworking of a wider heroic tradition in which the individual, solitary no more, is immersed" (30). That he "escapes specificity" altogether seems to me a bit extreme. I would argue, rather, that he transcends mere specificity.

legwork on the part of the artist. There are two primary ways in which Catholicism enables Jones to articulate a unified idea of Europe in *In Parenthesis*. The first is that by invoking Catholic ritual as a shared European tradition and basis for cultural organization, the text demonstrates a unity that transcends national boundaries and, specifically, unites English and Welsh with French, German, Irish, and Italian. The second is that the centrality to Catholic practice of bodies in general and of physical action in particular leads Jones to represent this unity not as an abstraction, not even as mere language signifying a concept, but concretely in the enactment of a ritual uniting an idea and a physical fact.

In addition to providing this conceptual link between Europe and the British Isles, Catholicism unites them in quite concrete historical terms, and not only by virtue of their common Christianization within the Roman Empire. Jones was fond of recalling that monks from the British Isles and Ireland had once been responsible for the preservation of the Catholic faith during the years after the Empire fell, and that they had led the re-Christianization of Europe from their remote outposts in Ireland, Wales, Scotland, and England. Moreover, he believed that the Celtic world might again spearhead such a spiritual reunification. In his 1938 essay "The Roland Epic and Ourselves," he laments "the falling into dis-usage of a petition [from the Good Friday office, asking for the redemption of barbarian nations (*barbaras nationes*)] that has such interesting historical associations and such abiding metaphorical validity" (DG 100). Once again, his thoughts tend toward Nazi Germany:

> It is, conceivably, for a baptized Führership that we may yet have cause to pray, if only in the sense that a sophisticated Roman of The Province would have asked heaven's prevenience for the difficult barbarian invested with The Purple; or a Celtic Christian might, just conceivably, have prayed for Edwin, with his assumed insignia of the *Dux Britanniarum*. (DG 100)

In Jones's Europe, not even a barbarous people seemingly bent on the subversion or destruction of the fabric of European cohesion (and on replacing it with an imposed and homogeneous unity) can fall entirely outside the Catholic fold, no more than Britain and its three islands, or the Welch Fusiliers, regardless of historical accidents, can be divided.

Given the rich constitution of the London-Welsh regiment, their happily mixed voices and customs, the text of *In Parenthesis* could limit its exploration of unity in diversity to life within the regiment based on purely local and national affiliations. Instead, in several key passages, it presses beyond those mobile confines into alternative territories of identification. Catholicism is repeatedly cited as the channel through which British soldiers are united to Europe. For example:

> On Sunday:
> they fell out the fancy religions; the three Jews were told off for fatigue at the latrines. Mr. Jenkins was detailed to march the R.C.s four kilometres to the next village to mass; because of Father Larkin being up at the Aid Post, with his Washbourne *Rituale*, and the saving Oils. (IP 107)

"Fancy religions," Jones explains, denotes "Any religious denomination other than C. of E." (IP 213). Army idiom, then, implicitly, and, one has the sense, reluctantly, acknowledges Catholicism as a tradition that takes British soldiers out of Britain, here into a French village. Judaism does the same, although the Jews of the regiment being sent to latrine duty strikes one here as rather bullying, particularly, recalling Corcoran's argument, since *In Parenthesis* is more a poem of 1937 than 1915. William Blissett makes an important comparison between the Jews and the Welsh, noting, for instance, that "by second nature, the Welsh think of their country as a small holy highland, like Judaea. The Welsh, like the Jews, are a small nation, many of their number in various degrees assimilated, others very jealously and zealously not assimilated" (114).[20] Were Jones's focus less restricted in religious terms, the ways that Judaism, as a non-national religion, unites Europe might have been brought into clearer focus, as those of Roman Catholicism certainly are.

In Parenthesis situates its British regiment within a network of other Europeans loyal to "the fancy religions." Most immediately visible is the Catholic tradition among the French. The narration pauses in one place to consider the life of nearby townspeople, among them "girls with baskets, linen-palled, children dawdling from the Mysteries on a Sunday morning" (IP 30), that may be going on, unseen, up the road. Such, cruelly, will become the victims of indiscriminate artillery: "Tomorrow, before daybreak, a ranging heavy fire will find the foundations and leave the kitchen flooring pounded like red-pepper, with Cecile's school satchel still hanging at its peg; and the Papal Blessing punctured in its gimcrack frame, poking from the midden" (IP 96). One "man from Rotherhithe" sits in a French café and looks "through the Sacred Heart, done in wools, through the wall, … through all barriers, making as though they are not, all things foreign and unloved" (IP 112). A bit later, Private Ball and Private Thomas exchange a few words with a French priest out walking his garden and praying: "Allemands—no bon—eh? / They tried to tell him it was British gunfire; that the war would soon be over— but he paid no heed. / Allemands—beaucoup de bombardment—plenty blessés. / He turned between where the bees hived, between low plants, to his presbytery" (IP 118). The text does not dwell upon such observations and encounters at length; rather, it offers them briefly but recurrently as the evidence, the deposits, as it were, of an identity beyond the narrow nationalism that has led to estrangement and war.

The poignancy of this identity—and the failure to respect it—becomes greater still when it is extended to the enemy. Germany is the country of Luther, but the Germans on whom the focus of the text lands are as Catholic as young Cecile. The cemetery described below is French, but the text makes little distinction between French and German deaths and prayers:

---

[20] For several other sources dealing with the Welsh-Jewish connection, see Blissett 114 n.36.

And the grave-yard huddled—silver black and filigree Mary-Helps and the funerary glass shivered where they ask of your charity. And the civvy dead who died in the Lord with *Libera nos* and full observance, churned and shockt from rest all out-harrowed and higgledy-piggledy along with those other—wood white with heavy script for mortuary monument, for these shovelled just into surface soil like dog—with perhaps an *Our Father* said if it was extra quiet.

But all the old women in Bavaria are busy with their novenas, you bet your life, and don't sleep lest the watch should fail, nor weave for the wire might trip his darling feet and the dead Karl might not come home.

Nor spill the pitcher at the well—he told Josef how slippery it was out there. O clemens, O pia and
turn all out of alignment the English guns amen. (149)

The juxtapositions are ironic in the best Great-War-poetry style. However, the irony derives from more than the incongruity, to recall Fussell, between elegant words and the dumb brutality of mechanized warfare. It derives from the fact, often remarked upon in wartime, that both sides are praying to God for help, and for victory, expecting their prayers to be answered. When people of different nations share the same religious tradition, when their common rituals make them seem more like family than enemies, and when the underlying unity is for more than a moment shown forth, irony gives way to pathos. The effect is the same when the narrative tells of German soldiers singing Christmas carols in the opposing trench and, in the same moment, calls them "barbarians" and "bastards" (IP 68); irony has the first word but not necessarily the last.

A kind of European trinity is completed when the text puts Italian soldiers, too, in the picture. This moving passage opens with reference to a priest hearing confessions, but the names are enough to suggest the soldiers' commonality as members of one Church:

Father Martin Larkin is available to all ranks between 3.30 and 5.0; that's where the Dagoes slip fatigue—that's not so healthy, that conforms to the general trend. When Bomber Mulligan and Runner Meotti approach the appointed channels you can count on an apocalypse, you can wait on exceptional frightfulness—it will be him and you in an open place, he will look into your face; fear will so condition you that you each will pale for the other, and in one another you will hate your own flesh. Your fair natures will be so disguised that the aspect of his eyes will pry like deep-sea horrors divers see, from the portage of his rigid type of gas-bag—but more like you'll get it in the assembly-trench—without so much as a glimpse at his port and crest. (IP 121)

Like the London-Welsh, this Mulligan and Meotti, with names from opposite ends of Europe but who partake of the same sacraments, bear "in their bodies" a tradition of unity. Kept apart from their German enemy, they are free not to consider a brotherhood that extends beyond the British forces; they bear in their bodies the new tradition of disconnection. In close enough physical proximity, the realization that they are so close to the enemy as to be one flesh would be overwhelming. The war, though, even the front line, affords few opportunities for such needful contact. Indeed, in the context of the war, to meet in this way would be apocalyptic, the horror of ultimate separation brought unbearably home. Nor is the pain of severance the soldiers' alone. Mulligans and Meottis and their German counterparts are Europe's scapegoats. In the "wilderness" of the war, the "appointed scape-beasts come to the waste-lands, to grope; to stumble at the margin of familiar things—at the place of separation" (IP 70). They are the very image of a sundered Europe, her islands no longer adjacent.

Keeping the islands adjacent, as well as the various deposits of Catholic culture in the landscape of *In Parenthesis*, are good, hard images for the concept of unity in diversity that Jones champions. The tools of his religion, though, enable him to concretize the concept even further. Dai's exhortation is full of pathos and, in the specificity of its references, nearly makes a European thing out of European words. On its own, however, it does not quite obtain to the level of ritual which is a sub-theme of, and has the last word in, *In Parenthesis*.[21] Not until the final scene do Dai's words achieve the effectual quality Jones attributes to military commands and Catholic liturgy, "in which the spoken word effected what it signified" (IP 3). Until it is manifested in bodily action, Dai's boast lacks a crucial aspect of ritual, to which the soldier is everywhere subject:

The immediate, the nowness, the pressure of sudden, modifying circumstance— and retribution following swift on disregard; some certain, malignant opposing, brought intelligibility and effectiveness to the used formulae of command; the liturgy of their going-up assumed a primitive creativeness, an apostolic actuality, a correspondence with the object, a flexibility. (IP 28)

A passage later in the text again describes a word effecting what it signifies, speech becoming action: "But how intolerably bright the morning is where we who are alive and remain, walk lifted up, carried forward by an effective word" (IP 163; see Dilworth, *Shape* 122–39). Jones's perception of a correspondence between words and "actuality," "object," and action derives from his understanding of the logic of sacrament, by which, according to Catholic doctrine, the work of divine grace is made real and present in the world through the ritual words of a priest, most vividly

---

[21] Thomas Dilworth, in his foundational book *The Shape of Meaning in the Poetry of David Jones*, makes two important points about ritual worth noting here. One is that the rhythms and structures of military life create a further ritualistic current in the poem, a virtual secular liturgy ordering an otherwise chaotic frontline experience (see especially 122–39). The other is that the poem itself challenges the reader to participate in a ritualistic unfolding of meaning (see 114–15, et seqq.). I have not pursued these ideas in depth here first because they extend somewhat beyond the narrow anthropological limits of ritual I have set myself (collective action, sacred space, tradition) and because Dilworth's analysis is so thorough as to preclude my doing anything but directing interested readers to the book named above as well as to Dilworth's somewhat difficult to obtain pamphlet *The Liturgical Parenthesis of David Jones*.

in the transformation of bread and wine into Christ's body and blood through the priest's "effective words" in the supreme Catholic sacrament of the Eucharist. With sacrament, words are most often accompanied by physical actions—bowing, kneeling, the signing of a cross in the air or on the body—but Jones sees the saying of the words themselves as actions of the same order. In a scene in Part 5 of *In Parenthesis*, the French priest comes under Private Ball's scrutiny:

> Down behind low walls at the further end of the village, man in black walked between his vegetable beds; he handled his small black book as children do their favourite dolls, who would impute to them a certain personality; he seemed to speak to the turned leaves, and to get his answer ...
>
> Private Ball loitered at the wall, where he passed on his fatigue, with Private Thomas ... to watch the lips move beneath the beaver's shade, where a canonical wiseness conserved in an old man's mumbling, the validity of material things, and the resurrection of this flesh. (117–18)

As the text emphasizes the physical action of the priest's speech, so Jones points out in the note to the passage: "It is required of priests, that they say with their lips the words of the Divine Office, the eye alone is not sufficient; a rule indicative of the Church's instinct as to the efficacy of bodily acts" (IP 215). This instinct is visibly alive in Jones's text as it moves from the spoken unity of Dai's boast to the enacted unity of the concluding ritual. *In Parenthesis* owes much to the oral tradition, which "easily telescopes history and transposes geography," but ritual is its goal. Just as, in Jones's scheme, only in the body can the words be made effective, only in ritual can the abstraction of unity in diversity be made actual.

Barry Spurr specifies this sacramental "actuality" as the key difference between Eliot's religious vision and Jones's: "It is that between a philosophical Christianity speculating and meditating upon the intersection of time and timelessness, and a sacramental one, always alert to the divine presence in creation, with its consummation in the mass" (23). He quotes a letter from Jones to Blissett in which Jones, addressing this difference, once again shifts between religion and art. Jones writes:

> It is a real distinction ... it may be to do with my being first a visual artist & so terribly concerned with tangible, contactual 'things'—not 'concepts' really, except in so far as the concrete, creaturely material 'thing' is a *signum* of the concept & that it must be that way now because we are creatures with bodies. (Spurr 23)

The combination of body and sign leads Jones to ritual, where concepts are replaced by bodies and numinous objects. Dilworth identifies an important aspect of Jones's purpose when he writes: "Only a widespread appreciation of symbolic activity which communicates spiritual values can, [Jones] thought, fill the vacuum at the heart of technological civilization" ("Fascism" 158). The final scene of *In Parenthesis*, in which symbolic activity momentarily fills the spiritual vacuum of the Somme battlefield (which itself came to be seen as a kind of microcosm of modern civilization) is Jones's attempt to foster such appreciation on a small scale.

In "Art and Sacrament" Jones is explicit about the centrality of the body to human experience, both physical and spiritual. He insists that, whereas other religions tend to view the body as "an infirmity or a kind of deprivation," Catholicism sees it as "not an infirmity but a unique benefit and splendour; a thing denied to angels and unconscious in animals. We are committed to body and by the same token we are committed to Ars, so to sign and sacrament" (EA 165). One may say that the commitment to body as "a unique benefit and splendour" is present in the Catholic belief in the resurrection of the body, in the belief that the body has a role to play in life after death; and that Christ's and Mary's bodily assumptions into heaven exemplify the Catholic conviction that the body is not a mere encumbrance keeping human souls from heaven. Just so, the Catholic respect paid to a dead body affirms its importance as a conduit and aid to the spiritual. Even death, that is, does not end the body's significance in the supernatural schema, a Catholic view that provides Jones with another tradition of life-from-death to match the Celtic one. They combine to form the context in which Jones's poetry, especially his war poetry, must be read, a context in which meaning always begins from but does not end with Corcoran's "unaccommodated and irreducible human fact" (225). Critics who do not share Jones's views of the body tend to disapprove of Jones's ritualization of death at the conclusion of *In Parenthesis*, of his making a pattern and a sign out of the carnage of Mametz wood. They seem to ask, with one of the poem's narrators, "But why is Father Larkin talking to the dead?" (IP 173). Jones suggests it is not a question Catholics, or Celts, need to ask.

The Queen of the Woods

The final pages of *In Parenthesis* contain a scene in which the mysterious "Queen of the Woods" adorns a small group of dead soldiers—German, English, Welsh—with "bright boughs of various flowering" (185). The scene represents the lyric climax of the poem (indeed, "a lyrical high point in modern literature," in Dilworth's estimation (*Shape* 139)), but it is also remarkable for how it intervenes in the narrative arc of the story. In the midst of the fiercest fighting in Mametz wood, bullets flying, mortars and bodies exploding, trees being shredded by artillery, there is a pause and momentary peace, and "[t]he secret princes have diadems given them" (IP 185). It is surely one of the strangest episodes in the literature of the Great War, running absolutely contrariwise to irony, despair, or the emotional vacuity brought on by mindless technological destruction. It also represents the ritual consummation of Jones's vision of European unity in diversity.

Although this ritual benediction comes as a surprise, even in the context of the poem's meanderings through time and space, the material and the supernatural, the scene is long in preparation. It takes place within a grove of trees, concluding the motif of trees and men that runs throughout the poem. In a letter to Blamires, Jones writes that the images of "wounded trees and wounded men" (qtd. in Blamires 3) are the dominant ones from his soldiering days, and they are everywhere joined in *In Parenthesis*. Here, the reference is to the Scandinavian myth of Odin as related in Sir James Frazer's *The Golden Bough*:

> His eyes turned again to where the wood thinned to separate broken trees; to where great strippings-off hanged from tenuous fibres swaying, whitened to decay—as swung
>
> immolations
> for the northern Cybele
> The hanged, the offerant:
>   himself to himself
>   on the tree. (IP 67)

The theme of sacrifice associated with trees is further developed by its association with the story of Christ's death on the cross or Tree: "de la Taille's *Immolatio victimae oblatae* (of the Tree)" (DGC 232). And again: "I served Longinus that Dux bat-blind and bent; / the Dandy Xth are my regiment; / who diced / Crown and Mud-hook / under the Tree, / whose Five Sufficient Blossoms / yield for us" (DGC 83), referring to the Roman "Xth Fretensis," thought in Italian legend "to have provided the escort party" at Christ's execution (DGC 210). Jones, though, sees the pattern alive in the Old Testament as well. Part of Dai's boast is the declaration: "I was with Abel when his brother found him, / under the green tree" (IP 79). Thus far, trees are trees of death, betrayal, and separation, the sacrifice of Christ (and Odin) registered on the landscape but not yet fulfilled as reconciliation.

Part 7 takes up these early references and hardens them into the setting for the final scene, at the same time shoring up the intended religious associations. The section begins with these lines deriving from Psalm 131:

> Invenimus eum in campis silvae
> and under every green tree.
> Matribus suis dixerunt: ubi est triticum et vinum? Cum deficerent quasi vulnerati
> … cum exhalarent animas suas in sinu matrum suarum. (153)

The first two lines foreshadow a subsequent reference to "trees of the wood … / and under each a man sitting" (184). "[U]nder every green tree" is taken from Isaiah 57:4–5: "Are you not children of transgression, the offspring of deceit—you that burn with lust among the oaks, under every green tree; you that slaughter your children in the valleys, under the clefts of the rocks?" The second two lines translate as: "They ask their mothers, / 'Where is the wheat?'—in vain, / As they faint away like the wounded … And breathe their last in their mothers' arms." This image combines with the recollection of the originary fratricide to become a picture of opposed armies:

> Each one bearing in his body the whole apprehension of that innocent, on the day he saw his brother's votive smoke diffuse and hang to soot the fields of holocaust; neither approved nor ratified nor made acceptable but lighted to everlasting partition.

Who under the green tree

had awareness of his dismembering, and deep-bowelled damage; for whom the
green tree bore scarlet memorial, and herb and arborage waste. (IP 162)

Through the associations with scripture, the sequence of images of men under
trees builds a theme of the fatal separation of brothers. At the same time, a place
is being arranged for the brothers' ultimate reconciliation, if only some ordering
actor will intervene.

The text repeatedly highlights the absence of some means of ordering and
redeeming the scene. Prior to the arrival of the Queen of the Woods, there is only
solitary "Father Larkin talking to the dead" to suggest some frame of meaning
beyond the immediate one of dying bodies and "herb and arborage waste." In Part
7, soldiers of Private Ball's regiment begin to fall, alone, mechanically, and without
the consolations of ritual: "No one to care there for Aneirin Lewis spilled there / ...
/ unwholer, limb from limb, than any of them fallen at Catraeth" (IP 155). Private
Ball is rebuked for lingering too long over a friend who dies in his arms:

And get back to that digging can't yer—
this aint a bloody Wake
        for these dead, who soon will have their dead
for burial clods heaped over.
Nor time for halsing
nor to clip green wounds
nor weeping Maries bringing anointments
neither any words spoken
nor no decent nor appropriate sowing of this seed
nor remembrance of the harvesting
of the renascent cycle
and return
nor shaving of the head nor ritual incising for these *viriles* under each tree.
        No one sings: Lully lully
for the mate whose blood runs down. (IP 174)

With all these bodies arranged under the trees, having fallen out of the current
of battle into another temporality, "like no-man's land between yesterday and
tomorrow" (IP 181), the stage is nearly set for a ritual action of some kind. Two
things remain: someone to sing, as it were, "Lully lully" for the bleeding men, and
the designation of a sacred space in which her words can be made effective.

That such a space is in the offing is made clear by the epigraph to Part 7, from
Y Gododdin: "Gododdin I demand they support. It is our duty to sing: a meeting
place has been found" (IP 151). As Private Ball advances, he comes upon the
meeting place, a kind of chapel carved out of the trees:

and in the very navel of the wood there seemed a vacuum, if you stayed quite
still, as though you'd come on ancient stillnesses in his most interior place. And
high away and over, above the tree-roofing, indifferent to this harrowing of

the woods, trundling projectiles intersect their arcs at the zenith—pass out of hearing, like freighters toil to gradients when you fret wakefully on beds and you guess far destinations.

Down in the under-croft, in the crypt of the wood, clammy drippings percolate—and wide-girth boled the eccentric colonnade, as perilous altar-house for a White Tower, and a cushy place to stuff and garnish and bid him keep him—or any nosy-bloody-Parker who would pry on the mysteries. (IP 181–82)[22]

Here is the space to be filled with ritual action, and the men of both sides and several nationalities, "these long strangers, / under this vaulting stare upward" (IP 182), seeming to wait in anticipation, "their seemly faces carved in a sardonyx stone; as undiademed princes turn their gracious profiles in a hidden seal, so did these appear, under the changing light" (IP 184). Some are dead, some perhaps not quite, but none of them is excluded from the benediction that follows.

"I suppose," Jones wrote much later, "all my stuff has on the whole been central round the Queen of Heaven" (DGC 227). The Queen of the Woods is most certainly, in part, Catholicism's Mary, Queen of Heaven, but also a great deal more. Her fluidity and multiplicity are an example of the way Jones's Catholicism constantly interacts with and contains much that is not, strictly, Catholic. His Queen is a host of archetypal mother figures, mostly pagan, imaginatively aligned with the figure of the mother of Christ. "She is," writes Dilworth, "the dryad of the forest, the Acorn-Sprite of its flora-fall ... She is the Celtic triple goddess: the mother, the lover, the presider over the dead" and "the composite goddess Sir James Frazer had written about at the start of the century" (*Shape* 139–41). Her coming has been prefigured throughout the text. As Dilworth affirms, "No empty or ironic symbol, she is sustained by the theological implication of the poem's ritual associations" (*Shape* 141). During an early march, Private Ball "raised up his head" to consider the moon (IP 39), which, Jones points out, is associated "with the Mother of God" (IP 196), and to reflect upon those at Chartres who, in legend, anticipated the Mystery of the Incarnation: "[I]n the cleft of the rock ... served Her in anticipation—and over the hill-country that per-bright Shiner stood for Her rod-budding" (IP 39). In Dai's boast, she is invoked by way of the Catholic prayer, *Salve Regina*—"She's clement and loving, she's Friday's child, she's loving and giving; / O dulcis / imperatrix' (IP 81). She is the representative figure of all mothers, all women. "Her ample bosom holds," Dai proclaims, a litany of women, lowly and great, from all of history. "She's the girl with the sparkling eyes, / she's the Bracelet Giver" (IP 81). She is also "Elen Luyddawg (Helen of the Hosts), who is the focus of much obscure legend" (IP 208), and the Welsh Rhiannon, "the Celtic Mother Goddess, 'Rigantona', the 'Great Queen' ... and so much more" (DG 32). She is, writes Pagnoulle, "a goddess who is simultaneously one and

---

[22]   The religious aspect of the language is self-evident, but Jones indicates, for good measure, that "Mordred's siege of the Tower, and memories of the Norman chapel there and Gothic tombs in a dozen churches directed me here" (IP 223).

many" (70). If she seems to be a goddess in *In Parenthesis*, it is not in a heretical sense. The poem's ultimate frame of reference, after all, is Roman Catholic, and its Queen is not so much power as an agent bestowing diadems (crowns) on others; she delivers a kind of judgment, but she also brings comfort to the sacrificed. She is often associated with the maid in the fifteenth-century Corpus Christi Carol who kneels by the bedside of a wounded knight-Christ, the carol beginning "Lully, lullay, lully" (IP 89, 186, 212).

Her presence and activity in *In Parenthesis* are inflected as Christian, but, because of Jones's overriding sacramentalism, the evidence of her role in the Christian scheme of redemption is visible in a host of other cultural material. In what Wootten calls the "synchronic medieval time" (29) at work in the sacramental view and in *In Parenthesis*, all time is one and thus all time, regardless of historical sequence, is redeemed by Christ's sacrifice. As Spurr argues, Jones is "an Incarnational poet ... and holiness, for him, could be experienced in pagan and prehistoric religion" (23). Thus, when Jones writes, "[i]n some battle of the Welsh ... a whole army ate grass in token of the Body of the Lord" and "somewhere in Malory, a single knight feeling himself at the point of death makes this same act" (IP 221), these men are demonstrating the sacramental mindset in which divine revelation pervades everything. "[T]he Sacraments of the Church are a total, [*sic*] impossibility, wholly unaccountable, unless man is essentially a creature of sign and *signa*-making, a 'sacramentalist' to the core' (DGC 222). In a late letter to Harman Grisewood, Jones writes that "the Church can't have seven Sacraments with a cap 'S' unless man is a user of sign and sacrament with a small 's'" (DGC 233). For Jones, according to Watson Holloway, this kind of religion represents one of the "indispensable components of the West's cultural core ... from paleolithic times to our present 'phase' of civilization" (48). Holloway argues that passages in *The Anathemata* "resonate with 'pagan' as well as Christian ritual intensity; in a synergism of anthropology and Eucharist which draws together many threads of archaic as well as modern life" (51). Precisely the same can be said of the Queen's intervention *in In Parenthesis*. Just as she gathers all the West's divine and human women into herself, her benediction seems to compress all the world and all time into the small sacred space of this grove, these few French "boughs of various flowering."

The help of this queen is invoked in the words, "Responde mihi?" ("Answer me"), uttered just prior to the final battle and corresponding to lines from the Office of the Dead from the Little Office of the Blessed Virgin Mary (IP 157, 220). Finally, a stretcher bearer lays down the wounded Dai, presses himself to the ground, and prays for this Queen to intercede for him and his friends:

> curroodle mother earth
> she's kind:
> Pray her hide you in her deeps
> she's only refuge against
> this ferocious pursuer
> terribly questing.
> Maiden of the digged places

> let our cry come unto thee.
> *Mam*, moder, mother of me
> Mother of Christ under the tree
> reduce our dimensional vulnerability to the minimum—
> cover the spines of us
> let us creep back dark-bellied where he can't see
> don't let it.
> There, there, it can't, won't hurt—nothing
> shall harm my beautiful. (IP 176–77)

The final two lines seem to indicate that his prayer is answered, and, indeed, when one man moves, it is like the Virgin herself, "in your private bright cloud like / one assumed / who is borne up by an exterior volition" (IP 164). Yet we are told of the incoming ordinance, "But on its screaming passage / their numbers writ / and stout canvas tatters drop [...] and the shaped ash grip rocket-sticks out of the evening sky right back by Bright Trench / and clots and a twisted clout" of a dead man on the back of a living one (IP 177). The assurances of protection from the blast have been fantasy; this maiden's intervention concerns something besides the reduction of dimensional vulnerability, and she cares equally for German and British.

She has also heard, after all, the pleas of the enemy. Earlier, Private Ball has managed to "scramble forward and pretend not to see" where "the other one cries from the breaking-buckthorn. / He calls for Elsa, for Manuela / for the parish priest of Burkersdorf in Saxe Altenburg" (IP 169). Ball registers just how absurd the distinction between countries in the face of death is when, in the worst confusion of the battle, he hears "someone shouting rhetorically about remembering your nationality" (IP 180). The Queen of the Woods makes no such distinctions. As Ewan Clayton writes, "Saxon and Celt, Gaul and German" are all equally entitled to her services (64). "Just as Jones weaves the language out of allusions to the different cultures ... and makes something new of this space, so she also creates a greater whole in her tangled kingdom in which all are united" (Clayton 64). She completes in action what has been arranged by Jones's poetry, Dai's speech.

Jones later wrote that the Queen of the Woods, "no less than any other sacral award-giver, cannot function without what the earth yields," hence her choice of "sacramental signa of daisy chains and floral crowns" (DGC 256). These she distributes with great care to each soldier in the sacred grove, and with a respect for "The exact disposition of small things" (IP 24) common to the sacramentalist and the soldier:

> Some she gives white berries
>   some she gives brown
> Emil has a curious crown it's
>   made of golden saxifrage.
> Fatty wears sweet-briar,
> he will reign with her for a thousand years.
> For Balder she reaches high to fetch his.
> Ulrich smiles for his myrtle wand.
> That swine Lillywhite has daisies to his chain—you'd hardly credit it. (IP 185)

As her ritual adornment continues, its signification of cultural unity becomes more acute: "She plaits torques of equal splendour for Mr. Jenkins and Billy Crower" (IP 185); the Dying Gaul dies again in Mametz wood, here in an Englishman and a Welshman, both equally possessed of the Celtic thing. Next, German and Welsh become one in death, wearing one garland: "Hansel and Gronwy share dog-violets for a palm, where they lie in serious embrace beneath the twisted tripod" (IP 185). Private Ball is compliant as his body is fitted into the ritual as a sign of reconciliation: "Lie still under the oak / next to the Jerry / and Sergeant Jerry Coke" (IP 187). These are the images of reconciliation in which Corcoran, whose historical materialist approach tolerates neither myth, nor mystery, nor true diversity, finds a politics "neither credible nor honorable" (216). The separated brothers of Europe are signed and sealed as family in this ritual that stitches together geography and history, men and nature, the "contactual" and the supernatural.

When the Queen comes to Dai's gift, however, the spell is momentarily broken: "Dai Great-coat, she can't find him anywhere—she calls both high and low, she had a very special one for him" (IP 186). The one whose words, likewise seeming to gather in all of Europe, had anticipated this final reconciliation is denied his due blessing because his body is absent (or, more specifically, blown to unrecognizable bits). It is a "fragile prize" (IP 185) the Queen has to give, and it cannot travel far. Corcoran rightly points out that this is partly Jones's "good Catholicism" requiring that one be bodily present to receive benediction (225). The Catholic commitment to body is certainly at work here. Even for Dai, Jones will not accede to what he calls the "*essential* protestant belief" that one "can do no more than make petition 'spiritually' 'mentally' with words maybe ... in direct contradiction to what is crucial and central to the Catholic faith" (DGC 256). It seems a cruel turn, but, as Jones wrote to Hague decades later, "Her awarding is not be questioned" (DGC 257).[23]

More than only "good Catholicism," though, the emphasis on body and ritual is, Jones insists, "inescapable to us as creatures with bodies, whose nature is to *do this*, or that, rather than *think it*" (DGC 222).[24] He argues that "certain manual cult-actions and verbal formulae are of the essence of the Christian religion, not *primarily* because such actions are 'commanded' or appear to be commanded in the Gospels and were the practice of the 'Early Church', but because such is the nature of man" (DGC 222).[25] This view of the primacy of ritual goes beyond Catholic

---

[23] In light of another comment, Jones's choice of a female figure to perform this closing rite seems entirely consistent with his other guiding themes: "I suppose," Jones wrote to Hague and his wife, "that's why one has always thought of women as more 'brave' than men, because they take for granted these things of the body (as childbirth and all that) whereas we think and can more easily endure active pains, as in war etc." (DGC 227).

[24] One remembers Yeats's pleasure at living "in a country [Ireland] where men will always act. Where nobody is satisfied with thought" (*Letters of W.B. Yeats* 812).

[25] "The nature of man" is altogether too broad for the present discussion. Conveniently, though, Jones never goes far with such grandiosity without grounding it in the small and local. "[W]e have," writes Hague, "a geographical concentration, and as man emerges in his fulness, so emerge the British Isles and finally Wales" (72).

dogma; indeed, it begins to look more like Greene's "religion of the earth." It enables Jones to move beyond the institutional church into the lived experience of the West at all times and places. As one might expect, it also brings him right back to a crucial aspect of the Welsh thing.

A traditional Welsh proverb, Jones writes, is "'He who would be head, let him be the bridge', *A fo ben bid bont*, still in actual use in Wales" (EA 160):

> It derives from the myth of Bendigeidfran who bridged the Irish Sea with his own body for his army to march upon. It seems a startling foreshadowing of what was achieved by the Incarnation. At the same time it offers from remote Celtic antiquity a theme familiar to us in the Roman title Pontifex Maximus and the title Servus Servorum Dei. (EA 160)

In more humble and local terms, the myth seems a startling foreshadowing of what was achieved by the London-Welsh, especially those who star in *In Parenthesis*, who bridged not the Irish Sea but the English Channel with their bodies. Jones's fallen soldiers enact the keeping of the islands and Europe adjacent, according to the logic of both sacramental ritual and the Welsh thing. They accomplish the binding of geographically distant places imagined by Rupert Brooke in "The Soldier," perhaps the most famous poem of the war, only without the exclusive nationalist tones or the sentimentality:

> If I should die, think only this of me:
>   That there's some corner of a foreign field
> That is for ever England. There shall be
>   In that rich earth a richer dust conceal'd;
> A dust whom England bore, shaped, made aware,
>   Gave, once, her flowers to love, her ways to roam,
> A body of England's, breathing English air. (3)

Jones's British soldiers die in France alongside their German counterparts within the enclosure of a sacred space and wearing the signs of their communion, rendering the words of Dai's great boast "effective." The corner of a foreign field they occupy will be forever Britain, but one remembers that "they bore in their bodies the genuine tradition of the Island of Britain," which is unity in diversity for the British but also for Europe.

The European dissolution that Jones addresses with such urgency and precision in *In Parenthesis* did not abate much during his career. Shortly before World War II, he noted the sad condition of "our tumbled European Humpty Dumpty" (DG 99); obviously Europe at that moment was not nearly finished cracking up. Other parts of Europe no doubt shared the desire evident in all of Jones's writing, noted by Allchin, "that all should be safely gathered in" (82). How difficult it was to do so, however, while still preserving the demarcations and deposits that give Europe its cultural texture, is measured by the possibility that *In Parenthesis* may be the only British interwar literary work to have tried and succeeded.

Conclusion
Writing Ritual

As anyone who has ever witnessed a verse play, a bullfight, or a Mass can attest, the wordless economy of witnessing usually comes coupled with an equally tantalizing desire to translate that experience into language, through speech and through writing after the fact. One constantly senses this tension within the work of the authors discussed in the preceding chapters. Their creation of and participation in ritual experience—their making, watching, and using ritual—although nearly ends in themselves, are as though incomplete without accompanying aesthetic—and, of even greater exigency—cultural criticism. As ever, the cultural lessons that true ritual had to offer these writers were to be found firstly in the action of the rituals themselves, but also and undeniably in the writing about them. Transmuted into writing, ritual, like any other cultural form, accretes meaning. Firsthand experience is essential to the meaning of ritual, but the literary mediation of firsthand experience can have a clarifying, not only a diluting, effect. It has the capacity both to refine and to expand the cultural, political, religious, or artistic implications the firsthand observer might be able to sense but not name. This function is particularly important in terms of the relationship between ritual and European identity. The unanswerable moment of ritual action contains a detail and a specificity that are impossible to translate into other forms, yet one can see that the rituals of Europe communicate with, for instance, a political voice because of the consistent interweaving of ritual experience and political reflection in writing.

The necessary ambiguity that inheres in the process of writing ritual is a unique benefit, rather than a hindrance, to the articulation of a nuanced idea of Europe. The position of ritual between the closed self-referentiality of its enactment and the inevitable entanglements of culture and history make possible a more flexible notion of the meaning of Europe than many other paradigms can provide. Such a notion bridges the divide between, for instance, the model of European integration that Timothy Reiss applauds, "based … on common economic and political interests" (25), and the "*esprit*" favored by Paul Valéry (*L'avenir* 10). A "spirit" of Europe is obviously closer to what has been emerging in the preceding chapters than is any purely political-economic model, but, absent the kind of contactual evidence that ritual provides, *esprit* remained for British and Irish writers rather too infirm a basis from which to make sense of European complexity. Virtually every writer covered in this project, regardless of religion, nationality, or political leaning, seemed convinced that no spiritual identity is possible for Europe without some corresponding political unity, and that material unity would be meaningless without the richer, stranger imaginative identification with which ritual maintains a living contact.

The problem of European unity is at once as vexing and as tantalizing today as it ever was, and the arena for its contestation is not limited to international debates. The intra-national divisions and discord that have marked the European landscape for as long as nations have existed seem at the moment of this writing to be waxing, rather than waning, in urgency. Within Spain, for instance, the guerrilla organization Euskadi ta Askatasuna (ETA) has officially ceased fire, but neither the violence nor the political pressure for Basque independence has disappeared. In another part of Spain, Catalonia continues to assert its cultural independence as a stepping-stone to political independence. In the summer of 2010, this movement found dramatic expression in the outright banning of the bullfight in all of Catalonia, a remarkably vivid contemporary example of the tendency of the Spanish national ritual to serve as the ground on which cultural and political identities are performed. Italy, a reluctant latecomer to the nation-state model, is likewise riven by cultural as well as economic disunity between its northern and southern regions. Other examples abound. Such divisions within sovereign European nations are almost always accompanied by a clash of outlooks regarding European unity and the role of the European Union. The allegiance of the local community is increasingly vied for by the province, the region, the nation, and the E.U. Perhaps most tellingly, even Belgium, the very seat of official European unity as the headquarters of the E.U., finds the divide between its two main constituent regions, Flanders and Wallonia, growing wider and deeper, the country's historical religious and linguistic differences having been exacerbated by economic and cultural ones to the point that violent conflict, once unthinkable, is actually beginning to appear plausible.[1] Brussels, routinely invoked as a synonym for the E.U. and even for the idea of European unity, is itself the site of a very real European-style culture clash. The voice of nationalism, too, has sounded again recently in the latest elections in Finland, a European nation far from unique in its anxiety about the growing presence of immigrants from all places but especially Africa and the Middle East.[2] [3]

So the questions of identity and allegiance, of identification and difference, of the claims of the local against those of the collective, are at least as alive in the young twenty-first century as they were in the 1920s and 1930s. And what of

---

[1]   See "Le Divorce," by Ian Buruma. *The New Yorker*, January 10, 2011.

[2]   As Finland is situated in Europe's extreme north, one is reminded by such developments there of Hegel's theory of World History and the Universal Spirit with its implicit assumption that these move not only globally from East to West but also, in Europe, from South to North, an assumption shared by Habermas but ably challenged by Dussel. Under the Hegelian model, when events tied to European identity occur in the far northern countries—as, for instance, in twentieth-century Germany—they must either suggest an ending or something more like a boomerang action. Under an alternative model, like Dussel's Ibero-centric one, events in Germany or Finland just happen in another part of Europe.

[3]   The July 2011 shooting massacre in Norway was also the work of an apparent anti-Muslim right-wing fanatic.

ritual? As evidenced in the intense debate leading up to the Catalonian decision, the bullfight retains its power to receive and represent all manner of Spanish identity questions. While it is likely—as was claimed by Catalan opponents of the bullfight—that more tourists than Catalonians had been attending bullfights in Barcelona, the hundreds of *plazas de toros* throughout the rest of Spain are filled with Spanish aficionados all season long—with the usual adjustments for economic downturns. True, more Spaniards than ever profess indifference to the corrida, yet the industry seems in no danger of perishing except in individual provinces which might follow Catalonia's lead and ban the bullfight as a political gesture of defiance against the perceived hegemony of the Spanish state. In the meantime, the bullfight goes on, and lyrical meditations by English-speaking writers continue to appear: Had the present study's scope extended to the end of the twentieth century, Scottish author A.L. Kennedy's *On Bullfighting* might have merited a chapter of its own.

Catholicism, of course, remains the dominant single religion in Europe, but it is no secret that its reach and visibility have diminished to the point of crisis for the Church. Still, there has been no pope from a non-European country for more than twelve centuries, although one might expect that to change within the current generation. The overall secularization of European culture, the growth of Europe's Muslim population, and the scandals within the Church all challenge the influence of Catholicism as a meaningful part of European identity. Still more germane to the present discussion, Catholic rituals and sacred spaces themselves have changed. The meaning of ritual, after all, derives primarily from the particulars of its enactment, and the enactment of a Mass in a contemporary parish in Europe is likely to differ in instantly perceptible ways from the same ritual eight or nine decades previous. The essential elements will be the same, but the language, the position of the priest, and potentially the church architecture, the music, and the disposition of the audience will have changed, and along with them the signification of the ritual to the attendant observer. In what ways and to what extent on a cultural or political level, given the generally receding prominence of the Mass as a marker of European experience? These questions must be, and are being, addressed by others.

In assessing the fate of the three ritual forms under discussion here, one is perhaps least surprised by the lack of new plays in verse. As suggested in the early chapters, the project of a renewal of English-language verse drama seems to have fizzled in approximately 1939—with the single major exception of T.S. Eliot, who kept the flame alive for another two decades but whose later plays, as shown in Chapter 1, had less and less of ritual in them.[4] The (very) rare British or Irish play in verse appears, of course, but never as more than a curiosity, an exercise, and certainly never as part of a concentrated effort to restore the form to something like the mind of Europe.

---

[4]   There are, of course, others, Louis MacNeice among them. In the United States, Archibald MacLeish (among others) also wrote some notable verse plays after 1939.

The last example would seem to suggest most strongly that the literary reinvigoration of ritual so important to writers of the 1920s and 1930s was, if not a failure, at least a program that ran its course long ago. The gradual de-Catholicization of Europe, though not quite a foregone conclusion, carries with it the near certainty that any voice with which the Church might beckon a creative writer attentive to ritual and the idea of Europe will be more muted. For the bullfight, if the writing cannot exactly be said to be on the wall, it is undeniable that indicators of a certain kind of decline are manifest.

However, one must be careful not to extrapolate from these three versions of decline to inevitably diminishing returns for writers interested in ritual, the idea of Europe, or both. From one point of view, things may not have changed so much. For all the writing that has appeared in recent years on an ostensible British Catholic revival in the late nineteenth and early twentieth centuries, Jones, Waugh, and Greene were hardly swept up in a sea change of popular feeling regarding Roman Catholicism in Britain. Even Eliot's conversion to Anglo-Catholicism was undertaken entirely in the teeth of a powerful and well-documented contemporaneous movement away from orthodoxy, even more acute among the literati than the general public. As biographer Lyndall Gordon writes: "It seemed to many of Eliot's contemporaries that he … took refuge in obsolete institutions. The *Times Literary Supplement* called Eliot a kind of traitor. Edmund Wilson deplored 'the unpromising character' of the ideals and institutions [Eliot] invoked" (226). Virginia Woolf stated the case in more biting terms:

> I have had a most shameful and distressing interview with dear Tom Eliot, who may be called dead to us all from this day forward. He has become an Anglo-Catholic believer in God and immortality, and goes to church. I was shocked. A corpse would seem to me more credible than he is. I mean, there's something obscene in a living person sitting by the fire and believing in God. (*Letters* 457–58)

Britain between the wars was no particularly congenial environment for those pursuing a return to the older forms of Christianity. Nor did there exist amongst these converts even the solace of a group consciousness or any program of solidarity and mutual support, other than the most incidental kind. Indeed, each writer's decision to embrace Catholicism must be understood as far more individual and counter-cultural than symptomatic of some upwelling of positive interest in Britain about the religion of Rome.

The rich legacy of plays by Yeats, Eliot, and Auden notwithstanding, serious verse drama, as has been explained in the first section, never actually established itself in the mainstream. Even at its height in, say, the mid-to-late 1930s, plays in verse remained a marginal, if important, sub-current of modern drama. And the upsurge of curiosity about Spain and its *fiesta nacional* among British writers of the interwar years, productive and exhilarating as it may have been, did not attain to the level of sustained interest of the American Hemingway or his legions of devotees. All of which is to say that the rich, deep, and complex body of literature described in the preceding pages belongs yet and truly to a project undertaken at margins, fashioned out of remainders, met with resistance, enjoying a general enough renewal of interest in its aims and materials to sustain it for a time but characterized more by its pursuit of elusive and neglected objects than by any guarantee of its solidity or worth for the modern world. Yet we possess the most reliable measure of the latter in the plays, poems, and prose themselves. If the ghosts of ritual dream themselves back—to invoke Yeats—into the contemporary consciousness, the writers who entertain them may face difficulties finding material in Europe with which to work, but this would not distinguish them so much, after all, from their predecessors, and other sources of material, new and old, persist.

The picture sketched here of European unity and diversity is painfully, if necessarily, limited. Even within the narrow frame of ritual, much more remains to be said, not least because Europe boasts a great many other true rituals: pagan, secular, Jewish, Muslim, Christian. What of the fiery summer festival of Beltane in Scotland, the pagan rites and ancient ritual enclosures spanning the Celtic world from Portugal to the Outer Hebrides, Balkan rainmaking rituals, the harvest rituals of Bavaria, the Jewish ritual tradition linking every European country; or the marching season in Northern Ireland, the impact of the rituals and ritual spaces of Islam on the cultural landscape of countries from Spain to the Netherlands? Great swaths of European culture have had to be left out of the present study, although I hope to have made clear in the Introduction the specific reasons for their exclusion. It is to be hoped that they will receive due attention in subsequent projects by others. Critical writing has the potential to make the often inexplicable cultural memories contained in Europe's rituals relevant to recent history by making them precise. Often in the interwar years, European ritual's potential for such relevance remained hidden because of the strangeness with which true ritual struck the twentieth-century eye. Behind that strangeness, though, lie parts of the mind of Europe that, when recalled, momentarily clarified and deepened Europe's vision of its present possibilities.

Bibliography

Abel, Christopher. "Latin America, c.1914–1950." McLeod 179–96.

Ackroyd, Peter. *T.S. Eliot: A Life*. New York: Simon and Schuster, 1984.

Adamson, Judith. Introduction. *Reflections*. By Graham Greene. London: Penguin, 1990. ix–xvii.

Adorno, Theodor W., and Max Horkeimer. *Dialectic of Enlightenment: Philosophical Fragments*. Ed. Gunzelin Schmid Noerr. Trans. Edmund Jephcott. Cultural Memory in the Present. Stanford: Stanford UP, 2002.

Allchin, A.M. "On Not Knowing Welsh: David Jones and the Matter of Wales." Humfrey and Price-Owen 75–82.

Alvarez, Carlos Luis. "The Public Square and the Bullring." *Los Toros* 41–43.

Anderson, Benedict. *Imagined Communities: Reflections on the Origin and Spread of Nationalism*. New Edition. London: Verso, 2006.

Arkins, Brian. *Builders of My Soul: Greek and Roman Themes in Yeats*. Irish Literary Studies 32. Gerrards Cross: Colin Smythe, 1990.

Auden, W.H. *The Chase*. 1934. *Plays* 109–88.

———. *The Dance of Death*. 1933. *Plays* 81–108.

———. "The Future of English Poetic Drama." 1938. *Plays* 513–22.

———. "Missing Churches." Cunningham, *Spanish Front*. 305–06.

———. "On *In Parenthesis*." Matthias 43–45.

———. *Paid on Both Sides*. 1928. *Plays* 3–34.

———. *Plays and Other Dramatic Writings, 1928–1938 by W.H. Auden and Christopher Isherwood. The Complete Works of W.H. Auden*. Ed. Edward Mendelson. Princeton: Princeton UP, 1988.

———. Rev. of *Modern Poetic Drama*, by Priscilla Thouless. *The Listener* 9 May 1934. In *The Complete Works of W.H. Auden: Prose: Volume II: 1939–1948*. Ed. Edward Mendelson. Princeton: Princeton UP, 2002. 69–70.

———. "Spain." *Selected Poems*. Ed. Edward Mendelson. New York: Vintage, 1989. 51–55.

Auden, W.H., and Christopher Isherwood. *The Ascent of F6*. 1936. Auden, *Plays* 293–356.

———. *The Dog Beneath the Skin*. 1935. Auden, *Plays* 189–292.

———. *The Enemies of a Bishop*. 1929. Auden, *Plays* 35–80.

———. *On the Frontier*. 1938. Auden, *Plays* 357–418.

———. "Preliminary Statement." 1929. Auden, *Plays* 459–63.

From *Authors Take Sides on the Spanish War*. *Left Review*, 1937. Cunningham, *Spanish Front* 51–57, 226–30.

L'avenir de l'esprit européen. Paris: Société des Nations, Institut International de Coopération Intellectuelle, 1934.

Balibar, Ètienne. "World Borders, Political Borders." *PMLA* 117 (2002): 71–78.

———. "Europe, an 'Unimagined' Frontier of Democracy." *Diacritics* 33.3–4 (2003): 36–44.

Barker, George. *Collected Poems, 1930–1955*. London: Faber, 1957.

Barzini, Luigi. *The Europeans*. New York: Simon and Schuster, 1983.

Bell, Catherine. *Ritual Theory, Ritual Practice*. New York: Oxford, 1992.

Benjamin, Walter. "The Work of Art in the Age of Mechanical Reproduction." *Illuminations*. Ed. and Intro. Hannah Arendt. Trans. Harry Zohn. New York: Shocken, 1969. 217–51.

Bhabha, Homi K. From "The Commitment to Theory." *New Formations* 5 (1988). Rpt. in *The Post-Colonial Studies Reader*. Ed. Bill Ashcroft, et al. New York: Routledge, 1995. 206–09.

Blamires, David. *David Jones: Artist and Writer*. N.p.: U Toronto P, 1972.

Blissett, William. "The Welsh Thing in Here." Hills 101–21.

Boehm, Deborah A. "Our Lady of Resistance: The Virgin of Guadalupe and Contested Constructions of Community in Santa Fe, New Mexico." *Journal of the Southwest* 44:1 (Spring 2002): 95–104.

Bonnerot, Louis. "David Jones 'Down the Traversed History-Paths.'" *Agenda* 5.1–3 (1967): 124–27.

Bosco, Mark, S.J. "From *The Power and the Glory* to *The Honorary Consul*: The Development of Graham Greene's Catholic Imagination." *Religion and Literature* 36.2 (Summer 2004): 51–74.

———. *Graham Greene's Catholic Imagination*. New York: Oxford UP, 2005.

Bottomley, Gordon. "His Legacy to the Theatre." *The Arrow: W.B. Yeats Commemoration Issue* (Summer 1939): 11–14.

Brady, Owen E. "Chorus and Character in Auden and Isherwood's *The Dog Beneath the Skin*." Izzo151–71.

Brecht, Bertold. *Brecht on Theatre: The Development of an Aesthetic*. 1957. Ed. and trans. John Willett. New York: Hill and Wang-Farrar, 1999.

Brennan, Michael G. "Graham Greene, Evelyn Waugh and Mexico." *Renascence* 55.1 (Fall 2002): 7–23.

Bronowski, Jacob "The Death of Garcia Lorca." Cunningham, *Penguin* 208.

Brooke, Rupert. "The Soldier." *World War One British Poets*. Ed. Candace Ward. Mineola: Dover, 1997. 3.

Brooker, Jewel Spears. *Mastery and Escape: T.S. Eliot and the Dialectic of Modernism*. Amherst: U Massachusetts P, 1994.

Burke, Kenneth. *The Philosophy of Literary Form: Studies in Symbolic Action*. 3rd ed. Berkeley: U California P, 1973.

Bynner, Witter. *Journey with Genius: Recollections and Reflections Concerning the D.H. Lawrences*. New York: Octagon-Farrar, 1974.

Cahill, Thomas. *How the Irish Saved Civilization*. New York: Doubleday, 1995.

Calhoun, Craig. "The Virtues of Inconsistency: Identity and Plurality in the Conceptualization of Europe." Cederman 35–56.

Camp, Roderic Ai. *Crossing Swords: Politics and Religion in Mexico*. New York: Oxford UP, 1997.

Campbell, Roy. *Collected Poems*. London: Bodley Head, 1949.

Carlson, Matthew Paul. "Auden and Britten's *Paul Bunyan* and the Frontiers of Opera." *Modern Drama* 54 (Winter 2011): 409–34.

Carpenter, Humphrey. *W.H. Auden: A Biography*. Boston: Houghton Mifflin, 1981.

Carroll, David. *French Literary Fascism: Nationalism, Anti-Semitism, and the Ideology of Culture*. Princeton: Princeton UP, 1995.

Cau, Jean. "Left and Right." *Los Toros* 35.

Cavano, A. Thomas. "Elesin, Cuchulain, and the Kingdom: The Culture Hero's Sacrifice." *Modern Drama* 45 (Fall 2002): 409–29.

Cederman, Lars-Erik, ed. *Constructing Europe's Identity: The External Dimension*. Boulder: Lynne Rienner, 2001.

Chadwick, Joseph. "Violence in Yeats's Later Politics and Poetry." *ELH* 55 (Winter 1988): 869–93.

Chadwick, Owen. *A History of Christianity*. London: Weidenfeld, 1995.

Chesterton, G.K. *Orthodoxy*. 1908. New York: Random House-Shaw, 2001.

Chinitz, David E. *T.S. Eliot and the Cultural Divide*. Chicago: U Chicago P, 2003.

Chua, Cheng Lok. "The European Participant and the Third-World Revolution: André Malraux's *Les Conquérants* and D.H. Lawrence's *The Plumed Serpent*." *Discharging the Canon: Cross-cultural Readings in Literature*. Ed. Peter Hyland. Singapore: Singapore UP, 1986. 101–11.

Clayton, Ewan. "The Inscriptions of David Jones." Humfrey and Price-Owen 56–64.

Clifford, James. "Traveling Cultures." *Cultural Studies*. Ed. Lawrence Grossberg, et al. New York: Routledge, 1992. 96–112.

Collins, Larry, and Dominique Lapierre. *Or I'll Dress You in Mourning*. New York: New American, 1968.

Conrad, Barnaby. *La Fiesta Brava: The Art of the Bull Ring*. Boston: Houghton, 1953.

Conway, Martin. "The Christian Churches and Politics in Europe, 1914–1939." McLeod 151–78.

Coogan, Tim Pat. *Michael Collins: The Man Who Made Ireland*. Boulder: Roberts Rinehart, 1992.

Cooper, John Xiros. *T.S. Eliot and the Politics of Voice: The Argument of* The Waste Land. Ann Arbor: U Michigan Research Press, 1987.

Corcoran, Neil. "Spilled Bitterness: *In Parenthesis* in History." Matthias 209–25.

Cousineau, Thomas J. *Ritual Unbound: Reading Sacrifice in Modernist Fiction*. Newark: U Delaware P, 2004.

Craft, Linda J. "Goddesses at the Borderlands: Mexican-American Women's Narrative and the Rediscovery of the Spiritual." *Language and Literature* 24 (1999): 31–42.

Crick, Bernard. Foreword. Fendler and Wittlinger ix–xiv.

Croce, Benedetto. *History of Europe in the Nineteenth Century*. Trans. Henry Furst. New York: Harcourt, 1963.

Cullingford, Elizabeth. *Yeats, Ireland and Fascism*. New York: New York UP, 1981.

Cunningham, J.S. "Pope, Eliot, and 'The Mind of Europe'." *The Waste Land in Different Voices*. Ed. A.D. Moody. New York: St. Martin's, 1974. 67–85.

Cunningham, Valentine. *British Writers of the Thirties*. New York: Oxford, 1988.

———, ed. *The Penguin Book of Spanish Civil War Verse*. Middlesex: Penguin, 1980.

———, ed. *Spanish Front: Writers on the Civil War*. New York: Oxford, 1986.

Dahl, Mary Karen. *Political Violence in Drama: Classical Models, Contemporary Variations*. Theater and Dramatic Studies, No. 36. Ann Arbor: U Michigan Research Press, 1987.

Dainotto, Robert M. *Europe (In Theory)*. Durham: Duke UP, 2007.

Dames, Michael. *Mythic Ireland*. London: Thames, 1992.

Daniel, Julia. "'Or It Might Be You': Audiences in and of T.S. Eliot's *Sweeney Agonistes*." *Modern Drama* 54 (2011): 435–54.

Darras, Jacques. "Sleep of the Tongue: Pound, Eliot, Jones and Europe." Hills 122–31.

Davies, Hilary. "Why David Jones Matters." *New Welsh Review* 30 (Autumn 1995): 23–25.

Davis, Derek H. Introduction. *Church-State Relations and Religious Liberty in Mexico: Historical and Contemporary Perspectives*. Ed. Davis. Waco: JM Dawson Institute, 2002.

Day Lewis, Cecil. *The Nabara*. Cunningham, *Penguin* 236–45.

Déak, František. *Symbolist Theatre: The Formation of an Avant-Garde*. Baltimore: Johns Hopkins UP, 1993.

Deane, Seamus. *Celtic Revivals: Essays in Modern Irish Literature 1880–1980*. Boston: Faber, 1985.

———. Introduction. *Nationalism, Colonialism, and Literature*. By Terry Eagleton, Frederic Jameson, and Edward W. Said. Minneapolis: Field Day-U Minnesota P, 1990. 3–19.

De Rougemont, Denis. *The Idea of Europe*. Trans. Norbert Guterman. New York: Macmillan, 1966.

Derrida, Jacques. *The Gift of Death*. Trans. David Wills. Chicago: U Chicago P, 1995.

———. *The Other Heading: Reflections on Today's Europe*. Trans. Pascale-Anne Brault and Michael B. Naas. Bloomington: Indiana UP, 1992.

Díez-Medrano, Conchita. "Fictions of Rape: The Teller and the Tale in D.H. Lawrence's 'None of That'." *Forum for Modern Language Studies* 32 (1996): 303–13.

Dilworth, Thomas. "David Jones and Fascism." Matthias 143–59.

———. *The Liturgical Parenthesis of David Jones*. London: Golganooza Press, 1979.

———. *The Shape of Meaning in the Poetry of David Jones*. Toronto: U Toronto P, 1988.

Donoghue, Denis. *The Third Voice: Modern British and American Verse Drama*. Princeton: Princeton UP, 1959.

Dorn, Karen. *Players and Painted Stage: The Theatre of W.B. Yeats*. New Jersey: Barnes and Noble, 1984.

Douglass, Carrie B. *Bulls, Bullfighting, and Spanish Identities*. Tucson: U Arizona P, 1997.

Douglass, Paul, ed. *T.S. Eliot, Dante, and the Idea of Europe*. Newcastle upon Tyne: Cambridge Scholars, 2011.

Durkheim, Emile. *The Elementary Forms of Religious Life*. 1915. Trans. J.W. Swain. Surrey: Unwin Hyman, 1976.

Dussel, Enrique. "Eurocentrism and Modernity (Introduction to the Frankfurt Lectures)." *Boundary 2* 20:3 (Fall 1993): 65–76.

Eksteins, Modris. *Rites of Spring: The Great War and the Birth of the Modern Age*. Boston: Houghton-Mariner, 2000.

Eliot, T.S. *After Strange Gods: A Primer of Modern Heresy*. New York: Harcourt, 1934.

———. "The Aims of Poetic Drama." *Adam International Review* (Nov. 1949): 10–16.

———. "American Literature and the American Language." *To Criticize the Critic and Other Writings*. Lincoln: U Nebraska P, 1991. 43–60.

———. "The Ballet." *Criterion* 3 (1924–1925): 441–43.

———. "The Beating of a Drum." *Nation and Athenaeum* 6 Oct. 1923: 11–12.

———. *Christianity and Culture*. New York: Harcourt-Harvest, 1977.

———. "A Commentary [Apr. 1926]." *Criterion* 4 (1926): 221–23.

———. "A Commentary [Aug. 1927]." *Criterion* 6 (1927): 97–100.

———. "A Commentary [Mar. 1928]." *Criterion* 7 (1928):193–94.

———. "A Commentary [June 1928]." *Criterion* 7 (1928): 289–94.

———. "A Commentary [Apr. 1929]." *Criterion* 8 (1929): 377–81.

———. "A Commentary [Jan. 1930]." *Criterion* 9 (1929–1930): 181–84.

———. "A Commentary [Jan. 1932]." *Criterion* 11 (1931–1932): 268–75.

———. "A Commentary [July 1932]." *Criterion* 11 (1931–1932): 676–83.

———. "A Commentary [Oct. 1935]." *Criterion* 14 (1934–1935): 610–13.

———. "A Commentary [Jan. 1937]." *Criterion* 16 (1936–1937): 289–93.

———. "A Commentary [Oct. 1937]." *Criterion* 17 (1937–1938): 81–86.

———. "A Commentary [Apr. 1938]." *Criterion* 17 (1937–1938): 478–85.

———. "A Commentary [July 1938]." *Criterion* 17 (1937–1938): 686–92.

———. "A Commentary [Jan. 1939]." *Criterion* 18 (1938–1939): 269–75.

———. *The Complete Poems and Plays, 1909–1950*. New York: Harcourt, 1971.

———. *The Elder Statesman*. 1959. New York: Farrar-Noonday, 1964.

———. *Essays on Elizabethan Drama*. New York: Harcourt-Harvest, 1956.

———. *The Family Reunion*. 1939. New York: Harcourt-Harvest, 1967.

———. *Four Quartets*. 1943. New York: Harcourt-Harvest, 1971.

———. *The Letters of T.S. Eliot, Vol. I: 1898–1922*. Ed. Valerie Eliot. San Diego: Harcourt, 1988.

———. "The Literature of Fascism." *Criterion* 8 (1928): 280–90.

———. "London Letter" [Nov. 1922]." *Dial* Dec. 1922: 659–63.

———. "The Man of Letters and the Future of Europe." *Horizon* 10.60 (Dec. 1944): 382–89.

———. *Murder in the Cathedral*. 1935. New York: Harcourt-Harvest, 1963.

———. "The Nature of Cultural Relations." *Friendship, Progress, Civilisation: Three War-time Speeches to the Anglo-Swedish Society*. 1943. 15–20.

———. "A Note of Introduction." *In Parenthesis*. By David Jones. vii-viii.

———. *On Poetry and Poets*. New York: Farrar-Noonday, 1961.

———. *The Sacred Wood: Essays on Poetry and Criticism*. 1920. New York: Barnes & Noble, 1967.

———. *Selected Essays, 1917–1932*. New York: Harcourt, 1932.

———. *Selected Prose*. Ed. Frank Kermode. New York: Harcourt, 1975.

———. *Sweeney Agonistes: Fragments of an Aristophanic Melodrama. The Complete Poems and Plays* 74–85.

———. *To Criticize the Critic and Other Writings*. 1965. Lincoln: U Nebraska P, 1992.

———. "Tradition and the Individual Talent." *Selected Essays* 3–11.

———. "The Unity of European Culture." 1946. *Christianity and Culture* 187–202.

———. *The Use of Poetry and the Use of Criticism*. Charles Eliot Norton Lectures given at Harvard University 1932–1933. London: Faber, 1933.

———. The Waste Land *and Other Poems*. Ed. Frank Kermode. New York: Penguin, 1998.

Esty, Jed. *A Shrinking Island: Modernism and National Culture in England*. Princeton: Princeton UP, 2003.

Fendler, Susanne, and Ruth Wittlinger, eds. *The Idea of Europe in Literature*. New York: St. Martin's, 1999.

———. "The Idea of Europe—the Contribution of Literature." Introduction. Fendler and Wittlinger xix–xxi.

Fischer, Eileen. "Dionysus in the Afternoon: Bullfighting as Ritual Sacrifice and Tragic Performance." *Themes in Drama* 14: *Melodrama*. Cambridge: Cambridge UP, 1992. 245–54.

Fleming, Deborah, ed. *William Butler Yeats and Postcolonialism*. West Cornwall: Locust Hill, 2001.

Foster, R.F. *Modern Ireland, 1600–1972*. London: Penguin, 1989.

Frantzen, Allen J. *Bloody Good: Chivalry, Sacrifice, and the Great War*. Chicago: U Chicago P, 2004.

Freud, Sigmund. *The Freud Reader*. Ed. Peter Gay. New York: Norton, 1989.

Fuentes, Carlos. *The Buried Mirror: Reflections on Spain and the New World*. New York: Houghton Mifflin, 1992.

———. "Europe's Other Face." *Liber* (Nov. 1989): 20.

Fussell, Paul. *Abroad: British Literary Traveling Between the Wars*. New York: Oxford, 1980.

———. *The Great War and Modern Memory*. New York: Oxford, 1975.

Gambaudo, Sylvie. "Europeans: Foreigners in Their Own Land." Fendler and Wittlinger 225–39.

García Lorca, Federico. "Lament for Ignacio Sanchez Mejias." Trans. Stephen Spender and J.L. Gili. John Miller 54–62.

Garrett, John. Rev. of *The Dog Beneath the Skin*, by W.H. Auden and Christopher Isherwood. *Criterion* 14.57 (July 1935): 687–90.

Gates, Larry. "The Reconciliation of Opposites in *The Plumed Serpent*." *Journal of Evolutionary Psychology* 15 (1994): 274–82.

Girard, Rene. *The Scapegoat*. Baltimore: Johns Hopkins UP, 1986.

———. *Things Hidden Since the Beginning of the World*. Stanford: Stanford UP, 1987.

———. *To Double Business Bound: Essays on Literature, Mimesis, and Anthropology*. Baltimore: Johns Hopkins UP, 1978.

———. *Violence and the Sacred*. Trans. Patrick Gregory. Baltimore: Johns Hopkins UP, 1977.

Goldpaugh, Tom. "To Make a Shape in Words: The Labyrinthine Text of David Jones." Humfrey and Price-Owen 132–52.

Gordon, Jan B. "Charlotte Brontë's Alternative 'European Community.'" Fendler and Wittlinger 3–30.

Gordon, Lyndall. *T.S. Eliot: An Imperfect Life*. New York: Norton, 2000.

Gordon, Philip, and Omer Taspinar. "Turkey's European Quest: The EU's Decision on Turkish Accession." U.S.-Europe Analysis Series. The Brookings Institution. Sep. 2004.

Gould, Evlyn, and George J. Sheridan, Jr., eds. *Engaging Europe: Rethinking a Changing Continent*. Lanham: Rowman and Littlefield Publishers, 2005.

Greene, Graham. "Eric Gill." *The Lost Childhood and Other Essays*. New York: Viking, 1951. 133–35.

———. *The Lawless Roads*. 1939. London: Penguin, 1982.

———. *The Power and the Glory*. 1940. London: Penguin, 1991.

———. *Ways of Escape*. New York: Simon and Schuster, 1980.

Grene, Nicholas. *The Politics of Irish Drama: Plays in Context from Boucicault to Friel*. Cambridge Studies in Modern Theatre. Cambridge: Cambridge UP, 1999.

Griffin, Roger. "Staging the Nation's Rebirth: The Politics and Aesthetics of Performance in the Context of Fascist Studies." *Fascism and Theatre*. Ed. Günter Berghaus. Providence: Berghahn, 1996.

Habermas, Jürgen. "Why Europe Needs a Constitution." *New Left Review* 11 (Sep.-Oct. 2001): 5–26.

Habermas, Jürgen, and Jacques Derrida. "February 15, or What Binds Europeans Together: A Plea for a Common Foreign Policy, Beginning in the Core of Europe." *Constellations* 10 (2003): 291–97.

Hague, René. "Myth and Mystery in the Poetry of David Jones." *Agenda* 15.2–3 (1977): 37–79.

Haldane, Charlotte. "Passionaria." Cunningham, *Penguin*. 252–53.

Hall, J.C. "Postscript for Spain." Cunningham, *Penguin* 457.

Hamnett, Brian. *A Concise History of Mexico*. Cambridge: Cambridge UP, 1999.

Hastings, Selina. *Evelyn Waugh: A Biography*. Boston: Houghton Mifflin, 1994.

Hayes, Richard. "His Nationalism." *The Arrow: W.B. Yeats Commemoration Issue* (Summer 1939): 10–11.

Heer, Friedrich. *The Intellectual History of Europe*. New York, Doubleday, 1968.

Heinemann, Margot. "On a Lost Battle in the Spanish War." Cunningham, *Penguin* 251–52.

Hemingway, Ernest. *Death in the Afternoon*. 1932. New York: Scribner's, 1960.

Hernández, Miguel. "The Winds of the People." Trans. A.L. Lloyd. Cunningham, *Penguin* 285–87.

Hills, Paul, ed. *David Jones: Artist and Poet*. Warwick Studies in the European Humanities. Hants: Scolar-Ashgate, 1997.

Hitchens, Christopher. *Why Orwell Matters*. New York: Basic, 2002.

Hogg, James. Preface. *Poetic Drama Interviews: Robert Speaight, E. Martin Browne, and W.H. Auden*. Poetic Drama and Poetic Theory 24. Salzburg: U Salzburg, 1976.

Holloway, Watson L. "The Pagan Liturgy of David Jones." *Antigonish Review* 53 (Spring 1983): 47–53.

Hooker, Jeremy. "David Jones and the Matter of Wales." Humfrey and Price-Owen 11–25.

Hopkins, Chris. "Mixed Languages: David Jones's *In Parenthesis*." *Swansea Review* 1994: 318–25.

Hubert, Henri, and Marcel Mauss. *Sacrifice: Its Nature and Function*. Trans. W.D. Halls. 1898. Chicago: U Chicago P, 1964.

Hughes, Langston. *I Wonder as I Wander: An Autobiographical Journey*. Columbia: U Missouri P, 2003.

Humfrey, Belinda and Anne Price-Owen, eds. *David Jones: Diversity in Unity: Studies of his Literary and Visual Art*. Cardiff: U Wales P, 2000.

Husserl, Edmund. *The Crisis of European Sciences and Transcendental Phenomenology*. Studies in Phenomenology and Existential Philosophy. Evanston: Northwestern UP, 1970.

Izzo, David Garrett, ed. *W.H. Auden: A Legacy*. West Cornwall: Locust Hill, 2002.

Jackson, Gabriel. *The Spanish Republic and the Civil War, 1931–1939*. Princeton: Princeton UP, 1972.

Jacobs, Alan. "Auden and the Dream of Public Poetry." *Literature and the Renewal of the Public Sphere*. Ed. Susan VanZanten Gallagher and M.D. Walhout. New York: Macmillan, 2000. 83–104.

Jay, Paul. "Beyond Discipline? Globalization and the Future of English." *PMLA* 116.1 (2001): 32–47.

Jeffares, A. Norman. "Theatre and the Visual Arts: A Panel Discussion." (With W.H. Auden, Marshall McLuhan Buckminster Fuller, and Jack MacGowran). *Yeats Studies* 2 (1972): 127–38.

Johnsen, William A. *Violence and Modernism: Ibsen, Joyce, and Woolf*. Gainesville: UP of Florida, 2003.

Jones, David. *The Anathemata: Fragments of an Attempted Writing*. 1952. London: Faber, 1972.

————. *Dai Greatcoat: A Self-Portrait of David Jones in his Letters.* Ed. René Hague. London: Faber, 1980.

————. *The Dying Gaul and Other Writings.* Ed. Harman Grisewood. London: Faber, 1978.

————. *Epoch and Artist: Selected Writings.* Ed. Harman Grisewood. London: Faber, 1959.

————. *In Parenthesis.* 1937. New York: New York Review, 2003.

————. *The Sleeping Lord and Other Fragments.* London: Faber, 1974.

Keal, W.B. "For the Fallen." Cunningham, *Penguin* 195–96.

Kerr, Douglas. "*Journey to a War*: 'A test for men from Europe'." Izzo 275–96.

Kertzer, David I. *Ritual, Politics, and Power.* New Haven: Yale UP, 1988.

Kiberd, Declan. *Inventing Ireland: The Literature of the Modern Nation.* Cambridge: Harvard UP, 1995.

Korg, Jacob. *Ritual and Experiment in Modern Poetry.* New York: St. Martin's, 1995.

Koster, Jan. "Ritual Performance and the Politics of Identity." *Journal of Historical Pragmatics* 4 (2003): 211–48.

Kostopulos, Dan S. "Mexico Imagined: *Robbery Under Law* and the Lessons of Mexican Travel." *Waugh Without End: New Trends in Evelyn Waugh Studies.* Ed. Carlos Villar Flor and Robert Murray Davis. Bern: Peter Lang, 2005. 115–29.

Kramer, Hilton, and Roger Kimball, eds. *The Future of the European Past.* Chicago: Ivan R. Dee, 1997.

Lawrence, D.H. *Kangaroo.* 1923. New York: Viking, 1951.

————. *Mornings in Mexico.* 1927. London: Heinemann, 1950.

————. "None of That!" *The Works of D.H. Lawrence: "The Woman Who Rode Away" and Other Stories.* Ed. Dieter Mehl and Christa Jansohn. Cambridge: Cambridge UP, 1995.

————. *The Plumed Serpent.* 1926. Hammondsworth: Penguin, 1971.

Lehmann, John. *The Whispering Gallery.* New York: Harcourt, 1955.

Levernier, James. "Including Catholic Texts in the Re-Formation of the Early American Canon: The Case of the Virgin of Guadalupe." Ninth Annual St. Charles Borromeo Conference on Catholicism in Literature. Little Rock, AR. 8 Nov. 2002.

Lévi-Strauss, Claude. "From *The Savage Mind*." *Theory of the Novel: A Historical Approach.* Ed. Michael McKeon. Baltimore: Johns Hopkins, 2000. 94–99.

Lewine, Edward. *Death and the Sun: A Matador's Season in the Heart of Spain.* Boston: Houghton Mifflin, 2005.

Lindsay, Jack. "Looking at a Map of Spain on the Devon Coast (August, 1937)." Cunningham, *Penguin* 396–99.

————. "On Guard for Spain! (A Poem for Mass Recitation)." Cunningham, *Penguin* 253–63.

————. "Requiem Mass: for the Englishmen fallen in the International Brigade." Cunningham, *Penguin* 179–83.

————. "Two Days." Cunningham, *Penguin* 450.

Littlejohns, Richard, and Sara Soncini, eds. *Myths of Europe.* Amsterdam: Editions Rodopi B.V., 2007.

Londraville, Richard, and Janis Londraville. "*Paid on Both Sides*: Auden and Yeats and the New Tragedy." Izzo 173–96.

Los Toros, or Bullfighting. Madrid: Indice, 1974.

Lyons, F.S. *Culture and Anarchy in Ireland, 1890–1939.* Oxford: Oxford UP, 1982.

MacNeice, Louis. *Out of the Picture.* London: Faber, 1937.

————. *Selected Literary Criticism.* Ed. Alan Heuser. New York: Oxford, 1987.

Malamud, Randy. *Where the Words are Valid: T.S. Eliot's Communities of Drama.* Contributions in Drama and Theatre Studies 58. Westport: Greenwood, 1994.

Malmborg, Mikael af, and Bo Stråth, eds. *The Meaning of Europe: Variety and Contention Within and Among Nations.* New York: Berg, 2002.

Massis, Henri. "Defence of the West." Trans. F.S. Flint. *Criterion* 4 (1926): 224–40.

Matthias, John, ed. *David Jones: Man and Poet.* Orono: National Poetry Foundation, 1989.

Matthiessen, F.O. *The Achievement of T.S. Eliot: An Essay on the Nature of Poetry.* 3rd ed. New York: Oxford UP-Galaxy, 1958.

McCormack, W.J. *Ascendancy and Tradition in Anglo-Irish Literary History from 1789–1939.* New York: Oxford UP, 1985.

McCormick, John. *Bullfighting: Art, Technique, and Spanish Society.* New Brunswick: Transaction, 2000.

McDiarmid, Lucy. *Saving Civilization: Yeats, Eliot, and Auden Between the Wars.* New York: Cambridge, 1984.

McLeod, Hugh, ed. *World Christianites c.1914–2000.* Vol. 9 of *The Cambridge History of Christianity.* Cambridge: Cambridge UP, 2006.

Mendelson, Edward, "The Auden-Isherwood Collaboration." *Twentieth-Century Literature* 22.3 (Oct. 1976): 276–85.

————. Introduction. *Plays and Other Dramatic Writings, 1928–1938, by W.H. Auden and Christopher Isherwood. The Complete Works of W.H. Auden.* Ed. Mendelson. Princeton: Princeton UP, 1988. xiii–xxx.

Merwin, W.S. Foreword. *In Parenthesis.* By David Jones. i–vi.

Meyers, Jeffrey. *D.H. Lawrence: A Biography.* New York: Knopf, 1990.

————. "Greene's Travel Books." *Graham Greene: A Revaluation. New Essays.* Ed. Meyers. New York: St. Martin's, 1990. 47–67.

Michel, Andreas. "Eurocentrism and *The Idea of Europe.*" *The Image of Europe in Literature, Media, and Society: Selected Papers from the 2001 Conference of the Society for the Interdisciplinary Study of Social Imagery.* Pueblo, CO: The Society, 2001. 232–37.

Millay, Edna St. Vincent. "Say That We Saw Spain Die." John Miller 221–22.

Miller, John, ed. *Voices Against Tyranny: Writing of the Spanish Civil War—on the 50th anniversary of the event.* New York: Scribner, 1986

Miller, Liam. *The Noble Drama of W.B. Yeats.* Atlantic Highlands: Humanities, 1977.

Mitchell, Timothy. *Violence and Piety in Spanish Folklore*. Philadelphia: U Pennsylvania P, 1988.

Moody, A. David. "The Mind of Europe in T.S. Eliot." *T.S. Eliot at the Turn of the Century*. Ed. Marianne Thormahlen. Lund: Lund UP, 1994. 13–32.

Morford, Mark P.O., and Robert J. Lenardon. *Classical Mythology*. 4th ed. New York: Longman, 1991.

Morrison, Paul. *The Poetics of Fascism: Ezra Pound, T.S. Eliot, Paul de Man*. New York: Oxford UP, 1996.

Moses, Michael Valdez. "The Rebirth of Tragedy: Yeats, Nietzsche, the Irish National Theatre, and the Anti-Modern Cult of Cuchulain." *Modernism/ modernity* 11 (2004): 561–79.

Mosse, George. *The Nationalization of the Masses: Political Symbolism and Mass Movements in Germany from the Napoleonic Wars through the Third Reich*. Ithaca: Cornell UP, 1975.

Murry, John Middleton. *Son of Woman: The Story of D.H. Lawrence*. New York: Jonathan Cape, 1931.

Nehls, Edward, ed. *D.H. Lawrence: A Composite Biography*. Madison: U Wisconsin P, 1958.

The New Oxford Annotated Bible. New Revised Standard Version with the Apocrypha. New York: Oxford UP, 2001.

Nietzsche, Friedrich. *Beyond Good and Evil*. 1886. Trans. Helen Zimmern. Radford: Wilder, 2008.

———. *The Birth of Tragedy*. 1872. Trans. Clifton P. Fadiman. New York: Dover, 1995.

O'Brien, Conor Cruise. *Passion and Cunning: Essays on Nationalism, Terrorism, and Revolution*. New York: Simon and Schuster, 1988.

O'Faolain, Sean. *The Irish: A Character Study*. Old-Greenwich: Devin-Adair, 1949.

O'Malley, Ernie. *On Another Man's Wound: A Personal History of Ireland's War of Independence*. 1936. Boulder: Roberts Rinehart, 1999.

Orwell, George. *Collected Essays, Journalism, and Letters*. Vol. 2. Ed. Sonia Orwell and Ian Angus. New York: Harcourt, 1968.

———. *Homage to Catalonia*. Intro. Lionel Trilling. San Diego: Harcourt-Harvest, 1952.

Ostrem, William. "The Dog beneath the Schoolboy's Skin: Isherwood, Auden, and Fascism." *The Isherwood Century: Essays on the Life and Work of Christopher Isherwoood*. Ed. and Intro. James J. Berg and Chris Freeman. Madison: U Wisconsin P, 2000.

Pagden, Anthony, ed. *The Idea of Europe: From Antiquity to the European Union*. New York: Cambridge UP, 2002. Reprinted 2007.

———. "Europe: Conceptualizing a Continent." In Pagden 33–54.

Pagnoulle, Christine. "David Jones's Wales: A World of Difference." *Pays de Galles, Ecosse, Irlande*. Brest, France: Université de Brest, 1987. 63–75.

Parsons, Geoffrey. "Lorca." Cunningham, *Penguin* 206–207.

Patey, Douglas Lane. *The Life of Evelyn Waugh: A Critical Biography*. Blackwell Critical Biographies. Oxford: Blackwell, 2001.

Payne, Robert, ed. *The Civil War in Spain, 1936–1939*. New York: Capricorn, 1970.

Pearson, Sheryl L. "'Is There Anybody There?': Graham Greene in Mexico." *Journal of Modern Literature* 9 (1992): 277–90.

Plá y Beltran. "Ballad of Lina Odena." Trans. Rolfe Humphries. Cunningham, *Penguin* 276–78.

Raine, Kathleen. "Fata Morgana." Cunningham, *Penguin* 401–04.

———. "The Sacred and Profane." Rev. of *The Anathemata*. *New Republic* 12 (Jan. 1953): 19.

Read, Herbert. "Bombing Casualties in Spain." Cunningham, *Penguin* 165–66.

———. "A Song for the Spanish Anarchists." Cunningham, *Penguin* 248.

Reiss, Timothy J. Introduction. *PMLA* 108.1 (Jan. 1993):14–29.

Rexroth, Kenneth. "The Poetry of D.H. Lawrence." *D.H. Lawrence: A Collection of Criticism*. Ed. Leo Hamalian. Contemporary Studies in Literature. New York: McGraw-Hill, 1973.

Roberts, Neil. "The Novelist as Travel Writer: *The Plumed Serpent*." *D.H. Lawrence Review* 25 (1993–1994): 130–39.

Roderick, J.T. "Memory." Cunningham, *Penguin* 452.

Rossman, Charles. "D.H. Lawrence and Mexico." *D.H. Lawrence: A Centenary Consideration*. Ed. Peter Balbert and Philip L. Marcus. Ithaca: Cornell UP, 1985. 180–209.

Sagar, Keith. *The Life of D.H. Lawrence*. New York: Pantheon, 1980.

Said, Edward W. *Culture and Imperialism*. New York: Knopf, 1993.

Schmitt, Natalie Crohn. "'Haunted by Places': Landscape in Three Plays of W.B. Yeats." *Comparative Drama* 31 (Fall 1997): 337–66.

———. "The Landscape Play: W.B. Yeats's *Purgatory*." *Irish University Review* 27 (1997): 262–75.

Schwartz, Adam. *The Third Spring: G.K. Chesterton, Graham Greene, Christopher Dawson, and David Jones*. Washington: Catholic U America P, 2005.

Schweizer, Bernard. *Radicals on the Road: The Politics of English Travel Writing in the 1930s*. Charlottesville: U Virginia P, 2001.

Sekine, Masaru. "What is Noh?" *Yeats and the Noh: A Comparative Study*. Ed. Sekine and Christopher Murray. Irish Literary Studies 38. Gerrards Cross: Colin Smythe, 1990.

———. "Yeats and the Noh." *Irish Writers and the Theatre*. Ed. Sekine. Irish Literary Studies 23. Gerrards Cross: Colin Smythe, 1986.

Shakespeare, Nicholas. Introduction. *Waugh Abroad: Collected Travel Writing*. By Evelyn Waugh. ix–xxv.

Shakespeare, William. *The Tragedy of Coriolanus*. Baltimore: Penguin, 1956.

Sherry, Norman. *The Life of Graham Greene. Volume One: 1904–1939*. London: Lester and Orpen Dennys. 1989.

Shubert, Adrian. *Death and Money in the Afternoon: A History of the Spanish Bullfight*. New York: Oxford, 1999.

Sidnell, Michael J. *Dances of Death: The Group Theatre of London in the Thirties.* Boston: Faber, 1984.

Sitwell, Edith. "Lullaby." *Chief Modern Poets of Britain and America.* Ed. Gerald DeWitt Sanders, et al. 5th ed. London: Macmillan, 1970. 1-268–69.

Smith, Grover. *T.S. Eliot's Poetry and Plays: A Study in Sources and Meaning.* Chicago: U Chicago P, 1956.

Smith, Stan. "Unreal Cities and Numinous Maps: T.S. Eliot and W.H. Auden as Observers of Central Europe." *Images of Central Europe in Travelogues and Fiction by North American Writers.* Ed. Waldemar Zacharasiewicz. Tubingen: Stauffenburg, 1995. 167–81.

Solterer, Helen. "The Waking of Medieval Theatricality, Paris 1935–1995. *New Literary History* 27.3 (1996): 357–90.

Sontag, Susan. "Fascinating Fascism." *Under the Sign of Saturn.* New York: Farrar-Picador, 1972.

———. "The Idea of Europe (One More Elegy)." *Where the Stress Falls: Essays.* New York: Farrar, 2001. 285–89.

Spender, Stephen. "The Bombed Happiness." Cunningham, *Penguin* 163.

———. Introduction. *Voices Against Tyranny.* Ed. John Miller. 1–16.

———. "Port Bou." John Miller 159–60.

———. "Two Armies." John Miller 151–52.

Spurr, Barry. "'I Loved Old Tom': David Jones and T.S. Eliot." *Yeats Eliot Review* 17.1 (2001): 19–25.

Stannard, Martin. *Evelyn Waugh: The Early Years, 1903–1939.* New York: Norton, 1986.

———. *Evelyn Waugh: The Later Years, 1939–1966.* New York: Norton, 1994.

Stansky, Peter, and William Abrahams. *Journey to the Frontier: Two Roads to the Spanish Civil War.* 1966. Chicago: U Chicago P, 1983.

Stewart, James C. Q. "An Auden Repudiation." *Notes and Queries* 36 (June 1989): 204.

Sykes, Christopher. *Evelyn Waugh: A Biography.* New York: Penguin, 1977.

Taspinar, Omer, and Henry J. Barkey. "Turkey: On Europe's Verge?" *Great Decisions 2006.* Foreign Policy Association. (Feb. 7, 2006).

Taylor, Richard. *A Reader's Guide to the Plays of W.B. Yeats.* New York: St. Martin's, 1984.

Taylor, William B. "The Virgin of Guadalupe in New Spain: An Inquiry into the Social History of Marian Devotion." *American Ethnologist* 14:1 (Feb. 1987): 9–33.

Thomas, Hugh. *The Spanish Civil War.* New York: Harper and Brothers, 1961.

Thompson, Theresa Mae. "Unlearning Europe: Postcolonial Questions for Teaching *The Plumed Serpent.*" *Approaches to Teaching D.H. Lawrence.* Ed. M. Elizabeth Sargent and Garry Watson. New York: MLA, 2001. 221–25.

Todd, Ruthven. "Poem (For C.C.)." Cunningham, *Penguin* 407–408.

Tomalin, Miles. "Down the Road." Cunningham, *Penguin* 384.

Tuñon, González. "Long Live the Revolution." Trans. A.L. Lloyd. Cunningham, *Penguin* 295.

Turner, Victor. *From Ritual to Theatre: The Human Seriousness of Play*. New York: Performing Arts, 1982.

Updike, John. Introduction. *The Power and the Glory*. By Graham Greene. v–xii.

Wahl, William B. *Poetic Drama Interviews: Robert Speaight, E. Martin Browne, and W.H. Auden*. Poetic Drama and Poetic Theory 24. Salzburg: U Salzburg P, 1976.

Warner, Rex. "The Tourist Looks at Spain." Cunningham, *Penguin* 393–95.

Waugh, Evelyn. *The Essays, Articles and Reviews of Evelyn Waugh*. Ed. Donat Gallagher. Boston: Little, Brown, 1983.

———. *Robbery Under Law: The Mexican Object-Lesson*. 1939. *Waugh Abroad* 713–917.

———. *Waugh Abroad: Collected Travel Writing*. New York: Knopf-Everyman, 2003.

———. *When the Going Was Good*. Boston: Little, Brown, 1947.

West, Rebecca. *Black Lamb and Grey Falcon: A Journey through Yugoslavia*. 1941. New York: Penguin, 1994.

Wexler, Joyce. "Realism and Modernists' Bad Reputation." *Studies in the Novel* 31 (1999): 60–73.

Wintle, Michael. *The Image of Europe: Visualizing Europe in Cartography and Iconography Throughout the Ages*. Cambridge: Cambridge UP, 2009.

Wintringham, Tom. "Monument." Cunningham, *Penguin* 304–07.

Woolf, Virginia. *The Letters of Virginia Woolf. Vol. III: 1923–28*. Ed. Nigel Nicholson and Joanne Trautmann. New York: Harcourt, 1977.

Wootten, William. "Basil Bunting, British Modernism and the Time of the Nation." *The Star You Steer By: Basil Bunting and British Modernism*. Ed. James McGonigal and Richard Price. Amsterdam: Rodopi, 2000. 17–34.

Worthen, W.B. "*Murder in the Cathedral* and the Work of Acting." *T.S. Eliot: Man and Poet*. Vol. 1. Ed. Laura Cowan. Orono: National Poetry Foundation, 1990. 253–73.

Wright, George T. *W.H. Auden*. New York: Twayne, 1969.

Yeats, William Butler. *At the Hawk's Well. Collected Plays* 135–46.

———. *Autobiographies*. N.p.: Trans-Atlantic, 1980.

———. *Calvary. Collected Plays*. 287–94.

———. *The Cat and the Moon. Collected Plays* 295–302.

———. *Collected Plays*. 1934. New Addition. New York: Macmillan, 1970.

———. *Collected Poems*. Revised 2nd ed. Ed. Richard J. Finneran. New York: Scribner, 1996.

———. *The Death of Cuchulain. Collected Plays* 437–46.

———. *The Dreaming of the Bones. Collected Plays* 275–86.

———. *Essays and Introductions*. New York: Macmillan-Collier, 1961.

———. *Explorations*. Sel. Mrs. W.B. Yeats. New York: Macmillan-Collier, 1973.

———. *A Full Moon in March. Collected Plays* 389–96.

———. *The King of the Great Clock Tower. Collected Plays* 397–404.

————. *The Letters of W.B. Yeats*. Ed. Allen Wade. London: Rupert Hart-Davis, 1954.

————. *Letters on Poetry from W.B. Yeats to Dorothy Wellesley*. Intro. Kathleen Raine. New York: Oxford UP, 1964.

————. *The Only Jealousy of Emer*. *Collected Plays* 183–94.

————. *Purgatory*. *Collected Plays* 429–36.

————. *The Resurrection*. *Collected Plays* 363–72.

————. *Sophocles' King Oedipus*. *Collected Plays* 303–28.

————. *Sophocles' Oedipus at Colonus*. *Collected Plays* 329–62.

————. *A Vision*. 1937. New York: Collier, 1965.

————. *The Words Upon the Window-Pane*. *Collected Plays* 375–88.

Index